PLUN]

M000165782

How Progressive Ideology is Destroying America

Plundered is the book I have always intended to write, tying "it" all together. A marvelous, marvelous job. You and your wife share the passion of me and my wife Pam—"truth telling" about Agenda 21, Maurice Strong, the New World Order, regional planners, California's cap and trade, the overhaul of education in America to omit our Christian heritage, et al. That makes you our hero.

Meantime - congratulations to you and your wonderful wife for committing the time and resources to get this book into print. And be encouraged—momentum is changing, the public is becoming both educated and aware and more and more citizens are becoming educated, activated and motivated to return America back to being "one nation under God."
Duffy and Company—Live from LA, Warren Duffy

Book Overview

America is at war, and doesn't even know it. Americans have been indoctrinated by our public education system, along with the progressive mainstream media, to accept progressive ideas as valid and part of the American Way. They are not. They are diametrically opposed to the Constitutional Republic established by our Founding Fathers. Right-left politics are bad enough. What is happening today, however, is much, much worse than that. Liberal progressives—this does not include liberals—hate capitalism, property rights, your liberty, and everything else that made America the greatest nation in the history of the world. There is no such thing as compromise in the progressive ideology. Progressives may seem to compromise, but it is an illusion. It is merely part of their strategy to eventually win. Those steeped in the ideology are convinced that they are right and everyone else is wrong.

Progressives are generally nice people—as long as you agree with them. However, they have succeeded for decades by relentlessly lying, intimidating, bullying, mocking, demonizing, and even destroying anyone or anything that stands in their way. Their strategy is based on "the end justifies the means," including class warfare. Progressives constantly accuse everyone else of hatred and bigotry in order to hide in plain sight their own hatred and bigotry that is usually far worse than those they accuse. They admit amongst themselves that they are at war with the American legal system and tradition so they can implement their utopian ideals using the Soviet model of governance.

Progressive ideology infects both political parties and manifests itself in different ways. Progressive ideology has given America a deeply divided nation that is $15-plus trillion in debt with another $118 trillion unfunded liability that can never be paid. Worse, progressive liberals believe debt is irrelevant so they constantly fight every effort to rein in our debt. For over a hundred years progressives in both political parties have been manipulated by a global elite to systematically undermine America's constitutional foundation in order to create a world government.

Although things may seem to be as they always have been, that is a deliberately created mirage. Americans can't see it because our public education and media have slowly but systematically indoctrinated us to accept the progressive version of reality.

Liberty in America as established by our Founders is in its death throes. The current "solutions" to our economic woes and high unemployment are actually making America's economy worse because they are based on an ideology that has *always* failed. Worse, America's moral fabric is being shredded as Christianity and Judaism are systematically extinguished. America is in a moral free-fall that is increasingly narcissistic, bigoted and hate-filled, demanding things that tear down rather than build civilization.

Plundered details how this progressive agenda has slowly but systematically strangled this great nation. It details who, why and how it is being done. Early psychiatrists in the 19th century were even then sounding the alarm. Progressivism is a cancer. It is part of a global agenda that is destroying America. It is evil. The November elections are perhaps the last, best hope of beginning to eliminate this cancer and the disaster it has created.

For additional information and breaking news go to
AmericaPlundered.com

PLUNDERED

How Progressive Ideology is Destroying America

John,
Keep up the good work!

Michael Coff

3-19-2013

Michael S. Coffman, Ph.D.

Published by Environmental Perspectives, Inc.
Bangor, Maine

PLUNDERED

How Progressive Ideology is Destroying America

Michael S. Coffman, Ph.D.
©2012 Michael Coffman, Ph.D. All rights Reserved

Cover: Background photo is of Occupy Wall Street protesters that joined a labor union rally in Foley Square before marching on Zuccotti Park in New York's Financial District, Wednesday, Oct. 5, 2011. (AP Photo/Jason DeCrow, by permission)

ISBN-13: 978-0-61563077 -9
ISBN-10: 0-615-63077-4
BISAC: Political Science/Political Ideologies/ Communism & Socialism

Environmental Perspectives, Inc. Publishing
6 Heather Rd.
Bangor, Maine 04401

DEDICATION

This book is dedicated to The Grandchildren,

Audrey, Nyssa, Ted, Nina, Eddie, Johnny, Jacquie and Alexander
And those yet to come—that they will have a future

May you live in a Constitutional Republic with liberty and freedom

ACKNOWLEDGEMENTS

To my wife Suz, whose tireless help made this book what it is and who forced me to follow the KISS method (Keep It Simple Stupid) and otherwise supported me in ways that cannot be described. And to Kristie Pelletier who worked tirelessly conducting research and writing, as well as cheerfully helping Suz and me keep our sanity while working on a very dark subject. And finally, to all those who contributed to the laborious job of editing—with special thanks to Becky McGlauflin and Don Folkers.

CONTENTS

FOREWORD

Former British Prime Minister Margaret Thatcher once said, "The problem with Socialism is that you eventually run out of other people's money." The fact is Socialism cannot exist without free market income to prop it up and pay its debts. Money must first be "made" before it can be plundered. A complete victory of Socialism would mean no money is being made – only that existing wealth is being redistributed. Eventually that must come to an end in a disastrous collapse of the economy.

That is exactly the point Michael Coffman is making in *Plundered*, and he reveals in great detail HOW it is being done in America and WHO is behind it. Dr. Coffman clearly shows it's not a Democrat vs. Republican issue and it's not Left vs. Right. America is under siege from a fully bipartisan effort of non-stop spending programs, ever higher tax schemes, and public funding to pay private groups to indoctrinate the American public to accept it all. In addition, he shows how these plans and schemes have evolved for more than a hundred years from both national and international sources.

Perhaps the most important message Dr. Coffman conveys in *Plundered* is the vast difference between the philosophies of the producers who grasp the virtues of a free market versus the looters of Socialism. The Progressive ideology is in full force in government at all levels; in business through global corporations and public/private partnerships, and now as the foundation of public education curriculum where future Americans learn nothing positive about free markets and limited government. They are instead daily indoctrinated for global citizenship and the need for government to make all of life's decisions for us. That's the reason why facts don't seem to matter in political debates; why scientific proof that global warming policy is wrong is ignored; why economic proof that the nation is bankrupt doesn't matter. There is no debate; no discussion; no discouraging word against an ideology that has become unquestioned globally-acceptable truth, no matter how wrong or disastrous.

The second vital lesson of *Plundered* is the absolute necessity of private property ownership as a means to build wealth and a sound economy. Private property ownership has been the centerpiece of American wealth since the United States was founded. The U.S. is virtually the only nation that has fully recognized and protected private property ownership. Because of that fact, Americans have been free to use their property as collateral to finance new business ventures, creating more than 60 percent of American jobs, building wealth and stability for a vast middle class. Private property ownership is also a major source of individual independence, the root of America's unique free society. So it is no surprise that the assault on private property is the centerpiece of "progressive" policy, particularly through the United Nations' *Agenda 21* that is now being systematically introduced into virtually every American city disguised as local planning.

In the pages of *Plundered*, Dr. Coffman has provided the source and the solution to the possible (perhaps inevitable) collapse of what was once the world's greatest example of freedom and prosperity. He names the names of the guilty and the details of how it's being done. He provides the root philosophy of freedom and the changes necessary to save us. The choice for Americans—take back what's yours or continue to be plundered into economic destruction. There is no middle ground.

For more than 100 years the free market economy of the United States has been used to prop up the failures of Socialism throughout the world. Over-taxed Americans have been forced to pay for it through foreign aid schemes and professional charity cartels. Armed with plundered American capital, global looters have had free rein to pillage some of the naturally richest nations in the world, now destroyed by socialism. Yet, all the while the socialists were gleefully accepting the cash to finance their failures. Americans were derided for being so rich. Now, America is the last stand; the last source of funds for the plunder. When the lights go out in America's once shining abundance of freedom and riches, what will these locusts have left but darkness?

Tom DeWeese, President
American Policy Center
Editor, The DeWeese Report, author of "Now Tell Me I Was Wrong."

PREFACE

Although the radical progressive agenda is obvious once a person understands what is happening, most Americans are blind to it. A corrupted educational system and a progressive mainstream media have trained most Americans not to see it. Progressive ideology is *extremely* dangerous to the future of America and progressives now control almost every political institution in America.

I don't sugarcoat anything they do in ***Plundered***. It took me a long time to come to realize that in the long run there is no possibility of compromising with the progressive ideology. It is not just right-left politics; it is war. That's their definition. Those steeped in the ideology are right and everyone else is wrong. Their modus operandi is to lie, intimidate, bully, mock, demonize, sue, and even destroy anyone or anything that stands in their way. It is time to expose their destructive ideology for what it is—the king has no clothes. I take apart and expose their agenda in a way that clearly shows how extremely dangerous they are to America's future.

Back when I was a naïve scientist doing research in ecosystem biodiversity and leading a multi-million dollar research effort in global warming, I never imagined in my wildest dreams I would be writing a book like this. At that time I followed politics by reading the mainstream media and voted, but otherwise was about as apolitical as they come. I detested the constant bipartisan and right/left infighting. Like most other Americans, I was blind to what was really happening. However, when the Clean Air Act was reauthorized in 1991 after completely ignoring about 10 billion taxpayer dollars in research, I realized there was an agenda. I started to investigate by following the money trail and realized there was a huge global agenda to turn the United States into a socialist, maybe even communist state reporting to a world government run by a global elite.

It was obvious that these elites knew exactly what they were doing. One of the foremost and respected historians of the twentieth century who had access to the records of these elites said, "In this group were persons whose lives have been a disaster to our way of life." As you read this book, you will see why that is an understatement. Initially, I believed the liberals who were advancing this agenda were mere dupes like the rest of us. As an environmental scientist, I saw their nefarious agenda in environmental issues like global warming and biodiversity. As I studied further, I realized the agenda was even more developed in arenas outside environmental issues. The agenda was huge, touching on every aspect of human life.

I quit my well-paying research job in 1992, and together with my wife, we have devoted our energies and personal resources to exposing this agenda to the American people. I began to realize that the agenda was being advanced, not by liberals in general, but by a certain class of liberals called progressives. On the Republican side there were the neocons (neoconservatives) or rinos (Republicans in name only) as they are popularly called. Even so, I still believed they were innocently misled and manipulated. I gave them the benefit of doubt. After all, as detailed in **Plundered**, almost every American has been dumbed-down by our public school system. That includes myself until I woke up and realized the horror that was about to overtake the greatest nation in the history of mankind.

That was my understanding when I wrote my most recent book *Rescuing a Broken America; Why America is Deeply Divided and How to Heal It Constitutionally.* To be sure, progressives had a very divisive worldview that somehow unhinged them in a way that they could not connect to reality. This led them to believe they must control everything. However, I thought they believed this because they were indoctrinated and living in delusion. Although misguided, they believed what they were doing was the right thing. Therefore, when writing *Rescuing a Broken America*, I wrote it from the perspective that while progressivism was dangerous and anti-American, it was so because of being misled.

My understanding changed radically when I read a description of what would later be called progressivism by a nineteenth century psychiatrist named Gustav Le Bon. He was writing about an emerging and violent belief system based on the philosophy of Jean Jacques Rousseau.

Reading Le Bon and finding that progressive liberal and neocons/rinos were quietly and secretly trying to destroy America and replace it with a Soviet-style government was an eye-opener.

In other words, this isn't new. Progressives have been actively doing this for a hundred years. However, I, like millions of other people, had trouble accepting they could be deliberately doing this evil. With this new information, my understanding of progressives changed radically. Le Bon and modern psychiatrists describe progressives as being capable of being very violent and dangerous in exactly the way we are graphically witnessing the past four decades, especially during the Obama administration.

Progressives are blind to their arrogance, hatred and violent nature. They will accuse (blame-shift) everyone else of doing exactly what they are doing. They truly believe they are the real Americans and the benchmark of all truth. Every indication suggests that many, if not most progressives are so deluded that they make the perfect patsies for the global elite to manipulate to advancing their agenda to create global governance.

Plundered will shock most readers by exposing how the global elite have used progressives to slowly, but systematically reverse the form of government given to us by our Founders. We are one short step away from losing our freedoms and Constitutional protections. I know that if this book is successful, I will be demonized, called a bigot, intolerant, racist and dozens of other vile names—or worse. However, there is no group of people as hate-filled, intolerant and bigoted as full-blown progressives. The need to expose the ideology for what it is doing is long overdue.

The best chance to begin reversing the devastating changes the elite and progressives have made to our laws over the past one hundred years, and especially the last forty, is the next election. It is imperative that progressives be voted out of office at every level of government, and then we need to slash the size of government. The next election may be the most important election the United States has ever had.

1 – A WAR OF WORLDVIEWS AND CRUSHING DEBT

A merica is in a war to the death. Not a war of nation against nation, but a culture war. Yet, it is every bit as deadly as if the former Soviet Union attacked the United States. Depending on which worldview wins, America will continue as the greatest nation in human history, or we will have a radically different nation plagued by conflict, loss of liberty and bankruptcy.

The Civil War was also a war of two cultures. Although most people believe it was primarily over slavery, it was importantly the first step in moving the United States (U.S.) from a decentralized government to a centralized one.[1] Even so, the people of both the Northern and Southern states held most other very foundational beliefs in common.

Contrary to the Civil War, the culture war being waged in the early twenty-first century is based on ideological beliefs that are radically different from one another. These two worldviews are rapidly moving in diametrically opposite directions and are tearing the heart out of America. They are so different that compromise between them is a complete impossibility. One *will* win out and utterly obliterate the other. One represents what is left of our Constitutional liberties and the other most closely resembles the old Soviet model that was so unworkable that it collapsed in 1992.

As will be detailed later in the book, these radical cultural differences are what define the deep division that dominates U.S. politics today. It is not historical Republican vs. Democrat political partisanship. It is about the ideological war that now dominates in both the Democratic and Republican Parties. It is leading to a completely different form of government than was established by our Founders. If it prevails, it will inevitably lead to a failed government and a loss in individual liberty. Conversely, returning to the Constitutional Republic originally established by our Founders will lead to a successful government, albeit imperfect, with increased individual liberty.

America is at a pivotal point in her history. The 2012 election will likely decide the ideology and form of government we embrace in future generations. This is so serious that America's future, or lack thereof, could be determined this year. This is the time. Those in the Tea Party, Patriot or Constitution Movements generally understand this and are America's greatest hope. However, even they do not fully understand what is happening. Although these groups have partial understanding, the vast majority of Americans don't have a clue as to what is really happening. Nor do they understand what could happen to them personally unless they make a radical turnabout. Providing that information is what this book is about.

Our institutions of public education and media have so indoctrinated our voting generation that many no longer have the knowledge and skills that are required for the type of critical thinking needed to make sound choices in the voting box. Many Americans vote for whatever candidate sounds the best, promises the most, or is even the one who looks the best on TV. Although this book will detail how indoctrination has occurred by design, the results of Obama-Boehner-Pelosi-Reed leadership has been shocking enough to wake up millions of Americans who are directly or loosely associated with the Tea Party, Patriot or Constitution Movements.

PROGRESSIVISM

THE NEW IDEOLOGY that is taking the United States over the cliff is called progressivism. Progressives can be either Democrats or Republicans and favor big government (although a progressive Republican will never admit it). Both progressive Democrats and progressive Republicans favor unconstitutional programs. Both favor drawing more power to a central government, or even a global government. Although progressive Democrats and neocons favor similar goals, they do so for different reasons and in different ways. Both are completely opposite of what the Founders intended in our Constitutional Republic.

1 – A War of Worldviews and Crushing Debt

Most readers will be surprised to learn in later chapters that the Founders specifically constructed the Constitution to prevent men with a lust for power from doing exactly what progressives are doing today! These progressives do not truly represent the average Democrat or Republican voter in America. Every poll that has been taken recently shows elite politicians and mainstream media do not believe the same things the average American believes, regardless of political affiliation. Each chapter in this book builds on the previous to shockingly reveal how progressivism is deliberately used to destroy America, especially through public school education.

Many readers will identify with some of the descriptions of progressives, and will ask themselves 'what's wrong with that?' That doesn't automatically mean that those readers are progressives. As shall be discussed later in the book, it might be nothing more than the result of indoctrination by the public school system, mainstream media and the fact they have been exposed to only one side of the story. If they knew the other side of the story, they would understand the enormous dangers of progressivism to America and reject it outright. Many liberal Democrats, moderate Republicans and independents fall into this group. This book gives you the other side of the story.

Progressivism infects, even controls, both political parties. Republican and Democratic progressivism is not identical in every detail, but each group tends to have a generally shared ideology.

Progressive Democrats vs. Republicans

Progressive Democrats are generally fixated on big environmental and social programs, as well as *big* government; the bigger the better. Some even call themselves communists. They believe only the government can solve problems; the more efficient the government and the more professionals and experts running it, the better. They dislike capitalism and Christianity, sometimes to the point of vitriolic hatred. Conversely, they believe in income redistribution, using the power of big government to plunder those who have, and give it to those who don't. This, they believe, will solve all problems. It is said tongue-in-cheek that a progressive Democrat/liberal never saw a social, environmental program, or a tax he or she didn't like.

The Occupy Wall Street protests in the fall of 2011 illustrate this point. The protesters had a very difficult time expressing their goals. They typically hated the Wall Street bailouts and blamed it on capitalism. Most of them claimed they wanted small government, but when cornered, they wanted their college education paid for, cradle to grave health care and government programs to save them if they can't make it in the real world. Yet, it was a socialist/Marxist bailout plan that rescued the banks in TARP. True capitalism would have let the banks fail. Their health care/welfare demands were socialist/big government plans. It was obvious they had no idea of economic reality and what they were demanding.

Historically, Presidents Woodrow Wilson and Franklin D. Roosevelt were progressive liberals. Bill and Hillary Clinton, President Obama, Nancy Pelosi and Harry Reid are all self-identified progressive Democrats today. Progressive Democrats are often called liberals, although not all liberals are progressives.

Progressive Republicans, on the other hand, are harder to define. They evolved from President Lincoln and his Hamiltonian political tradition of a more centralized government.[2] In general, they favor huge military budgets and the use of force in executing foreign policy. They often favor neo-fascist public-private partnerships whereby favored corporations team up with the government to accomplish some defined goal. Today progressive Republicans are often called RINOs (Republican in Name Only), or neocons (Neoconservatives).

Progressive Republicans or neocons are not just a little more liberal than conservative Republicans. Irving Kristol, the godfather of neoconservatism, defined the purpose of neoconservatism is; "to convert the Republican Party, and American conservatism in general, against their respective wills, into a new kind of conservative politics suitable to governing a modern democracy."[3] The Constitution set up a republic where government has very limited powers. Neocons want a democracy whereby, through lying and persuasion, they can get the majority to do what they want. As will be discussed in Chapter 2, our Founders almost unanimously declared that a pure democracy is the worst form of government possible.

Neocons are destroying America as quickly as are progressive Democrats. Of the two, the progressive Republicans are the most dangerous because conservative Republicans and moderates actively support them. As if to prove the point, the October 16, 2011 New York Times Magazine published a 10 page article subtitled, "The G.O.P. Elite Tries to Take Its

Party Back." The establishment neocons, according to the article, favored either Perry or Romney because "either man can be counted on to steer the party back toward the broad center next fall, effectively disarming the Tea Party mutiny."[4]

In what has to be the height of ignorance, 37 percent of the Tea Party vote in the New Hampshire primary on January 10, 2012 went to Romney.[5] It is obvious that many in the Tea Party movement have little understanding of the dynamics of progressivism and how neocons can persuade them to vote for the very candidate they philosophically reject.

If you expect the neocons to safeguard our liberties, forget it. The National Defense Authorization Act for 2012 (S. 1867)[6] passed by Congress on December 15, 2011 was strongly supported by Senators John McCain (R-AZ), Lindsey Graham (R-SC) and Jeff Sessions (R-AL), all neocons. The bill grants absolute power to the president to use the military to arrest and detain U.S. citizens without informing them of any criminal charges, without a trial on the merits of those charges, and without due process in violation of the Fifth Amendment to the Constitution.

In addition to terrorists, Subtitle D, Section 1031 b(2) of the law applies to "A person who was a part of or substantially supported al-Qaeda, the Taliban, or associated forces that are engaged in hostilities against the United States or its coalition partners, including any person who has committed a belligerent act or has directly supported such hostilities in aid of such enemy forces," the Taliban al-Qaeda or associated forces.[7] The way the sentence is structured, it can be interpreted to mean *any citizen*, even if there is no connection to any terrorist organization.

What does belligerent mean? This book, and therefore this author, would definitely be considered belligerent to the current administration. The fact that it is factually based would not make any difference in executing the law. Congressman Justin Amash, (R-MI) warned that the act would "permit the federal government to indefinitely detain American citizens on American soil, without charge or trial, at the discretion of the President." The act he continued, "does not preclude U.S. citizens from being detained indefinitely without charge or trial; it simply makes such detention discretionary."[8]

At a minimum this bill guts the Bill of Rights of its provisions protecting free speech, due process, and speedy trial. Senator Mark Udall (R-UT) correctly warned that the bill would effectively repeal the Posse Comitatus

Act of 1878, which forbids the use of military in law enforcement. The last ditch effort to protect American citizens from the law was an amendment proposed by progressive Democrat Diane Feinstein (D-CA) that added a paragraph that prevents the Act from affecting existing law "relating to the detention of United States citizens, lawful resident aliens, or any other persons who are captured or arrested in the United States."[9]

Lest you think Feinstein is standing up for the Constitution, the wording of her amendment not only protects U.S. citizens, but anyone, including illegal aliens, one of her favorite constituencies. Many believe this wording is worthless. Progressive Senator Carl Levin (D-MI) dismissed the clause, saying "We think that the law is clear…that there is no bar to this nation holding one of its own citizens as an enemy combatant, and we make clear whatever the law is, it is unaffected by this language in our bill." Unlike the misleading statements made by neocons McCain, Graham and Sessions, at least Levin was honest. Not to worry though, President Obama has promised he will never use this power.[10]

Scott Reed, a veteran Republican strategist and lobbyist, proudly asserted when asked if the neocons were slowly co-opting the Tea Partiers, "Trying to…. And that's the secret to politics: trying to control a segment of people without those people recognizing that you're trying to control them." The Tea Party congressional freshmen have not fallen for it, however. Rather than being co-opted, the Tea Party freshmen typically lament some version of "This is not what I'd want to be doing, but I've got to do it for the country."[11] True conservatives want to save their country. Neocons want to enjoy the power and prestige as they compromise their way to the New World Order.

As a neoconservative most of his adult life, C. Bradley Thompson understands this damning ideology. He abandoned neoconservatism in disgust thirty years after graduating from college because of their secret agendas to create The New World Order, and deliberate efforts to deceive the American people.[12] Thompson writes in the preface of his 2010 book *Neoconservatism: An Obituary for an Idea*, co-author "Yaron Brook and I have written this book to alert Americans—and especially those who value our nation's founding principles—to the threat posed to this country by neoconservatism."[13]

Thompson refutes once and for all the idea that neocons are just a variation of conservatism, "The obvious temptation is to suggest that the neoconservatives are confused or that neoconservatism is just a patchwork hash of ideas and policies that have no essence or defining principle—but that would be wrong.... By way of analogy, neoconservatism might be compared to a Faberge egg that contains multiple layers, some of which are intentionally hidden."[14] Thompson warns the reader at the end of the book:

> In conclusion, the neoconservatives are the false prophets of Americanism, and neoconservatism is America's Trojan horse. Those who wish to defend America's Enlightenment values and the individual-rights republic created by its revolutionary Founders must therefore recapture from the neocons the intellectual and moral high ground that once defined the promise of American life.[15]

Presidents Teddy Roosevelt and Herbert Hoover are examples of early Republican progressives. Both of the Bush Presidents as well as Senators John McCain and Lindsey Graham are Republican progressives today. Not surprisingly, presidential candidate Mitt Romney is also a neocon. That is why so much money and media exposure is given him compared to any of the other candidates.

In summary, progressive Democrats are far more socialist, even communist in nature, while progressive Republicans tend to be more fascist in nature (to the extent they favor public-private partnerships), although neither description is adequate. In reality, both have roots in the philosophy of Jean Jacques Rousseau, which will be explained in depth in Chapter 2. The fact that progressive ideology has effectively permeated both major political parties explains why nothing seems to change regardless of who is running things in Washington. Both tend to favor centralized control and globalism today as will be detailed in later chapters.

Irving Kristol, the well-known twentieth century columnist who was dubbed the "godfather of neoconservativism," made the case in his 1983 book *Reflections of a Neoconservative* that:

> A socialist elite…was indispensable to mobilize the masses for their own ultimate self-transformation. And the techniques of such mobilization would themselves of necessity be scientific—what moralists would call "Machiavellian"—in that they had to treat the

masses as objects of manipulation.... The appeal of any such movement to intellectuals is clear enough. As intellectuals, they are qualified candidates for membership in the elite that leads such movements, and they can thus give free expression to their natural impulse for authority and power.[16]

Kristol's observation is true for progressives from both sides of the aisle. The easy acceptance of progressivism by intellectuals explains why our colleges and universities are infested with progressives. It also explains how the progressive ideology has been taught by these professors to education majors and ultimately to society as a whole. It's called indoctrination.

The Behavioral Science Teacher Education Program (BSTEP)

Lest you find this hard to believe, in 1965 the U.S. Department of Health, Education and Welfare, as well as the who's who of private foundations and businesses,[a] funded a report entitled, "The Behavioral Science Teacher Education Program" (BSTEP) Published in 1970, BSTEP laid out the goal of this education process claiming, "We are getting closer to developing effective methods for shaping the future and are advancing in fundamental social and individual evolution." This evolution was to be done by "technological-scientific elite" planners and "long-range planning:"

Most people will tend to be hedonistic, and a dominant elite will provide bread and circuses to keep social dissension and disruption at a minimum. A small elite will carry society's burdens. The resulting impersonal manipulation of most people's lifestyles will be softened by provisions for pleasure-seeking and guaranteed physical necessities.[17] ...The *controlling elite will engage in power plays largely without the involvement of most of the people.* The society will be a leisurely one. *People will study, play, and travel; some will*

---

[a] Not only did the U.S. Health, Education, and Welfare fund BSTEP, but so did the American Academy of Arts and Sciences—Commission of the Year 2000; American Academy of Political and Social Science; United Nations Future-Planning Operation in Geneva, Switzerland, World Future Society of Washington, D.C., General Electric Company, The Air Force and Rand Corporation, The Hudson Institute, Ford Foundation's *Resources for the Future and Les Futuribles,* University of Illinois, Southern Illinois University, Stanford University, Syracuse University, and IBM.

be in various stages of the drug-induced experiences.[18] Each individual will be saturated with ideas and information. Some will be self-selected; other kinds *will be imposed overtly by those who assume responsibility for others' actions. Relatively few individuals will be able to maintain control over their opinions. Most will be pawns of competing opinion molders.*[19] (Italics added for emphasis)

This goal of the education establishment should shock most readers. More on this will be discussed in later chapters. For now, it is chilling enough to realize this seemingly impossible goal laid out in the late 1960s is now a reality. Unless you belong to the class of progressive elites, the rest of us are nothing more than "pawns" to blindly help them advance their evil agenda; or as Joseph Stalin once said of the dupes who supported him, "useful idiots."

THE FORGOTTEN DEPRESSION, 1920-1921

PROGRESSIVISM EMERGED in the late 1800s in the United States and led to the first major depression in the twentieth century from 1920-1921. Known as the Forgotten Depression of 1920, it resulted from the progressive policies implemented by President Woodrow Wilson from 1913 to 1920. Wilson advocated what later became known as Keynesian economics. Keynesian economics is derived from the economic theories of John Maynard Keynes in the twentieth century, who, during Wilson's presidency and WWI, was considered a brilliant economist in the British Treasury.

The Keynesian theory argues that private sector decisions sometimes lead to inefficient macroeconomic outcomes and therefore active government intervention in the marketplace and monetary policy is the best method of ensuring economic growth and stability. A supporter of pure Keynesian economics believes it is the government's job to smooth out the bumps in business cycles. Intervention would come in the form of government spending and tax breaks in order to stimulate the economy; and government spending cuts and tax hikes in good times in order to curb inflation.[20] In short, it means government control.

Keynesian economics sounds so logical, especially to intellectuals. Intellectuals know that if the task of running the economy is given to them, they, and they alone can run the government smoothly, increase prosperity and avoid economic downturns that are so painful to society. That was a key justification for the creation of the U.S. Federal Reserve in 1913[a] during Woodrow Wilson's presidency.

Keynesian economics has not lived up to its promise, however. In 1913 federal spending was 2 percent of the Gross National Product (GNP); about the same as the preceding one hundred years. During the Wilson administration, it jumped to over 7 percent. The non-defense federal budget went from about $25 billion annually (in 1990 dollars) to a whopping $478 billion.[21] Wilson also raised the income tax rate from 7 percent to 73 percent for the rich during his administration, while only increasing from 1 percent to 4 percent for the lowest tax bracket earning $2,000 a year or more.[22]

The whiplash effect of Wilson's wild increase in non-defense spending and tax increases resulted in the 1920-1921 depression. Just like President Obama today, President Wilson attempted to spend his way out of the depression by dramatically increasing federal spending and taxing the rich. Like Obama, he failed. By 1920 unemployment had jumped to nearly 12 percent,[b] and GNP declined 17 percent—the same general pattern as experienced from 2008-2011. In spite of the Federal Reserve, or because of it, the economy was a disaster.

When Warren Harding was elected President in 1921, he imposed an anti-Keynesian solution by slashing taxes from 73 percent in 1921 to 25 percent by 1925. Taxes were cut for lower incomes starting in 1923.[23] Instead of trying to stimulate the economy like Wilson had done and Herbert Hoover (Harding's Secretary of Commerce) advised; Harding cut

---

[a] The Federal Reserve Act passed on December 22, 1913, just as Congress was adjourning for Christmas and in no mood for debate. President Wilson signed it into law the next day. It was the same old fractional-reserve system that had been responsible for all the banking horrors of the past three efforts at having a central bank. Now, however, the Federal Reserve (Fed) was under the total control of a small group of families in the banking cartel with roots back to the Rothschild dynasty through Paul Warburg. The Fed is not part of the federal government, nor is it accountable to the federal government, other than the governing board is appointed by the president and confirmed by the Senate. However, the federal government (i.e. you and me) are responsible for any debt or default the Fed makes. It was created and is still controlled by a small group of international bankers/financiers, mostly from Europe. Source: G. E. Griffin. *The Creature From Jekyll Island* (Appleton, Wisconsin: American Opinion Publishing, Inc., 1994-1995), Pp. 4-5, 223; 437-438; 457; 465-466; 466-468.

[b] Although unemployment in the first half of 2011 hovered around 9 percent, the number did not include those who were no longer on unemployment, or underemployed. The real unemployment in mid-2011 was around 16 percent.

the government's budget nearly in half between 1920 and 1922. The result? The national debt was reduced by one-third. By 1922 unemployment was down to 6.7 percent and by 1923 it had dropped to 2.4 percent.[24] The depression had vanished and The Roaring Twenties were launched.

As a comparison, Japan introduced a planned economy in 1920 similar to the Keynesian model. Instead of prosperity, Japan created "chronic industrial stagnation and at the end in 1927, she had a banking crisis of such severity that many great branch bank systems went down, as well as many industries."[25] The contrast between Japan and the U.S. in the 1920s is staggering. A state-controlled model of economics was an in-your-face failure. Yet, progressives have continued to blindly, or deliberately, use it right through the current Obama administration.

Economic historian Thomas Woods Jr. reflects on Harding's enormous success, "The federal government did not do what Keynesian economists ever since have urged it to do: run unbalanced budgets and prime the pump through increased expenditures. Rather, there prevailed the old-fashioned view that government should keep taxation and spending low and reduce the public debt." [26] It speaks volumes as to why President Obama's Keynesian economic plan of increased expenditures and enormous deficit spending have not worked. The only thing Obama and other modern-day progressives in Congress have done is to bring us to the brink of total economic collapse—just like President Wilson did in the early 1920s.[27]

Why don't these modern-day progressives learn from the Harding miracle? A large part of the answer comes from the progressives' efforts to re-write history. Progressives throughout the twentieth century have revised U.S. history with a vengeance to conform it to their unworkable ideology. Progressive historians have reduced Harding's miracle to a footnote in history books, if it is mentioned at all. Incredibly, progressive historians usually label Harding 'the worst president in history.'[28]

Harding suffered from what is now a well-established strategy practiced by progressives—demonize and marginalize anyone who disagrees with the progressive view of reality, in this case Keynesian economics. Since Harding's miracle is essentially erased from economic history and can't challenge Keynesian dogma, progressives today are doomed to repeat the same failed policies over and over again. In a very real way, progressives are trapped in their own distortions of history.

When Harding died in office in 1923, Calvin Coolidge continued his free-market policies which fueled the Roaring Twenties. Eugene Trani and David Wilson report in their book, *The Presidency of Warren G. Harding* that progressives believe this huge prosperity is what caused the Great Depression of 1929:

> The tax cuts, along with the emphasis on repayment of the national debt and reduced federal expenditures, combined to favor the rich. Many [Keynesian] economists came to agree that one of the chief causes of the Great Depression of 1929 was the unequal distribution of wealth, which appeared to accelerate during the 1920s, and which was a result of the return to normalcy. Five percent of the population had more than 33 percent of the nation's wealth by 1929. This group failed to use its wealth responsibly.... Instead, they fueled unhealthy speculation on the stock market as well as uneven economic growth.[29]

This classic progressive anti-capitalist view of the cause of the Great Depression is now entrenched in the history books and has fueled the Keynesian economic theory of progressives since then. Yet, if this were true, we would be in a constant state of depression because most wealth has always been in the hands of the entrepreneurs. In contrast, wealth in communist or totalitarian countries is always in the hands of the ruling elite.

Much of the wealth in prosperous times is in the hands of those who are *creating* the wealth to begin with, through increased capital investment and job creation. "In fact," explains economic historian Thomas Woods, "the Great Depression actually came in the midst of a dramatic *upward* trend in the share of national income devoted to wages and salaries in the United States—and a downward trend in the share going to interest, dividends, and entrepreneurial income."[30]

Woods is an advocate of the Austrian School of Economic Theory. In its simplest form, the theory holds that both supply and demand and the resulting price of goods is the result of *individual personal preferences* expressed in a "free" marketplace. This, in turn, is dependent on strong private property rights to protect the economy from government intervention.[31] In its purest form it is laissez-faire economics constrained only by a few laws that protect the businesses and consumer from harming one another. All economic theories have their deficiencies. The Austrian School is no exception. However, of all the economic theories it has historically worked best.

It wasn't the free market that caused the Great Depression as claimed by Keynesian economists; it was government interference distorting the free market—just as it is today. Discussing British economist Lionel Robbins' 1934 book *The Great Depression*, Woods explains,

> Given that the market, via the profit-and-loss system, weeds out the least competent entrepreneurs, why should the relatively more skilled ones that the market has rewarded with profits and control over additional resources suddenly commit grave errors—and all in the same direction [that caused the Great Depression]? Could something outside the market economy, rather than anything that inheres in it, account for this phenomenon?[32]

The answer is a resounding 'YES.' Woods continues, "Artificial credit expansion…at the hands of a government-established central bank [is] the non-market culprit…. When the central bank expands the money supply—for instance, when it buys government securities—it creates the money to do so out of thin air."[33] Austrian School economist Murray Rothbard, in his *America's Great Depression*, provides compelling evidence the stock market crash of 1929 was the inevitable outcome of the easy credit policies by U.S. Federal Reserve (Fed—the U.S. central Bank) during the latter 1920s that fueled over-speculation.[34] It is also exactly what the Fed did from October of 2008 to June of 2011 with nearly two trillion dollars of Quantitative Easing 1 & 2 (QE1 and QE2).[35]

Calvin Coolidge served the balance of Harding's term following his death in 1923 and won the 1924 election for an additional four years as president. During his presidency he kept taxes low and government small. He declined to run for a second term in 1928. He claimed he had given enough to his country, but it may be that he saw the easy credit policies of the unconstitutional Fed were undermining his economic policies. At any rate, he knew Herbert Hoover, his popular Secretary of Commerce, was a big spender wolf in fiscally conservative clothing. He did not want to endorse Hoover for president and remarked "for six years that man has given me unsolicited advice—all of it bad."[36]

When Herbert Hoover accepted the Republican nomination in 1928 he predicted that "We in America today are nearer to the final triumph over poverty than ever before in the history of any land. The poorhouse is vanishing from among us."[37] The booming economy resulting from low taxes and small government of Harding and Coolidge seemed to put that dream in reach. However, the easy credit policies of the Fed had already hollowed out the economic boom and in less than eight months after Hoover's inauguration, Wall Street crashed.

It wasn't the stock market crash that caused the Great Depression, however. Coolidge scholars point out that the crash occurred in "October and by December of that year the economy was once again calm and remained so for the next six months…"[38] Ironically, according to President Regan's economist Milton Friedman,[a] the Fed reacted to the stock market crash caused by its easy money policy by immediately contracting the money supply. This led to runs on banks and a catastrophic, cascading bank failure, turning a depression into the Great Depression. The money supply shrank by one-third from 1929-1933.[39] The-Fed-caused-the-Great Depression argument is now accepted by most economists, including the Fed's current chairman, Ben Bernanke.[40]

Hoover didn't help. In his efforts to combat the depression, Hoover took the tried and true path to failure being used by Obama when he increased federal spending and dramatically increased taxes, especially on the rich. In 1930 he had signed the Smoot-Hawley Tariff Act against the advice of economists. The Act imposed a high tax on imports in a desperate effort to create more jobs at home. All it did, however, is cause foreign

---

[a] Milton Friedman, originally a Keynesian economist, abandoned the theory when he realized it caused high inflation and slow economic growth. He vehemently opposed pure Keynesian economics. He developed the Monetarism Economic Theory. Monetarism is an economic theory that focuses on the macroeconomic effects of the supply of money and central banking. Although he opposed the Fed, as long as it existed, he argued that it should focus solely on maintaining price stability, which is equilibrium between supply and demand for money. Because of this, Monetarism is more closely aligned to the Austrian School of Economics and free market capitalism than the government-controlled Keynesian School. Friedman was President Reagan's economic advisor.

nations to also raise tariffs on American exports, bringing international trade to a standstill and greatly worsening the depression.[41]

Unemployment reached 24.9 percent by 1932, businesses and families had defaulted in record numbers, and more than 5,000 banks had failed. Tens of thousands of Americans were homeless. In desperation, Hoover signed the Emergency Relief and Construction Act, which authorized funds for public works,[42] not unlike Obama's "shovel-ready" stimulus plan. To pay for it, Hoover signed the Revenue Act of 1932 which increased taxes across the board, but especially on the rich. After hovering around 25 percent during the Harding/Coolidge years, tax rates for top earners skyrocketed back to 63 percent of their net income and from 1 percent to 4 percent for lower income brackets.[43]

In one of the ironies of history, Hoover's opponent during the 1932 presidential race, Franklin D. Roosevelt attacked Hoover for taxing and spending too much, increasing the national debt, raising tariffs that blocked trade, and placing millions of Americans on the government dole. He even attacked Hoover for trying to "center control of everything in Washington."[44] Roosevelt's running mate, John Nance Garner, even accused Hoover of leading the country into socialism.[45] The irony is in the fact that Roosevelt's New Deal actually did everything he accused Hoover of doing and so much more. The lesson learned is that this seems to be a hallmark of progressivism—accusing the opposition of doing exactly what the progressive is guilty of doing.

Roosevelt's rapid expansion of federal taxes and regulations, along with his intimidation of "the rich," encouragement of labor strikes, and a host of other applications of progressive ideology, discouraged employers from hiring new workers. He also provided disincentives to new business investment, and turned the 1929 stock market crash into the long-lasting Great Depression after he became president. Not only did his actual policies raise havoc with the economy, the *fear* of not knowing what future policies would be concocted froze the economy.[46] That's exactly what has happened during the Obama administration.

In contrast, President John F. Kennedy cut all tax brackets by 30 percent, reducing the top rate for the rich from 91 to70 percent before his assassination in 1963. As a result of JFK's tax policies the nation saw business investments increase, the economy jump 50 percent, and a million jobs created. Unemployment dropped to its lowest peacetime level in 30 years.

Likewise, President Ronald Reagan slashed the top marginal tax rate for the rich from 70 percent to 55 percent, then to 28 percent, and exempted most of the poor from paying *any* income tax. The corporate income tax was reduced from 48 percent to 34 percent, capital gains from 28 percent to 20 percent. The result? A 25-year boom in which the nation's net worth went from $25 trillion in today's dollars during 1980 to nearly $57 trillion in 2007.[47] Even subtracting the $6.4 trillion loss due to the housing collapse,[48] as much wealth was created from Reagan's free market policies as was seen in the previous 200 years.[49] Yet, Obama claimed in a December 6, 2011 speech in Osawatomie, Kansas, "But here's the problem: It [free enterprise] doesn't work. It has never worked."[50] Really? Apparently, Obama has a serious disconnect from reality.

REPEATING WILSON'S DISASTER IN THE 21ST CENTURY

The depressions of 1920 and 1929 are being repeated in 2010 and 2012. Obama's solution, just like Wilson's, Hoover's and Roosevelt's, is much, much more of the same. Their solutions, like Obama's, just made it worse. The economic disaster in Europe clearly shows us the endgame. Yet, it's full steam ahead for Obama. Every one of these presidents was blinded by ideology. One of the many root causes of the unfolding disaster in Europe and the U.S. is overregulation. And, as of mid-fiscal year 2011, Obama has given us $38 billion in new costs brought on by a tsunami of new regulations. That's more than any other comparable period of time.[51]

The High Cost of Regulations and Taxes

The U.S. business climate has been drastically undermined by over-regulation. Many businesses have been taxed to the point of being incapable of doing business in the U.S. and have moved offshore taking their jobs with them. Business has also been hamstrung so much by regulations and taxes that many closed up shop altogether. It shouldn't surprise anyone that one of the primary reasons for the disappearing middle class in the U.S. is the regulatory strangulation of businesses that historically have created the middle class. Progressive liberals, however, will adamantly deny it, claiming it is corporate greed that is the cause.

1 – A War of Worldviews and Crushing Debt

The cost of regulations in the U.S. is not trivial. Annual regulatory compliance costs hit a whopping $1.75 trillion in 2008.[52] That is a "hidden tax" of over 50 percent of the entire 2010 budget! It exceeds all 2008 corporate pretax profits of $1.36 trillion. Worse, businesses had to wade through **81,405** pages of proposed regulations in the Federal Register in 2010, 24,914 pages of which were final rules. Federal regulations added more than $231 billion in hidden regulatory costs requiring 122 million man hours of paperwork in 2011 alone.[53] As long as this uncertainty remains, especially with Obamacare, high unemployment will continue and the economy will flounder.

In spite of overwhelming evidence, Senate Majority Leader Harry Reid made this unbelievable assertion on November 16, 2011, "My Republican friends have yet to produce a single shred of evidence that the regulations they hate so much do the broad economic harms they claim. That's because there aren't any."[54] Although we do need some regulation to protect one another, to say that overregulation does not cause harm to the economy is absurd. No, it is a psychotic disconnect from reality. Chapters three and four will explain this mind-blowing disconnect.

If all this causes you to yawn and say "so what," think of it this way. Say you inherited $50,000 from Uncle Big Bucks. Assuming you wanted to save it, would you put it in a bank that may go out of business at any time, or one which pays low interest because their overhead is so high? Or, would you put it in a bank whose future is assured and is known for reliably paying a high interest rate? It's a no-brainer. You certainly wouldn't put your money in a bank whose future is uncertain. The same is true for business. Business owners have to make these kinds of decisions all the time. Businesses are not going to expand or hire new employees if uncertain regulations may drive up their costs so that they are uncompetitive, no matter how noble the regulation.

Raising taxes on those businesses has a similar negative effect on job creation. A chilling poll of small businesses across America released on July 11, 2011 clearly proves these points. The poll found that an incredible 76 percent of small businesses either have no plans to hire over the next year, or plan to lay employees off. The overwhelming reason for this is because of the concerns outlined above. Eighty-four percent say Obama's economic policies are on the wrong track. Over 80 percent want Washington to get out of the way and less than 15 percent want Washington's help—

17

exactly the opposite of what progressive Democrats believe.[55] Yet, progressive Democrats dogmatically claim big government is the answer to everything.

It is obvious that the ideology of progressive Democrats has blinded them, and they don't have a clue as to what makes the American economy tick. Needless to say, this is causing the U.S. to invite economic disaster. That is because in recent decades progressive liberals control the presidency, Congress, most state and local elected positions, and the mainstream media. Yet, an August, 2011 Gallup poll reveals the astonishing fact that that there are twice as many people who call themselves conservatives than liberals, 41 vs. 21 percent. (Moderates make up the balance of 36 percent.)[56]

Of the 21 percent who call themselves liberal, only 6 percent call themselves very liberal. This 6 percent are most likely the true progressive liberals. Think about that for a moment. Roughly 6 percent of the American population is in control of government, courts, education and the media. These progressives are literally driving the nation over the cliff to economic catastrophe because of a blind and arrogant ideology and an inability to deal with reality. [57]

That's the progressive liberals. The progressive Republicans are doing the same thing. The U.S. Federal Reserve (Fed) is controlled by neocons who gave us Quantitative Easing (QE1 and QE2.) One of the purposes of QE2 was to keep interest rates down on the U.S. debt. It worked.[58] As just noted, the interest rate on the debt is at historical lows. QE2 was also supposed to make money available to small businesses. That was apparently a lie. It seems the Fed intended that only part of QE2 be used to increase money available to small businesses in the U.S. Even the part that was intended for small business never reached these businesses because the bank immediately made loans impossible to get and deposited the money back into the Federal Reserve to earn interest without any risk.

According to Zerohedge.com documents obtained using a Freedom of Information Act request, the Fed used some of QE1 and most of QE2 to bail out failing European banks in a desperate attempt to forestall the collapse of the euro and the European Union.[59] Even so, most economists now predict that Greece cannot be saved even with the gyrations of the EU to allow "restricted defaults" and partially-backed securities.[60] By October of 2011, Greece was technically in default even though Germany and France announced they would save Europe.[61]

By October 11, 2011, Greek bond holders had already forgiven 21 percent of Greek debt in a vain attempt to save the country. That was followed on October 26 with a 50 percent writedown by bondholders of Greek debt.[62] Even that was not enough. Prior to this, Greece was paying an astonishing 159 percent interest on two-year bonds.[63] To say that Greece is not already in default is ridiculous, but that claim is designed to hide the looming disaster that is all but certain. By May of 2012, Greece couldn't even put a viable government together after the citizens voted to reject austerity measures imposed by the EU. The fear of economic collapse threatened a run on the banks that could spread to other euro nations.[64]

Spain and Italy are also on the brink, having a combined debt of over $3.3 trillion, and that is on the edge of default. If any of these nations default it is likely to cause a chain reaction that would cause the euro and EU to fail, and could result in total financial collapse of the Western World.[65] More on this in later chapters.

Not all European nations were so foolish. Sweden, for instance, did exactly the opposite of what the EU and U.S. did. While most countries in Europe borrowed massively to get out of their recessions, Sweden's finance minister Anders Borg did not. Instead of spending, he pared back government. His 'stimulus' was a permanent tax cut. To critics, this was fiscal lunacy. Borg, on the other hand, thought lunacy meant repeating the economics of the 1970s and expecting a different result.[66]

By 2012, it was pretty clear who was right. "Look at Spain, Portugal, or the UK, whose governments were arguing for large temporary stimulus," Borg said. "Well, we can see that very little of the stimulus went to the economy. But they are stuck with the debt."[67] Tax-cutting Sweden, by contrast, had the fastest growth in Europe in 2011. Amazingly, it also celebrated the abolition of its deficit. Borg continued to cut taxes and cut welfare-spending to pay for it, just like Harding and Coolidge did to get out of the 1921 depression in the United States. Borg even cut property taxes for the rich to lure entrepreneurs back to Sweden.

Not surprisingly, the growth rates of Gross Domestic Product (GDP) for Sweden vs. the U.S. from 2002 to 2011 shows that Sweden's economy has outperformed the U.S. economy over the last ten years by 0.8 percent per year on average. Over the last two years (2010 and 2011), Sweden's real GDP growth has averaged 5 percent, or more than twice the U.S. average of 2.35 percent, and provides evidence that Sweden's supply-side approach to the 2007-2009 recession has been more successful than the demand-side Keynesian approach in the United States.[68]

The important thing to realize is that the entire European financial collapse was caused by progressive overregulation, excessive taxation, and unsustainable health/retirement benefits. It broke the bank. The only solution that will work is much less government and taxation. There was never any hope of Europe surviving their socialist behemoth any more than there is any hope of the U.S. surviving the nightmare that progressives have created in America—unless radical policy changes are made in Congress, state legislatures and local governments. Yet, as we shall see in the next few chapters, progressives are either literally blind to this or they are doing it deliberately. There is very strong evidence for both.

2 – PHILOSOPHICAL ORIGINS OF THE TWO WARRING WORLDVIEWS

P rogressivism now dominates almost every political, educational and judicial institution in America. Progressives are proud of their self-appointed superior intellect—to the point of arrogance. But where did it originate and why is it seemingly always associated with big government, strife and confrontation? To understand this, a brief discussion of the founding roots of America must be compared to the radically different roots of the progressive movement that is now threatening to destroy the greatest nation in the history of mankind. It is necessary because America's history, especially its founding principles, has been revised, even erased from the history books used in public schools.

Although these two major worldviews can be traced back to Aristotle (384-322 B.C.) and Plato (428-347 B.C.), America is now engaged in a war between two philosophies that have been struggling for supremacy for the past 230 years; those of English philosopher John Locke and French philosopher Jean Jacques Rousseau.

America's Declaration of Independence and Constitution are rooted in the thoughts of John Locke (1632-1704), whose *Two Treatises on Government* (1689) provided a framework for England's Glorious Revolution of 1688 and the American Revolution of 1776. This political philosophy, with its basis in individual rights and individual sovereignty, has been under attack in America for nearly two centuries by the ideology of Jean-Jacques Rousseau (1712-1778) and his *Social Contract* (1762).

The Social Contract focuses on an abstract "general will" of the people and *forced* state control.[69] Today the general will is called the "public good" and forms the heart of socialism and communism. It depends on a "statist" approach to government in which the all-powerful state is sovereign *over* the individual and all individual rights come from the state.

It is the exact opposite of the form of government given to Americans by the Constitution. Tragically, it is also a history filled with unbelievable bloodshed and carnage.

JOHN LOCKE, NATURE'S GOD AND PROPERTY RIGHTS

JOHN LOCKE DEMONSTRATED that the foundation of a progressive civilization, as outlined in his *Second Treatise of Government*, begins with God-given natural rights called the law of nature and nature's God:

> The state of nature has a law of nature to govern it, which obliges every one: and reason, which is that law, teaches all mankind… being all equal and independent, no one ought to harm another in his life, health, liberty, or possessions…. For men being all the workmanship of one omnipotent, and infinitely wise maker; all the servants of one sovereign master, sent into the world by his order, and about his business; they are his property…made to last during his, not one another's pleasure. …Being furnished with like faculties, sharing all in one community of nature, there cannot be supposed any such subordination among us, that may authorize us to destroy one another, as if we were made for one another's uses, as the inferior ranks of creatures are for ours.[70]

All men are created with *equal opportunity* and no person has a right to suborn the rights of another by denying that person their natural rights—rights to what Locke terms "life, liberty and estate." These rights do not derive *from* government, according to Locke, but are God-given natural rights inherent to all men. Thus, these rights have existed *before* government. Sir William Blackstone (1723-1780), who established the first law school and wrote the first legal dictionary, and others refined these ideas until Thomas Jefferson made them the cornerstone of the Declaration of Independence, which, Jefferson claimed, is based entirely on the "Laws of Nature and of Nature's God."

The underlying principle of this enlightenment was simple. Certain natural laws govern civilization. Violating them does not break nature's physical laws, but only results in man eventually breaking himself. Blackstone claimed that this natural law is "superior in obligation to any other. It is binding over all the globe, in all countries, and at all times; no human laws are of any validity if contrary to this.... no human legislature has power to abridge or destroy them, unless the owner shall himself commit some act that amounts to a forfeiture."[71]

If Locke, Blackstone and our Founders are right, then a nation *must* fail if it begins to deviate from God's law to man's law. I submit to the reader, isn't that exactly what is happening in Europe and the U.S. right now? As we shall see, we have abandoned God's law that gave us freedom and adopted man's law that is stripping away our once-guaranteed freedoms one by one; all justified in what seem to be good ideas.

Our nation is founded on the belief in God, regardless of all the convoluted efforts by the progressives to convince Americans otherwise. The belief in God primarily rested in Judeo-Christian beliefs. John Adams warned in a letter in 1798, nine years *after* the start of the French Revolution;

> While our country remains untainted with the principles and manners which are now producing desolation in so many parts of the world [especially France]; ... we shall have the strongest reason to rejoice in the local destination assigned us by Providence. But should the people of America once become capable of that deep simulation towards one another, and towards foreign nations, which assumes the language of justice and moderation, while it is practising iniquity and extravagance, and displays in the most captivating manner the charming pictures of candour, frankness, and sincerity, while it is rioting in rapine and insolence, this country will be the most miserable habitation in the world. Because we have no government, armed with power, capable of contending with *human passions, unbridled by morality and religion. Avarice, ambition, revenge and licentiousness would break the strongest cords of our Constitution, as a whale goes through a net. Our Constitution was made only for a moral and religious people. It is wholly inadequate to the government of any other.*[72] (Italics added)

Other letters by Adams at the time he wrote the above letter, strongly suggest he was referring to the horror of the French Revolution that wiped out Christianity in France. Adams claimed that without the moral framework of Christianity, society would devolve into the same morass as led to the French Revolution. Many other Founders and writers at the time were equally as adamant as John Adams. Tragically, his warning is now coming true even in America where citizen is pitted against citizen and there is rioting in the streets.

The foundation for the Declaration of Independence and Constitution is foreign to most progressive liberals and neocons. Like Rousseau, most progressives at best have only a "form of religion"[73] devoid of a living God acting in humanity's lives. If they don't believe in God, how can they accept that there is a God-given natural law that yields natural rights that no man can abridge? They can't. Progressive liberals believe man is the final arbiter of right and wrong. Therefore government is the grantor of civil rights as well as economic well-being. Progressive liberals call these *positive rights*. There is one fatal flaw, however. These rights are not unalienable. What the government giveth, the government can taketh away.

The Purpose of Government—Protect Property Rights

Locke then goes on to say the purpose of government is to join with others to "unite, for the mutual preservation of their lives, liberties and estate, which I call by the general name, property. The great and chief end, therefore, of men uniting into commonwealths, and putting themselves under government, *is the preservation of their property*."[74] (Italics added) Therefore, when Jefferson penned the Declaration of Independence, he forevermore established this now famous fundamental principle, "That to secure these Rights, [of life, liberty and the pursuit of happiness] Governments are instituted among Men, deriving their just Powers from the *Consent* of the Governed." (Italics added)

Except for a very few instances, such as the government of the Anglo Saxons, the American form of governance based on property rights and individual sovereignty within a Constitutional Republic has stood alone in history. Property always accompanied words such as *life* and *liberty* throughout the writings of Locke and our Founding Fathers. Conversely, progressives believe, as did Rousseau, property rights are evil and had to be controlled by the state. So, who is right and why are property rights so important?

In their book, *Property Rights*, constitutional attorneys Nancie and Roger Marzulla explain: "The Constitution places such a strong emphasis on protecting private property rights because the right to own and use property was historically understood to be critical to the maintenance of a free society."[75] The Marzullas continue by saying that property is more than just land. It includes buildings, contracts, money, retirement funds, savings accounts, machines and even ideas. "In short," say the Marzullas, "property is the fruit of one's labor. The ability to use, enjoy, and exclusively possess the fruits of one's own labor is the basis for a society in which individuals are free from oppression."[76] The U.S. Supreme Court agrees. In Lynch v Household Finance Corporation (1972), the Court ruled:

> [T]he dichotomy between personal liberties and property rights is a false one. Property does not have rights. People have rights. The right to enjoy property without unlawful deprivation, no less than the right to speak or the right to travel, is in truth, a 'personal' right, whether the 'property' in question be a welfare check, a home, or a savings account. In fact, a fundamental interdependence exists between the personal right to liberty and the personal right in property. Neither could have meaning without the other.[77]

Whether the property is one acre or twenty-thousand acres of land, a home, the money earned in wages, a car, a contract, or royalties from a book, the form of property is irrelevant. According to the Constitution all of it has equal protection. It is the basis of the "pursuit of happiness" portion of "life, liberty and the pursuit of happiness" in the Declaration of Independence. Perhaps Noah Webster says it best:

> On reviewing the English history, we observe a progress similar to that in Rome—an incessant struggle for liberty from the date of Magna Charta, in John's reign, to the revolution. The struggle has been successful, by abridging the enormous power of the nobility. But we observe that the power of the people has increased in an exact proportion to their acquisitions of property... Let the people have property, and they *will* have power—a power that will for ever be exerted to prevent a restriction of the press, and abolition of trial by jury, or the abridgement of any other privilege.... Wherever we cast our eyes, we see this truth, that *property* is the basis of *power;* and this, being established as a cardinal point, directs us to the means of preserving our freedom."[78] (Italics added)

Without the right of private, unencumbered property, a person cannot have liberty. People argue that there can be no true freedom for anyone if they are dependent upon the state for food, shelter, and other basic needs. When the state, not the individuals, owns the fruits of the citizens' labors, nothing is safe from *either* a democratic majority or a tyrant. "Ultimately, as government dependents," argue the Marzullas, "these individuals are powerless to oppose any infringement on their rights…due to the absolute government control over the fruits of their labor."[79]

Nowhere is this more apparent than in the old Soviet Union, where all property belonged to the state. No one could speak out against the government for fear of their family being evicted from their state-owned apartment, or fired from their state provided job. The local commissar had the people by the throats.

JEAN JACQUES ROUSSEAU, STATE CONTROL AND GODLESSNESS

IN CONTRAST TO THE LOCKE MODEL, various forms of the statist approach have dominated the governments of almost every nation for millennia. In more recent history Rousseau provided the foundational philosophy that spawned the incredibly bloody French Revolution as well as inspiring the writings of Immanuel Kant, Georg W. F. Hegel, Karl Marx[80] and many others. Rousseau also planted the seeds in America for the European model of socialism and Russian communism.

Rousseau based much of his philosophy on the writings of Englishman Thomas Hobbes. Hobbes believed man was so greedy and selfish that the enlightened state should control all property and make a social contract to keep peace and order. Rousseau refined these ideas into a *Social Contract* that set the stage for the war of world views that is now occurring in America.

Rousseau seeks to achieve equality of man through a vague socialist metaphysical concept called the "general will." To overcome the tension between individual interests and the community, Rousseau argues for the creation of the common good as embodied through an abstract, objective public will; a will that is supposedly free (but never is) from our subjective selves and personal interests.

Progressives try to convince us that Locke and Rousseau's philosophies were quite similar and equal in securing democracy and liberty. They are not. They are not even close. Rather, it is classic progressive revisionist history. Rousseau's ideas are in utter opposition to those of Locke.

The key fundamental difference between Rousseau and Locke is the role that "participation" and "community" play in Rousseau's "general will." According to the Rousseau model, individuals give up their freedom for the *good of all*, not just for the *protection of individuals* as is the case for the Locke model. "The good of all" is today's "positive rights."

"Positive rights" are rights granted *by* the government. Positive rights spell out what the government must do for the people as well as what the people can and cannot do. Positive rights were the basis of the Soviet Union's Constitution. History has not been kind to the actual practice of positive rights. Yet, progressives hold them up as the Holy Grail.

As an example, positive rights include the right of every citizen to have a job, or if not, have the government provide them a base income. This is a *government right* to happiness. All rights are granted and controlled by the government. Conversely the Locke/Constitutional model is based on negative rights or natural rights that *limit* what the government can do. The Locke model holds that everyone has a *God given right* to seek the best job they can find or create, free from government interference, a business in the *pursuit* of their happiness. It is imperfect because people are imperfect, but it is the best form of government in the history of mankind.

Rather than a government 'Of the People, By the People, and For the People,' described by Locke and enshrined in our Constitution, it is the enlightened state which determines the general will, or common good of the people. Progressives likewise place strict social control on private property to prevent the inequalities that they believe will lead to social division and private interest.

In the *Social Contract*, Rousseau acknowledges the great power of the state by admitting that raw force can bring consent to the general will; "That whoever refuses to obey the general will shall be *constrained to do so by the whole body*.... In this lies the key to the working of the political machine; this alone legitimises civil undertakings."[81] (Italics added) In doing so, Rousseau states the individual is supposedly "*forced* to be free"[82] by the government from his own selfishness. That is exactly what we are seeing today being implemented by *both* progressive Democrats and Republicans in laws like Obamacare and the Endangered Species Act. The difference between the Locke and Rousseau model of governance is huge (See table).

Comparison Between the Lock and Rousseau Models of Government	
Locke	**Rousseau**
The individual is sovereign. Unalienable individual rights form the basis of the U.S. Constitution and private property rights. Focuses on self-government where all men have equal opportunity. Strongly limits the right of government to intervene in the lives of individuals. Administered by a minimum of government.	The government is sovereign. The "general will" (public good) as defined by the state (Nation). All people supposedly share equally (equal outcome) in the wealth called social justice today. Based on positive rights that are defined by the government. Administered by collectivist & ever-growing government.
Power to make decisions primarily in the hands of the people thereby encouraging risk-taking. The only laws needed are those to enforce the golden rule that no person can conduct activities that cause harm to another person or their property. Creativity to find new and better ways of doing things is encouraged by minimal regulatory structure.	Power to make most decisions primarily in the hands of government bureaucrats. It is a breeding ground for government corruption and arbitrary enforcement of ever expanding regulations. Stifles creativity to find new and better ways to do things because there is no incentive. Considers capitalism and profits as wrong, even evil.
Establishes and protects private property rights which allows the creation of needed capital and provides the only proven way to eliminate poverty. It is why capitalism works in America and doesn't within centrally controlled nations.	Minimizes property rights to only those allowed by the state to reduce all risk. Places nature's perceived needs ahead of man's real needs. By controlling property rights there is little incentive to build a better widget.
Encourages individual protection of asset value of privately owned property because of pride of ownership and the need to maintain environmental health for continued production or use.	Invokes the Law of the Commons where property is held in common by the state through deed or regulation. No one person, family or organization has a vested interest in protecting the property for the benefits it can provide.
Depends on free markets with minimum of regulations to create incentives to maximize efficiencies of production through creativity and entrepreneurship.	Depends on controlled markets by government to achieve predetermined social and environmental goals based on precautionary principle which, in turn, stifles creativity and entrepreneurship.

Property Rights Are Evil

Rousseau wrote this *before* the French Revolution, when feudalism still ruled France and only a few wealthy noblemen could own property—

at the expense of the serfs whom they forced to work the land for a pittance. Thus, Rousseau saw private property as an evil that repressed man. So much was Rousseau against property rights that he stated that no one should own anything; "You are undone if you forget that the fruits of the earth belong to us all, and the earth itself to no one!"[83] The rich, claimed Rousseau, designed property rights to place:

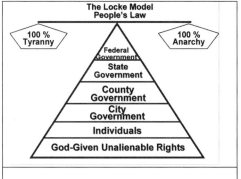

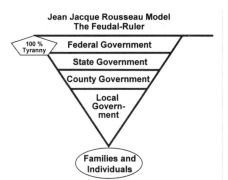

> new fetters on the poor, and gave new powers to the rich; which irretrievably destroyed natural liberty, eternally fixed the law of property and inequality, converted clever usurpation into unalterable right, and, for the advantage of a few ambitious individuals, subjected all mankind to perpetual labour, slavery and wretchedness.[84]

Top: In the Locke Model, sovereignty lies with the individual with decreasing power up the levels of government until the federal government has the least power of all. This provides a balance between anarchy and tyranny. Jefferson called this the People's Law. Bottom: In the Rousseau Model sovereignty supposedly lies with the individual, but in practice lies in the federal government. Power decreases down until families and individuals only have the power granted by the governments ruling them. Jefferson called this the Feudal-Ruler Law that leads to tyranny. He saw this in France. *Source: W. Cleon Skousen. The Making of America, the Substance and Meaning of the Constitution. The National Center for Constitutional Studies, Washington, D.C. 1986.*

To avoid this perceived wretchedness, Rousseau insists that the public good is served only when the state owns or controls all land. However, there is a terrible flaw in Rousseau's logic. A major problem arises from government ownership of land. Everyone shares land owned by the government, but *no one* is responsible to take care of it. This principle is known as the law of the commons. The Pilgrims tried it and it failed miserably. So did the Soviets under communism.

Without pride of ownership, there is no motivation to care for or optimize property held in common with millions of other citizens. Everyone sinks to the lowest common denominator, the economic structure stagnates, and the infrastructure collapses, just as happened in the former Soviet Union. Although private property owners receive the blame for environmental destruction, ironically, in the mid-twentieth century Americans polluted their air and waterways because *no one* owned them. It was cheaper to dump pollution into the air or water since they were in the public domain.

The inevitable adverse consequence of common ownership to a large degree explains why Communism and Marxism, both products of Rousseau ideology, have been such dismal failures.[85] The environmental devastation revealed in Eastern Europe and Russia as the Iron Curtain and the Soviet Union collapsed in the early 1990s evidences a lack of motivation to protect the environment. America's waterways and air, unlike its land, are not under Locke's model of property rights. Consequently, like Eastern Europe and the former Soviet Union, America's air and water suffered the same fate as the tragedy of the commons.

Although Rousseau was also an atheist, he saw how religion controls the masses. He coined the term civile or civil religion in *The Social Contract* for what he believed was the essential secular moral and spiritual foundation of any modern society. Rousseau hated Christianity as portrayed at that time by corruption he perceived in the Roman Catholic Church; "the humble Christians changed their language, and soon this so-called kingdom of the other world turned, under a visible leader [Jesus], into the most violent of earthly despotisms."[86] Of course, some in the Catholic Church made a very poor representation of Christ during that era, but there was no way Rousseau could have known it unless he really wanted to; and from all accounts he didn't want to find out.

Rousseau continues, the church "being founded on lies and error, ...deceives men, makes them credulous and superstitious... becomes tyrannous and exclusive, and makes a people bloodthirsty and intolerant, so that it breathes fire and slaughter, and regards as a sacred act the killing of every one who does not believe in its gods."[87] While there are periods in history where Rousseau was right, tragically, his form of government has resulted in some of the greatest slaughter of human life in modern history.

In any case, this same anti-Christian belief is found in the writings and beliefs of modern progressive liberals. They try to label any nutcase as a Christian extremist. Immediately following the mass murder of more than 76 adults and children in Norway on July 22, 2011, The New York Times ran a front-page headline "AS HORRORS EMERGE, NORWAY CHARGES CHRISTIAN EXTREMIST."[88] It continued printing the label a week after the killings.[89] It was later determined that there was absolutely no evidence that terrorist Anders Belin Brevik was a Christian or had any Christian connections.[90] As with Jared Lee Loughner, the would-be assassin of Congresswoman 'Gabby' Giffords, progressives also tried to label Brevik a right-wing extremist—again with no evidence that he had any right wing leanings or affiliations before they knew anything about him at all.

If Rousseau was referring to the Catholic Inquisitions, he was correct. But those dark days were 200 years before Rousseau penned his words. The Catholic Church maintained power into the eighteenth century in France and French royalty and the church (at least the "upper clergy") reinforced each other at the expense of the common man.[91] In Northern France, the clergy owned as much land as the royalty. The poor saw the Church as oppressors equal to the royalty.[92] It must be noted, however, that the "lower clergy" were as poor and powerless as the people.[93]

Civil Religion

Because of the Church's corruption of power, Rousseau believed he must establish a civil religion in the place of Christianity. It would be a religion controlled by society with a profession of faith. It would allow leaders to invoke god in political speeches, quote religious texts, allow worship and establish cultural morality. In other words, as Paul warned in 2 Timothy 3:1-5, Rousseau's civil religion would have "a form of godliness but denying is power."[94]

Although Rousseau allowed that no one could be forced to adhere to this civil religion, the government "can banish from the State whoever does not believe them." Why? For being "anti-social, incapable of loving the laws and justice, and of sacrificing at need, his life to his duty." Rousseau concludes with this prophetic statement, "if he does not believe them [the civil religion tenets of faith], let him be *punished by death*: he has committed the worst of all crimes."[95] (Italics added). That's exactly what happened to thousands of priests when they were hacked, dismembered and guillotined in the French Revolution. Many churches were destroyed. Christianity was virtually wiped out during the Reign of Terror.

That's not all. Rousseau attacked Locke's model in the name of the wholeness of man, arguing that focusing on self-interest, individual rights, and property divides man. Rousseau sees "man as a malleable creature" to be molded by an "enlightened government." He "favors primitive man, the noble savage who lives in simple equality with his fellow man, with few needs, a limited appetite, over man in civilized society."[96] That is exactly what the modern progressive environmentalist believes today. This belief that the primitive man and noble savage forms the highest form of equality between men is what Gustave Le Bon, a late nineteenth century French physician and early psychiatrist, attacks with utter distain:

...the mere fact that he forms part of an organised crowd [mob], a man descends several rungs in the ladder of civilisation. Isolated, he may be a cultivated individual; in a crowd, he is a barbarian—that is, a creature acting by instinct. He possesses the spontaneity, the violence, the ferocity, and also the enthusiasm and heroism of primitive beings, whom he further tends to resemble by the facility with which he allows himself to be impressed by words and images—which would be entirely without action on each of the isolated individuals composing the crowd—and to be induced to commit acts contrary to his most obvious interests and his best-known habits.[97]

Le Bon wrote this after studying the destructive nature of what would later be called the progressive movement. Specifically, he was referring to the incredibly heinous and bloody French Revolution and the subsequent millions of deaths resulting from the Napoleonic Wars which would have never happened without the Revolution.[98] Rousseau's man was primitive and savage all right, but he was far from noble.

THE FRENCH REVOLUTION

AS ROUSSEAU'S IDEAS GRADUALLY SPREAD throughout France the royalty were forced to give more freedoms to the people. However, it was too little, too late. By 1789, the poor in the country were suffering from ruinous taxation to support the sumptuous, often gluttonous lifestyle of the aristocratic royalty. Louis XVI, the widespread French nobility and the Catholic Church had become immensely unpopular. The ideas of 'equality' and 'freedom of the individual' as presented by Voltaire, Denis Diderot, Turgot and especially Rousseau began to inflame the French lower class. A series of famines in the 1780s contributed to the unrest. Unfounded rumors that the royalty caused the famine deepened unrest.

The French Jesuit, the Abbé Augustin Barruel provides historical evidence to suggest that the stories were planted by provocateurs that used and eventually took over the Jacobin Society to rouse the peasants into revolution against the royalty.[a] Whatever happened to start the war, the Jacobin Society, led by Maximilien Robespierre, made it into one of the bloodiest, most heinous wars in modern history—all guided by the writings of Jean Jacques Rousseau. With raw brutality as the benchmark, the atrocities were beyond anything we in twenty-first century America can even grasp.

Le Bon specifically noted that Robespierre almost worshipped Jean Jacques Rousseau. Robespierre was "hypnotised by the philosophical ideas of Rousseau, and employing the methods of the Inquisition to propagate them."[99] Remember, Rousseau never defined his "general will," but did give all power to the state to crush, even put to death anyone who disagreed with the tenants of faith in the Social Contract's civil religion. Robespierre took it upon himself to be the leader of the Revolution and therefore define the general will for everyone else. He started the Reign of Terror by ruthlessly eliminating anyone and everyone who disagreed with him. During the entire French Revolution from 1789 to 1799, upwards of a 100,000 people were beheaded if they were lucky, or butchered and dismembered if they were not so lucky.[100]

Robespierre actually believed that his mission was based on virtue. Unfortunately for tens of thousands of Frenchmen who were literally butchered, chopped up or beheaded, Robespierre claimed that to become

---

[a] The *Memoirs Illustrating the History of Jacobism* by the French Jesuit, the Abbé Augustin Barruel provides historical evidence that the French Revolution was the result of a deliberate conspiracy to overthrow the throne, and alter aristocratic society in Europe. It was hatched by a coalition of Freemasons and the Order of the Illuminati (Yes, the Illuminati did exist. The debate that continues today is whether it was ever fully eradicated.) This coalition allegedly took over the Jacobin Society, which until the start of the French Revolution was made up of mostly moderate government officials in Brittany.

virtuous in Revolution terror is required, "Terror is nothing else than swift, severe, indomitable justice; it flows, then, from virtue."[101] In an incredibly twisted way, Robespierre's Reign of Terror from 1793 to July 28, 1794 slaughtered 40,000. It was all done to attain virtue, which in turn, was based in Rousseau's writings.

This serves to point out yet another huge difference between Locke and Rousseau. Our Founders guided by Locke believed that virtue came from obedience to a righteous God, while Robespierre, as guided by Rousseau, believed virtue came from terror and brute force. It should not be forgotten that Rousseau's ideology also spawned fascism and communism, under which governments slaughtered in excess of 150 million of its people. Future chapters will document how this terror and raw force is beginning to be seen in America today.

Rousseau has become known as the Father of the French Revolution.[102] Because modern progressive liberal philosophy is based in the same writings that resulted in incomprehensible atrocities, progressive liberals today are attempting to revise history to minimize or even eliminate Rousseau's contributions to the French Revolution as well as fascism and communism.

In fairness, Rousseau undoubtedly never expected his philosophies to generate such horror. However, the vague definition of the "general will," the promotion of the primitive man and the condemnation by death for anyone not complying with whatever definition is given to the general will, was and is a recipe for disaster. Hitler, Lenin, Stalin, Mao Zedong and many other lesser known butchers have applied philosophies derived from Rousseau's writings to justify the slaughter of hundreds of millions of people.[103]

Conflict, division, oppression and violence have dogged almost every nation historically where Rousseau's form of governance has dominated. The only major exception is modern-day Europe. However, even Europe seems to be changing as decades of socialist plundering have ravaged the economies of individual nations, resulting in violent riots when the citizens' bloated benefits are cut off. As perfectly described by Le Bon, the citizens don't care that their nation was bankrupt; they irrationally and violently demand that their benefits continue, even though doing so would bankrupt their country and they would ultimately get nothing at all. It is a massive disconnect from reality. Much more on Le Bon's findings in the next chapter.

Can It Happen In America?

Can it happen in America? Progressive liberals will adamantly deny the possibility and throw up all kinds of smoke screens to obscure it. However, put aside their hubris and look at what they actually do. They bully, denigrate, and vilify all opposition to focus the population on hatred—hatred of the Republicans, vitriolic hatred of the Tea Party, hatred of Wall Street, deep hatred of capitalism, hatred of the rich, hatred of the U.S. Constitution, hatred of the United States itself, hatred of anyone who disagrees with them. They claim that they are the only real Americans, yet since when is hatred an American value? Since when does America stand for intolerance? Since when is Marxism, or even socialism the foundation of American economics? These are all *anti-American* characteristics.

Progressive liberals use trigger words and slogans to evoke divisive emotions. Once a mob makes a decision based on emotion, facts and figures mean nothing. Reality is meaningless. That is exactly what the Jacobeans, led by Robespierre, did in the French Revolution. This inability of progressive liberals to connect to reality was obvious in their denial that entitlement programs need to be restructured and in the debt ceiling debacle in the summer of 2011.

Aren't these also the same tactics used by community organizers like ACORN (Association of Community Organizations for Reform Now), or unions like the SEIU (Service Employees International Union), the NEA (National Education Association), AFT (American Federation of Teachers), AFL-CIO and many more socialist and communist-based organizations? They all use militant tactics of intimidation through terror. The only difference from Robespierre's Jacobeans is that the Rule of Law more or less still prevails today. Robespierre was the Rule of Law. Today, progressives are once again eroding the Rule of Law. Can lawlessness be far behind?

Can there be any doubt that when these groups besiege banks, government buildings, even private homes, that they would not commit the same bloody terror found in the French Revolution if there were no fear of their being arrested or constrained in any manner? Le Bon gave this chilling warning about mob behavior, "Without the restraining presence of the representatives of authority the contradictor [the one that disagrees with the mob], indeed, would often be done to death."[104] Remember, that is exactly what Rousseau said an all-powerful government should do. [105] Greece, Italy and other collapsing nations were on the verge of this very thing in the summer of 2011, as unions violently protested the stringent austerity rules put on them by the IMF (International Monetary Fund) and the EU (European Union). As Greece's economy disintegrated, the violent protests of unions were taking the rule of law with them. Almost all, if not all, of Greece's debt (along with Europe), and the $15.8 trillion debt of the United States was created because of the siren song of socialist ideology derived from Rousseau. Tragically, anarchy and terror is exactly what the radical progressive liberals are seeking.

3 – WRONGLY USING THE LAW TO PLUNDER

When the law is not used to protect individual life, liberty and property, French economist, legislator and philosopher Frédéric Bastiat claims it becomes perverted—used by the unscrupulous to exploit the life, liberty and property of others.[106] In the process, they turn this perversion into a right, making criminals out of those who try to defend their right of property. Bastiat states:

> Unfortunately, the law by no means confines itself to its proper functions. And when it has exceeded its proper functions…it has acted in direct opposition to its own purpose. The law has been used to destroy its own objective: It has been applied to annihilating the justice that it was supposed to maintain; to limiting and destroying rights which its real purpose was to respect. *The law has placed the collective force at the disposal of the unscrupulous who wish, without risk, to exploit the person, liberty, and property of others. It has converted plunder into a right, in order to protect plunder. And it has converted lawful defense* [of life, liberty, and property] *into a crime, in order to punish lawful defense....*[107] Sometimes the law places the whole apparatus of judges, police, prisons, and gendarmes at the service of the plunderers, and *treats the victim—when he defends himself—as a criminal.*[108] (Italics added)

Nothing highlights Bastiat's warning more than what happened to Tony Martin. Martin, a Norfolk British farmer, had already had ten break-ins in his isolated home with £6,000 ($9,243) worth of furniture and other items stolen. Not surprisingly, he became paranoid. Awakened on August 20, 1999, he heard someone again breaking in, and he grabbed his unlicensed shotgun, shot blindly in the dark, killing a 16-year-old home invader and seriously wounded another 33-year-old. The 16-year-old had 29 previous arrests and had just been released on bail hours before committing the break-in.[109]

The Chief Constable testified Martin should have screamed for help, even though Martin's home was totally isolated. Additionally, citizens of the Norfolk area had been complaining for years that police protection was essentially non-existent. Police response time was as much as 50 minutes, resulting in an explosion of break-ins and other criminal activity.[110]

If there were no gun-control law in Britain, Martin would have been found not-guilty. Because of this counterproductive law, he was found guilty of murder and sentenced to life in prison. His sentence was reduced to manslaughter in 2001. However, the burglar who was not killed was out of prison in 18 months; whereupon he sued Martin for bodily harm. That was later dropped when Martin countersued. Martin was finally released in 2003. The case raised a huge and continuing outcry from British citizens that this was justice gone totally amok.

Just as Bastiat warned, Martin became a criminal by just defending his property.[111] The gun law became so controversial with the Martin case that restrictions against protecting yourself or your property were finally loosened in 2011. British citizens now can use "reasonable force" (whatever that means) to stop a crime without fear of prosecution.[112]

Progressive liberals have literally annihilated constitutional law as laid down by our Founders and described so eloquently by Bastiat. They have made it legal for the government to steal from those who have earned something by the sweat of their brow, and give it to those who have not earned it. It is called legalized plunder. One of the greatest examples of this is income redistribution.

Obama's socialist views came blazing to the forefront on October 12, 2008, when he was unknowingly caught on video responding to Sam Wurzelbacher, more commonly known as "Joe the Plumber." Wurzelbacher was a plumber who was concerned that some of Obama's ideas would greatly increase his taxes and perhaps put him out of business. Caught by ABC News cinematographer Scott Shulman, the world saw and heard Barack Obama's response:

"It's not that I want to punish your success. I just want to make sure that everybody who is behind you, that they've got a chance at success too… and I think when you spread the wealth around, it is good for everybody."[113]

While the comment was reported by every news organization, and ignited a firestorm with conservatives, the general attitude of the progressive mainstream media was, "so what, what's wrong with that?" Again, the liberal mainstream media protected him from any damage that would have meant certain political death if he had said the same things 25 years earlier.

As Obama told Joe the Plumber, Rousseau socialism is based upon the right of the state to *force* a person to give a portion of what they have earned to others who have not earned it. [114] Redistribution is also the basis of almost all environmental and social laws in the U.S. The state is superior to the individual in all matters. How do we know if a law really is legal plunder? Bastiat provides a simple answer:

See if the law takes from some persons what belongs to them, and gives it to other persons to whom it does not belong. *See if the law benefits one citizen at the expense of another by doing what the citizen himself cannot do without committing a crime.* The person who profits from this law will complain bitterly, defending his *acquired rights.* He will claim that the state is obligated to protect and encourage his particular industry; that this procedure enriches the state because the protected industry is thus able to spend more and to pay higher wages to the poor workingmen.[115] (Italics added)

Another way of looking at this is legal plunder takes from someone who is productive, thereby impairing future productivity and giving it to someone who is not productive, also impairing future productivity. Although Bastiat penned these words over 160 years ago, is not this the very essence of the income redistribution as put forth by Obama? Isn't this the basis of most lobbying in the United States today? Tragically, most laws passed by Congress in the past 100 years starting with the Federal Reserve Act are plundering America based on Bastiat's litmus test.

FREE MARKET CAPITALISM CREATES PROSPERITY FOR ALL

IRONICALLY, PROGRESSIVE LIBERALS claim it is the greed of capitalism and corporations that have caused the problems we have today. Because they don't believe in human nature, they don't believe that every person is tempted by greed, including the lazy, criminals, politicians, bureaucrats, unions, and yes, even progressive intellectuals. But human nature does exist and is at the heart of why free market capitalism is light years ahead of socialism or communism in improving the lot of man.

Perhaps economist Milton Friedman explained free market capitalism's enormous superiority over socialism best in an interview he had with Phil Donahue in 1979. Donahue tried to pin Friedman down by asking him, "When you see around the globe the mal-distribution of wealth, the desperate plight of millions of people in underdeveloped countries, when you see so few haves and so many have-nots, when you see the greed and the concentration of power, did you ever have a moment of doubt about capitalism and whether greed's a good idea to run on?"[116] Friedman calmly responded;

"Well, first of all, tell me is there some society you know that doesn't run on greed? You think Russia doesn't run on greed? You think China doesn't run on greed? ...*The world runs on individuals pursuing their separate interests.* The great achievements of civilization have not come from government bureaus. Einstein didn't construct his theory under order from a bureaucrat. Henry Ford didn't revolutionize the automobile industry that way. In the only cases in which the masses have escaped from the kind of grinding poverty you're talking about, the only cases in recorded history *are where they have had capitalism and largely free trade.* If you want to know where the masses are worst off, it's exactly in the kinds of societies that depart from that. So that the record of history is absolutely crystal clear: that there is no alternative way so far discovered of improving the lot of the ordinary people that can hold a candle to the productive activities that are unleashed by a free enterprise system."[117]

To this Donahue responded, "But it seems to reward not virtue as much as ability to manipulate the system."[118]Friedman answered,

"And what does reward virtue? You think the communist commissar rewards virtue? You think a Hitler rewards virtue? You think—excuse me, if you will pardon me—do you think American presidents reward virtue? Do they choose their appointees on the basis of the virtue of the people appointed or on the basis of their political clout? Is it really true that political self-interest is nobler somehow than economic self-interest? You know I think you are taking a lot of things for granted. Just tell me where in the world you find these angels who are going to organize society for us? Well, I don't even trust you to do that."[119]

Donahue was appropriately dumfounded and uncharacteristically had no further questions. What Friedman said was right; the free market unleashes a person's creativity. A manager works harder and smarter in order to get to be vice president. If a person can see a reward for developing a better widget, the reward provides the incentive to be creative. When something is produced that is in high demand, everyone benefits. It could be a store in a neighborhood that needs one, or a better form of transportation as was the case with Henry Ford.

A person with a good idea also needs capital to get started or to expand. He or she can get it via a loan on their private property, or someone with some money can invest in the business. Both are rewarded. Of course the business can fail and many do, so the potential reward has to be enough to make the risk worthwhile.

This is the power that the Constitution of the United States unleashed, making this nation the most successful in human history. It is based in *equal opportunity*, not equal outcome or social justice. All that was needed to make it work was the rule of law to keep a person, company or the government from taking what belonged to the individual or company building the better widget for personal gain, or to give it to another person who would squander it. The latter is exactly what socialism, fascism and communism do. Yet, repeating what Obama said in a December 6, 2011 speech in Osawatomie, Kansas, "But here's the problem: It [free enterprise] doesn't work. It has never worked."[120] Really? That's the mantra of Marxism and another example of a total disconnect from reality.

In fact, the principle of self-interest works for government equally as well. Instead of building a better widget, however, a government bureaucrat can only get a reward by building a bigger empire. That can't happen if the rule of law constrains government from growing, but will *always* happen if government is not constrained.

The entire purpose of an unconstrained socialist government becomes one of finding more efficient reasons and ways to take what belongs to one person and give it to another who has not earned it. The person or company that may have created a better widget, or improved it, won't bother because his or her reward is taken away and given to someone else. Everyone suffers. It is why socialism, fascism and communism always fail.

Misplaced Philanthropy

This is exactly what Bastiat goes on to explain. History reveals that Rousseau-type plundering is usually the result of misplaced greed and philanthropy:

> The law has been perverted by the influence of two entirely different causes: stupid greed and false philanthropy.[121] …There is…a tendency that is common among people. When they can, *they wish to live and prosper at the expense of others*. This is no rash accusation. Nor does it come from a gloomy and uncharitable spirit. The annals of history bear witness to the truth of it: the incessant wars, mass migrations, religious persecutions, universal slavery, dishonesty in commerce, and monopolies. This fatal desire has its origin in the very nature of man—in that primitive, universal, and *insuppressible instinct that impels him to satisfy his desires with the least possible pain*.… This process is the origin of plunder….(Italics added)[122]

In the case of philanthropy, those who wish to plunder often use the excuse that they are merely trying to help those in need. Bastiat explains, "When a politician views society from the seclusion of his office, he is struck by the spectacle of the inequality that he sees. He deplores the deprivations which are the lot of so many of our brothers."[123] While we should help those in need, there has been an increasing cacophony of cries in the U.S. about this injustice or that environmental disaster. The only remedy ever put forward to these alleged problems is Rousseau socialism and more state control. That is exactly what Milton Friedman told Phil Donahue will create the conditions "where the masses are worst off."

In trying to remedy these kinds of problems, Bastiat claims that a socialist politician's "mind turns to organizations, combinations, and arrangements—legal or apparently legal. He attempts to remedy the evil by income or asset redistribution, perpetuating the very thing that caused the evil in the first place: legal plunder."

There are more than enough people willing to accept such plunder: "Now since man is naturally inclined to avoid pain—and since labor is pain in itself—it follows that men will resort to plunder whenever plunder is easier than work. History shows this quite clearly..."[124] In this case of legal plunder, however, the person who receives the benefits is not responsible for the act of plundering. The responsibility for this legal plunder rests with the law, the legislator, and society itself. Therein lies the political danger.[125]

Taking Care of the Poor

Legitimate law as defined by the Declaration of Independence and the United States Constitution is based on the concept that "all men are created equal," which provides for the *equality of opportunity* to succeed or fail. Conversely, socialist law seeks *equality of prosperity*, which can only occur through plunder. In doing so it encourages greed and laziness while rewarding failure.

This may seem cold-blooded to many who have an honest desire to help the poor. Indeed, it is the common assumption that the U.S. welfare program has taken millions of people off the poverty rolls. But ask yourself, 'has the trillions of dollars spent on poverty in America since the Great Society program of President Johnson's really helped the poor?

In 1966, the first full year following the passage of the Great Society legislation, the percentage of all Americans below the poverty level was 15 percent. While it dropped to 11.1 in 1973—alleged proof that socialism worked—it increased back to 15 percent in 1982-83 and again in 1992-93.[126] In 2000 it was again 11.3 percent.[127] In 2010 it was once again 15.1 percent.[128]

Since Johnson instituted his Great Society, the percentage of Americans below the poverty level has varied from 11.1 percent to 15 percent several times. What brought the poverty level down in each case was an improving economy—an economy based on free markets and property rights, *not* socialist welfare programs. Yet, socialists despise capitalism and adamantly believe that more income redistribution is the only answer.[129]

The progressive view of endlessly subsidizing the poor is diametrically opposed to the observation of Benjamin Franklin,

> I am for doing good to the poor, but I differ in opinion of the means. I think the best way of doing good to the poor, is not making them easy *in* poverty, but leading or driving them *out* of it. In my youth I travelled much, and I observed in different countries, that the more public provisions were made for the poor, the less they provided for themselves, and of course became poorer. And, on the contrary, the less was done for them, the more they did for themselves, and became richer.[130]

This, of course, assumes the existence of human nature; the *natural* propensity of every human is to take the easy way out and blame others for their failings and weaknesses. This is diametrically opposite of the progressive liberal's worldview. There is no such thing as human nature to a progressive. To them there is no such thing as an evil person or nation, a criminal, or a lazy bum. These "symptoms" are merely the result of bad government. They believe that if these people were treated right in the first place, there would be no evil, criminals, or laziness in the world.

The socialist manipulators attack the Locke natural law of self-determination and equality of opportunity by creating the perception that the poor were treated as second-class citizens who were *victims* of the rich, rather than because of their own choices. As victims, they had the *equal right* to share the benefits enjoyed by the majority of middle and upper-income Americans who unfairly took advantage of them. The solution was to plunder the middle and upper classes in order to impose Rousseau socialism.

It is easy to test Franklin's observation that "the best way of doing good to the poor, is not making them easy in poverty, but leading or driving them *out* of it." [131] If progressive liberals are right, how do they explain two siblings brought up in exactly the same environment where one becomes a solid citizen who contributes to society while the other becomes a criminal, a tyrant or a lazy bum?

3 – Wrongly Using the Law to Plunder

Environment is important and should be made as positive as possible. However, unless human nature is controlled, society will degenerate into chaos as we are now seeing in the U.S. and Europe, just as observed by Franklin. The Bible admonishes us that "The one who is unwilling to work shall not eat."[132] At the same time the Bible admonishes us to "to visit orphans and widows in their trouble."[133] As discussed in Chapter 2, this forms part of God's law, that if broken will lead to the slippery slope of social collapse. If this is true, then no progressive welfare plan is going to work. The test then, is to ask whether our welfare state has improved social stability or deteriorated it.

While the social laws have certainly helped some individuals, the trillions of dollars spent by the Great Society and other social programs have done absolutely nothing to reduce poverty in America. Our economy is on the brink of total collapse and class warfare is tearing our nation apart. The Great Society and its numerous progenies have created an entire segment of our society that is now completely dependent on the government for their day-to-day survival.

Whether intentional or unintentional, huge voting blocs have become slaves to the government and are more than willing to vote for anyone who will promise them more plunder. In doing so, they have established a vicious cycle that increasingly and insidiously perverts the law that eventually leads to the implosion the U.S. is facing today.

It is true that many people really do want to get off welfare and become productive. But *Inc.* magazine reports that 50 to 60 percent of welfare hires disappear by the end of the first pay period. Even when training organizations help screen and train those who want productive jobs, the mountain of paperwork required by social services buries both the candidate and employer. "It's like social services doesn't really care if they have a job," TCA Fulfillment Service vice-president Lynn Giordano says. (TCA is a $1.2-million a year telemarketing and fulfillment company in New Rochelle, N.Y.)[134]

Truth be known, social services employees are too overwhelmed with the multitude of tragic stories—some legitimate, some illegitimate. Welfare workers have to distance themselves emotionally to keep their own sanity. The system devolves into a one-size-fits-all set of requirements that dehumanizes both the social worker and the recipient. Social workers often become jaded by the worst society has to offer and try to cover every possible contingency by creating mountains of rules and regulations that freeze victims into the system.

Bastiat claims that this tragedy is the natural result of the Rousseau model of socialism. He does not deny we should help our fellow man when they cannot help themselves, but insists that it should be done on a *personal* level. If families and local communities take responsibility for their brothers and fellow citizens, only the truly needy will get assistance. That assistance will usually come with the strong encouragement to find gainful employment, if possible.

Bastiat notes that the socialist will avoid personal responsibility for giving of himself or his own property to the needy, and instead will choose to plunder others to provide for the necessity. "It is demanded" by socialists, notes Bastiat, "that the law should directly extend welfare, education, and morality throughout the nation. This is the seductive lure of socialism."[135]

That is also true today. Of the top 25 states in which people give to charitable causes more than the average, 24 were states that voted Republican. Arthur Brooks, the author of *Who Really Cares*, says that "when you look at the data, it turns out the conservatives give about 30 percent more" than liberals. Equally significant, conservative-headed families earn slightly less income than do liberals.[136]

Critics will say that people will not take this personal responsibility, thereby necessitating government intervention to help those in need through forced taxation. This truth merely shows how far society has sunk into the socialist quagmire of state control over everything. It is also true for most of the Jewish synagogues and Christian churches. God commands these members to help the poor: "Whoever shuts his ears to the cry of the poor will also cry himself and not be heard." (Proverbs 21:13 NKJ)

The fact that Christians and Jews are willing to give this responsibility to the government reveals the insidious nature of socialism to numb the consciousness of believers to the point where they feel they have met their Biblical responsibilities. Even so, church people give four times the amount that liberals give to charitable, non-church causes; Arthur Brooks emphasizes that "The religious Americans are more likely to give to every kind of cause and charity, including explicitly non-religious charities."[137] In fact, the Jews and Christians have defaulted on their responsibilities, in part because the government takes such a large chunk of their income in taxes. In doing so, these hapless victims are turned over to a system that will enslave them for the rest of their lives, perhaps for generations.

PLUNDERING BY ENVIRONMENTAL LAW

AS NOTED EARLIER in this chapter, Bastiat said that if the state passes a law forcing a person to use his property for an arbitrary purpose that harms the owner, then the person automatically becomes a criminal if he attempts to protect it or use it in a normal or traditional way for him and his family. In fact, most social and environmental laws deny some people to use their land in certain ways that are allowed other citizens. It is usually arbitrary and capricious. Worse, it is often corrupt.

The Endangered Species Act (ESA) has fined or put many Americans into prison for merely defending themselves or conducting normal activities, just as Frédéric Bastiat said would happen with Rousseau socialism. Juanita Swanke was fined $1350 after she killed a grizzly bear that was chasing her horse into her corral. Initially, she shot around the bear in an attempt to scare it off. But when this failed, she had no choice but to kill the animal.[138]

In a similar case, Montana sheepherder John Shuler discovered four Grizzly Bears on his property. He went outside and fired warning shots that scared off three of the animals. Returning to his house, he found another one blocking his path. The huge beast reared on its hind legs. In fear for his life, Shuler shot and killed the animal. However, officials with the Department of the Interior fined Shuler $5,000, arguing that he couldn't claim self-defense because he purposely entered a "zone of imminent danger." That zone was his backyard.[139]

In both cases, the ESA turned Swanke and Shuler into criminals for merely protecting their lives and livestock. Had the law been obeyed, they would have had to volunteer themselves and their livestock as a food source for the endangered species. U.S. statutory law and common law has always provided that a person can defend his life and property from this kind of harm. The ESA, however, puts nature's rights before man, and in doing so it trashes more than two hundred years of U.S. constitutional law and nearly a thousand years of common law, not to mention decency and common sense.

A person does not even have to have an endangered species on their property to fall victim to this abuse of power. The United States Fish and Wildlife Service (USFWS) threatened to fine a Utah farmer $15,000 for farming his land and allegedly posing a risk to the Utah Prairie Dog, a protected species. The only problem is that a professional survey found that there were no Utah Prairie Dogs on his property, so the farmer worked his land.

The USFWS reasoned that since it is *theoretically possible* for Utah Prairie Dogs in the surrounding area to migrate onto the property, they have the right to issue a fine for harming a *potential* habitat.[140] This is known as the "precautionary principle" whereby zealous bureaucrats can justify anything they want as long as there is the remotest of chance that an action may cause harm sometime in the foreseeable, or even unforeseeable future.

It gets worse. In 1991 John Pozsgai purchased a 14 acre tract across the street from his business so he could expand. Used as a dump for 20 years, John's first effort was to clean up 7,000 old tires along with an assortment of rusting car parts, and replace them with clean dirt and gravel. The property was not a marsh, swamp or bog, and state officials told Pozsgai that he needed no permit.[141]

Unknown to Pozsgai, since a mostly dry stream bed was adjacent to the cleanup in progress, and since there were sweet gum trees present as well as skunk cabbage, John's land had the misfortune of falling under the 1989 wetlands jurisdiction definition.[142] The EPA obtained a restraining order to prevent the deposit of the fill, whereupon Pozsgai immediately erected barricades to keep the contractors he had hired from dumping any more fill. But, alas, John did not camp out on the site to forcibly stop the contractors.

Several contractors who had not yet gotten the word drove around the barricades and deposited their loads as prescribed in the contracts. The EPA video-taped these contractors placing the clean dirt on the land, which was then used to convict John of violating 41 counts of the "Navigable Waters" provision of the Clean Water Act. The trial bankrupted John, yet the court fined him $202,000 and sentenced him to three years in prison. The Court also ordered him to restore the land—not to its previous state—but to a pristine condition![143]

Pozsgai could not believe what had happened. This was America, home of the free, where even an immigrant from Hungary could start with nothing and, through hard work, build a solid business and a good life. Now, because he cleaned up some junk tires and started to build a garage, the government sent him to prison and robbed him of his life's savings.

This was just what he remembered happening to his neighbors first under Nazi occupation then at the hands of the Soviet Union!

Pozsgai was right. It was *exactly* like what he had experienced in Hungary, because both ideologies are based on the Rousseau model of governance! This is America's future if the progressive insanity is not stopped. These are but a few of the thousands of examples of normal, law-abiding citizens being turned into criminals by rightfully defending their life and property against government abuse. To be sure, we need to protect our environment, but in a way that employs the Locke model that protects the right of the citizen, not the Rousseau model whereby the citizen is turned into a criminal for merely trying to protect what is rightfully his.

Since Obama took office the EPA has become the high priest over all citizens of the United States. Mike and Chanteill Sackett found that out in 2007 when they attempted to build a home on their 0.63-acre lot. After securing all the necessary building permits they began preparing the land for building. Three EPA employees showed up and told them their land was a wetlands and to cease and desist all work. The EPA then ordered them to restore the land back into its original condition at their own expense and plant wetland species that had never grown on the property. If they refused, the EPA would fine them $37,000 a day! That was generous of the EPA apparently. They could have levied a fine of $75,000 a day. [144]

The land was not designated as wetlands on the EPA's wetlands map. The decision was apparently made on the spot by the three EPA zealots. After the EPA refused the Sacketts a hearing, they sued, and the Pacific Legal Foundation took it all the way to the U. S. Supreme Court. Even the progressive members of the Supreme Court were astonished at the seeming EPA abuse. When the Court heard the case on January 9, 2012, Justice Antonin Scalia condemned the "high-handedness" of the EPA while Justice Samuel Alito called it "outrageous,"[145] noting that most homeowners would say it "can't happen in the United States."[146]

Justice Elena Kagan joined in the apparent unanimous disbelief by the Supremes of the EPA's actions. Kagan called it a "strange position" for the government to insist the property owner has no right to a hearing.[146] Justice Ruth Ginzburg agreed. Justice Stephen Breyer noted, "For 75 years the courts have interpreted statutes with an eye towards permitting judicial review, not the opposite." Chief Justice John Roberts noted:

Because of the administrative compliance order, you're really never going to be put to the test, because most land owners aren't going to say, 'I'm going to risk the $37,000 a day," Roberts said. "All EPA has to do is make whatever finding it wants, and realize that in 99 percent of the cases, it's never going to be put to the test."[147]

Therein lies the problem. The government has unlimited time and money to bully and intimidate citizens into complying with arbitrary and capricious regulations. When it is finally revealed, it is likely the Sacketts spent a million dollars to take their case all the way to the Supreme Court—something that very few citizens can do. That is the first giant step to tyranny.

With the kind of questions asked during oral arguments by even the progressive Justices, it was not surprising the Supreme Court unanimously found in favor of the Sacketts on March 21, 2012.[148] In issuing a second concurring opinion, Justice Samuel Alito wrote the government's position in the case "would have put the property rights of ordinary Americans entirely at the mercy of…EPA employees."[149] Many observers are convinced that was exactly the precedent the EPA was attempting to establish.

That interpretation was exposed in April 2012 when a 2010 video surfaced showing EPA Region 6 Director Al Armendariz—an Obama appointee—telling an audience:

My philosophy of enforcement is kind of like how the Romans used to conquer little villages in the Mediterranean. They'd go into a little Turkish town somewhere, they'd find the first five guys they saw and they'd crucify them. And then, you know, that town was really easy to manage for the next few years.[150]

Although Armendariz was referring to how he is crucifying oil and natural gas companies, it nonetheless accurately depicts the culture of the EPA and why it tried to crucify the Sacketts. Armendariz tried to apologize, but there was no question that represented his—and the EPA's—true belief and he eventually had to resign.

Unfortunately, the Supreme Court's decision does not punish the arrogant EPA perpetrators who will do the same thing again and again because they are never held personally accountable. The only way to send a message is for the Sacketts to sue the *individual* EPA employees for violating the Sacketts constitutional rights in the Court of Federal Claims. That would send a strong message throughout all federal agencies.

THE HIGH COST OF SOCIALISM

SOCIALISM IS NEITHER CHEAP nor efficient. Government "one size fits all" solutions are enormously expensive and create huge bureaucracies that treat people like mindless automatons. The IRS reports that tax collections went up from $187 billion in 1969,[151] at the beginning of President Johnson's Great Society Program, to $2.35 trillion in 2010.[152] Most of the increase was due to socialist programs and inflation.

In 1900, before socialism seriously began to creep into the federal budget, "Americans paid a total effective tax rate of only 5.7%. Tax freedom day fell on January 20. In 2000…Americans paid a total effective tax rate of 33.3 percent—a full third of the national income.[153] Tax Freedom Day fell that year at the latest point ever—May 1."[154] In 2011, the tax freedom day was April 12, and the effective tax rate had dropped to 28 percent, in large measure do to the Bush tax cuts.[a] However, that isn't the entire picture. When the federal deficit is added in, the 2011 tax freedom day jumps to May 23.[155]

In short, nearly a third of the average working American's salary goes to feeding the Rousseau socialist behemoth originally created in the twentieth century. In 2011 alone, almost $2.1 trillion was budgeted for mandatory social programs—not touchable by Congress. That is up from $1 trillion in 2002.[156]

Bastiat noted also that a characteristic of socialist power in government is to demonize anyone who would question the need for their enlightened socialist programs. "If you suggest a doubt as to the morality of these institutions," warns Bastiat, "it is boldly said that 'You are a dangerous innovator, a utopian, a theorist, a subversive; you would shatter the foundation upon which society rests.'"[157] Bastiat continues, saying,

---

[a] The effective tax rate is determined by dividing per capita burden of all local, state and federal taxes by the per capita income. The tax freedom day is the day when the average American will have worked long enough to pay all his or her taxes.

Socialism confuses the distinction between government and society. As a result of this, every time we object to a thing being done by government, the socialists conclude that we object to its being done at all. We disapprove of *state* education. Then the socialists say that we are opposed to *any* education. We object to a *state* religion. Then the socialists say that we want *no* religion at all. We object to a state-enforced equality. Then they say that we are against equality.[158]

Nothing has changed in the 160 years since Bastiat penned these words. The same exact type of demonization continues unabated today. Bastiat also argues that these socialists believe, like Rousseau, that "people have within themselves no means of discernment; no motivation to action. They…assume that people are inert matter, passive particles, motionless atoms, at best a kind of vegetation indifferent to its own manner of existence. They assume that people are susceptible to being shaped—by the will and of another person—into an infinite variety of forms, more or less symmetrical, artistic, and perfected."[159]

Just who is "another person" or persons who will do the molding? Themselves, of course. They, after all, are far more intelligent than you and I. They are not just content with administering justice; they want justice to include *their* version of what is just, which is usually the opposite of the Judeo-Christian ethic that has prevailed in America since early colonial days;

They desire to set themselves above mankind in order to arrange, organize, and regulate it *according to their fancy.…* They think only of subjecting mankind to the philanthropic tyranny of their own social inventions. *Like Rousseau, they desire to force mankind docilely to bear this yoke of the public welfare that they have dreamed up in their own imaginations.*[160] (Italics added)

To socialist "intellectuals and writers," notes Bastiat, "the relationship between persons and the legislator appears to be the same as the relationship between the clay and the potter.… In all of them, you will probably find this idea that mankind is merely inert matter, receiving life, organization, morality, and prosperity from the power of the state."[161] If true, a socialist believes that other human beings are merely un-programmed computers who require their programming to create the model global citizen. How it was done is explained in Chapters 10 and 11.

Therefore everything has to be planned for the people by those who are enlightened to keep them from self-destructing; "Since the law organizes justices, the socialists ask why the law should not also organize labor, education, and religion." Bastiat then asks the next logical question:

> Why should not law be used for these purposes? Because it could not organize labor, education, and religion without destroying [true] justice. We must remember that law is force,…[and] when law and force keep a person within the bounds of justice,… they oblige him only to abstain from harming others…. They are *defensive*; they defend equally the rights of all.[162]
>
> But when the law, by means of its necessary agent, force, imposes upon men a regulation of labor, a method or a subject of education, a religious faith or creed—then the law… substitutes the will of the legislator for their own wills; the initiative of the legislator for their own initiatives. *When this happens, the people no longer need to discuss, to compare, to plan ahead; the law does all this for them. Intelligence becomes a useless prop for the people; they cease to be men; they lose their personality, their liberty, their property.*[163] (Italics added)

In other words, they become automatons. When the Western world attempted to introduce capitalism into the former communist nations in the 1990s, it failed miserably. They instituted all the structures of capitalism except private property rights. How were former Soviet citizens, for whom the state made all the decisions, going to understand how to retool and develop a dilapidated factory that was no longer state controlled? Indeed, why would they even want to? Where was the incentive?

However, if the introduction included private property rights, whereby their rewards would be dependent on the effort expended, there would suddenly be a big incentive to create a needed product. True, mistakes would be made because of lack of knowledge and experience, but it has been shown elsewhere that thousands of small businesses would have appeared overnight in the first step towards a flourishing capitalistic system. Instead, any new business had to operate extra-legally. Hernando de Soto reports in *The Mystery of Capital*, that:

> ...people who could not operate within the law also could not hold property efficiently or enforce contracts through the courts; nor could they reduce uncertainty through limited liability in insurance policies or create stock companies to attract additional capital and share risk. Being unable to raise money for investment, they could not achieve economies of scale or protect their innovations through royalties and patents.[164] ...The only "insurance" available to them is that provided by their neighbors and the protection that local bullies or Mafias are willing to sell them.[165]

Thus was born the Russian Mafia out of the former KGB, and other political forces left over after the Soviet system crumbled. The corrupt system of the Mafia only gutted the nation further. The "protection" fees levied by the Mafia plus the extortion by corrupt officials more than made up for the lack of taxes the new entrepreneurs would have paid if they had been operating within the system. The myriad of would-be entrepreneurs had all the disadvantages and none of the advantages of a legal property system. Says de Soto:

> The disastrous economic effects of this legal apartheid are most strikingly visible in the lack of formal property rights over real estate. In every country we researched, we found that some 80 percent of land parcels were not protected by up-to-date records or held by legally accountable owners.[166]

The Vicious Nature of Legalized Plunder

Tragically, this is but just the beginning of the vicious cycle of plunder. There is another natural tendency of men—when plundered unjustly, they fight back. "Thus," explains Bastiat, "when plunder is organized by law for the profit of those who make the law" and those who benefit from the law, "all the plundered classes try somehow to enter—organized by law for the profit—into the making of laws."[167]

When everyone wants to share in the plunder, the democratic process devolves into madness whereby "men seek to balance their conflicting interests by universal plunder.... As soon as the plundered classes gain political power, they establish a system of reprisals against other classes. Obama's vicious class warfare is the perfect example. They do not abolish legal plunder. Instead they emulate their evil predecessors by participating in this legal plunder, even though it is against their own interests."[168] In the United States, it makes little difference whether the Republicans or Democrats are in power. Both parties propose laws that plunder citizens without a second thought.

Bastiat explains this degeneration further. "Under the pretense of organization, regulation, protection, or encouragement the law takes property from one person and gives it to another; the law takes the wealth of all and gives it to a few—whether farmers, manufacturers, ship owners, artists, [or the poor]. Under these circumstances, then certainly every class will aspire to grasp the law, and logically so."[169] As various factions grasp powerful political positions to plunder for themselves, the law becomes vicious and destructive:

As long as it is admitted that the law may be diverted from its true purpose—that it may violate property instead of protecting it–then everyone will want to participate in making the law, either to protect himself against plunder or to use it for plunder. *Political questions will always be prejudicial, dominant, and all absorbing. There will be fighting at the door of the Legislative Place, and the struggle within will be no less furious....* Is there any need to offer proof that *this odious perversion of the law is a perpetual source of hatred and discord; that it tends to destroy society itself?*[170] (Italics added)

Does this sound like twenty-first century politics in the United States? The eventual result is paralysis and finally self-destruction. Our Founding Fathers understood this gruesome truth. That is why James Madison wrote in the Federalist Papers 10.21 and 10.22 that:

In all cases where a majority is united by a common interest or passion, the rights of the minority are in danger..... [A] pure democracy can admit of no cure for the mischiefs of [the majority] and there is nothing to check the inducements to sacrifice the weaker party. *Hence it is that such democracies have ever been spectacles of turbulence and contention; have ever been found incompatible with personal securities or the right of property; and have in general been as short in their lives as they have been violent in their deaths.* (Italics added)

Madison clearly identifies why Rousseau's model cannot work. It factionalizes an otherwise united people into special interest groups, each fighting to either take the other's rights or property for their own purpose, or defending their own rights or property from the other group. Instead of unifying the whole, as Rousseau postulates, his model invariably creates hostility and division within the whole, ultimately tearing itself apart—just as is happening in the United States in 2012.

It is why Thomas Jefferson, after witnessing the horrid results of the first French Revolution wrote, "When all government, domestic and foreign, in little as in great things, *shall be drawn to Washington as the center of all power*, it will render powerless the checks provided of one government on another and *will become as venal and oppressive as the government from which we separated.*"[171] (Italics added)

A pure democracy is nothing more than two wolves and a lamb voting on what to have for dinner. Almost all politicians and national leaders have told Americans that the U.S. is a democracy so many times that we now believe it and are acting like a democracy. Consequently, America is devouring itself through plundering.

To prevent this, our founders established a Constitutional Republic that divided power into three branches of government, legislative, executive, and judicial, and a minimum of three levels of government, local, state and federal. The founders *deliberately* intended to make government terribly *inefficient*. A government can only become efficient at the expense of the people's liberty. By definition, a government must be able to control the people to be efficient. It is for this reason that the founders included the Tenth Amendment, which states, "The powers not delegated to the United States by the Constitution, nor prohibited by it to the States, are reserved to the States respectively, or to the people."

The founders gave only eighteen powers to Congress in Article I, Section 8—most of which dealt with the national defense or foreign trade—specifically to keep the federal government weak thereby protecting the people from an abusive, plundering government. Progressives in Congress have slowly and insidiously expanded those eighteen powers to thousands, giving truth to the warning of Thomas Jefferson, "The natural process of things is for liberty to yield and government to gain ground."[172]

Our national leaders are transforming the United States from a republican government of the people, by the people, and for the people, into a democratic government whereby nearly all power to legally plunder resides at the federal level. It has been done through the siren song of making the government more efficient; of making our monetary supply more secure by creating the Federal Reserve; of helping the poor with vast welfare and social programs; of making our homeland more secure from terrorism; of creating wilderness areas of making the rights of animals more important than human rights; and a host of other actions taken in the past one hundred years.

Each legislative action has given more power to fewer people, slowly weakening our beloved Bill of Rights that protects our civil liberties. America's leaders have transformed this once solid nation, which was committed to serving and protecting its citizens, to a nation that is plundering its citizens and destroying the very foundation upon which they built the nation. Bastiat proclaims to all who would listen:

> It is impossible to introduce into society a greater change and a greater evil than this: the conversion of the law into an instrument of plunder. In the first place, it erases from everyone's conscience the distinction between justice and injustice. No society can exist unless the laws are respected to a certain degree. The safest way to make laws respected is to make them respectable. When law and morality contradict each other, the citizen has the cruel alternative of either losing his moral sense or losing his respect for the law.[173]

Could the reason politicians and corporate leaders in America today are losing their moral direction be because socialist dogma has morally perverted the law in America? Could the sudden appearance of the Tea Party, 9-12ers, constitutionalists, conservatives and property-rights advocates in America who decry the injustice of many federal laws be the result of socialist plundering? Of course they are. There can be no other explanation.

When does plunder stop? The only solution is to return the law to its original purpose—to protect each individual's right to life, liberty, and property. In the final analysis, plunder "stops when it becomes more painful and more dangerous than labor. It is evident then that the proper purpose of law is to use the power of its collective force to stop this fatal tendency to plunder instead of to work. All the measures of the law should protect property and punish plunder."[174] Doing so not only enhances economic growth and stability, but also social stability, "Since all persons seek well-being and perfection, would not a condition of justice be sufficient to cause the greatest efforts towards progress, and the greatest possible equality that is compatible with individual responsibility?"[175]

Bastiat would not recognize the United States today with nearly all laws plundering the people, causing factions and destroying the unity that once existed in America. Although he is speaking of nineteenth century France, he could have very well been talking about twenty-first century America when he said:

> The present-day delusion is an attempt to enrich everyone at the expense of everyone else, to make plunder universal under the pretense of organizing it. Now legal plunder can be committed in an infinite number of ways:...tariffs, protection, benefits, subsidies, encouragements (welfare), progressive taxation, public schools, guaranteed jobs, guaranteed profits, minimum wages, a right to relief, a right to the tools of labor, free credit, and so on, and so on. *All these plans as a whole—with their common aim of legal plunder—constitute socialism.*[176] (Italics added)

WHAT TO EXPECT

LED BY PROGRESSIVE LIBERALS, Rousseau socialism has invaded America. Progressive liberals claim their way is the American Way. It is not. Not even close. It has perverted the American Way into a cesspool of plunder. It dominates our culture and thinking, even of those who consider themselves conservatives. It has invaded everything in America, causing citizens to fight citizens as they try to plunder one another. As America moves ever closer to Rousseau socialism and away from the Locke constitutional republican government, we are tearing ourselves to shreds, just as warned by Frederic Bastiat and James Madison.

People may legitimately ask themselves, 'how come no one told me? How could I have missed it?' The answer is simple; people weren't supposed to see it. It is a matter of historical fact, but it is not in the newspapers or on the evening news. It is not in the classrooms. Yet, as shall be seen in this book, the evidence is everywhere—if people know what to look for. Powerful institutions have spent billions of tax dollars to very slowly create a new Rousseau socialist government that gives them more and more power while stripping America of its roots and Americans from their liberty.

The older generations can see the change and they know something is terribly wrong. Nevertheless they generally do not know what that problem is. For the younger generations, what they see today is reality to them. They know nothing different. Their revisionist history books do not tell them that America has a proud history of relative innocence, complete with real heroes.

How did this happen? One thing is certain—it absolutely, unequivocally DID NOT happen by accident. As will be seen in the next chapter, it has been creeping in since the nineteenth century. Late 19th century psychiatrists described it perfectly even though it was not called progressivism then. The social change artists have systematically stripped citizens of their ability to see the whole picture through the perversion and dumbing down of Americans by the progressive takeover of education and media outlets for the past one hundred years. How do we stop it? There is a way, but first people must understand the history of how evil invaded the shores of this great land.

4 – HISTORY OF PROGRESSIVISM

Mobs have been a plague on humanity virtually since humans first walked on the earth. They are dangerous because mob psychosis breaks down all the inhibitions in people necessary for civilization to thrive. People caught up in the emotion of the mob will do heinous things they wouldn't even consider doing by themselves. Unfortunately, late nineteenth century psychiatrists began to see these same symptoms emerging in a new worldview that was sweeping Europe. They defined what is now known as the ideology of the early progressive movement.

NINETEENTH CENTURY HISTORY AND TWENTIETH CENTURY REALITY

IN THE LATE NINETEENTH CENTURY, progressive thinking had become so sufficiently prominent that it attracted the attention of the well-respected French physician, scientist and social scientist named Gustave Le Bon. Le Bon conducted in-depth studies of the growing phenomenon which he termed *psychological crowd behavior*, or what is known today as mob behavior. Had Le Bon been an Englishman or American, he likely would have missed the origins of the progressive movement. As Le Bon himself acknowledged, the movement uniquely grew out of the writings of Jean Jacques Rousseau and the French Revolution. It didn't noticeably infect Britain or the U.S. until the late nineteenth century. The resulting progressivism defines the rancorous war of worldviews dividing America today.

Le Bon wasn't talking about a group of people, but a group where the "sentiments and ideas of all the persons" involved "take one and the same direction, and their conscious personality vanishes. A collective mind is formed,...but presenting very clearly defined characteristics."[177] Le Bon published papers and several books, but the book that became the standard for understanding crowd or mob behavior was his 1896 *The Crowd; A Study of the Popular Mind.*[178] (Today it would be entitled The Mob or Progressivism).

The Crowd describes a distressing picture of modern-day progressive liberal behavior. He called the progressive phenomenon "a psychological crowd... subject...to the law of the mental unity of crowds [mobs]."[179] In other words, the early progressive movement exhibited striking similarities to mob behavior. As we shall see, it still does today.

Stuart Jeffries, writing in The Guardian, a left-wing British newspaper, recently brought attention to the importance of *The Crowd*, "French social psychologist Gustave Le Bon described crowds as mobs in which individuals lost their personal consciences. Le Bon's book, *The Crowd...* influenced Hitler and led many later psychologists to take a dim view of crowds."[180] Le Bon was also Mussolini's favorite psychologist.[181] In his book, *The Roots of Nazi Psychology, Hitler's Utopian Barbarism*, author Jay Gonen noted that in *Mein Kampf* Hitler almost plagiarized Le Bon's book. "Many of Hitler's propaganda techniques for enforcing his will on the masses appeared to come from Le Bon.... [Hitler] reused [Le Bon's] ideas and manipulated them for political impact."[182] Both Hitler and Mussolini[183] used Le Bon's findings as a roadmap to whip up the emotions of a crowd.

Le Bon notes that mobs also worship their leaders.[184] Both of the Clintons are worshiped. Obama has been declared the Messiah so many times that people have lost track. Conversely, although President Reagan was held in high esteem by conservatives, many among even conservatives today are still critical of some of the things he did wrong—especially of his inability to cut the budget when he cut taxes.

Although Le Bon says it is impossible to describe every characteristic of a psychological crowd or mob, he does identify several that we see in action by liberal progressives today. First, there is a sense "of invincible power" to do things one would never do alone. Second, there is a "contagion" of thought—almost hypnotic—whereby the contagion is so strong "that an individual readily sacrifices his personal interest to the collective interest." A simplistic idea or thought introduced to the mob by its leaders spreads like wildfire and can be unjustified by reality. Third, is the immediate acceptance of an idea or action to commit "acts in utter contradiction with his character and habits," not unlike a "hypnotic" state.[185]

Le Bon concludes this description with the comment that the individual "is no longer himself, but has become an automaton who has ceased to be guided by his will."[186] All of us have observed that a sound bite or slogan introduced by a progressive liberal one day, is regurgitated by a million progressive liberals the next day. Le Bon found that the mob thinks in images that are interlinked and are contagious to all members of the group. How else can you explain very adamant statements by progressives and the mainstream press that Obama had put forward a "detailed plan" in his April 13, 2011 speech on how to address the deficits and debt, when in fact he had given absolutely no specifics? It was repeated over and over again.

Those in the mob accept images as real and actionable, "though they most often have only a very distant relation with the observed fact."[187] Hence, progressive liberals are extremely motivated by sound bites or slogans on signs. The sound bites and slogans become fact, no longer requiring critical thinking. Tragically, it requires no thinking at all. It stimulates an automatic reaction. Le Bon calls this "collective hallucination" and can be quite powerful.[188]

That's exactly how Obama manipulated progressives in his April 13 speech on deficits and debt. He used a massive amount of highly emotional word pictures and sound bites; all based in how we are all "connected" and must solve this together. He used the phrase Social Security 12 times and Medicare 17 times to show how concerned he was how they helped less fortunate Americans. He then stated "This is my approach to reduce the deficit by $4 trillion over the next *twelve* years," and then gave four steps of his plan to do it. There was only one problem. There was nothing new in those steps, and certainly nothing specific in how he was going to do it. Yet, the media gushed the next day about what a great detailed plan it was. By the following evening, the contagion spread to every progressive and most liberals in the country.

The contagion phenomenon likely explains the progressive disconnect from reality. During the debt ceiling debacle in July and early August of 2011, the progressive mantra was that the Tea Party congressmen and women were "holding the economy of the nation hostage." After the S&P downgrade on August 5, 2011, every progressive Democrat instantly parroted the sound bite that what happened was a "Tea Party downgrade."

Like automatons, within a day every progressive politician or pendant was faithfully regurgitating the sound bite of the day.

The "holding the nation hostage" sound bite was used so often that it became obnoxious. Fox and Friends hostess Gretchen Carlson had a panel discussion on the overused one-liner with one Democrat and one Republican. It was obvious Debbie Wasserman Schultz (D-FL), chair of the Democratic National Committee, hadn't done any critical thinking about the sound bite. In an increasingly shrill voice, she actually used the phrase itself to describe the phrase several times before being pinned down by Carlson.

That's circular reasoning. With a deer-in-the-headlights expression, she finally blurted out "because they did!" As if that explained everything.[189] Sadly, to progressive liberals it does say everything. It strikes at the very marrow of their bones. It would immediately evoke images of the evil George Bush who they *know* is responsible for all the problems in the world. According to Le Bon, this is classic mob mentality.

Progressives really do believe their own reality. Gretchen Carlson must love to have Wasserman Schultz on Fox and Friends, because their discussions are right out of the twilight zone. On December 12, 2011, Carlson mentioned in passing the fact that "unemployment has gone up precipitously since [Obama] took office. Before Carlson could move on to her main point, Wasserman Schultz interrupted her while shaking her head saying "that is simply not true." Incredulously, Carlson fired back, "Yes it is." To which Wasserman Shultz fired back, "In fact, unemployment has now dropped below 9 percent. It's continuing to drop. He's been focused on..."[190]

Carlson, now getting her stride, confronted Wasserman Shultz, "But it's higher than when they [the Obama administration] promised that the stimulus would lower it to 8 percent ..." Now in full combat mode, Wasserman Shultz shot back, "See, that narrative doesn't work for you anymore, though, because when President Obama..." Not giving an inch, Carlson interjected, "It's not my narrative. I'm just talking about facts, where the unemployment numbers are." To this Wasserman Shultz blurted out, "You just said that the unemployment rate has been going up since he took office, and it hasn't."[191] Really? It got worse from there. It was so bizarre you can't make it up.

Weeks after the exchange political analysts were still wondering what planet Wasserman Shultz was on during the dialog. But it is classic mob (progressive) mentality according to Le Bon. He observed that mobs characteristically exhibit impulsiveness, irritability (violence), incapacity to reason or deal in reality, lack of good judgment and a large capacity to exaggerate.[192] That describes both of the Carlson/Wasserman Shultz exchanges.

Exaggerated sound bites don't require any critical thinking. The progressive liberals blamed the Tea Party and their congressional representatives for the debt limit debacle while holding Obama up as a god. Progressive Democrats were outraged at the Tea Party for not allowing them to raise taxes in a "balanced approach" to reduce the deficit.

Congresswoman Maxine Waters (D-CA) even said the "Tea Party can go straight to Hell."[193] Apparently, she believes the U.S. can continue to increase its debt with no consequences whatsoever. She told the delegates at the California Democratic Convention that Republicans, especially John Boehner and Eric Cantor are "demons." With a shrill voice she said, "Don't ever let me see again, in life, these Republicans in our hall.... These are demons."[194]

Then there's Harry Reid's bizarre claim that, "My Republican friends have yet to produce a single shred of evidence that the regulations they hate so much do the broad economic harms they claim. That's because there aren't any."[195] Really? Tragically, the inability of progressives like Waters, Reid and Obama to deal with reality, even sanity, is a common and increasingly dangerous symptom.

That's not all. Incredibly, as discussed in Chapter 2, the progressive Democrats blamed the S&P downgrade squarely on the Tea Party. The day of the S&P downgrade an outraged John Kerry acidly made this outrageous statement on MSNBC's "Morning Joe" program,

The media in America has a bigger responsibility than it's exercising today. The media has got to begin *to not* give equal time or equal balance to an absolutely absurd notion just because somebody in the [tea party] asserts it...which everybody knows is not factual. It [the tea party] doesn't deserve the same credit as a legitimate idea.... America is losing any sense of what's real, of who's accountable, of who is not accountable, of who's real, who isn't, who's serious, who isn't?[196]

Really? The Tea Party shouldn't be heard because they have absurd notions? They are not factual? Not accountable? Not real? Isn't the out-of-control $15.8 trillion debt (it'll be much higher by the time you read this) due to the overspending by progressive Democrats and Republicans? Wasn't it the progressive Democrats who stonewalled every conservative proposal to rein in the out-of-control deficit spending? Weren't the progressives the ones who were, and still are, holding the nation hostage? Isn't the progressive liberal's take-no-prisoner determination to not make any changes to Medicare and Social Security insane, when these programs are about to bankrupt the country? Isn't their claim that these programs are solvent absurd—no, psychotic? Wasn't it the Tea Party delegation who forced the deficit and debt issue to finally be put on the table? Aren't the Tea Party/conservative representatives the first ones in decades to finally hold the progressive Democrats accountable?

Kerry meant every word of what he said. Like Wasserman Schultz, he really *believes* his own version of reality! No one could have made this up if he tried! It is absolutely bizarre. Progressives really believe they have the only truth and anyone who disagrees with them is an obstructionist and an idiot. This disconnect from reality is extremely dangerous. Le Bon concludes his book *The Crowd*, with this warning,

> "Its civilisation [now called progressive] is now without stability, and... tide of barbarism mounts. The civilisation may still seem brilliant because it possesses an outward front, ...but it is in reality an edifice crumbling to ruin, which nothing supports, and destined to fall in at the first storm.[197]

Progressives have hollowed out the economic and moral structure of America. America still seems like the beacon of hope and shining example to the world, but it is starting to crash in on itself. One stiff push can send the whole thing crumbling down.

One well-crafted sound bite evokes an avalanche of similar visual images within a progressive liberal without any critical thinking about the reality of what they are spouting off. By being part of a mob, individuals feel like they have "invincible power" which allows them to lose any sense of responsibility that would normally prevent them from doing outrageous things. Even to the extent of taking action against their best interest. [198]

Example: Wisconsin Public Employees' Union

Take for instance the public employee's unions in Wisconsin during the winter of 2011. Wisconsin Governor Scott Walker had to reconcile a $3.8 billion projected shortfall through 2013. Like many other states, this was just the tip of the iceberg of out-of-control deficits that would be piling up in four and five years if not solved immediately.

As with other states with huge deficits, Wisconsin's troubles were caused by a corrupt cycle of public unions voting for progressive Democrats, who then vote for better and better benefits for union workers to buy their votes in the next election. This rather obvious cycle of corruption is why public workers were never allowed to organize into unions until the last half of the twentieth century.

It was then that private-sector unions were going the way of the dinosaur, and progressive Democrats realized it could provide a built-in constituency to keep them in office.[199] To break this unholy cycle, the Wisconsin lawmakers had to pass legislation to restrict the public union's collective bargaining power.

Like Le Bon's description of automatons, progressive liberals across the country and Wisconsin public employee unions went ballistic, greatly exaggerating their complaints. Feeling invincible, public workers eventually stormed the state capital, causing millions of dollars of damage. The unions spent multi-millions of dollars fighting the legislation in a debacle that was on the evening news for months.

When the legislation finally passed, unions spent about $14 million more through the summer of 2011 to try to recall Republican legislators and then tens of millions more to recall Governor Scott Walker in 2012. All the while, they were distorting the truth that what the governor and legislature did was un-American, unjust and unfair (and much, much worse).

Although the Wisconsin and national media gave the impression the unions were the pitiable poorly paid underdogs with valid complaints, the Department of Labor reported a completely different story. Rather than being underpaid, Wisconsin teachers received an average salary of $51,676, compared to $38,625 for private sector employees in comparable positions.[200] Likewise, the average benefit package for Wisconsin teachers (not including administrators) was $25,596 for a total compensation package of $77,271.

Unlike almost all private sector Americans, Wisconsin public employees did not contribute *any* of their own income towards their pension fund and only 6 percent towards the cost of their health care insurance. All Governor Walker and the Republican legislature were asking the public employees was to pay 6 percent of their monthly pension costs and 12 percent of the cost of their medical insurance. This request was *still* below the average for the Midwestern states.[201]

In total, Wisconsin public employees received 25 percent more compensation than the private sector employees.[202] Yet, the unions repeatedly proclaimed their Cadillac plan was not out of line, and the public employees deserved every penny of it. Of course, the progressive media parroted the union's misinformation. Ironically, what these union officials and employees fail to see is their Cadillac demands are based in greed. The same greed they accuse the rich of having.

As Le Bon also observed, those caught up in this mental madness lost all connection with reality and actually did what is contrary to their best interest. The protesting union members knew that 1,500 of their coworkers would have to be laid off to balance Wisconsin's budget if the legislation didn't pass. It was not a fear tactic, it was a fact. Yet, the public employees ignored reality and went on a rampage rather than work out a compromise that was in their best interest.

That's not all. Like spoiled four-year olds, the Wisconsin Democratic legislators impulsively fled the state in a vain attempt to keep the Republican majority from getting a quorum needed to pass the legislation. It was insane and totally irresponsible. Worse, progressive Democrats and unions knew if they didn't get their state budget under control, Wisconsin would eventually go bankrupt, throwing tens of thousands of employees out of work.[203] It didn't matter to these progressives. They thought and acted exactly like the mob that Le Bon described over 100 years ago.

It turned out Governor Walker had bragging rights to the actions he took. He was applying the principles of Harding and Coolidge, with similar results. By July of 2011, five months after the legislation finally passed, the state went from a $3.6 billion deficit to a budget surplus. More importantly, his policies allowed Wisconsin to create 39,000 new private sector jobs; 14,000 being in manufacturing. These new jobs represented a quarter of the jobs lost in the 2008-2009 recession, with many of those losses occurring during the implementation of Obama's stimulus plan. The state even created 9,500 jobs in June 2011, alone—more than half of the 18,000 created in the entire country that month![204]

Governor Walker explained how he created the miracle on the August 3, 2011, episode of Fox and Friends: "We changed the business climate...by passing major tort reform, regulatory relief, reduced the tax burden on job creators, pulled away the tax burden on health savings accounts, and even created an Economic Development Corporation." Walker went on to explain that the key was in providing lower taxes and increased certainty for business.[205] In spite of this, however, the unions are spending tens of millions of dollars to recall him in 2012. Yet, no good deed goes unpunished. Rather than support Walker, 52 percent of the Wisconsin electorate supported his recall as late as April 2, 2012.[206]

Apparently, unions succeeded in convincing the citizens of Wisconsin that they somehow had an obligation to pay higher taxes so that public employees could dictate higher salaries and benefits for themselves than employees got in the private sector doing similar work. There is only one expression that expresses this insanity; mass delusion. Yet, we shouldn't be surprised. Early psychiatrist Gustave Le Bon warned us in 1895 that progressives have little connection to reality and will do things against their best interests.

Meanwhile, during the summer of 2011, the Tea Party/conservative members of Congress tried to emulate Walker to stop the hemorrhaging of deficit spending in Washington by Obama and the progressive Democrats. Like Walker, they were called terrorists, obstructionists and as noted earlier, they were accused of "holding the nation hostage." Yet, the only thing these conservatives were attempting to do was to try to get the progressives to deal with the unsustainable national debt—something that none of the progressive Democrats wanted to do—and still don't. Even the neocons had a few choice words. The truth is the Tea Party Republicans were the only ones in Congress that were trying to save the country. The eventual legislation that was finally passed with great fanfare was all show, and did nothing more than slightly slow down the hemorrhaging.

In spite of the heroic efforts by the Tea Party and conservative members of Congress trying to stop deficit spending, House Minority Leader Nancy Pelosi issued another of her extreme and over-the-top exaggerations on July 28, 2011, "What we're trying to do is save the world from the Republican budget....we're trying to save life on this planet as we know it today."[207]

Pelosi's over-the-top expression begs the question; is her statement merely an ill-advised exaggeration, or is it really how she feels? There is evidence that this is truly how she and other progressive liberals really think. She *knows with absolute certainty* that the Republican plans are cataclysmically ruinous; that we can continue adding to our huge debt and deficit spending with impunity; and that she and her colleagues must *never* take $1 away from Medicare and other entitlements, lest the world be destroyed. The progressive liberal solution to the debt and job crisis is to spend even more money! A lot more money. If that is what she and other progressive liberals really believe, then America is in deep trouble—not from conservatives and the Tea Party, but from progressive liberals. To say this is disturbing is an understatement.

PSYCHOLOGY OF PROGRESSIVISM IN THE 21ST CENTURY

THERE EXISTS STRONG EVIDENCE for this concern about progressive liberals. After forty years of observing the shocking characteristics of progressive liberals, author and psychiatrist Lyle Rossiter, M.D. makes this alarming observation,

> The degree of modern liberalism's irrationality far exceeds any misunderstanding that can be attributed to faulty fact gathering or logical error. Indeed, under careful scrutiny, liberalism's distortions of the normal ability to reason can only be understood as the product of psychopathology. So extravagant are the patterns of thinking, emoting, behaving and relating that characterize the liberal mind that its relentless protests and demands become understandable only as disorders of the psyche. The modern liberal mind, its distorted perceptions and its destructive agenda are the product of disturbed personalities.[208]

Rossiter's observation doesn't neatly fit into any modern-day psychiatric categories. Yet, if he is correct, nothing much has changed in the 115 years since Le Bon published *The Crowd*. It is exactly the behavior that Le Bon described. Having said that, later chapters will clearly show that at least some of these progressives know exactly what they are doing. That is not a psychiatric issue. That is evil.

Assuming Rossiter is correct, he warns that progressive liberals deny their "own propensity for hatred and violence. The liberal mind is an angry mind determined to force people into its stereotyped categories but unable to acknowledge that its own political coercion is a form of criminal violence."[209] Perhaps that is why they are quick to judge phantom acts of hatred by conservatives; yet do not see their own real vitriolic hatred in their violent statements and actions—even when it is pointed out to them. This will be described in greater detail later in the chapter.

Le Bon observed in 1895 that, "In crowds the foolish, ignorant, and envious persons are freed from the sense of their insignificance and powerlessness, and are possessed instead by the notion of brutal and temporary but immense strength."[210]

Rossiter provides insight into what the liberal mind is passionate about. He found their reality is,

...a world filled with pity, sorrow, neediness, misfortune, poverty, suspicion, mistrust, anger, exploitation, discrimination, victimization, alienation and injustices. Those who occupy this world are "workers," "minorities," "the little guy," "women," and the "unemployed." They bear no responsibility for their problems. None of their agonies are attributable to faults or failings of their own; not to poor choices, bad habits, faulty judgment, wishful thinking, lack of ambition, low frustration tolerance, mental illness or defects in character.... Instead the "root causes" of all this pain lie in faulty social condition: poverty, disease, war, ignorance, unemployment, racial prejudice, ethnic and gender discrimination, modern technology, capitalism, globalization and imperialism.... "Big business," "Big Corporations," "greedy capitalists," "U.S. Imperialists," "the oppressors, the rich," "the wealthy," "the powerful," and " "the selfish."[211]

Blame the Rich and the United States

Sound familiar? Interviews with people in the Occupy Wall Street protests in the fall of 2011 reveal a mish-mash of concerns that touch on every one of the progressive concerns listed above described by Rossiter. Certainly, like Le Bon, Rossiter's descriptions are generalizations and they don't fit all progressive liberals equally. Regardless, their ideology centers on the belief that the downtrodden are *always* victims. While some know exactly what they are doing, most of them seem to really believe that the downtrodden will do the right thing if just given the chance. Most of them completely discount human nature, especially its baser side. To solve the never-ending disparity they see between the "rich" and the poor, income redistribution is at the center of everything they do.

Progressive liberals hate the rich because they see them as greedy, always squashing the little guy. Unfortunately, that can be true in too many cases. However, what they refuse to acknowledge is that because of human nature, even the most poor among us can be just as greedy given the opportunity. As already noted, that is the basis of extravagant union demands and why public sector unions are bankrupting cities and states.

The glaring truth of this was revealed in the Occupy Wall Street tent cities where the homeless were not given shelter or food. Even more ludicrous, many of the richest Americans are progressive liberals who rarely give their wealth to the poor directly. Instead, they join in the class warfare to assuage their guilty consciousness by forcing others to pay for their misguided philanthropy.

Progressive liberals believe downtrodden people are prevented from doing the right thing because of evil corporations and greedy capitalists. The people are victims. The theme of victimization is constantly exploited and reinforced. Therefore, individuals are not responsible for the bad consequences of their behavior and should not suffer from them. The solution is common for every liberal: a very large authoritarian government having large social programs and choking regulations, all paid for with huge taxes; especially on corporations and the rich. In short, it is the *plundering of America by law.*

At the international level, global ills are the fault of the United States and its arrogance and bad behavior. Hence, if we just play nice with rogue nations like Iran, or Islamic Jihadists, they will no longer hate the U.S. and we can negotiate a lasting peace. That is why the Obama administration demanded that the phrase "War on Terror" be changed to "Overseas Contingency Operation." Surely we don't want to offend radical Islamists. After all, the progressive liberal thinking goes, the U.S. made otherwise peaceful Muslims into fanatics of hatred because of our bad foreign policy.

That explains why President Obama appears to be soft on terrorism and kept holding out olive branches to Iran while allowing Iranian citizens to be slaughtered and permitting ultimatums to pass without doing anything. Like anything based on progressive ideology, playing nice with

Iran backfired. Apologies for the bad behavior offered by the U.S. to enemies that hate us just increased their hatred of us even more, because they see us as weak. It is this mental psychosis on the part of the Obama administration that emboldened Iran to try to assassinate the Saudi and Israeli ambassadors to the U.S. on U.S. soil.[212]

Many progressive liberals literally cannot see that Jihadist terrorism or Iran's rush to become a nuclear power is not the result of U.S. policy. Instead, it is because of a fanatical religious ideology of world domination that even most Muslims reject.

Because everyone and everything is a victim of someone or something evil, progressive liberals NEVER accept responsibility. Their failures are ALWAYS someone else's fault. Over time they have developed blame-shifting to an art form. It's why President Obama never takes responsibility for his utterly failed economic policies. (The only alternative is that he is deliberately trying to destroy America, which will be discussed later.) Even upon nearing the end of his first term he still blamed President Bush, or hurricanes, or earthquakes or a dozen other things for his failures.

Worse, because of the progressive liberal's "victim" mentality, progressives are immune from any rational discussion that shows where they are wrong. Whenever the truth gets too uncomfortable, they escape behind some sound bite that clearly shows (to them) how they have been victimized or that demonizes the opposition. That's what DNC Chairman Debbie Wasserman Schultz tried to do to the Fox and Friends hostess Gretchen Carlson in both dialogues mentioned earlier in the chapter. It didn't work in her case, because she was so far out in the twilight zone that her ruse backfired.

Extreme intolerance is another unfortunate characteristic of a mob, i.e. progressive liberals. Le Bon notes, "At public meetings the slightest contradiction on the part of an orator is immediately received with howls of fury and violent invective, soon followed by blows, and expulsion should the orator stick to his point."[213] How many times have we heard of conservative speakers being booed and shouted from the speaker's podium by brain-washed liberal progressives? This is especially true on university campuses—supposedly the bastion of free speech. On October 14, 2011 John Stossel did a special on the Occupy Wall Street protests. When he tried to engage protesters to explain why they were so angry, they responded with vitriolic hatred and screams preventing any coherent discussion.[214]

Gun Control

As noted earlier, liberal progressives often act as automatons once an idea is implanted in their group-think. This single-mindedness and blindness to reality is another hallmark of the mob and can lead to dangerous policy. While the examples are as numerous as stars in the sky (admittedly an exaggeration), nothing speaks to this truth more than the near fanatical belief of progressive liberals that gun control reduces crime—in spite of overwhelming evidence to the contrary.

For instance, in the two years following the harsh 1997 handgun ban in England, handgun crime increased by 40 percent. That continues today. In just one time period, April to November 2001, the number of people robbed at gunpoint in London rose 53 percent. Moreover, the 53 percent is after progressive bureaucrats had manipulated the statistics downward.[215] Scotland also passed harsh gun control laws in 1997. By 2005, "the United Nations labeled Scotland the most violent country in the developed world, with people three times more likely to be assaulted than in America."[216]

Even the police secretly report that the gun ban is a total failure.[217] Yet, like automatons, progressive liberals totally ignore reality and, with few exceptions, continued blindly to accept the groupthink that demands gun control. This can result in a horrible policy. By the end of 2011, new documents began to provide strong evidence that the entire ATF Fast and Furious gun walking tragedy was concocted to justify stronger gun control laws. CBS News reported on December 8, 2011 that, "Documents obtained by CBS News show that the Bureau of Alcohol Tobacco, Firearms and Explosives (ATF) discussed using their covert operation "Fast and Furious" to argue for controversial new rules about gun sales."[218] Although that has not been proven, it would explain why there was *no* effort to track the guns after they entered Mexico.[219]

As of this writing, the massive cover-ups for the Fast and Furious debacle were still being exposed. Even so, it has now been demonstrated that Assistant Attorney General Lanny Breuer helped write a letter submitted to Congress in February 2011 that adamantly denied ATF had ever walked guns into Mexico. Contrary to his testimony, Breuer knew about the ATF gun-smuggling debacle as early as 2010.[220] Dennis Burke, a U.S. attorney vehemently denied ATF had walked the guns. In an email,

Burke blasted Senate Judiciary ranking member Chuck Grassley (R-IA) and Republicans in general:

> What is so offensive about this whole project is that Grassley's staff, acting as willing stooges for the Gun Lobby, have attempted to distract from the incredible success in dismantling [southwest border] gun trafficking operations ... but, instead, lobbing this reckless despicable accusation that ATF is complicit in the murder of a fellow federal law enforcement officer.[221]

It turns out Burke *did* know that ATF walked the guns and was throwing up smoke to blame-shift responsibility back to Republicans by demonizing them. After getting caught red-handed, Burke was forced to resign. Not so with Lanny Breuer. Attorney General (AG) Eric Holder refuses to fire him, in spite of his contribution to falsifying the February 2011 letter to Congress.

Internal documents show that former acting ATF Director Kenneth Melson "reassigned every manager involved in Fast and Furious after the scandal surfaced on Capitol Hill and in the press." Melson was then "ordered by senior Justice Officials to be silent regarding the reassignments." Thus, the silence of ATF managers having knowledge of Justice Department culpability was bought through "promotions to cushy bureaucratic jobs."[222]

While blatant cover-ups like Fast and Furious are not confined to progressives, they are more prone to it because of their propensity to play fast and loose with reality, their unfailing belief that they are always right and are therefore justified in bending the law, and their seeming inability of ever taking responsibility for any failure.

In spite of these flagrant violations of the rule of law, AG Holder continues to claim he and his office are victims of a modern-day McCarthy racist witch-hunt by Republicans. At the same time, the Department of Justice is viciously going after Arizona and other states for their new immigration laws that parallel federal laws. The states were forced to pass them because the AG's office refuses to enforce federal immigration laws.[223]

In spite of progressives' self-deception that they are deep, critical thinkers, many are in fact, simple minded, linear thinkers. In progressive reasoning, guns kill people and are used to commit crimes. Therefore guns are bad. If guns are bad, they must be banned. If guns are banned, they couldn't be used to commit crimes and kill people. It seems so obvious to many progressive liberals anyone who disagrees has to be an idiot. Yet, this is shallow linear thinking. Because of group-think, it never occurs to most progressive liberals that real criminals can buy all the guns they want on the black market where gun control laws don't apply.

There is good evidence that the reason that daylight crimes skyrocket after gun control laws are put into place is because criminals no longer fear an armed citizenry. Without gun control laws, criminals are afraid that citizens they encounter while committing their crime may pull their gun and shoot them. Being shot is not something criminals want to risk.[224] This understanding requires critical thinking, something most progressive liberals seem unable to do.

The National Rifle Association reported FBI statistics showing over time that as gun ownership increased in the United States, crime decreased. "The FBI estimated that the number of violent crimes decreased...more than 6 percent from 2009 to 2010, including a 5 percent decrease in the number of murders." This is a 37 year low for violent crime and a 47 percent low for murder.[225]

Our Founders included the Second Amendment to prevent the government from becoming totalitarian. George Mason warned, "The right to bear arms was clearly about self-defense."[226] Samuel Adams warned, "That the said Constitution shall never be construed to authorize Congress to infringe the just liberty of the press or the rights of conscience; or to prevent the people of the United States who are peaceable citizens from keeping their own arms ..."[227]

Those people who try to reason with progressive liberals have felt the progressives' intolerant scorn and attack rhetoric as if they were sub-human morons; vastly inferior to the self-ascribed superior intellect of the progressive liberal. The progressive liberal's superior ego is seriously misplaced. Le Bon describes them as being "mentally inferior" fifteen times in his book. However, that may be technically incorrect. Many of them are quite intelligent. Their irrationality is "guided almost exclusively by unconscious motives" of what we have come to call group-think.[228] That is why a single sound-bite or slogan can call up dozens of "truths," none of which is rooted in reality.

Hate Slogans

Take for instance the Wisconsin union protest slogans used on their February 15, 2011 protest in Madison; "Stop the Attack on Worker Rights;" "WI Dictator Must Go;" "Scott Walker=Adolf Hitler—Can You Tell the Difference? I Can't;" "Midwest Mussolini;" "Hosni Walker;" "Why Do Republicans Hate People;" "RAPE Is Never a Good Choice;" "Walker, the Mubarak of the Midwest;" "Walker Terrorizes Families;" "Dont (sic) Retreat; Reload, Repeal Walker;" "Raping Public Employees is not the way to balance the budget;" "One Dictator To Go;" "Death to Tyrants;" "Down With the Dictator." These are all from just one protest.[229]

Remember, that union protest was only *six weeks after* the January 8, 2011 attempted assassination of Congresswoman Giffords (D-AZ) in Tucson, Arizona. Giffords had barely reached the hospital when progressive liberals were spinning *false* accusations that her assassin, Jared Lee Loughner, was a right-wing extremist inflamed by Tea Party hate speech. It turned out that although he had slightly more left leaning credentials, he was mostly just a nutcase.[230] In any event, the speed of all that vitriolic rhetoric coming from progressive liberals was a classic illustration of Le Bon mob reaction.

Even before the Wisconsin public union chaos broke loose and showed who really used hate-speech, we heard news reports like "Violent political rhetoric…comes almost exclusively from the Right." White House spokesman Robert Gibbs said, "Imagine, just a few years ago had somebody walked around with images of Hitler." Congresswoman Nancy Pelosi (D-CA) lamented, "I have concerns about some of the language that is being used [by right-wingers]." Bill Maher spewed, "The Right-wing loves [to say]… 'Wouldn't it be fun to kill the people we disagree with?' Left-wingers don't talk that way." Even Democratic State Senator (WI) Lena Taylor said "In 1933, (Hitler) abolished unions and that is what our Governor is doing today."[231]

During a Labor Day speech just nine months after Giffords was shot, Jimmy Hoffa Jr. declared there's a "war on workers" and "We've got to keep an eye on the battle that we face—a war on workers. And you see it everywhere. It is the Tea Party, …and there's only one way to beat and win that war…keep the eye on the prize, let's take these son-of-a-bitches out."[232]

The above citations of progressive liberal hate mongering are just a few examples. Entire books could be written on the vitriolic hatred by progressives for anyone who disagrees with them. In her book *Demonic*,[233] Ann Coulter cites over 150 well-documented incidents of angry mobs of progressive liberals. Over 50 of these involved violence, and 20 involved murder. She also cited numerous efforts by progressive liberals to falsely blame violent incidents on conservatives, all without merit. It is time to expose the hatred and violent tendencies of progressive liberals.

In contrast, over *500,000* tea partiers peacefully attended a Glenn Beck rally in the Washington Mall on August 28, 2010. There were no hate slogans, just peaceful onlookers. After the event the only trash left in the Mall was overflow from trash cans. No litter was found anywhere.

The progressive liberal media was astonished at Beck's peaceful rally. They didn't know what to say, so they said as little as possible. That has not, however, stopped them from continuing their desperate effort to smear the Tea Party as terrorists, violent ignoramuses bent on destroying the country. Reality, however, is just the opposite. When progressive liberals and left-wing extremists hold similar rallies, hate signs are the rule and tons of trash and litter are scattered everywhere. The Occupy Wall Street demonstrations across the country resulted in murders, rapes, fights and tens of millions of dollars in damage and cleanup costs.

DESTINED TO FAIL

PROGRESSIVE LIBERALS CAN NEVER understand why their ideas always fail. It's not because progressive liberals are stupid. In general, they are quite bright. Yet, their actions, however noble sounding, usually produce negative results that can end up as catastrophic failures.

Their failures are always the fault of conservatives, or the Tea Party, or the hated George Bush, or wrong constitutional principles or some outside obstruction like the Japan earthquake. It is never because their basic worldview is bankrupt and will always lead to the wrong conclusions and solutions. Rather than solving problems, liberal progressives spend their time dreaming up one-liners to blame-shift responsibility to hated Republicans, especially Tea Party and conservative Republicans.

Social laws and international negotiations must be based on a realistic worldview that truly considers the dynamics of human nature. Reality, once understood, must always be tempered with compassion. That is why the Founders put severe limits on government in the Constitution. Yet, progressive liberals reject this limitation and demand bigger and bigger government.

The progressive liberal ideology has locked progressives into the insane position of fighting every effort to cut the budget. They do it because they *know* they must constantly increase legal plundering via income redistribution if the nation's failings are to be solved. They can't give up even one dollar of a program they designed to save the downtrodden (and buy votes)—even save humanity, as Pelosi claims. Progressives generally don't base policy on facts. As a rule, they base *everything* on emotion and group-think.

Presidents Harding and Coolidge and now Wisconsin Governor Walker, clearly showed us what works. The only way out of the nightmare the progressive liberals have created is to slash deficit spending, slash the size of government and reduce the regulatory burden; exactly the opposite of what the progressive liberals have done. These progressives demand *more* of what has clearly failed every time it has been applied. Doing the same thing again and again and expecting a different result is the very definition of insanity.

At the risk of repetition, Dr. Rossiter explains this irrationality; "…under careful scrutiny, liberalism's distortions of the normal ability to reason can only be understood as a product of psychopathology…. The modern liberal mind, its distorted perceptions and its destructive agenda are the product of disturbed personalities."[234] Le Bon observed the same general thing in 1895. This is nothing new. It has been a cancer eating at America for over a hundred years.

Clearly, progressive liberals need help. They are not getting it, in their unrealistic drive to solve every problem they have concocted in their dysfunctional minds. Yet, they have essentially taken control of many institutions in America—with devastating results. Wrong has become right, and right has become wrong. The inmates have taken over the asylum.

Dr. Rossiter warns, "At the dawn of the twenty-first Century [progressive liberal] attempts continue to fail in the stagnant economies, moral decay and social turmoil now widespread in Europe. An increasingly bankrupt welfare society is putting the U.S. on track for the same fate if liberalism is not cured….Yet, despite all the evidence against it, the modern liberal mind believes his agenda is good social science. It is, in fact, bad science fiction. He persists in this agenda despite its madness."[235] Rossiter is right. We are likely seeing the death throes of the euro and EU today.

This does not portend well for America's future. America can never spend enough money to correct all the social evils progressive liberals perceive. Europe has tried, and is now like a house of cards collapsing in slow motion. With every correction, they create even more inequity that needs to be corrected. It never ends until the economy and society collapses like the Soviet Union.

5 – Politics of Deceit and the U.S/Global Debt Crisis

Today, the plundering of America has put the United States on the brink of economic disaster that could be worse than the Great Depression. America's staggering trillion-plus dollar deficits and $15.8 trillion debt[a] threaten to sink us. Almost all of this debt is the direct result of the massive social programs and undeclared wars promoted by like-minded progressives over the past 60 years.

The Debt Crisis

China is the United States' largest lender and holds at least $1.2 trillion in U.S. government debt,[236] approximately 26 percent of all U.S. debt. It has become increasingly clear to China that inflation of the dollar is destroying the real value of the $1.2 trillion in bonds and securities that it holds. China is losing money. Yet, China must have dollars as the world's reserve currency to buy oil and other commodities from other nations. The only way out of this mess is to destroy the dollar as the world's reserve currency.

So that's what China is doing. It has started attacking the U.S. dollar as the reserve currency of the world by buying as much gold and as many gold mines as possible. As discussed in further detail in Chapter 9, if China is successful, it is almost certain the interest rates we pay on the debt (around $460 billion a year in 2010)[237] will skyrocket.

Interest on the debt in early 2012 is at historical lows; 1 to 3 percent, depending on the type of Treasury bond.[238] The low rate isn't because the bonds are risk free. It's because all other bonds carry far more risk. Therefore, demand for U.S. bonds is high, lowering the yields we have to pay. Raising the interest to 6 percent (last seen in 2000) would increase the

---

[a] as of January 2012

interest to $840 billion a year. An 8 percent rate (last seen in 1990) would increase payments to $1.1 trillion annually![239]

If the Chinese are successful in replacing the U.S. dollar with their yuan as the world's reserve currency (see Chapter 9), interest rates on our debt would be much higher as worthless dollars flood the global economy. It doesn't take a rocket scientist to realize these interest rates would devastate the U.S. economy.

There is another downside to the debt and deficit. When the government borrows money, that money can't be used by business to expand or build new production facilities in the private sector. The jobs that would have been created with the new or expanded facilities are lost.

Progressive liberals try to solve every perceived problem with a new government program. Progressives in Congress pass 300 to 500 new laws every year that create tens of thousands of pages of new regulations.[240] Many of these like Obamacare and the Dodd-Frank Financial Reform Act, for example, are taking years to implement and are creating massive uncertainty in the business world. Just as you would not open a savings account with a bank that won't tell you what interest rate you will earn, businesses will not hire new employees until there is more certainty in regulations, debt and deficit.

POLITICAL CHICKEN AND THE ART OF BLAME-SHIFTING

IN SPITE OF THE SERIOUSNESS of the debt and deficit, an unbelievable game of political chicken was played out in Congress during the summer of 2011. Much of the $15.8 trillion debt is the direct result of the massive social programs and undeclared wars over the past 60 years. President Bush increased federal spending by $1.7 trillion (including TARP) during his eight years, primarily because of the Afghan and Iraq undeclared wars.[241] Obama, on the other hand, has increased federal spending for social programs by $1.6 trillion in just the first three years of his administration.[242] As usual, both presidents are progressives.

The debt and deficit problem in the U.S. is not insufficient revenues as many in Congress and the media claim. The real problem is excessive spending that is spiraling out of control. The 2011 debt/deficit crisis provides an excellent case history of how progressive liberals think and act to get what they want.

'Tax the Rich' Class Warfare

The progressive liberals blindly call for tax increases on the rich demanding they pay their "fair share" even though they already pay one of the highest tax rates (33-35%) in the world, and pay about 55 percent of all taxes paid in the U.S.[243] At the same time, people in the bottom *half* income brackets pay only about 4 percent of all taxes. Most of those pay none at all. That's fair? Yet, it is easy to convince lower income voters who pay no tax at all that the rich should pay their "fair share," especially when the poor have nothing to lose and everything to gain.

That's not all. A stunning Heritage Foundation analysis found that the $700 billion the increased taxes on the rich would allegedly raise over ten years wouldn't put a dent in the $9 trillion deficit in Obama's budget over the same period.[244] The reason for the entire 'tax-the-rich' message is to redirect the public attention from the failed Obama economic strategy to destructive class warfare.

Senate Majority Leader Harry Reid used the class warfare mantra on the Senate floor by saying that the Republicans' claim that the rich create jobs was a "red herring" and that "every shred of evidence contradicts" it.[245] He cited a statement by National Public Radio that supposedly found no examples of millionaires creating jobs.[246]

However, citing NPR is like putting Occupy Wall Street in charge of scoring the ethics of banks. The question NPR asked was whether a marginal tax increase would keep them from hiring an employee. The typical answer from millionaires was that there were many more things that were important, such as whether they can even *get* a contract to sell whatever widget they produce, the business climate (certainty), and, of course, regulations.[247]

Nobody denies that these other factors drive a small business' decisions, but the bottom line is the bottom line. Taxes affect the bottom line, dampen demand and create uncertainty in the future. That doesn't mean millionaires don't create jobs. If millionaires don't create jobs, who does? The poor? The government? Based on Reid's insane comment, apparently progressives believe jobs just magically appear because of the good intensions of progressive liberals.

Besides, history has shown that raising taxes on the rich has never worked to raise revenues in a recession or depression. In the depressions of 1920 and 1929, raising taxes on the rich made the depression worse in each case. The reason is simple. Money that might have gone into creating jobs went instead to the federal government which, at best, can only create bureaucratic jobs that do little to nothing to actually create wealth. These federal employees often stifle business by enforcing smothering regulations. It is the classic case of killing the goose that lays golden eggs. Both problems existed in the debt/deficit crisis. They still do.

Between high tax rates and strangling regulations passed by progressive Democrats, most U.S. companies had already fled the U.S. to other nations. These nations provided a more favorable business climate. When the companies moved offshore to flee excessive U.S. regulations they took badly needed jobs with them. The progressive Democrats then claim that capitalism doesn't work because the middle class is being destroyed by fleeing corporations, when they themselves created the nightmare in the first place. Their ability to twist the truth so that right becomes wrong and wrong becomes right is mind-boggling.

A favorite "zinger" progressive liberals like to trumpet comes from a 2011 report from the Congressional Budget Office (CBO) that states, "The share of income received by the top 1 percent grew from about 8 percent in 1979 to over 17 percent in 2007."[248] This allegedly "proves" the rich are getting richer off the poor. But why did the CBO analysis stop at 2007? It is because, as the CBO report states in a footnote, "high income taxpayers had especially large declines in adjusted gross income between 2007 and 2009."

The CBO's footnote is an understatement. After doing what the CBO should have done, the Wall Street Journal's Alan Reynolds found that the top 1 percent's share plummeted from 17.3 percent to 11.3 percent from 2007 to 2010. [249] That should have been one of the main highlights of the report, but that is not what the CBO wanted to show because it would not highlight the disparity they wanted to point out. Reynolds goes on to explain that the share of income by the 1 percent has fluctuated widely over time as tax laws change. This makes any effort to compare one period to another impossible. The CBO's analysis proves nothing.

Finally, the effort by progressives to blame the rich has turned cause and effect upside down. The depression of 1921 clearly showed that big government is one of, if not *the* primary cause of economic recessions and depressions. President Wilson's efforts to tax the rich and apply the Keynesian theory of spending his way out of the depression he had created only made the depression worse. President Obama applied the same strategy with the same results as Wilson. The Keynesian approach clearly does not work. Yet, the progressive Democrats continue to apply it dogmatically and in the face of the overwhelming evidence that it was resulting in economic disaster.

When President Harding slashed federal spending by half in 1922, unemployment dropped like a rock and the federal deficit was reduced by a third within two years. The conservative Republicans have tried numerous plans to apply variations of Harding's strategy with Ryan's Cut, Cap, and Balance plan but all have been blocked by the progressive Democrats.

Because of blame shifting, the progressive Democrats and the mainstream media have at least partially convinced the public that it is the Republicans who are obstructionists. In fact, the conservative Republicans' efforts have backfired to the point that they may be guaranteeing Obama's reelection and the Democrats retaking of the House in 2012. The only thing saving Republicans is the continuing unraveling of the U.S. economy because of the upside-down economic policies of the Obama administration specifically and the progressives in general.

The Art of Blame Shifting

Progressive Democrats have turned misdirection and blame-shifting into an art form. Through decades of practice, they have learned how to misdirect people's attention from their own disaster to make themselves look like heroes and the Republicans appear as heartless morons.

For instance, the Medicare program has an unfunded liability of $80 *trillion*[250] and is rapidly climbing. It will *bankrupt* the U.S. in the not too distant future. When Congressman Ryan came out with his plan to restructure the popular Medicare program—without harming seniors—progressive democrats attacked it with a TV/internet ad that showed heartless Republicans wheeling grandma out to the edge of a cliff and throwing her off to her death.[251]

In thirty seconds the progressives totally destroyed Ryan's efforts to save America and allowed the progressive Democrats to continue the insolvent Medicare program. Medicare will doom America unless it is fixed, and fixed quickly. Yet, the progressive Democrats don't seem to care about destroying the country. It was all about winning. Rather than having a modified Medicare plan as a safety net, progressive Democrats are the ones destroying these programs and sentencing seniors to *total* abandonment! Ryan's plan may not have been the best one—some say it didn't go far enough—but at least it was a starting point.

President Obama used the same type of strategy in his June 29, 2011 press conference when he repeated six times during his talk that if we keep tax breaks for corporate jets, "then that means we've got to cut some kids off from getting a college scholarship." He painted a verbal picture that drove home the point that the rich get cushy tax breaks for luxuries and that somehow steals from poor children trying to go to college.

The use by Obama of corporate jets is another of thousands of classic misdirects. As syndicated columnist Charles Krauthammer observed, "If you collect that tax for the next 5,000 years—that is not a typo—it would equal the new debt Obama racked up last year alone."[252] In other words, the reality of Obama's point was absurd and the entire purpose was designed to mislead the listener, deepen the class warfare he is waging, and distract the people's attention from his failed economic policies.

Such reckless use of blame shifting and class warfare tactics can have unintended consequences. If Obama was successful in removing this tax loophole, it may actually cause the very same less fortunate to actually lose their jobs. When progressive Democrats in Congress imposed a luxury tax in 1990, thousands of people lost their jobs in facilities making or distributing the luxury items. The government lost more revenue in lost income taxes than they ever got out of the tax. The tax had such a negative affect that it was quickly repealed in 1993.[253] Obviously, Obama knew of this event, yet he still used the corporate jet example.

Obama and the progressive Democrats are succeeding because of the mainstream media's help. The Media Research Center conducted a survey of ABC, CBS and NBC stories that mainly blamed Republicans or Democrats for the gridlock from July 1 to 22, 2011. There were 56 stories that blamed Republicans and only 17 that blamed the Democrats.[254] With a 3 to 1 bias against Republicans by the mainstream media, Obama and the progressive Democrats have turned their abject failure into probable success—at least politically. Never mind that their policies have a history of proven failure and could cause the nation to go down in flames.

Progressive Democrats accuse the "right-wing" Republicans of obstructing a solution to the debt and deficit problem. Yet, they were unable to pass a budget since 2009, even though they controlled both Houses in 2010. It was the conservative Republicans that passed legislation in the

House to address the deficit spending. It was the progressive Democrats who blocked it, then demagogued the conservatives for putting the poor in jeopardy by being obstructionists.

The only way Republicans could be the obstructionists is if the progressive Democrats and Obama are gods, and everything they say is the absolute truth. It should be no surprise. That is exactly the way the mainstream media see it. Progressive ideology is their benchmark for truth, so it is little wonder they view conservative Republicans as obstructionists.

For example, it was President Obama who actually ignored the debt crisis for two years while dramatically increasing the likelihood for a catastrophic failure by creating the greatest deficit spending in history. He even passed the debt-deficit buck to the Simpson Bowls Commission, whose final report he totally ignored. Krauthammer noted that Obama then delivered a budget that was "so embarrassing (it actually increased the deficit) that the Democratic-controlled Senate rejected it 97 to 0."[255]

Obama's 2012 budget was so outrageous that it was called a "fantasy" by many analysts. Harry Reid would not let it come to a vote in the Senate because it would be rejected once again since it would increase the deficit by $1.3 trillion. Jack Lew, Obama's chief of staff actually said it was the Republican's fault it would not pass in the Senate because 60 votes were needed to pass and the Democrats had only 51 (53 if independents were counted). Really? As former Director of the Office of Management and Budget, he knows full well that it only takes 51 votes to pass the budget in the Senate, not 60.[256]

In other words, Lew lied by once again blame-shifting responsibility to the Republicans. He knew his progressive media friends would not challenge him. Except for ABC and Fox News, they didn't challenge him. The depths that this progressive administration will go to in order to confuse and mislead the public are positively breathtaking.

Obama gave a speech on April 13, 2011 that the mainstream media hailed as a major step forward in addressing the deficit and debt. Yet, when the Congressional Budget Office (CBO) was asked how it would affect the budget, CBO Director Doug Elmendorf replied with "We don't estimate speeches." In other words, Obama's speech was nothing but hot air. By not giving specifics, no one can pin Obama down, freeing him to demagogue the specific proposals laid out by the conservative Republicans while avoiding criticism himself.

This has become a hallmark of Obama. He won his presidency in 2008 by promising "change we can believe in," but never specified what he meant by change. When the voters found out what he meant in 2009-2010 by passing thousands of pages of new social changes, including Obamacare, the nation was outraged and the Tea Party movement began.

Obama used the same strategy in July, 2011 when he said he would tackle Social Security reform. The mainstream media went all gaga, praising Obama for his courage and leadership. Yet, Obama's promise was all rhetoric and no specifics. The one specific detail he provided was a huge cut in military spending. The only thing his plan did was to front load tax increases. He did not provide any serious budget cuts until the end of the ten year period – long after he was out of office. That is nothing but political misdirection, giving the impression of trying to find solutions when there was *never any intent* of actually doing it.

In a brilliantly executed misdirection in Obama's June 12, 2011, press conference, he chided the lesser mortals in Congress for not quickly dealing with the debt problem he had never dealt with at all. He then scolded Congress for being even less responsible than his own children who got their homework done on time. Yet, at best, the progressive Democrats have done nothing but make empty promises while demonizing the Republican's specific plans.

When the Gang of Six proposals came out on July 19, 2011, the progressive Democrats, many neocons and President Obama proclaimed that the ultimate solution to the crisis had been found. Why wouldn't the conservative Republicans agree? The proposals were nothing more than the same litany of empty promises the progressives love to hide behind. Both the immediate spending cuts and revenue increases were unspecified. It didn't touch entitlements, which were, and are, the main cause of the crisis. There were promises of future unspecified big budget cuts. The history of similar promises, however, has shown those cuts are never made.

The progressive Democrats have promised huge budget cuts before in the Reagan and Bush administrations if only the Republicans (mostly neocons) would just pass their tax hikes. The neocons foolishly passed the tax hikes only to have the progressive Democrats refuse to pass the promised budget cuts. How many times do even neocons need to have the progressive Democrats renege on their promise to make cuts to realize progressive Democrats never honor those agreements? Yet, it is the Republicans who are very successfully portrayed as the obstructionists.

On July 22, 2011 the debate entered the twilight zone when a visibly angry Obama accused the Republicans of walking out of his deficit reduction plan that he claimed "was an extraordinarily fair deal." Because he said he "was willing to take a lot of heat from a lot of interest groups around the country," Obama was applauded by the press for being the adult in the room. By putting on a sad face and saying, "It is hard to understand why Speaker Boehner would walk away from this kind of deal," he shifted the blame to the Republicans. He drove the final nail in the Republican coffin during the question and answer time by indignantly saying "one of the questions the Republican Party is going to have to ask itself; can they say yes to anything?"[257]

When one of the reporters asked if Obama had changed anything in his proposal to cause Boehner to walk away from the almost deal, Obama adamantly denied it—several times.[258] When Boehner gave his press conference about an hour and a half later, he claimed that Obama did in fact raise the revenue part of the deal from $800 billion to $1.2 trillion. That's huge. Boehner insisted that he refused to do that because it would require raising taxes on Americans. In frustration, Boehner once again reiterated a favorite comment that negotiating with the Democrats was like working with Jell-O, meaning the goal post was constantly shifting.[259]

One of them had to be lying. As will be discussed in the next chapter, progressive liberals are strong followers of Saul Alinsky's Rules for Radicals and the Cloward and Piven Strategy, both of which justify lying when it serves their purpose. Boehner finally had an epiphany just before Obama's 2012 State of the Union Speech on January 24. Whether intentionally or unintentionally, Boehner lamented, "We just come from two different planets. We speak a different language." Indeed, they are from two different worlds; worlds that are diametrically opposite. In Obama's case, he is from a world where government controls everything, where truth is optional and the policy of the day is whatever is expedient, regardless of reality.[260]

No Intention of Finding Solutions

Indeed, these tactics have been in the game plan of the progressive Democrats through the entire negotiation cycle—the same as they have for decades. There was *never any intention* to cut the budget. Their strategy was to stall, giving the appearance of wanting resolution until the crisis for not increasing the debt became so severe that conservative Republicans had to cave to the progressive Democrats or face an outraged public.

There is a reason progressive Democrats don't think it is necessary to cut the budget. It is now very obvious they don't believe debt matters. One of the psychopathologic misfires of not connecting with reality causes progressive liberals to believe debt is not important! In one of the most incredible, mind-bending articles ever published, New York Times economist/columnist Paul Krugman wrote on January 1, 2012, "when people in D.C. talk about deficits and debt, by and large they have no idea what they're talking about—and the people who talk the most understand the least."[261]

In classic progressive arrogance using linear reasoning, Krugman defends his thesis proclaiming, "Families have to pay back their debt. Governments don't—all they need to do is ensure that debt grows more slowly than their tax base."[262] Is there any doubt that this thinking either leads to, or justifies the progressive's insatiable desire to constantly raise taxes? After all, they claim everything would just be fine if the rich would just pay their share.

Krugman then points to the fact that the interest we are paying on the federal debt is at record lows.[263] He is right, but not for the reason he believes. In late 2011 and early 2012, investors and nations bought U.S. debt at record rates, pushing down the interest rates paid on the Treasuries. But they did not buy because the Treasuries were a great deal. Rather they bought because U.S. Treasuries are the best of the worst. In a stable market, U.S. Treasuries would have been a bad risk.

Krugman then goes on to explain the Keynesian theory of paying back debt with inflated dollars—something, he boasts, that the U.S. has always done. Besides, he claimed, "U.S. debt is, to a large extent, money we owe to ourselves."[264] Really? China vehemently disagrees and has launched an attack on the dollar's world reserve status because of our reckless spending.[265] Besides, inflation hurts the citizen, especially the poor, the most because it essentially steals their wealth by devaluing what they earn or save. Ignoring these arguments, Krugman concludes, "We need more, not less, government spending to get us out of our unemployment trap. And the wrongheaded, ill-informed obsession with debt is standing in the way." [266]

As discussed earlier, it is this tortured reasoning that led House Minority Leader Pelosi on July 28, 2011, to proclaim: "What we're trying to do is save the world from the Republican budget….we're trying to save life on this planet as we know it today!"[267] They give lip service to finding a compromise solution, but like Pelosi's lying quote, all their outrageous actions do is cause more division. They have successfully used this strategy for decades.

Progressive Democrats have *never* negotiated without a clear-cut goal to raise taxes and extend control over the American people. Their ideology prevents them from cutting the budget. If they did not succeed they would blame-shift the message so that the conservative Republicans are left holding the putrid bag of blame. It's all about politics. Dirty, rotten politics. These progressive Democrats don't care about what happens to America as long as they win. To be sure, Republicans do it too, but they are not in the same universe as the progressive liberals.

Moments after Obama was finished with his press conference, syndicated columnist Charles Krauthammer vehemently exposed Obama's blame-shifting on Fox News Special Report,

This is Obama at his most sanctimonious, demagogic, self-righteous and arrogant [self]; and given the baseline, it wasn't a pretty sight…. He said he has set forth a plan. He has set forth nothing, nor has the Democratic controlled Senate…. The Republicans have offered a detailed plan, the Ryan plan in the House, and they offered Cut, Cap and Balance this time around…. He [Obama] has never once spoken about real [specific] cuts…. Even at this late date where he [Obama] says the fate of the Republic hangs on the debt ceiling extension, he said, if given a short extension of say a half a year I won't accept it. Why? Cause he says I want this to go past Election Day. That is entirely self-serving and political, and he pretends he's the one not interested in politics.

In reading Krauthammer's opinion of Obama, understand that in the 1970s and 80s Krauthammer was a staunch liberal; a member of the Carter administration and speechwriter for Walter Mondale in his 1980 campaign. Longtime editorial page editor of The Washington Post, the late Meg Greenfield, called Krauthammer's column "independent and hard to peg politically. It's a very tough column." Indeed, he has received awards from the far-left People for the American Way, to the conservative Bradley Foundation. He won the 1987 Pulitzer Prize and is published weekly in 250 newspapers worldwide. The *Financial Times* named him the "most influential commentator in America."[268] Krauthammer sees right through the lies of Obama and the progressive Democrats.

Although some of the conservative Republican plans may not have been the best solution, at least they had the courage to publish specifics. Yet, it was Obama—after doing nothing but blowing hot air and blame-shifting—who was treated by the mainstream media as the hero and the only adult in the room. It would be laughable if the economic survival of America weren't at stake—and that so many Americans actually *believe* him. It is a testament to the effective dumbing down of the American people through indoctrination in our public school system. More on this in Chapter 10 and 11.

Incredibly, on October 4, 2011 a Barna Poll found that 48 percent of Americans thought Obama was basically honest, while only 36 percent said the same about Romney and a woeful 31 percent for Perry.[269] Of equal concern, 45 percent believed Obama's progressive ideology was excellent or good, compared to 36 and 31 percent for Romney's and Perry's, respectively.[270]

Both Romney and Perry are essentially progressive neocons, a fact which can partially explain their low scores. But for 48 percent of Americans to believe Obama is honest and 45 percent to accept his progressive ideology as good to excellent—after his continuous lying, misdirection and blame shifting—shows the stunning ignorance of the American people in the knowledge of U.S. history and what has made America great. Chapters 10 and 11 will explain why this is so.

Finally, after stalling for seven months, Congress made another back-room deal that was passed by both Houses and signed by Obama on August 2. If fully enacted, the OMB said it would save $2.1 trillion[a] over ten years. The legislation raised the debt cap by $900 million initially by cutting the budget by the same amount.

---

[a] The legislation called for a $2.4 trillion cut , but OMB scoring showed it to be only $2.1 trillion.

As with all the other proposals by the progressive Democrats, the final legislation was nothing but empty promises. Seventy percent of the budget cuts occur after 2017, while all the cap increases occur in 2011-2012. Only $28 billion is going to be cut in the 2012 budget. That is a proverbial drop in the ocean. Even if the entire $2.1 trillion was cut, it would only reduce the projected deficit spending from $10 trillion to $8 trillion.

An unconstitutional Super Congressional Committee was formed to find the last $1.2 trillion of the $2.1 trillion by November 2011 when the debt cap would be increased by another $1.5 trillion. There was no tax increase in the legislation, but the defiant Democrats said that their representatives to the Super Committee would make sure there were tax increases. Republicans claimed just the opposite. Once again gridlock prevailed and the Super Committee had to admit failure just before Thanksgiving in 2011.

It was another bait and switch job just like those the progressive Democrats have been using for decades. Although the media claimed the Tea Party congressional delegation won the standoff, it was actually the progressive Democrats who won. The Tea Party was blamed and the American people lost—big time.

Progressive Democrats, especially Secretary of Treasury Geithner, used constant fear-mongering to spin the lies that if we didn't raise the debt ceiling, surely holy hell would break lose. Geithner did assure the American people on April 19, 2011, however, that there is "absolutely…no risk" of losing the U.S.'s AAA credit rating.[271]

The last week before the legislation to increase the debt limit, Wall Street began to hemorrhage, giving believability to the lie. What actually happened, however, is that Wall Street took the big nose dive *after* Obama signed the legislation. The Dow Jones lost over 7 percent for the week.[272] Then late Friday evening, August 5, 2011, the other shoe dropped; S&P lowered the U.S. credit rating from AAA to AA+. That is the first time in U.S. history that the U.S. has lost its triple A rating.

S&P blamed Congress for its gridlock and the dismal inability of the U.S. to deal with the debt. The S&P stated that they were "pessimistic about the capacity of Congress and the administration to be able to leverage their agreement…into a broader fiscal consolidation plan that stabilizes the government's debt dynamics anytime soon…. The political brinksmanship of recent months highlights what we see as America's governance and policymaking becoming less stable, less effective, and less predictable than what we previously believed." The S&P report continued, "The downgrade reflects our opinion that the fiscal consolidation plan that Congress and the Administration recently agreed to falls short of what, in our view, would be necessary to stabilize the government's medium-term debt dynamics." [273]

In other words, the S&P wasn't as concerned about getting the debt ceiling raised as making hard cuts to the budget and reversing the *instability* that was being created by Congress. S&P also noted that the outlook on the U.S. debt was still negative, which means the U.S. credit rating could be lowered again if Congress doesn't get its act together within six months. [274]

The progressives' spin machine activated immediately, and with unbelievable, but classic hubris, blamed the entire fiasco on the Tea Party congressional delegation. "I believe this is without question the Tea Party downgrade," claimed Senator John Kerry, (D-MA). "This is the Tea Party downgrade because a minority of people in the House of Representatives countered even the will of many Republicans in the United States Senate who were prepared to do a bigger deal." [275] Among many other progressive liberals, White House top strategist, David Axelrod proclaimed on Face the Nation, this is a "Tea Party downgrade." Tea Party Republicans "played brinksmanship with the full faith and credit of the United States. And this is the result of that." [276]

What deal? There was never any deal. The progressive Democrats *never* offered a specific plan. Think about it. It was the deficit/debt problem that caused the S&P downgrade; not the timing of the debt ceiling increase. It was the progressives of both parties who ran up the $14.5 trillion debt in the first place.

Conversely, it was the Tea Party and conservative congressional delegation who forced the loudly protesting progressive Democrats to at least discuss the deficit/debt problem. It was the progressive Democrats who stonewalled every effort to reduce the deficit; even a little. Yet, like a well-choreographed concert, every progressive liberal spontaneously parroted the same its-the-tea-party's-fault in continuing to blame-shift the downgrade to the Tea Party. Of course, the progressive mainstream media dutifully reported the party line and many Americans believed it hook, line and sinker.

Once again, it is incredible how Obama and the progressive liberals, with the help of the mainstream media can so easily convince the American people that a lie is the truth and the truth is a lie. In fact, it would be dazzling if it weren't so disturbing.

The only plan that even comes close to resolving S&P's concern that has been proposed in Congress is the Ryan Plan. Congressman Paul Ryan's (R-WI) plan reduces federal spending by $6 trillion over 10 years—from the current 24 percent of GDP to the historical post-World War II average of about 20 percent.[277] Among its key provisions, the plan;

- Provides a flat tax to eliminate all the loopholes currently used by the rich to avoid taxes.
- It provides a standard deduction of $39,000 (for a family of four).
- Replaces the corporate income tax—currently the highest in the industrialized world—with a business consumption tax of 8.5 percent.
- For entitlements it provides a "means" test for eligibility to receive benefits, creates a voucher system for Medicare, and preserves the existing Social Security program for those 55 or older.[278]

Ryan always considered his plan a starting point, not the final plan. Nonetheless, progressive Democrats went ballistic, decrying the plan as the end of the world. Conservative critics said it didn't do enough. In spite of the desperate need to restructure entitlement programs to avoid bankruptcy, the progressive Democrats blindly refused to even consider restructuring the programs.

These progressives claimed they were saving the programs and the people dependent on them. That claim borders on criminal malfeasance. These were the same progressive Democrats who gave us Obamacare, which was supposed to reduce the federal deficit by claiming it would only cost $940 billion over ten years. However, progressive Democrats rarely, if ever, tell the truth to the American people. As usual, they frontloaded all the benefits and back loaded all the costs to get the $940 billion estimate. By 2012, the ten year estimate included more of the back loaded costs and the CBO's (Congressional Budget Office) ten year estimate almost doubled to $1.76 trillion.[279] When all the beans were counted and the fuzzy math removed, Obamacare is now going to cost Americans over $2 *trillion* according to the CBO.[280]

Obama used the same fuzzy math to calculate his $4 trillion cut to the deficit in the next 10 years. When the Committee for a Responsible Federal Budget analyzed Obama's math, they found the savings were only about $2.5 trillion.[281] As usual, the spending is front loaded for now, and the budget cuts are back loaded for later—long after Obama is out of office even if he gets two terms. Worse, the Obama plan does not address entitlement programs in any meaningful way. There is simply no way the deficit/debt crisis can be resolved unless entitlements are addressed.

Such blindness defies common sense. It is obvious these progressives are willing to destroy the lives of those Americans dependent on these programs while claiming to help them. It is bizarre at best and insane at worst. This glaring disconnect defies logic for all except progressive liberals. The reasons were discussed in Chapters 3 and 4. Worse, their disconnect from reality threatens the entire country with bankruptcy and total economic collapse just like what is happening to many of the European countries in 2011and 2012.

Americans hate gridlock in Congress and don't have a clue about what really happened to cause it. There is enough blame to go around for everyone, but the real villains of the gridlock were and are the progressive Democrats. What the public does not understand is that these progressives will *never* compromise. If they can't win, they obstruct. As will be discussed in chapters 6 and 7, they believe they are at war with traditional American values and laws and they purpose to destroy them. That's right— systematically destroy the Constitutional Republic that has made this nation the greatest in human history.

We have been taught in our public education system to not see what these progressives are doing right before our eyes. (See Chapters 10 and 11) That leaves us wide-open to what can only be described as the unabashed blame-shifting lie the media and Obama are spinning. A July 18, 2011 CBS poll found that 71 percent of the American people disapprove of the Republican handling of the debt limit crisis. Only 48 percent disapprove of Obama's handling of the crisis,[282] even though the facts show he has offered absolutely nothing but empty promises and more debt. Yet, how can a truly conservative Republican ever compromise on legislation he or she *knows* from historical evidence will seriously harm the American people. The truth is; they can't.

A CNN poll two days later found similar results. In this poll, 52 percent believed Obama has acted responsibly, while 63 percent believe Republicans have acted irresponsibly. Even more disturbing, the CNN poll showed that 73 to 76 percent believed the mainstream media about the alleged need for raising taxes on oil and gas companies, businesses that own jets, and on people who earn more than $250,000 a year.[283] Yet, as discussed earlier in this chapter, this is a red herring that has no basis in reality. The progressive Democrats and media could be proud of themselves; they had won the blame-shifting game once again. By doing so, they are sealing the financial disaster that is surely coming to America.

These polls graphically illustrate the enormous disconnect the American people have with the reality of the danger faced by the U.S., and the true identity of who is really putting America at risk. Even half of the Republican respondents in the CBS poll disapproved of their party's handling of the crisis.[284] That is astonishing because most of the freshmen congressional representatives were voted into office in November of 2010 to stop the spending.

On the other hand, the CNN poll showed 74 percent want a Constitutional Amendment requiring a balanced budget, and 60 percent thought it would be necessary to pass a Constitutional Amendment for Congress to ever get the budget under control.[285] It is obvious the American people know there is a big problem, but at the same time are very vulnerable to the manipulative tactics of the progressive Democrats and mainstream media.

With the loss of the ability of many Americans to think critically, they are blind to the blatant fear mongering, demagoguery and manipulation used by the progressive Democrats. It is not that Americans are unintelligent; they are very intelligent. What they don't have is the needed learned mental skills to be able think critically because of the dumbing down of public school education. Because of this, it is possible that the Tea Party candidates who were voted into office in the 2010 Republican landslide to get America's financial house in order may not survive the next election. Unless we citizens act, both Houses of Congress and the presidency could once again be totally controlled by the progressive Democrats and neocons—and any chance that America can be saved would be lost.

There is hope. A July 20, 2011 Fox News poll found that 62 percent of the American people from all age groups do not trust the government. If they only knew how they were being used like Stalin's useful idiots, they would stop this insanity instantly. Unfortunately, fewer Americans think the federal government is generally trying to do too much. It dropped from 57 percent in February of 2010 to 43 percent in the July 20 Fox News poll. At the same time, the percentage of voters who believe the government is doing too little almost doubled from 17 percent in February 2010 to 30 percent in the July 20th Fox poll.[286]

These almost schizophrenic polling results show that the American people understand there is something seriously wrong in America, but have been taught to believe the government can actually solve our economic crisis. It can't. History is clear; only low taxes, less government, and as few regulations as possible to protect each of us from one another, can improve the economy.

Even though Obama either blindly or deliberately does the very things that make the economic recovery worse, another Fox poll taken on January 12-14, 2012 shows that 45 percent of voters approve of the job he has done, while 47 percent do not approve. This is an improvement for Obama over the 44/51 percent approve/disapprove poll taken on December 5-7, 2011. If taxpayers really knew what Obama has done, his approval-disapproval score would be closer to 0-100. Many voters seem to be catching on, however. The same Fox poll showed only 34 percent think the country is going in the right direction. Yet, if the election was held that day, Obama would win over Romney, Gingrich or Santorum.[287]

The general public's ignorance of the real dangers facing America makes them vulnerable to the siren song that it doesn't really matter who is in control and how they govern. It matters. It matters so much that their very lives and the lives of their children and grandchildren will be radically affected in very negative ways if the progressives of either party remain in power.

In the case of the progressive Democrats, nothing they have done is about solving the deficit/debt problem. Rather, it is about winning the next election. Everything Obama has done is about politics. Everything! He has never stopped campaigning since 2007.

The Danger of Policy Based on Emotion

As discussed earlier, progressive Democrats in general have always made decisions on the basis of their emotions, not reality. Truly conservative Republicans tend to make decisions on facts. Think about it. Your eyes probably glazed over when reading the polling statistics in the above paragraphs. Right? Likewise, the ears of voters become deaf when conservative Republicans cite statistics showing that America is heading for a disaster. Obama's message of Hope, Change and Progress strikes a positive emotional chord in everyone. Tragically history shows that basing policy on deceitful rhetoric only leads to Sorrow, Regret and Despair.

Any society that makes decisions on emotion, even when it is noble, will soon fail. For decades we have been taught, "If it feels right do it." That belief has resulted in a disaster because it is not based on reality. Only when policy is formed on facts and reality can a nation prosper. Only then can the policy be tempered with emotion and compassion, knowing full well the real cost or impact of the emotional or compassionate change in policy. That is what defines us as human. A hundred years of decisions based mostly on emotion has blinded us to the stark reality (in facts and figures) that America is in a deep economic and moral crisis. It is prolonged and made worse by the actual quicksand of Obama's campaign promise of Hope, Change and Progress.

The progressive group Environics or AE describes how it is done. It uses social-values surveys, cognitive linguistics, and political psychology to help progressive NGOs (non-governmental organizations) and politicians. By using these emotional touchstones, they reframe what would normally be an offensive, radical message to most Americans into something acceptable, even desirable. AE argues the best way to garner yes votes on progressive issues is to focus on shared "a fundamental belief, even if the targeted parties don't necessarily share progressivism's every last goal."[288]

In softening the American people for Obamacare, the progressive Herndon Alliance said, "…it truly matters how we talk about health care reform. In focus groups, we could lose the issue 8:1 or win it 9:0 depending on what values, images, and feelings we evoked. Well-crafted progressive messages substantially outperform the strongest conservative counter messages, whereas weakly crafted messages fail to gain support. Now is the time to go on offense on health care reform, using language we know in advance works. We also know that simply changing our words is not enough."[289]

Understand what these progressive liberals are admitting. They use *emotional* bridges to trick people to accepting as truth and desirable what they would otherwise outright reject as false and undesirable. It is the proverbial ability to "sell freezers to Eskimos in January." It is based entirely on manipulation and deception. It has nothing to do with truth and accuracy. It is fundamentally dishonest. It also is clearly a case of the ends justifying the means. The end is about winning and destroying the Constitution and the free market system that has created the most successful nation in human history.

Progressives have been enormously successful in destroying any conservative message that is based on fact and reality. The only defense is to dig behind the emotion and find the facts. In other words, use critical thinking. Most Americans can no longer do that because it has been deliberately programed out of them in public schools. More on that in Chapters 10-11.

In the case of our debt and deficit, progressive Democrats and neocons spin it like a stage-four cancer patient who refuses surgery because it will *feel* painful, and will not believe he or she will surely die if surgery is delayed. This inability to deal with reality makes progressive Democrats, liberals and neocons very dangerous to the well-being of the nation. As will be discussed later, socialist nations in Europe are financially collapsing like a house of cards because socialism opens a nation to the cancer of corruption and policies based on nothing but thin air. America is following the same path to destruction. In the next two chapters we will take a hard look at the specifics of progressivism and its bankrupt theory of governance.

America is at a crisis stage. We cannot play politics any longer. As obvious as that is to some Americans, progressives *don't seem to believe it*. Their game of politics has reached an *extremely* dangerous level. Either progressive Democrats are such ideologues that they literally cannot see the reality of the situation, or they are deliberately attempting to destroy the economic base of the United States to create a utopian society based on their unworkable ideology. If the latter, they couldn't be following a better strategy to get it done. Unfortunately, subsequent chapters will provide overwhelming evidence that that is exactly what they are doing.

Progressive Democrats and Republican neocons in both parties must be voted out of office at *every* level of government in the 2012 election and replaced with those candidates who understand the problem and will turn the nation back to a Constitutional Republican form of government that leads to prosperity.

6 – COLLAPSING AMERICA

Along with all the other problems that the U.S. and the world are facing in 2012, there is alarming evidence that the entire world is hemorrhaging and falling apart because of this type of plundering. Worse, it appears to be deliberate. Two main things are driving it; the creation of anarchy and terror to bring down entire nations, and the seeming economic collapse of the Western World. In the cover flap of their in-depth book, *Red Army,* best-selling authors Aaron Klein and Brenda Elliott warn:

> For decades, a radical socialist movement has been quietly infiltrating the major institutions of American power: our schools, our military, our economy, our media, and Congress itself. This progressive Red Army is an organized network consisting of numerous specialized groups that target specific policy areas while cooperating more broadly in a concerted decades-long campaign to transform America.[290]

Klein and Elliott are the authors of the best-selling *The Manchurian President* in 2008. In the following 485 pages of their new book, Klein and Elliott detail a myriad of plans in which hundreds, if not thousands of nongovernmental organizations (NGOs), the media, members of Congress and university professors have cooperated and coordinated on an unimaginable level to transform America into their shared vision of a socialist/fascist/communist utopia.

SAUL ALINSKY—RULES FOR RADICALS

SAUL ALINSKY'S 1971 *RULES FOR RADICALS* is generally accepted as the blueprint progressive liberals use to radically change American culture[291] to a Rousseau-based form of governance. *Rules for Radicals* is often called the radical "bible" of liberal progressives. It should surprise no one that Alinsky dedicated the book to Lucifer—the father of discord and rebellion. Alinsky makes it clear that progressives are at war with the American system and capitalism; "In war," asserts Alinsky, "the end justifies almost any means."[292] Alinsky identifies twelve civilization-destroying rules to win the war. They call for lying, intimidation, ridicule, threats, blackmail, and even violence to name a few.[293]

Alinsky also knew emotional sound bites would be far more effective than reason and logic. He even said in *Rules for Radicals* that Americans have been "trained to emphasize order, logic, [and] rational thought."[294] Therefore when the average American attempts to explain his or her reasons for doing something, "they are compelled to fabricate...logical, rational and structured" explanations, claims Alinsky.[295] In other words, use logic, facts and figures to explain their position. Using an emotional sound bite to make a point always trumps a long complicated explanation of reality, hence, the progressive's almost exclusive use of emotion and disconnect from reality.

Not surprisingly, in addition to Alinsky's "the end-justifies-any-means" method of destabilizing the existing system, he advocates, "The first step in community organization is community disorganization. ...All change means disorganization of the old and organization of the new."[296] That is exactly what we are witnessing in America in the twenty-first century. These radicals are experts in tearing down and destroying, but because they are disconnected from reality, what they try to build always ends in disaster.

Like Robespierre, Alinsky called for creating a mass army to intimidate the government and society into capitulating to their demands,[297] "In this book we are concerned with how to **create mass organizations to seize power** and give it to the people."[298] (bold original) Alinsky advocates a totalitarian government to force Marxist ideals onto the populace, "The only place you really have consensus is where you have totalitarianism," claimed Alinsky.[299] "A Marxist," Alinsky continues, "begins with his prime truth that all evils are caused by the exploitation of the proletariat by the capitalists. From this he logically proceeds to the revolution to end capitalism, then into the third stage of reorganization into a new social order of the dictatorship of the proletariat, and finally the last stage—the political paradise of communism."[300]

6 – Collapsing America

Is Alinsky's belief so farfetched? Obama's manufacturing Czar, Ron Bloom, proclaimed that "We know that the free market is nonsense.... We know this is largely about power, that it's an adults only, no limit game. We kind of agree with Mao [Zedong] that political power comes largely from the barrel of a gun."[301] Force is the final means of achieving the progressive Marxist/Fascist/Communist goals. Lying, distortion, misdirection, and yes, blame-shifting is at the heart of getting there.

What that means is that you can never take anything a liberal progressive says at face value. They will say anything to achieve their goal to strip Americans of their liberties and destroy the free market system that has been the most successful in all of human history.

Community organizing groups and unions use this strategy. Groups like environmental organizations, ACORN, National Education Association (NEA), American Federation of Teachers (AFT) and SEIU have been extremely successful in their attacks on American institutions.[302] Obama worked with or for ACORN to actually train their employees in these tactics. He actually bragged about it in his 2008 campaign before unpleasant links to ACORN were made.

Both ACORN and SEIU have used intimidation and barely legal protests of banking institutions to force them to grant what became toxic mortgages to people who could not afford them. When they were only partially successful they turned to noisily protesting at the homes of senior banking officials. They were highly successful because the terrorized family members demanded their spouses give in to the demands of ACORN or SEIU.

These intimidating practices are still used. On May 16, 2010 an army of fourteen busloads carrying more than 500 angry SEIU union members descended on the home of Greg Baer, the deputy general counsel for corporate law at Bank of America. Located in a normally quiet neighborhood, the highly agitated mob hurled exaggerated angry epithets and slogans. The only family member home was the Baer's terrified 14-year-old son who locked himself in the bathroom. Nina Easton, a neighbor across the street said:

> ...this event would accurately be called a 'protest' if it were taking place at, say, a bank or the U.S. Capitol. But when hundreds of loud and angry strangers are descending on your family, your children, and your home, a more apt description of this assemblage would be 'mob.'

103

Intimidation was the whole point of this exercise, and it worked—even on the police. A trio of officers who belatedly answered our calls confessed a fear that arrests might "incite" these trespassers.[303]

This was not a media event. No media were notified. It was designed specifically to create terror, so SEIU did not want the media to record it. Nina just happened to be the Washington Bureau Chief at *Fortune* magazine and was able to get the event videotaped. The video showed an angry, barely constrained mob trespassing on the Baer property right up to their front door. The police refused to intervene for fear of further inciting the trespassers to violence.

That left the SEIU mob free to terrorize other homes before they quit for the day. The police were there, but did nothing to protect the residents. Do you really believe if there wasn't the threat of arrest that this mob would have stopped at just angry protesting? Other than Fox News, the mainstream media said nothing.

The Obama administration not only agrees with this kind of barely controlled mob action, it actually plans it. When Tea Party protests in Town Hall meetings became embarrassing to President Obama in 2009, Health and Human Services Secretary Kathleen Sebelius called SEIU to solicit their help to neutralize accusations and perceived distortions from opponents of Obamacare. The next day the White House issued a "battle plan" to Senate Democrats to quell the protests by "punch[ing] back twice as hard."[304] The mainstream media yawned and turned a blind eye.

Just as *Rules for Radicals* advises, SEIU sent large numbers of counter-demonstrators to intimidate and speak in favor of Obamacare at several town hall meetings. At a St. Louis Town Hall meeting, four SEIU members surrounded and physically attacked Obamacare protester Kenneth Gladney.[305] Video of the attack showed Gladney's SEIU attackers (wearing SEIU shirts) violently kicking him in the head and back. Even though the attack was violent and Gladney is a diabetic weighing only 130 pounds, the SEIU thugs were never prosecuted.[306] As usual, the mainstream press ignored the blatant attack on Gladney's civil rights.

Does this sound a bit unbelievable? It shouldn't. Remember, progressive liberals believe they are at war with traditional American values.

Another thing *Rules for Radicals* advocates is that the greater the resistance to the radical agenda the harder its advocates must work to *force* its implementation. When it looked like Obamacare would fail to pass, House Majority Leader Nancy Pelosi uttered another of her over-the-top statements on January 28, 2010, "We'll go through the gate. If the gate's closed, we'll go over the fence. If the fence is too high, we'll pole-vault in. If that doesn't work, we'll parachute in."[307] While it perhaps wasn't the wisest things to say publicly, it was the perfect description of what the progressive liberals did. Just as Alinsky advised, they bulldozed their way to success even though 60 percent of the American people were adamantly against it.

President Obama actually grew up in the Alinsky culture. After graduating from college, where very few people remember him, President Obama actually represented ACORN and helped train community activists in the Alinsky model. Likewise, he has always been united with SEIU in their goals.[308] He proved his faithfulness to unions when he gave unions preferential treatment over investors during his bailout of General Motors and Chrysler. He trampled the property rights of the stockholders in the process—essentially stealing what was rightfully theirs to give to his favored unions. Again, the mainstream media said very little about this direct attack on well-established rule of law.

Ideology Trumps America's National Security

Obama did it again with Solyndra by providing a $535 million loan guarantee to the company after President Bush recommended against making the loan.[309] The Office of Management and Budget even warned Obama in spite of the loan; Solyndra would run out of money and head for bankruptcy court by September 2011.[310] It actually declared bankruptcy on September 6th.

Solyndra was the centerpiece of Obama's "clean energy" future. As the dirty details of the Solyndra scandal trickled out, it was determined that U.S. Department of Energy (DOE) employee Steve Spinner had helped monitor the Solyndra loan guarantee. Spinner was previously one of Obama's top fundraisers.[311] Worse, as it became clear Solyndra would fail, the DOE allowed private creditors, including many big Democrat donors, to get paid first when Solyndra's assets were sold, in violation of procedure. The investors got some of their money back, but the U.S. taxpayer got none.[312] Besides the cloud of corruption, the Solyndra scandal shows why the government shouldn't be in the business of picking winners and losers. Most of these kinds of loans have been losers.[313]

No sooner did the Solyndra scandal begin to die down when it was revealed that the Energy Department provided a $529,000,000 loan to Fisker Automotive to develop an electric luxury sports car. This benefits Al Gore and his venture capital business partner John Doerr. Both men, but especially Doerr, are big donors to the Democrats. As investors, Gore and Doerr also benefited from a $560 million grant to utilities which have contracts with Silver Spring Networks, a company developing electrical smart grids.[314]

After Vice President Joe Biden hailed electric car battery maker Ener1 as the best example of paving the way to for a new industry, Ener1 filed for Chapter 11 bankruptcy on January 27, 2012. But not before receiving a $118 million stimulus grant from the Obama administration.[315]

Biden had proudly told the press just a few months before that, "Everyone is catching on folks, the industry is transforming itself. And we believe Americans are ready to embrace that transition. And you folks standing here on this floor, Enron1 (sic), are on the ground floor of that transition."[316] This is pure hubris. The industry is not transforming. Germany and Great Britain announced they are dramatically slashing their alternative energy subsidies because it is money down a rat hole. German solar equipment companies are dropping like flies without the ability to leech off the taxpayers. Solon, Solar Millennium, and Solarhybrid, and as of April 2012, Q-Cells have joined the ranks of companies to fall to bankruptcy.[317] More companies will surely follow.[318]

After spending tens of billions of dollars on subsidies to green energy wind and solar farms Obama's Clean Energy Program, the nation's use of green energy has barely changed, from about 1.5 percent 10 years ago to 2 percent today. Worse, in his new book, *Throw Them All Out*, Peter Schweizer details how 80 percent of DOE funds for clean energy have gone to Obama backers:

> ...In the...government-backed loan program [alone], for example, $16.4 billion of the $20.5 billion in loans granted as of Sept. 15 [2011] went to companies either run by or primarily owned by Obama financial backers—individuals who were bundlers, members of Obama's National Finance Committee, or large donors to the Democratic Party.[319]

This type of crony capitalism runs throughout Obama's tenure. It has nothing to do with capitalism and everything to do with corruption.[320] Taxpayers lose, and friends of the Obama administration either do not lose if the projects fail, or get richer if they succeed. It calls into question whether Obama is pushing green energy because he believes in it, or to pay off his supporters with taxpayers' money.

Even while all of this was going on, Obama refused to issue the permit to build the Keystone XL oil pipeline from Canada down to Texas. The pipeline would have delivered 1.2 million barrels of oil a day—the amount of oil the U.S. currently gets from Saudi Arabia and 46 percent more than all the wind and solar energy currently produced in the U.S. each day.[321] The XL pipeline is but one of a long list of outright attacks by Obama on the coal, oil and natural gas industries, costing America tens of billions of dollars and hundreds of thousands of jobs.

Although U.S. reserves of oil, natural gas and coal are inexpensive and very abundant, Obama has done all he can to shut down every plan to develop these sources of economically cheap energy.[322] Progressive Democrats have blocked every effort to drill in ANWR (Arctic National Wildlife Refuge), Alaska, and develop the enormous oil and natural gas shale deposits in the Northern Rockies since 2000. They have claimed ANWR is part of the beautiful pristine Arctic National Wildlife Refuge that would be fatally harmed by drilling.

However, the 2,000 acres that would be developed for drilling is only 0.001 percent of the entire ANWR wildlife refuge. If the progressive Democrats had allowed ANWR to be developed, it would now be producing more than a million barrels of oil per day, greatly reducing our dependence on foreign oil.[323] Besides, the Prudhoe Bay oil development on Alaska's North Slope has greatly enhanced the wildlife population.[324] This is just one more example of how progressive liberals cannot deal with reality.

Likewise, the largest oil deposit in the world is located in the Northern Rockies in the form of oil shale. Much of that oil can be recovered at today's market prices with new technology in an environmentally safe way. There is enough shale oil to meet all of America's current need for at least 100 years. There are 1.2–1.8 *trillion* barrels of oil available in Wyoming's Green River Formation alone. Again, progressive Democrats have blocked every effort to develop it. The main reason? It would take 10 years to develop, which was too long to wait. That was in 2000. We would have access to that oil today if President Bush's plan was passed in Congress.[325]

Obama even defied a court order requiring the Department of Interior to grant deep water drilling permits for oil. Meanwhile, Cuba contracted several companies, including China, to conduct exploratory drilling within 60 miles of the Florida coast; something Obama would not let U.S. companies do.[326] By the end of 2011, Cuba had brought in a Chinese deep water drilling rig and started drilling some 60-70 miles from Florida.[327]

America has more than a hundred-year supply of oil. Yet, in March 2012 President Obama made the absurd statement in every speech about energy:

> As a country that has 2 percent of the world's oil reserves, but uses 20 percent of the world's oil — I'm going to repeat that — we've got 2 percent of the world oil reserves; we use 20 percent. What that means is, as much as we're doing to increase oil production, we're not going to be able to just drill our way out of the problem of high gas prices. Anybody who tells you otherwise either doesn't know what they're talking about or they aren't telling you the truth."[328]

Really? Technically he is right. The U.S. does only have 2 percent of the world's *proven* reserves. Proven reserves are those that are already well-defined and essentially producing oil. That's about 22 billion barrels of oil. Of course, all the sources of oil mentioned above are not included because they are *politically* not available, or are just now becoming economically available. If only those that are known to be economically available are included but politically blocked, the known reserves would be 160 billion barrels, or almost eight times the amount Obama always quotes.[329] Add oil shale and it becomes 45 times more than Obama quotes.

Obama knows this of course. He is deliberately using it to mislead the American people. It is disingenuous at best and an outright lie at worst. It is nothing more than his plan to hide the fact that his administration is actually trying to drive up the cost of energy, putting national security at risk, and greatly harming the American people in the process; especially the poor.

The EPA is also refusing to grant new permits to open new coal mines and has gone so far as to revoke existing permits.[330] Once again, the federal court ruled against the efforts of the Obama administration, in this case the EPA, charging that the EPA exceeded its authority under Section 404 of the Clean Water Act.[331]

While Obama gives lip service to reducing the dependence of the U.S. on foreign energy and creating jobs, he is actually making America more dependent on foreign energy, thereby potentially jeopardizing U.S. national security. This author has been warning of this for years. It now is happening with Iran's threat to block the Strait of Hormuz which could raise the price of gasoline to $5 a gallon in late 2012.[332] It is also killing hundreds of thousands of jobs in the process.

None of this would be happening if progressive Democrats and Obama had not blocked development of these sources of domestic fossil energy. It borders on being criminal, yet the mainstream media are strangely quiet about this negligence. However, they are more than happy to promote yet another misdirection—that Obama has increased domestic oil production. It's just not true. Obama's claim that domestic oil production is up since he took office is not due to anything he did. The increased production is the result of more drilling on state and private lands that can't be stopped by Obama. Production on federal lands and the Gulf of Mexico actually declined 11 and 17 percent respectively in 2011.[333]

The decline in oil production would have been much worse in the Gulf and federal land if it were not for the Bush administration granting new permits during his administration. It takes 4 to 8 years from getting permits to begin pumping oil. Permits granted by Bush finally came into production in 2010 and 2011. There is no way Obama had anything to do with the increase in production.[334]

Likewise, Obama blatantly misled the American people by falsely taking credit for approving the southern end of the Keystone XL pipeline after he denied approval for the northern end. That section of the pipeline did not need Obama's approval, yet he tried to make people believe it did in order to take the spotlight off the political disaster resulting from his denial of the permit for the northern part of Keystone. Like Alaska's infamous "bridge to nowhere," the Oklahoma to Texas part of the Keystone will remain almost empty until the northern part is built.

Rather than providing Americans with cheap energy, Obama is committed to forcing Americans to use very expensive wind and solar energy. He will tolerate no plan or program that will slow his efforts to achieve his goal—even with overwhelming evidence that it is destroying

America. However, not only is wind and solar power economically ruinous, it just doesn't work. Simply put, wind energy only works when the wind blows—about 25 percent of the time. Likewise, solar power is even less effective because it doesn't work when the sun doesn't shine or it's cloudy. The technology to store electricity when it can't be produced is decades away, if it is ever developed. There are a host of other technical reasons why wind and solar won't be economically competitive with carbon-based energy on a large scale for a long time into the future.[335]

Europe is already reeling from the realization that green energy is bankrupting them. British companies are threatening to move to other countries that are not forcing green energy to be used. Some are already moving. Great Britain estimated in July 2011 that 25 percent of their population already suffered from "energy poverty" as British energy costs skyrocketed by 71 percent.[336]

An in-depth study in Spain found that for every job green energy creates, 2.2 jobs are lost in the rest of the economy as the enormous subsidies required for green energy sucks jobs out of the private sector. Research in Italy found that they lost an incredible 6.9 jobs in the industrial sector and 4.8 jobs across the entire economy for every green job created.[337] As one European nation after another realizes the enormous costs of alternative energy, they systematically shut off their astronomic subsidies that propped up green energy. By 2012 green energy is in a death spiral in Europe as the EU and the euro face total collapse.

The European evidence means nothing to Obama. His clean energy plan is an utter failure that has cost the American people tens of billions of dollars, killed hundreds of thousands (perhaps millions) of jobs, threatened national security and opened the door to what appears to be rampant corruption. Yet, the Obama administration and the progressive Democrats in Congress continue to force-feed us its failed policy. Republican primary presidential candidate Newt Gingrich even joined radically progressive Nancy Pelosi in a 2008 ad claiming they can reduce global warming through clean energy technology.[338] And the mainstream press either says nothing, or supports the administration's twisted and extremely dangerous goals.

Worse, along with thousands of pages of other rules, allegedly to make us more "sustainable," the EPA is morphing into a high priesthood for an emerging new environmental religion. This new religion is based on nothing more than pseudoscience created to justify its fear that mother earth is supposedly being destroyed by capitalism and the free market system. Obama and the progressive liberals couldn't have chosen a better way to bring the U.S. to its knees and destroy it economically.

CLOWARD AND PIVEN

IN MANY RESPECTS, WHAT OBAMA and the progressives are doing is irrational. When all things are considered, Obama seems to be deliberately driving the U.S. right into the ground. While some of it can be explained by blind ideology, Obama and the progressives in general cannot be that blind.

Enter Richard Cloward and Frances Piven. Radical socialists at Columbia University, professors Richard Cloward and his wife Frances Piven wrote a 1966 article titled "The Weight of the Poor: A Strategy to End Poverty" in The Nation.[339] Now known as the Cloward-Piven Strategy, the strategy took off like wildfire among the progressive liberals. Using Rousseau as their foundation and Alinsky as their inspiration, the Cloward-Piven Strategy "seeks to hasten the fall of capitalism by overloading the government bureaucracy with a flood of impossible demands, thus pushing society into crisis and economic collapse."[340] The strategy calls for creating a massive movement employing intimidation so that the rest of society fears them.

After decades of studying the Cloward and Piven Strategy, DiscovertheNetworks.org found that Cloward-Piven initially wanted to collapse the welfare system by overwhelming welfare rolls. The result, they said, would be "a profound financial and political crisis" that would unleash "powerful forces…for major economic reform at the national level." They would do this by the "collapse of current financing arrangements," thereby creating a "climate of militancy" and fear.[341] The strategy did this by:

Carefully orchestrated media campaigns, carried out by friendly, leftwing journalists, who would float the idea of "a federal program of income redistribution," in the form of a guaranteed living income for all—working and non-working people alike. Local officials would clutch at this idea like drowning men to a lifeline. They would apply pressure on Washington to implement it. With every major city erupting into chaos, Washington would have to act.[342]

The strategy was extremely successful from the start. Cloward and Piven recruited an organizer named George Wiley to lead their movement. In 1967, he created the National Welfare Rights Organization (NWRO). His very militant followers invaded welfare offices around the United States, sometimes violently. Social workers were always intimidated. Other tactics involved signing up people who were eligible, but not on welfare. They intentionally wanted to overload the system.[343] One of their early targets was New York City. The New York Times commented on September 27, 1970,

> There have been sit-ins in legislative chambers, including a United States Senate committee hearing, mass demonstrations of several thousand welfare recipients, school boycotts, picket lines, mounted police, tear gas, arrests - and, on occasion, rock-throwing, smashed glass doors, overturned desks, scattered papers and ripped-out phones.[344]

The protests were so successful that one out of two New York City residents was on welfare by the early 1970s. Just as planned, New York City was overwhelmed and was forced to declare bankruptcy in 1975. New York City Mayor Rudy Giuliani attempted to expose the effort in the late 1990s and again in 2009-2010 when ACORN became front-page news. He accused them of deliberate economic sabotage. Not surprisingly, the mainstream media turned a deaf ear.[345]

The strategy has proven to be so successful that Cloward and Piven began to use it on other fronts as well. In 1982, they, along with their supporters, branched into the voting rights movement. ACORN (Association of Community Organizations for Reform Now) grew out of George Wiley's NWRO. ACORN was created by Wade Rathke, who was a NWRO organizer and a protégé of Wiley. Rathke also organized the militant Students for a Democratic Society (SDS) during the same period.

It was only when ACORN was videotaped offering tax advice to what it thought was a prostitute and her pimp in 2009 that a small fraction of ACORN's moral corruption was finally exposed to America. Federal grants were outlawed and donations dried up, forcing ACORN to declare bankruptcy on November 2, 2010. The date is especially satisfying in that it occurred on Election Day after ACORN had been embroiled in dozens of election fraud cases.[346] ACORN lives on however, because it has morphed into hundreds of front groups. All of these groups have used the same militant/violent tactics as NWRO did in New York City.

One of these offshoots, Affordable Housing Centers of America (AHCOA) received an illegal $80,000 grant from the U.S. Department of Housing and Urban Development (HUD). The grant was exposed by the Washington DC-based Judicial Watch, a conservative legal watchdog. Both AHCOA and the GAO (Government Accounting Office) denied any connection to ACORN, allowing the grant to stand.[347]

Judicial Watch wondered how the GAO could keep a straight face in this bald-faced lie. After all, the grant was issued to "ACORN Housing Corporation, Inc." The grant also was sent to ACORN's New Orleans' address. Even more shocking, a September 2010 HUD report states that ACORN Housing is "now operating as Affordable Housing Centers of America" and has misappropriated funds from a $3.2 million federal grant.[348] Has the federal government become so corrupt that it can do whatever it likes and give money to whomever it wants at will? It seems so—and it must be stopped.

The 2009 Stimulus Plan

Whether in Europe or America, the Rousseau progressive worldview, Alinsky's *Rules for Radicals*, or the Cloward Piven Strategy is based on emotions and feelings, not reality. In every case the secret of their success is the use of political correctness, followed by intimidation, bullying, and if they can get away with it, outright violence. If their program fails, they believe it just needs *more* government control or *more* money and it will surely work. Welfare is a classic example.

Although it was barely reported by the mainstream press, one of the 2009 American Recovery and Reinvestment Act's (i.e. the stimulus bill's) most important provisions was its repeal of the key provisions in the highly successful Personal Responsibility and Work Opportunity Reconciliation Act of 1996. This is the welfare-reform legislation passed by the Republican Congress and signed by President Clinton that reduced the welfare rolls by two-thirds.[349] Progressives apparently hated the 1996 legislation and waited for the opportunity to reinstate the bloated welfare program they wanted. The 2009 Stimulus Plan was their opportunity. We may never know whether it was because of blind ideology or a deliberate plan to once again overload the system in order to bring it down, or both. In the final analysis, it doesn't matter.

The Heritage Foundation did an in-depth analysis following the passage of the stimulus legislation. Their findings were stunning. Heritage found that the claim that the stimulus funding was temporary was a red herring. Rather, it represented a "massive permanent expansion of the welfare state."[350]

For instance, every poor person in the U.S. receiving welfare saw a $6,700 increase in their benefits from stimulus money. This welfare benefit accounted for 32 percent of the entire $816 billion stimulus pot of gold. It was earmarked for such programs as Temporary Assistance to Needy Families; Medicaid; food stamps; the Women, Infants, and Children food program; public housing; Section 8 housing; the Community Development Block Grant; the Social Services Block Grant; Head Start; and the Earned Income Tax Credit.

The Heritage report claimed that, "this welfare spending is only the tip of the iceberg.... Once the hidden welfare spending in the bill is counted, the total 10-year fiscal burden (added to the national debt) will [be] $1.34 trillion! This amounts to $17,400 for each household paying income tax in the U.S."[351] Another stunning example of increased welfare spending in the stimulus bill was Obama's "Make Work Pay" refundable tax credit. According to the Heritage Foundation:

> This credit represents a fundamental shift in welfare policy. At a cost of around $23 billion per year, this credit will provide up to [$400] in cash to low income adults who pay no income taxes. For the first time, the government will give significant cash to able-bodied adults without dependent children. Since most of these individuals have little apparent need for assistance, the new credit represents 'spreading the wealth' for its own sake. The lack of connection between this credit and 'economic stimulus' is evident in the fact that the first payments under the program [were] not...made until April 2010.[352]

Don't ever think the misrepresented stimulus bill was a stealthy effort to try to help the poor. As was shown in the passage of the Personal Responsibility and Work Opportunity Reconciliation Act of 1996, all this income does is to encourage recipients to stay on welfare. No, the real reason was and is much worse than that. In fact, it is a diabolical, but common practice for progressives.

In their 2009 book, *Catastrophe*, former Clinton political advisor Dick Morris and Eileen McGann provide key insights into the monumental significance of President Obama's $400 refundable tax credit:

> Under the guise of a stimulus package to bring the economy out of recession, the Obama administration [was] reworking the fundamental politics of our country, passing out checks like heroin to create a constituency addicted to public handouts, and concentrating the tax burden of paying for it all on a smaller and smaller number of Americans. A larger percentage of the American population is paying no income taxes at all…making them unlikely to complain when taxes are raised on those who do. At the same time, they're getting checks from Washington as part of a concerted effort to build a constituency that supports big government and big handouts.... The hard progressive left demanded the solution to the slumping economy following the 2009 stimulus was more, much more, stimulus money.[353]

Like the public union scandals that are now threatening to bankrupt states, welfare is being used to buy votes for progressive Democrats while overloading the system. The same reasoning applies to the progressive agenda to open the floodgates to illegal aliens to enter the U.S. and eventually get citizenship. In the highly controversial illegal alien issue, the progressive liberals are not alone. Neocons promote the same thing, but for a slightly different reason. They want to break down national borders to hasten the progress to global governance. That's why the illegal alien issue is never solved. Progressives on both sides of the aisle don't want it solved until we open the door to illegal aliens to flood the nation.

Although any effort to stimulate the economy using Keynesian economics was bound to fail, it is a siren song to any progressive, even those who have self-serving motives for creating stimulus plans. Except for the administration lackeys, very few economists thought the Stimulus Plan would work. They were right. It didn't. The only thing the Stimulus Plan did was to increase our debt by $816 billion, plus another $787 billion over ten years in additional hidden welfare costs.[354] Once again the system is being overloaded.

In spite of administration efforts to put a positive spin on the Stimulus Plan, the Obama administration had to finally admit it cost $278,000 per job created or saved.[355] Jeffrey Anderson of the Weekly Standard laments, "In other words, the government could simply have cut a $100,000 check to everyone whose employment was allegedly made possible by the "stimulus," and taxpayers would have come out $427 billion ahead."[356] In short, the Stimulus Plan was a horrible policy. On the other hand, if your goal is to overwhelm and bankrupt the system, it was a perfect policy.

Stimulus 2.0

Although Obama said there would not be a Stimulus II, he finally succumbed to this overwhelming ideological pull by announcing his jobs bill on September 8, 2011. However, this time there was an ulterior motive: to back the Republicans into a corner. It allowed Obama to go into campaign mode focused on class warfare and demonization of all opposition—a classic Alinsky/Cloward-Piven strategy. He did it to take the spotlight off of his self-created, catastrophic economic train wreck and to go on the offensive by blaming the Republicans for sacrificing jobs and the middle class by keeping taxes low for their wealthy friends.

Like Stimulus 1, Stimulus 2 focused on the public sector jobs rather than private jobs. Much of it in the private sector was crony capitalism; giving money to friends and supporters. It also focused on things like extending jobless benefits and the payroll tax holiday that are already in effect. These measures have not, nor will they ever add new jobs or help the economy.[357] Extending the jobless benefits merely encourages the unemployed to stay on unemployment. The payroll tax holiday represents a perfect way to buy votes while further exacerbating the Social Security Crisis that was already serious. Once again, it was about politics, winning and overstressing entitlements rather than what is good for America.

Obama's American Jobs Act is supposed to work by throwing money at much needed infrastructure improvements. However, these are no more "shovel-ready" than they were in Stimulus 1, so they won't have any impact for at least 9 months to a year. Worse, just like the sugar high resulting from Stimulus 1, all the gains made by flooding the economy with money would crash when the money runs out. Obama's American Jobs Act was so bad that even the Democrat-controlled Senate refused to vote on it because Senate Majority Leader Harry Reid knew many Democrats would vote no.[358]

There was, however, one bright spot. The only shovel-ready infrastructure project that was really ready to go was the Keystone XL pipeline project that would bring cheap oil from Canada to Texas. It would create 20,000 new jobs and perhaps 120,000 additional supporting jobs. However, the XL plan did not fit Obama's plans to stop *all* development of carbon-based fuels like oil, coal and natural gas. He was making good on his campaign promise to make coal and oil so expensive that America would be forced to go to alternative green energy no matter what the cost.[359] So he postponed any decision twice on the project until after the 2012 election, thereby appeasing his very powerful environmental base.[360] By doing so, he showed he couldn't care less about the jobs it would have created.

The Keystone XL project was a significant step to improving our national security by helping the U.S. to wean itself from unstable supplies from the Mideast and Venezuela. Obama postponed the decision the second time a week after Iran threatened to close the Strait of Hormuz. Yet, Obama still insisted the decision was based on the national interest.[361]

Obama also justified his decision on the need for additional environmental impact studies, even though it had already been studied for three years and been found to be safe! There are already 50,000 miles of crude oil pipeline built in the U.S., out of two million miles of energy pipeline that crisscross America. These have an extremely small environmental effect.[362] Canada's Prime Minister Harper even warned that if Obama nixed the pipeline he would sell the oil instead to China.[363]

THE RADICAL ARMY OF NGOS, POLITICIANS AND MEDIA

THE INCESTUOUS INTERCONNECTIONS between ACORN, AHCOA, HUD and even the GAO are but the tip of the iceberg. Like Klein and Elliot in their book *Red Army*, Discoverthenetworks.org has uncovered thousands of interconnections between non-governmental organizations (NGOs) who cooperate and collaborate to undermine the constitutional, economic and moral foundations of the United States and the American way of life. This sickening array of social malcontents/anarchists and their evil agenda can only be described as a conspiracy to secretly destroy the United States and create a utopian society based on their Rousseau ideology. Chapter 8 unveils those who are behind this sinister plot.

The Discoverthenetworks.org website even details the step-by-step process of how these NGOs were largely responsible for first pressuring the U.S. Congress into passing the Community Reinvestment Act (CRA) in 1977. Using the CRA, they then *forced* banks into loaning mortgage money to unqualified borrowers. When these borrowers could no longer pay their monthly mortgage, the housing crash in 2007 resulted. This in turn led the way to the financial collapse of 2008.[364]

More than just these NGOs were involved. Progressive politicians like Barney Frank (D-NY) were also deeply involved, forcing Freddie Mac and Fannie Mae to lower standards in buying up these toxic mortgages and bullying anyone who questioned the soundness of what they were doing. Congressman Frank angrily proclaimed that Freddie Mac and Fannie Mae were sound financially right up until they collapsed.[365]

Politicians and NGOs

Perhaps the most significant far-reaching and expensive legislation ever passed by Congress was the 2700-page Patient Protection and Affordable Care Act, or Obamacare as it is now called. For most people, Obamacare immediately brings to mind one of the most moronic, yet prophetic utterances by a politician ever made. On March 9, 2010, Nancy Pelosi proclaimed, "We have to pass the bill so that you can find out what is in it."[366] It was passed less than two weeks later with 60 percent of the American people against it. The percentage against it was still almost as high in 2012.

In classic Alinsky/Cloward-Piven strategy, Klein and Elliot note, "the legislation, deliberately masked by moderate, populist rhetoric, was carefully crafted and perfected over the course of decades and is a direct product of laborious work by the same radical network,"[367] of NGOs, politicians, and media that have created so much havoc in other areas of American society. As with any progressive assault on constitutional principles and the American Dream, 30-50 progressive organizations joined weekly conference calls to plan the week's activity and keep everyone on message.[368]

The template for Obamacare was the George Soros-funded Economic Policy Institute's Agenda for Shared Prosperity. Its centerpiece, *Health Care for America* was written by Jacob Hacker who was Hillary Clinton's and Barack Obama's advisor during the 2008 presidential campaign. Hacker, in turn, is a third generation liberal progressive with roots in

Fabian Socialism. Hacker's plan is the culmination of many evolutions of a socialist, single-payer healthcare plan. The plan was promoted by not only a slew of radical NGOs, but by four major progressive groups in the 11th Congress; the Congressional Progressive Caucus as well as the Progressive, Black, Hispanic, and Asian Pacific American Caucuses.[369]

In their first two chapters of *Red Army*, Klein and Elliott detail what can only be described as a mind-numbing array of connections between these congressional caucuses and socialist, communist, union, environmentalist and other radical organizations. As will be discussed in Chapter 9, multi-billionaire George Soros provides a significant source of funding to these radical NGOs.

The ultra-radical SDS (Students for a Democratic Society) and Fabian Society-affiliated Michael Harrington founded the Democratic Socialists of America (DSA). The DSA in turn founded the Congressional Progressive Caucus (CPC) with the able help of avowed socialist, Vermont Senator Bernie Sanders. Its purpose, according to Klein and Elliot, is to "infiltrate a political system using innocuous-sounding titles and stealthy tactics."[370]

The DSA and CPC were joined at the hip, sharing identical goals and even sharing a website until at least 2002.[371] The DSA "is still the principle branch of the Socialist International (SI), one of the planet's most influential socialist organizations…"[372] SI has never deviated from its goal of global governance and socialism. Former Speaker of the House Nancy Pelosi (D-CA) was a member of both the DSA and CPC in 2001. She is also a longtime member of CPC's executive committee.[373, a]

Many conservatives believe the 82-member CPC was damaged in the 2010 election. It wasn't. It only lost a couple of seats. It was the Blue Dog Democrats—the original Democrats of 30 to 50 years ago—that lost half of their seats.[374] Although the Democrats lost control of the House, those that remained were even more radical than before the 2010 election. That has certainly been evident in never-seen-before animosity and gridlock in 2011. Creating gridlock and blaming it on the conservative Republicans is their strategy, and it is being supported by the mainstream media.

The gridlock is no accident. John Podesta, former chief of staff for Bill Clinton and now CEO of the Center for American Progress—another

---

[a] Other members of the CPC can be found at:
http://cpc.grijalva.house.gov/index.cfm?sectionid=71.

George Soros funded NGO—has proposed that "Barack Obama should employ all the executive authority available to him and circumvent Congress by any and all means possible to push his radical agenda." The details of how to do this, in the Center's report *The Power of the President,* which "enumerates the types of executive authority available to Obama: executive orders, rulemaking, agency management, convening and creating public-private partnerships, commanding the armed forces and diplomacy."[375] The report was written specifically to allow Obama to create and implement policy while Congress is conveniently gridlocked.[376] He has taken full advantage of it.

The Mainstream Media

In earlier chapters it was obvious the mainstream media now has a blatant bias in their reporting against anything conservative or Tea Party related, while they support anything progressive liberals promote. Klein and Elliott note that "Central to advancing the agenda of President Obama and the progressives who helped to craft White House policy has been the U.S. news media, which has largely failed to report on the glaring radicalism of the president and the company he has sought to keep."[377]

A report issued by the Business and Media Institute at the Media Research Center revealed that when the "networks talked about tax cuts, ABC, CBS and NBC have portrayed Obama as a tax cutter more than four times as often as they talked about him raising taxes. Those potential tax increases are almost 20 times the size of the $214 billion temporary tax cuts Obama included in the stimulus bill."[378]

More recently, the Media Research Center analyzed 723 campaign segments broadcast from January 1 through October 31, 2011 by the three networks on their weekday morning programs. The network reporters employed 49 "conservative" labels to describe the Republican candidates, compared with only one "liberal" label for President Obama. The morning shows used an "adversarial liberal agenda" when questioning Republican presidential candidates by a 4 to 1 margin. Even more blatant, the questions asked of Obama were "liberal-themed," which played right into what Obama wanted to say. The questions asked of the Republican candidates bordered on being caustic. Instead of asking Obama about his disastrously failed domestic policies, they tended to focus on positive feature stories or his family, treating the president as a celebrity.[379]

Writing in The Daily Caller, Jonathan Strong exposed JournoList—an email list comprising several hundred journalists who actually conspired to mute any stories that treated Obama negatively. Strong cited the firestorm of hatred on JournoList when ABC News anchors Charles Gibson and George Stephanopoulos had the audacity to politely ask Obama why it took a year for the president to dissociate himself from the extreme hate rhetoric of his spiritual guide, the Reverend Jeremiah Wright, Jr. It was a softball question, but it set off a tirade of responses from JournoList members.[380]

Stephanopoulos was "a disgusting little rat snake," fumed Richard Kim of The Nation. Michael Tomasky, a writer for the Guardian, and fellow member of JournoList wrote, "Listen folks–in my opinion, we all have to do what we can to kill ABC and this idiocy in whatever venues we have. This isn't about defending Obama. This is about how the [mainstream media] kills any chance of discourse that actually serves the people." Tomasky continued, "Richard Kim got this right above: 'a horrible glimpse of general election press strategy.' He's dead on. We need to throw chairs now, try as hard as we can to get the call next time. Otherwise the questions in October will be exactly like this. This is just a disease."[381]

The dialog of JournoList members goes downhill from here. It is obvious that hate has blinded many, if not all, of these members. Just how does a softball question like this "kill any chance of discourse that actually serves the people?" Isn't that what the media is supposed to do at a minimum? Is this a "disease" that justifies "throwing chairs?" By any measure, this is blind hatred, and if it prevails in the mainstream media it will open the door to a tyrant to take control, just like Napoleon did following the French Revolution discussed in an earlier chapter. In fact, that door has already been blown wide open. It is the same mentality discussed by Dr. Gustav Le Bon when describing the early progressives in 1895, and more recently by psychiatrist Lowell Rossiter, Jr., MD.

JournoList members include reporters and employees of Time, Politico, the Huffington Post, the Baltimore Sun, the Guardian, Salon and The New Republic. According to Strong, they participate in "outpourings of anger over how Obama had been treated in the media, and in some cases plotted to fix the damage."[382] Sarah Spitz, a producer for National Public Radio even went so far as to say she would "Laugh loudly like a maniac and watch his eyes bug out" if Rush Limbaugh writhed in torment dying from a heart attack in front of her. She went on to say, "I didn't know I had this much hate in me, but he deserves it."[383] What more needs to be said.

At the risk of repetition, Dr. Rossiter warns that progressive liberals deny their "own propensity for hatred and violence. The liberal mind is an angry mind determined to force people into its stereotyped categories but unable to acknowledge that its own political coercion is a form of criminal violence."[384] Progressive liberals are incapable of seeing their own vitriolic hatred, even when it is pointed out to them. After all, like Ms. Spitz above, they think they are justified because they are always right and the world is wrong. Strong concludes his series on JournoList by saying, "In the view of many who've posted to the [JournoList], conservatives aren't simply wrong, they are evil. And while journalists are trained never to presume motive, JournoList members tend to assume that the other side is acting out of the darkest and most dishonorable motives."[385]

In *Red Army*, Klein and Elliott point out that JournoList included activists with ties to the White House through the New America Foundation (NAF). The NAF is funded by George Soros' Open Society Institute (OSI) and the Tides Foundation. Like peeling an onion, the two investigators uncovered connection after connection. Suffice it to say that Klein and Elliott describe a veritable cesspool of congressional/socialist/ media/communist, and Islamic interconnections that have done enormous damage to the U.S. Constitution and the liberties of all Americans.[386] All these interconnections are beyond the scope of this book, but they are spelled out in detail in *Red Army*.

Needless to say, to support the progressive/socialist/communist ideology, every one of the congressmen and women involved in this agenda had to violate their oath of office to uphold the Constitution of the United States. It is now clear why the mainstream media are strangely quiet about this outright war against traditional America and our U.S. Constitution.[387]

7 – THE FINAL COLLAPSE?

America is being torn apart by the progressive liberal ideology that follows the very destructive Jean Jacques Rousseau model of government control of everything. That model led to the very violent and bloody French Revolution, Marxism and communism. Psychiatrists described the progressive liberal ideology and its destructive plundering as early as the late 1800s as the progressive movement began in the United States. Little has changed since then.

The Rousseau/progressive/socialist/communist ideology has spawned hundreds of highly militant, sometimes violent progressive organizations like ACORN and SEIU, that purpose to collapse the financial and social system of America. They intend to institute an entirely different system of government, most closely resembling fascism and communism. They are being protected by Rousseau progressive liberals in Congress, the White House, the courts and the media.

According to *The Coming Insurrection*, a 2007 booklet that calls for global revolution to bring down capitalism and Western Way of Life, the revolution is imminent. While paralleling Alinsky's *Rules for Radicals*, it calls for overt violence to *"Take up arms*.... There is no such thing as a peaceful insurrection. Weapons are necessary: it's a question of doing everything possible to make using them unnecessary."[388] (Italics original) In short, these radicals don't want to use guns, but they will if they have to. They don't mention how they reconcile taking up arms and using them against innocent people and their never ending demand for gun control. One can only assume that if they do take up arms, they don't want to have anyone else armed.

The Coming Insurrection is written by the "Invisible Committee" for obvious reasons. In addition to taking up arms, the book calls for bringing down governments by "mak[ing] the most of every crisis," "sabotage[ing] every representative authority," "block[ing] the economy," "liberat[ing] territory from police occupation," and "depos[ing] authorities at a local level."[389]

The strategy is sweeping Europe with the protests and riots resulting from the economic collapse of the PIIGS nations; Portugal, Italy, Ireland, Greece and Spain. Until 2011, however, the U.S. seemed to escape it. That changed with the Occupy Wall Street protests.

OCCUPY WALL STREET

DURING THE SEVERAL YEARS BEFORE 2011, there had been a growing sense throughout the radical NGOs and progressives in America and around the world that there was going to be a time of mass protests that would overwhelm the governments of not only the U.S. but most of the Western world. The 2008 financial crisis and the subsequent massive bailouts of the banks seemed to provide the catalyst. People were angry that Wall Street and the banks were bailed out with $700 billion in taxpayer dollars while Main Street suffered through near depression-like conditions. Millions of workers lost their jobs and many lost their homes. Resentment and anger were growing.

The anger and frustration was not enough for Frances Fox Piven, however. She called for even more anger and outrage in the December 22, 2010, issue of The Nation, "So where are the angry crowds, the demonstrations, sit-ins and unruly mobs? After all, the injustice is apparent. Working people are losing their homes and their pensions while robber-baron CEOs report renewed profits and windfall bonuses. Shouldn't the unemployed be on the march? Why aren't they demanding enhanced safety net protections and big initiatives to generate jobs?"

Piven called on the unions to create the unruly mobs. They did, starting the following month, in both America and Europe. In Europe, Greek unions took the lead as the government was forced to take draconian austerity measures to prevent sovereign bankruptcy. More on that later.

In America, the unions violently protested state governments that forced public workers to pay for part of their retirement and health benefits, or passed right to work laws. (See Chapter 4) Glenn Beck initially revealed the first solid hint of a much larger protest March 22, 2011. Beck had secured video of Stephen Lerner explaining a massive protest against major banks called Justice for Janitors.[390]

Lerner is the former director of SEIU's banking and finance campaign. SEIU claimed Lerner was on a leave of absence. At the Left Forum held at Pace University on March 19, 2011, Lerner was introduced as partnering with unions and groups in Europe and South America. In his speech, Lerner laid out his recommendations to bring the kind of economic collapse that Cloward and Piven promote, *"There are actually extraordinary things we could do right now to start to destabilize the folks that are in power and start to rebuild a movement."*[391] (Italics added)

Lerner's plan called for a carefully coordinated attack on home mortgages, student loans, and local government debt payments. Basically, the plan called for people who asked for and committed to these loans, to stop paying. If enough people did this, reasoned Lerner, it would cause bank insolvency, which would theoretically cause the banks to renegotiate the terms of the loans. The attack would cause the destabilization that Lerner longed for and bring about a stock market crisis that would facilitate the transfer of power that the radical left wants.[392]

Lerner's plan was supposed to start by having union thugs attack JP Morgan Chase in early May 2011 with demonstrations on Wall Street and protests at the stockholders' meeting. Lerner cautioned that although unions would benefit from this strategy and could participate in the background, they cannot be seen as having orchestrated the disruption.[393]

Lerner's effort fizzled after Beck exposed it, but he revealed some key principles that would be applied in a planned September protest. Lerner said:

> I don't think this kind of movement can happen unless actually the community groups and other activists take the lead. And that's a big reversal of how a lot of these coalitions have even thought about it, so unions helping community groups…. if we really believe that we're in a transformative stage and what's happening in capitalism, …we need to confront this in a serious way and develop a real ability to put a boot in the wheel, then I think we have to think not about labor community alliances. We have to think about how together we're building something that really has the capacity to disrupt how the system operates.[394]

Lerner continues, saying that the unions can't lead it, because as soon as an injunction is issued they have to back down. Therefore, asserts Lerner:

So we need to build a movement based on [what] we know [about] the oppression we're going to face.... What does the other side fear most? They fear disruption, they fear uncertainty. Every article about Europe says [when they rioted] in Greece, the markets went down. The folks that control this country care about one thing: how the stock market does; how the bond market does; and what their bonus is. So I think we weed out a very simple strategy: how do we bring down the stock market, how do we bring down their bonuses, how do we interfere with their ability to, to be rich? And...that means you have to politically isolate them, economically isolate them and disrupt them.[395]

Creating this kind of fear is exactly what *Rules for Radicals* and *The Coming Insurrection* both call for to cause maximum disruption.

Things more or less quieted down for the summer as the congressional budget and debt limit debates took over the headlines. Almost unnoticed (at first), a protest called Occupy Wall Street (OWS) began on September 17, 2011, sponsored by another radical nongovernmental organization (NGO) called Adbusters.

It wasn't long before the progressive mainstream media and liberals began to hail OWS as being the same as the Tea Party, with some of the same goals. It was allegedly an uncoordinated, spontaneous protest made up primarily of an amorphous cross section of youth in college or who couldn't find jobs. OWS was allegedly protesting Wall Street, the bailouts, and the rich who made up one percent of the population but controlled 25 percent of the wealth.

While some of these OWS goals were vaguely similar to those of the Tea Party, it was soon obvious there was a huge difference. Interviews of actual protestors quickly revealed their demands were all over the map, some demanding the government pay their student loans, others were about making the rich pay for more government spending, still others about getting rid of capitalism, and much more. These weren't Tea Party goals at all. The Tea Party focused specifically on reducing the size and scope of government by reducing taxes and government spending and returning to the Constitution.

By the time the progressive media and liberals gave up trying to convince the public that OWS was like the Tea Party, the unions, socialist NGOs, Nazis and even Marxist/communists joined the fray—just as Stephen Lerner had recommended. As it spread across the country, crime and violence increased, protestors defecated and urinated on lawns, sidewalks and even police cars. Mountains of trash were strewn everywhere.[396] Cleanup costs were in the tens of millions of dollars. Although police "brutality" did occur, most of it was the result of extreme provocation by the protestors.[a] More than 5,000 protestors were arrested from October 2011, to early 2012.[397]

The usual progressive hate-filled placards appeared demanding "Class Warfare Now," "Marx Was Right," "Smash Capitalism," "Capitalism Must Be Destroyed," and "Build Socialism." Images of Marx, Lenin, Mao, and Che Guevara were plentiful. Publications of the Communist Party Revolutionary, Communist Workers Party, Socialist Party, Socialist Workers Party, Young Communist League Democratic Socialists of America, and many more were everywhere.

Although Jefferson and Madison's names were invoked on a few occasions, their names were not used to promote constitutional intent, but to fuse the statements of the Founders into an absurd endorsement of anarchism, communism, or socialism.[398] Some protesters even screamed the need of "killing and eating the rich."[399] Yet, nary was a word of this hate speech covered on the evening news or by other mainstream media.

Another critical connection to the OWS demonstrations ignored by the popular media was the intellectual inspiration, organization and direction provided by a long list of professional revolutionaries. These were the "quiet" revolutionaries operating out of New York City's colleges, universities, publicly funded think tanks and centers of counter-culture activism.

The Brecht Forum/New York Marxist School is one of the more important in this group. An activist hub for communist/socialist/anarchist organizers, the school is located a short three miles from Zuccotti Park; the

---

[a] While police brutality should never be condoned, the mainstream media deliberately did not show or discuss the provocation by the protesters that usually precipitated the police response.

private one-acre park that became ground zero for OWS.[400] Writing in the New American, William Jasper noted:

> The Brecht Forum/New York Marxist School "faculty" includes a rotating lineup of 1960s celebrity activists from the SDS, the terrorist Weather Underground, the Communist Party USA, the Socialist Workers Party, the Democratic Socialists of America, the Black Panther Party, and the like: Angela Davis, Cornell West, Bill Ayers, Todd Gitlin, Frances Fox Piven, Van Jones, Leslie Cagan, and Stanley Aronowitz, to name a few who have been providing intellectual direction to the OWS agitators.[401]

Even as OWS was showing itself to be a hate group, despite glowing reports from the mainstream media, progressive liberals directly or tacitly endorsed OWS. After denigrating the Tea Party for two years for being anti-big government, Obama sympathized with OWS, "I think people are frustrated and the protesters are giving voice to a more broad-based suspicion about how our financial system works."[402] Democratic Leader Nancy Pelosi told reporters, "The message of the American people is that no longer will the recklessness of some on Wall Street cause massive joblessness on Main Street..."[403] The Democrat Congressional Campaign Committee issued a petition to support OWS.[404]

Typical of Alinsky styled protests, none of the OWS across the country had to pay anything to occupy and trash public parks. Worse, they stuck the taxpayers with millions of dollars of cleanup and repair costs. Conversely, Tea Party rallies and protests had to pay for permits, police, security, and porta-potties even though they typically left the parks cleaner than when they arrived. The contrast between the progressive OWS and the conservative Tea Party could not be greater.

Rather than the heroes painted by the mainstream media, OWS groups were parasites sucking the lifeblood out of America for the express purpose of destroying it. Ironically, it wasn't Wall Street and the banks (although there was plenty of blame to go around) which were the problem, it was the laws passed by progressives of both parties in Congress at the behest of the international banking cartel that has set America up to fail. More on this in a future chapter.

7 – The Final Collapse?

OWS Highly Organized and Funded

After Glenn Beck received a dozen or so phone calls from heads of state, CEOs and religious leaders asking what was happening and what OWS's true goals were, he did research, found links and video explanations and aired them on GBTV on October 24, 2011. The first video he showed was of a *big* protest being organized by former ACORN Communication's Coordinator, Dave Swanson. Swanson laid out a plan on August 28, 2011:

> We're planning to model our behavior on the actions that happened earlier this year in Tahrir Square in Cairo Egypt, in Tunisia, and the actions you see in Spain and Greece and countries around the world when governments get even a fraction as bad as ours has gotten. And so we're going to go to Freedom Plaza in Washington D.C., whose name is quite similar to Tahrir Square translated, and we're going to occupy it beginning October 6th, and we're going to remain and we're going to non-violently interfere and shut down the offices of our government until we begin to get some movement.[405]

OWS actually started with Steve Lerner on September 10, 2011 when he revealed, "I know in Seattle, in LA, in San Francisco and Chicago, in New York and Boston we've got some stuff in Boston and New York that is going to really be spectacular. This is about building and creating power. We're not going to convince the other side through intellectual argument. We need to create power and…create a crisis for the super-rich." In other words, the protests were not spontaneous, but a planned event organized months in advance.[406]

Lerner didn't do this by himself. One of his SEIU colleagues, Lisa Fithian, appeared to be the master organizer of OWS. Fithian had organized the 1999 World Trade Organization protest in Seattle. She brags about organizing violent protests in Seattle, San Francisco, Boston, Los Angeles, Chicago, New York, Minneapolis, Denver, Honolulu, and St. Louis. Apparently, she is one of the most famous radical organizers on the radical left. Like Lerner, she was once employed by SEIU.[407]

Fithian adores the 1960s radical hippy Abby Hoffman, who was arrested and tried as one of the Chicago Eight. The Chicago Eight incited violent riots at the 1968 Democratic National Convention. She republished Hoffman's 1960s book, *Steal This Book*, which provides instructions on how to build a bomb, make Molotov Cocktails and trash things in a protest. She released the reprint of Hoffman's book a month after 9-11.

Her dedication is a love letter to Hoffman in which she extols 9-11 as wonderful because "the old order was cracked open." She goes on to trash American institutions which most Americans hold dear. "Everything Abby," she claims, "is still up for grabs, and *we are winning*! This resurgence of activism has radically changed the political landscape.... It's a coming together of all strands of reform and resistance."[408]

This is only a portion of Fithian's activist resume. During an interview with Education Action Group Foundation EAGtv, Fithian said, "When people ask me, 'What do you do?' I say, I create crisis, because crisis is that edge where change is possible."[409] Fithian had earlier said:

Nonviolence is a strategy. Civil disobedience is a tactic.... Direct action is a strategy. Throwing rocks is a tactic.... I guess my biggest thing is that as people who are trying to create a new world, I do believe we have to dismantle or transform the old order to do that.[410]

This is right out of Alinsky's *Rules for Radicals*. Remember, Fithian is organizing the OWS protests. It is ludicrous to say that the intent of OWS is merely to make minor corrections to America's Constitutional Republic. Their long-term goal is to destroy capitalism and our Constitutional Republic, and replace it with some variation of Rousseau's totalitarian model where force is used to make the citizens obey.

Even though OWS *seemed* like there was no real organization because empty-headed college students and deadbeats act as if it were just a big game, its purpose is tightly organized, right down to deciding who and when someone gets arrested. EAGtv caught the teacher's union protestors discussing who would be the best person to be filmed getting arrested next by TV networks.[411]

If there remains any doubt, The Working Families Party, another radical NGO, took out an ad on September 26 on Craig's List that they would pay protesters up to $650 a week to join OWS. That's like honey to flies for brainwashed college students and deadbeats. It is doubtful that the Working Families Party is the only one offering cash to protest. Unions do it all the time. Even so, it is doubtful that all protesters were being paid.

Many came for the "fun." Others came because they have been taught to hate America and all that she stands for.

The OWS was well funded. Some of the funding came from thousands of small donors, but multi-billionaire George Soros funded OWS's organization through a host of radical NGOs. As of October 19, 2011, OWS had taken in $435,000.[412] Soros will be discussed in detail in a future chapter, but for this discussion, understand he is deeply involved in funding the destruction of the United States to the tune of at least $450 million annually.[413]

In the case of OWS, the Tides Foundation and the Alliance for Global Justice were the primary distributors of Soros' funding. Soros has given Tides over $24 million since 1998 for radical activism.[414] Adbusters Media Foundation was the front organization for OWS. Adbusters is a Canadian NGO and publishes an ad-free anti-consumer magazine. It also published a full-color newspaper for OWS.

The next chapter will discuss how Soros is part of an international financial cartel seeking to implement global governance—with them in control, of course. For decades this cartel has been angling for a global tax on all international financial transactions, called the Tobin Tax, to fund the UN independently. Once done, the UN would no longer be dependent upon the member nations, especially the U.S. for funding. It became obvious the cartel was pulling the strings on OWS in mid-October when Adbusters began to demand that a 1 percent tax on all international financial transactions be imposed. Adbusters called it a Robin Hood tax although it was clearly the Tobin Tax.[415]

The OWS followed the classic mob/progressive mantra of violence, vitriolic hatred, class warfare, racism and extreme civil disobedience. Anti-Semitism was commonly spewed forth. What shocked most Americans (or should have) were the unmitigated class warfare, gunfire, rape, and even murders that accompanied the protests. Black conservative Deneen Borelli of Project 21 was so disgusted, she issued a demand to the progressive leadership like Obama, Pelosi and others to apologize for supporting OWS:

> The behavior of the Occupy Wall Street protesters is boorish and violent, and it has no place in civil society. It's shocking that the very same people who tried and failed to tie the Tea Party

movement to racism and radicalism are now embracing the Occupy mob despite the reports of widespread violence, anti-Semitism and general lawlessness. If these people hope to retain any shred of credibility, they must take responsibility for their poor judgment and condemn the Occupy protests.[416]

Project 21 is an initiative of The National Center for Public Policy Research to promote the views of African-Americans whose entrepreneurial spirit, dedication to family and commitment to individual responsibility has not traditionally been echoed by the nation's civil rights establishment.

If nothing else, OWS proved beyond any doubt that it is not the Tea Party or conservatives that are hate-filled, racist and violent; rather, that disgrace and dishonor is held by progressives. Yet, if you were a viewer or reader of the mainstream media, all you would know is that while there may have been a few acts of un-civility, OWS was mainly a peaceful protest attempting to bring fairness to all Americans.

Was OWS effective in bringing down capitalism? Not yet. Although the protests had died down by the beginning of 2012, activity was still ongoing. Were these hangers-on merely die-hards that did not want to give up on the failed dream, or are they part of a larger strategy to cause OWS to flare up again in the spring of 2012? Although as of this writing it is too early to tell, the latter scenario is probably the correct one. Every indication is that by mid-summer 2012, a perfect storm of economic desperation—even chaos—will provide the necessary unrest to ramp up OWS into major riots in Europe, the U.S., and perhaps around the entire world.

THE BRINK OF TOTAL FINANCIAL COLLAPSE

THE COLLAPSE OF THE WESTERN WORLD is no longer just a concern. It now seems likely, and may even be happening as you read this. The unmanageable U.S. debt and unfunded liabilities were briefly discussed in Chapter 5. Although China seemed to be in good financial health, there is growing evidence the Chinese boom is imploding. The Daily Bell reported on December 15, 2011:

The property market is swinging wildly from boom to bust, and...the Shanghai index has fallen 30 percent since May. The Chinese miracle appeared to be nothing but a concoction of central bank monetary stimulation and the relaxation of state controls on market-driven family businesses.... China's $3.2 trillion foreign reserves are shrinking as "hot" money leaves the country.... China jammed about a trillion dollars of phony money into its economy in 2008. It hasn't worked any better than Obama's Keynesian stimulus.[417]

This raises the question of whether China can still buy U.S. debt, and if not, who is going to buy America's enormous and growing debt?

As serious as these issues are, they are a walk in the park compared to the financial collapse underway in Europe. European banks have loaned Greece more than $140 billion. For most of the summer in 2011, these banks rolled over the debt into new loans hoping for the impossible—that Greece will recover or that they can shed their debt to some other institution, preferably the EU's central bank. Then it becomes the liability of the people. (We've already seen how that works out with TARP—the banks profit, the people suffer). In other words, it was a fool's attempt to paper over the hemorrhaging.

By early September, European banks were forced to quietly forgive 21 percent of the Greek debt they held to help Greece stay afloat.[418] It was not nearly enough. By early October, interest paid by Greece on a two-year bond was 155 percent. Greece was technically in default and had been for most of the summer, but couldn't declare it because the EU banks holding their paper would go down like dominos.

Writing for the *Financial Times*, Chris Giles had already warned in June 2011 that even under the best of circumstances Greece is predicted to default by 2013. This would send shockwaves through Europe that certainly will find their way to the United States. Giles predicted that not only would Greece be kicked out of the EU, but Spain, Ireland, Italy and Portugal (the so-called PIIGS nations) would also default and lose their membership in the EU.

Hyperinflation will likely grip these defaulted nations as they lose the protection of the EU, cascading into a severe depression for the rest of Europe.[419] It is also likely the euro either would cease to exist or would no longer be a serious contender with the U.S. dollar. If the euro goes, it is also likely the resulting chaos would break the EU apart as well.

Unbelievably, that's the good news. Greece, along with the rest of Europe, is highly socialistic with most people depending on the government for their benefits, and indeed, their livelihoods. Outrageous benefits and corruption are the norm. Losing even some of those socialist benefits has caused frequent riots. However, with the passage of the austerity laws in late June 2011, Greek unions are rioting with increasing frequency and violence.[420] By March 2012, violent riots had spread to other EU nations although it's rarely in the U.S. mainstream news.

As discussed in previous chapters, violence of this type seems to accompany the Rousseau model of governance wherever it dominates, whether it is called progressivism, socialism, fascism or communism. As discussed in Chapter 4, it is increasing even in the U.S. with violent union protests and now the Occupy Wall Street demonstrations discussed earlier in this chapter.

A Series of Failed "Solutions"

The plan was to have the backing of the U.S. Federal Reserve so that the European Central Bank (ECB) could provide unlimited liquidity to the banks suffering runs or default on Greek loans, thereby limiting the damage.[421] Analysts believe that default may still happen in 2012 regardless of what happens in Greece.[422] The world could ride out the storm; albeit with some significant belt tightening.

The downside is that the PIIGS nations may still fall like dominos. By late summer 2011 that appeared to be the case, with Italy and Spain very close to total collapse. By the spring of 2012, Italy's and Spain's bank debt had grown to $2.4 trillion dollars with fears of default. It forced the ECB to print another $670 billion out of thin air to hopefully prevent that default.[423]

All summer and early 2012, the EU would take an action to stem the collapse of the euro and the EU banking system. The supposed "solution" would cause ecstatic joy in the New York Stock Exchange with stock prices surging, only to collapse days or a week or so later as it finally sank in that the action was only a band aid that would solve nothing. Meanwhile each crisis gets a little worse. By January 23, 2012, Greek bondholders were willing to take a 70 percent loss. It was still not enough to save Greece.[424]

By mid-October things were desperate and the global financial structure was holding on by a thread. On October 27, Bloomberg reported the European Union forced a one-time, 50 percent write down on EU banks on all Greek debt.[425] The huge $1.4 trillion write down was made possible by the announcement by Secretary of Treasury Tim Geithner that the U.S. Fed (Federal Reserve) would underwrite the International Monetary Fund (IMF) trillions of dollars needed to eventually bail out the EU central bank.[426] All that debt by the IMF would then be on the backs of U.S. taxpayers if Greece still defaulted.

The ECB would in turn capitalize the EU banks that would otherwise default if they wrote off 70 percent of the Greek debt. Unfortunately, the 70 percent write down was still too low.[427] Some analysts believe that 100 percent might be necessary.[428] Greece was technically in default and Italy's long-term interest rate on its bonds went over 7 percent. Historically, 7 percent was the turning point in which nations went into a financial death spiral. Things were desperate. Yet, to read reports by the mainstream media, things were going to be fine.

By November 2011, Greece and Italy's financial situation was so bad that Prime Ministers George Papandreou of Greece and Silvio Berlusconi of Italy were forced to resign as heads of their respective governments. It was announced that things were so bad there was no time to elect replacements, so new prime ministers were *appointed*! That's right, appointed!

The citizens of both nations woke up on November 10, 2011 with new, unelected governments led by Greek PM Lukus Papademos, and EU heavyweight Italian PM Mario Monti. Both are technocrats and long-standing members in the Trilateral Commission. Both have backgrounds in central banking![429] The significance of this will be explained in the next chapter.

Nothing like this had happened before in modern history. Politically, it was earthshaking. Yet, the mainstream media downplayed it as if it were a disturbing, but everyday event. Regardless, both nations experienced extreme austerity measures, with concurrent union riots. By November 28, 2011, Moody's warned, "The continued rapid escalation of the euro area sovereign and banking credit crisis is threatening the credit standing of all European sovereigns...The euro area is approaching a junction, *leading either to closer integration or greater fragmentation.*"[430] (Italics added)

Again, that proved to be a band-aid. By the end of 2012, Europe's banks will have to refinance more than $8 trillion in wholesale funding, mostly from U.S.-based money market funds. Money was already fleeing the EU bond and money market funds for the marginally "safer" U.S. dollar, raising the EU's interest rates on their bonds, and lowering them for

U.S. Treasuries.[431] Things became even more desperate. On December 9, 2011, the other shoe finally dropped. All 17 European Union nations except Britain agreed to set up a new "fiscal compact" that required them to give up crucial powers over their own budgets in an attempt to overcome their crippling debt crisis.[432]

The new "fiscal compact" obliged Eurozone countries to incorporate a balanced budget provision into their national constitutions, committing them to keeping annual structural deficits at or below 0.5 percent of nominal GDP. The provision also included an automatic correction mechanism that kicks in if the deficit exceeds the ceiling.

The Court of Justice of the European Union, which is in charge of ensuring that state laws are in line with EU regulations, would be in charge of ensuring that legislation adopted on a national level complies with the treaty. In short, the Eurozone countries surrendered their financial sovereignty to an unelected central European authority to manage future budgets and austerity measures. Severe penalties would be imposed if the terms were violated.[433]

The compact also directs $267 billion to the International Monetary Fund (IMF) to be parceled out to ailing European economies. Again, it was too little, too late. Italy by itself must refinance 168 billion euros in 2012, and another 100 billion in 2013. Italy's public debt is 1.7 trillion euros—seven times larger than Greece's public debt. Even after the "fiscal compact" was agreed to, Italy's yield on its 10-year bonds rose to 6.7 percent, once again playing tag with the magic 7 percent limit after which interest rates escalate upward in a financial death spiral.[434] In effect, the Eurozone nations gave up their financial sovereignty for a plan that was bound to fail.

Finally, the ECB overrode German Chancellor Angela Markel's strong resistance and agreed on December 21, 2011, to print 489 billion Euros ($645 billion) out of thin air (read Quantitative Easing) to bail the banks and national sovereign debt. The interest the 523 banks would have to pay was only 1 percent.[435] However, financial analyst Porter Stansberry's S&A Digest warns:

…this is on top of $3.2 trillion already loaned. Goldman Sachs estimates the latest bailout amounts to nearly 63% of all European bank debt maturing in 2012. Remember, *In Europe, the 90 largest banks must finance a 5.4 trillion euro debt over the next 24 months—45% of GDP. That's not counting any of the European sovereign debt that must be refinanced over the next two years, which I estimate will add another 1.5 trillion-2 trillion euros to the credit required.*[436] (Italics original)

Stansberry has accurately predicted almost all of the global financial trends and crashes in recent history. He is convinced that to succeed, this is but the first in trillions of euros that must be printed out of thin air. "It's quantitative easing, plain and simple. We bet it's not enough... We'll see another, larger bailout before the end of next year."

Lest you think this will have minimal impact on the U.S., Forbes reported on December 30, 2011:

European banks hold as much as $10 trillion in claims against their U.S. counterparts, which reflects how vulnerable the North American financial system is to Europe's debt crisis.... European banks have made direct loans to U.S. businesses but also hold U.S. money-market deposits and U.S. mortgage securities. So while U.S. banks might not hold too much sovereign debt issued by troubled European governments, should a default in Europe take place and banks there go under, they could take U.S. financial institutions with them due to counterparty exposure.[437]

What that means is the U.S. Federal Reserve will also have to secretly crank up the printing presses for QE3, in spite of Obama's assurances we will not bail out Europe's banks. To not have QE3 would mean a certain catastrophic depression, worse than the Great Depression of 1929. With QE3, most analysts are predicting high inflation at a minimum. The worst case scenario would be hyperinflation, which would be as catastrophic as a Great Depression.

There is precedent for sending QE money to Europe under the table. The Fed recently complied with a Freedom of Information Act request that seemed to show that much of the $630 billion Second Quantitative Easing (QE2) ending June 30, 2011, directly, or indirectly went to bailing out defaulting European banks, not to U.S. banks to help the U.S. economy. It is small wonder small businesses could not get loans! Tyler Durden, writing for zerohedge.com made this staggering conclusion:

In summary, instead of doing everything in its power to stimulate reserve, and thus cash, accumulation at domestic (US) banks,-which would in turn encourage lending to US borrowers, the Fed has been conducting yet another stealthy foreign bank rescue operation, which rerouted $600 billion in capital from potential borrowers to insolvent foreign financial institutions in the past 7 months. QE2 was nothing more (or less) than another European bank rescue operation![438] (Original in bold)

Even with the rescue, the Financial Times reported that "almost $6.3 trillion (12.1 percent) was erased from global stock markets in 2011 as the Eurozone financial crisis reverberated across the world."[439] That's money taken out of the global economy. It is the dead canary in the coal mine, warning the EU debt crisis is about to kill the global economy.

There is no way either private or central banks can weather a full-blown PIIGS default storm. Many trillions of dollars would soon disappear from the balance sheets of hundreds of private and central banks in the Western World. As banks directly affected by the PIIGS' defaults begin to fail themselves, their failure will set off a domino effect, seriously affecting banks not directly involved. In the case of the Fed, American citizens are liable for any bad debt incurred by the Fed.

All but a few economies of the Western world are teetering already. The real concern is whether a default chain reaction would result in a severe depression for the Western world, or if the financial structure of the world would completely collapse. In either case the United States and its citizens would suffer as well. Even more sobering; rather than this scenario not playing out until 2013, it could actually happen much sooner in 2012.

By the end of 2011 this realization may have started affecting the U.S. Treasury market—even though U.S. Treasury bonds were considered the safest among all the bad choices. By the last week in December foreign holders of U.S. Treasuries dumped a record $69 billion in Treasury Notes.[440] By January 12, 2012 an additional $8 billion was dumped. Most of this was China because "it does not trust the US financial system," claimed Anton Zhukov, an analyst with the Moscow Stock Center.[441]

If continued for a full year, it would be equal to $3.6 trillion. Although, it probably won't continue at that rate, it graphically illustrates how vulnerable the U.S. debt really is to pushing the U.S. off the economic cliff. China's action may be a warning shot off the bow of Obama's reckless spending. If so, it hasn't worked. Congress increased the debt cap an additional $1.2 trillion on January 26, 2012 after a weak objection by the House.[442] The Obama administration hopes that it will be enough time to get him past the November elections.

This will raise the U.S. debt to an unsustainable $16.4 trillion. When both the U.S. and the EU crises are considered, it is obvious now the Fed and the ECB are going to print money out of thin air to keep the economy afloat. Rather than a severe depression, we will have very high inflation, perhaps even hyperinflation. As noted earlier, that would be as bad as a severe depression. The choice seems to be between bad and worse. Yet, the central banks seem to be desperately trying to keep things afloat for a while longer, which will only make the consequences worse.

Some analysts believe we are already heading into hyperinflation. So why aren't we seeing it? We are; it's just hidden. The way inflation is calculated has changed dramatically in 1980 and 1990 when things like food, gasoline and other items that affect each of us every day were removed from the calculation. If it were calculated the way it was before 1980, the inflation in early 2012 would have been over 6 percent, not the 3 percent we are told.[443]

There is another reason inflation isn't skyrocketing. Besides much of QE2 going to European banks, $1.47 trillion made available to American banks for loaning to small business. The money was never loaned out by the banks. Instead the banks deposited it into the Federal Reserve to earn interest without risk. In other words, the $1.47 trillion was never put into circulation where it would cause inflation. At least not yet.[444]

We have to hope this does not happen. Yet, we are told very little by either the government or by the mainstream media. Why? Time is extremely short. There is no doubt that excessive progressive/socialist spending has created this nightmare in the U.S. and Europe. Yet, the same progressives in Congress are attempting to block every effort to deal with it, guaranteeing the worst collapse possible. Again, why?

As of the writing of this book there is no simple answer. There are, however a couple of possibilities. Ask yourself this question; "What would happen in the 2012 elections if the global financial collapse happened in August or September, just before the U.S. election? The 2008 financial collapse occurred on September 18 when John McCain was ahead in the polls. The collapse guaranteed Obama's election. Could it happen again? Would Obama declare Martial Law, "postponing" the election indefinitely?

The New Global Financial Architecture

There is another reason for the herculean efforts to paper over the global financial crisis. A new global financial architecture has been underway since the mid-1990s and it may not be ready yet for implementation.

On January 21, 1999, the UN issued a new report entitled, *Towards a New International Financial Architecture* (IFA). The report focuses on correcting many global financial deficiencies of the day, "*The recent* [Asian] *crisis has demonstrated a fundamental problem in the global economy*," asserts the IFA. The primary cause of the global crisis, alleges the report, is "the enormous discrepancy that exists between an increasingly **sophisticated and dynamic international financial world, with rapid globalization of financial portfolios, and the lack of a proper institutional framework to regulate it.**"[445] (Bold original) The same dialogue exists in 2012.

The IFA plan is to "create a world financial authority...in charge of setting the necessary international standards for financial regulation and supervision, and of supervising their adoption at the national level." All of this would be administered through "a network of regional and sub-regional organizations to support the management of monetary and financial issues."[446] Individual economic regions would operate under a strengthened UN Economic and Social Council or a newly created Economic Security Council. The new institution would establish and manage global macro-economic policy and the regions and sub-regions would implement the policy.

The IFA is designed to overcome the failings of a single, global financial/trade structure like the WTO-by using regional institutions patterned after the European Union, but with much stronger central control. G.W. Bush's Security and Prosperity Partnership of North American (SPP) in 2005 was an initial effort to do just that. Tagged the North American Union (NAU) by critics, strong opposition caused the effort to fail by the end of Bush's term. Since economic regions are planned to be the heart of the new global financial architecture, it is not surprising that President Obama is continuing the dialogue with Canada and Mexico, albeit on a much lower key.[447]

Within this structure, the International Monetary Fund (IMF) would be restructured so that it would increasingly serve as *a world central bank.* A world central bank "would require, in particular, the surrender of more economic autonomy and powers of intervention in national policies than countries are willing to accept at present."[448] At the same time in 1999, the G7 created the Financial Stability Forum (FSF) "to promote stability in the international financial system." The FSF was supposed to bring together:

- "national authorities responsible for financial stability in significant international financial centres, namely treasuries, central banks, and supervisory agencies;
- sector-specific international groupings of regulators and supervisors engaged in developing standards and codes of good practice; international financial institutions charged with surveillance of domestic and international financial systems and monitoring and fostering implementation of standard;
- committees of central bank experts concerned with market infrastructure and functioning."[449]

The mandate of the FSF (renamed the Financial Stability Board, or FSB, in 2008) was to:

- assess vulnerabilities affecting the financial system and identify and oversee action needed to address them;
- promote co-ordination and information exchange among authorities responsible for financial stability;

In addition to the mandate of the FSB, it has these additional mandates:

- monitor and advise on market developments and their implications for regulatory policy;
- advise on and monitor best practice in meeting regulatory standards;

- undertake joint strategic reviews of the policy development work of the international standard setting bodies to ensure their work is timely, coordinated, focused on priorities, and addressing gaps;
- set guidelines for and support the establishment of supervisory colleges;
- manage contingency planning for cross-border crisis management, particularly with respect to systemically important firms; and
- collaborate with the IMF to conduct Early Warning Exercises.[450]

The emerging financial architecture was formalized at the UN's March, 2002 International Conference on Financing for Development in Monterrey, Mexico. Supporting documents called on The Bank for International Settlements (BIS) and FSF (now FSB) to work closely with individual nations and the UN to restructure the global financial architecture.

The Monterrey Conference tasked the IMF, BIS and FSF (now the Financial Stability Board) with strong oversight responsibilities of the financial dealings of every nation, including the United States. For this to be accomplished required that the records of every nation be open to the BIS and FSF. With this requirement, the IMF and BIS could control the world at the international level.[451] As noted earlier, their goals include dividing the world into economic regions patterned after the European Union with centralized command and control.[452]

With oversight like this, how did IMF, BIS, FSF and then the FSB totally miss the coming financial catastrophe the world is now embroiled in? The only viable answer is—they couldn't have missed it. They must have seen this train wreck coming. Perhaps the 2008 reorganization of the FSF into the FSB was a response to the soon-to-happen crisis. It doesn't matter. The fact is that no warning was ever issued, either in 2008 or 2011-12. Why? Could it be that the globalists (defined in the next chapter) are deliberately allowing this to happen? Is there any evidence for that?

The following chapters define how powerful global institutions have systematically corrupted the Locke-based United States Constitution. They created the Rousseau-based all-powerful federal government—without Americans understanding what was happening. If we are given the time, our only hope is to vote every possible progressive out of office of both parties at every level of government and replace them now with those who understand the U.S. Constitution and are committed to systematically restore America to the Constitutional Rule of Law.

8 – THE ANGLO-AMERICAN ESTABLISHMENT

Most Americans have a tough time believing there has been an agenda to shift the republican constitutional basis of government in the United States into a socialist government based on plundering inherent with the Rousseau model. Even harder to believe is that those behind this agenda may be deliberately sabotaging the economies of the Western world and funding radical nongovernmental (NGO) organizations to destabilize America to bring about her destruction. Even if these Americans have heard rumors of this agenda all their lives, they *know* it could not possibly be true. After all, this is America!

Some will say that no one they trust who has researched this supposed evil agenda has found any evidence of it. But if they think carefully about it, they will realize that their sources are the major progressive media or big political figureheads. If this is the case, they need to read this book. They have been lied to.

AN EXPLANATION OF A DIFFICULT SUBJECT

ALTHOUGH THE STRUGGLE started the moment the Founders signed the Constitution, Rousseau's ideas initially did not gain much headway. French judge, statesman and political writer Alexis de Tocqueville explains why after he visited America in 1831:

> If you question [an American] respecting his own country...he will inform you what his rights are and by what means he exercises them.... You will find that he is familiar with the mechanism of the laws.... The American learns to know the laws by participating in the act of legislation.... The great work of society is ever going on

before his eyes, and, as it were, under his hands. In the United States, politics are the end and aim of education. [453]

As discussed in Chapter 2, Locke's model of "natural" sovereignty of citizens over the state was the foundation of the Constitution and culture of the United States. It created the "American Way" which was unique in the history of mankind. In early America, these principles were so strong and generally known by every American that the lie contained in Rousseau's philosophies could not take root.

However, a group of men who coveted power gradually introduced the Rousseau model into the American education system. They had a goal. The same goal that megalomaniacs have had throughout history—to rule the world.

These would-be rulers knew they could never attain that goal as long as the people understood the Constitution and the principles upon which it stood. As students of history, they knew that nations ruled by the Rousseau model were populated by citizens who could be easily manipulated to do what the rulers wanted. After all, socialism and communism train people from early childhood to obey the government—the source of all power.

That constitutional understanding began to change in the late eighteenth century when Christopher Langdell was hired by Harvard University expressly to change the direction of the highly influential Harvard Law School. Prior to Langdell, law schools taught law by lecturing from the Constitution and law itself. When Langdell became Dean of the Harvard Law School, he taught law by reviewing previous case law. In doing so the Constitution and the actual legislated law was ignored. By the twentieth century, the case law approach was adopted by all U.S. law schools.[454] Court cases were no longer decided by the Constitution or the written law, but by previous cases. Small changes could be made in each successive decision to actually reverse the original intent of the Constitution or legislated law. It is legislation from the bench.

No longer were students forced to dig into Constitution wording and constitutional intent, but instead were taught how appellate courts *ruled* in specific cases. Tragically, actual teaching of the Constitution in law schools is almost nonexistent today. This is not an exaggeration.

Take the First Amendment to the Constitution; "Congress shall make no law respecting an establishment of religion, or prohibiting the free exercise thereof; or abridging the freedom of speech…" There is nothing in the Amendment to justify the now parroted foundational principle of "separation of church and state." The First Amendment merely states that the federal government cannot declare a state religion like what England did in establishing the Church of England as the official church of Britain. But by using case law, agenda driven attorneys and judges have turned freedom of religion into freedom *from* religion, denying the right of free speech in almost every place—except behind the doors of a church.

Once law schools no longer taught constitutional law from the Constitution, the bedrock constitutional anchor was severed from American intelligentsia and government leaders. Without a constitutional anchor, court decisions and even legislation soon began to drift away from the Constitution. By the first quarter of the twentieth century, the trend was becoming apparent. At the same time, industrialist bankers like J. P. Morgan and J.D. Rockefeller began wielding tremendous power and funded numerous Rousseau socialist efforts. In the early 1900s Rockefeller funded Marxist-humanist John Dewey's efforts to infuse socialism into the nation's public schools through his Progressive Education system (See Chapter 10).

In 1909, Congress ratified the Sixteenth Amendment instituting the federal income tax and giving the federal government the ability to grow like cancer. In 1913, the Seventeenth Amendment was ratified, thus trashing the constitutional requirement that state legislatures directly elect federal Senators. Thus, states no longer had a direct voice in federal policy. The Seventeenth Amendment seriously weakened the Founding Father's intent by dramatically shifting the balance of power from the states to the federal government. It also effectively nullified the Tenth Amendment that was designed to strictly limit the power of the federal government.

The creation of the Federal Reserve (Fed) in 1913 transferred the federal government's power to create money to a powerful group of international *private* bankers. There were no checks and balances to keep the Fed reined in, and the citizens of the United States were totally responsible for *any* debt incurred by it.

In 1917, J. P. Morgan took control of the 25 largest news media organizations in America. In 1919, the Round Table groups of Sir Alfred Milner, successor to the Cecil Rhodes fortune, created the Royal Institute of International Affairs in England. Together with Colonel Edward

Mandell House, they created the Institute of International Affairs in the United States. In 1921, Colonel House, President Wilson's close advisor, changed the name to the Council on Foreign Relations, which immediately endorsed world government as a goal.[455]

Much of the subversive activity resulting from these events was hidden for decades to come. Nonetheless, they stand out as key turning points for the implementation of the Rousseau plan for world government.

President Woodrow Wilson openly revealed this cabal in his self-published *The New Freedom*. He spoke of this agenda and the cartel behind it just prior to the passage of the Federal Reserve Act in 1913:

> Since I entered politics, I have chiefly had men's views confided to me privately. Some of the biggest men in the U.S., in the field of commerce and manufacturing, are afraid of somebody, are afraid of something. They know that there is a power somewhere, so organized, so subtle, so watchful, so interlocked, so complete, so pervasive, that they had better not speak above their breath when they speak in condemnation of it.[456]

A decade after he signed the act creating the so-called Federal Reserve, Wilson confessed:

> I am a most unhappy man. I have unwittingly ruined my country.... The growth of the nation... and all our activities are in the hands of a few men. We have...come to be one of the worst ruled, one of the most completely controlled and dominated, governments in the civilized world—no longer a government by free opinion, no longer a Government by conviction and the vote of the majority, but a Government by the opinion and the duress of small groups of dominant men.[457]

Wilson isn't the only president to admit this. On November 21, 1933, President Franklin Roosevelt wrote in a letter to Colonel House, "I had a nice talk with Jack Morgan the other day.... The real truth of the matter is, as you and I know, that a financial element in the larger centers has owned the Government ever since the days of Andrew Jackson–and I am not wholly excepting the Administration of W. W. [Woodrow Wilson]."[458]

This begs the question: Who among us, even those of us we consider 'schooled,' knew of Wilson's lament?

By the mid-1900s, the Rousseau model began to dominate that of Locke's in the American education system. Rousseau's ideas also crept in culturally and politically through the labor and civil rights movements. However, it was not until the counterculture and environmental movements in the 1960s and 1970s that Rousseau socialism began to overwhelm the Locke foundation upon which the Founding Fathers had established the United States. The leadership of Saul Alinsky, Cloward-Piven, and their poisonous progressive ideology found a willing audience with the indoctrinated and ignorant youth.

CARROLL QUIGLEY—THE INSIDER HISTORIAN

THE MOST CONCLUSIVE PROOF of a global agenda came in 1966 with President Clinton's mentor, Professor Carroll Quigley. Quigley had impeccable credentials. He was a highly respected professor of history at Georgetown University, a frequent lecturer, and consultant for groups like the Industrial College of the Armed Forces, the Brookings Institution, the U.S. Naval Weapons Laboratory, the Naval College, the Smithsonian Institute, and the State Department.

The British-American Anglophile Network

In his astonishing 1300-page magnum opus book, *Tragedy & Hope, A History of the World in Our Time*, Quigley admitted that he had studied this international cartel in depth:

There does exist, and has existed for a generation, an *international Anglophile network* which operates, to some extent, in the way the radical Right believes the Communists act. In fact, this network, which we may identify as the *Round Table Groups*, has no aversion to cooperating with the Communists, or any other groups, and frequently does so. I know of the operations of this network because *I have studied it for twenty years and was permitted for two years, in the early 1960's, to examine its papers and secret records.* I have no aversion to it or to most of its aims and have, for much of my life, been close to it and so many of its instruments.[459] (Italics added)

147

Quigley was included in the inner circle of this elite group. He even agreed with their goals and was given access to their secret records. This isn't his speculation; it is his first-hand knowledge. As a Harvard and Georgetown University history professor, his credentials cannot be denied. Just what does this group of high rollers plan for the world? Quigley also answers that question:

> ...the powers of financial capitalism had another far-reaching aim, nothing less than to *create a world system of financial control in private hands able to dominate the political system of each country and the economy of the world as a whole*. This system was to be *controlled in a feudalist fashion by the central banks of the world acting in concert*, by secret agreements arrived at in frequent private meetings and conferences. The apex of the system was to be the *Bank for International Settlements in Basel, Switzerland*, a private bank owned and controlled by the world's central banks which were themselves private corporations. *Each central bank...sought to dominate its government* by its ability to control Treasury loans, to manipulate foreign exchanges, to influence the level of the economic activity in the country, and to influence cooperative politicians by subsequent economic rewards in the business world.[460] (Italics added)

In one paragraph Quigley admits that there exists a secret financial cartel which rules in a feudalistic manner from the Bank for International Settlements (BIS) in Basel, Switzerland. They needed the Federal Reserve "to dominate [the United States] by its ability to control Treasury loans." Their goal was to literally control the world. With the passage of the Dodd-Frank Financial Reform Act of 2010, Quigley's prediction is nearly complete in the U.S. The Act gives unbelievable oversight powers to the Federal Reserve, the *private* central bank of the U.S., which along with the Bank of England, is a key player in the BIS.

In the previous chapter we discussed how the BIS was working closely with the UN to restructure the global financial architecture so it could be better controlled from the international level, with the BIS administering most of the oversight responsibilities.[461] The restructuring of the world would also include establishing a global tax to fund the UN. Called the

Tobin Tax, it would impose a 0.5 to 1 percent tax on all international financial transactions.

The late Nobel Laureate James Tobin originally conceived the Tobin Tax in 1978 as a mechanism to tax all international investment exchanges to help control speculative investing thereby stabilizing the global financial structure. It evolved into a means of funding UN global governance by taxing at a rate of 0.1 to 0.5 percent all international monetary exchanges.[462]

These exchanges amount to $1.5 trillion per business day, which would yield around $1-$2 trillion a year in taxes to fund UN global governance—one to two hundred times more than the current annual budget of the UN![463] Even if the U.S. were to withdraw from the UN at that point, the UN could build a big fence around America and gradually strangle it until the U.S. capitulated or died.

Although Adbusters—who played a key role in Occupy Wall Street (OWS)—called the Tobin Tax a Robin Hood tax,[464] its intent and origins fooled no one. As noted in the previous chapter, it could have only originated from the global banking cartel, which has been attempting to get it implemented in dozens of ways over the past 30 years. There is little doubt the OWS was a tool sponsored by this global elite.

Quigley's story gets even more bizarre. He wrote in a second book entitled, *The Anglo-American Establishment,* which was not published until after his death in 1977, "I have been told that the story I relate here would be better left untold, since it would provide ammunition for the enemies of what I admire. I do not share this view. The last thing I should wish is that anything I write could be used by the Anglophobes and isolationists of the *Chicago Tribune.* But I feel that the truth has a right to be told…"[465]

Quigley continues, "It is not easy for an outsider to write the history of a secret group of this kind, but…it should be done, for this group *is…one of the most important historical facts of the twentieth century.*" (Italics added) He admits "In this group were persons whose lives have been a disaster to our way of life."[466] The front cover of the book shows the U.S. flag upside down—a sign of distress. It also shows the U.S. flag inside the British flag.

Quigley shares in *The Anglo-American Establishment* that the members of the organization call it "the Group," or "the Band", or simply "US," among others.[467] Ironically, it was the various members of the Group that helped finance the writing of *The Anglo-American Establishment*, "...it would have been very difficult to write this book if I had not received a certain amount of assistance of a personal nature from persons close to the Group. For obvious reasons, I cannot reveal the names of such persons..."[468] Former Hoover Institute Research Fellow Antony Sutton, who has studied this agenda all of his life, agrees with Quigley. However, he claims the American players are called "the Order" because the majority of the players are members of the Order of the Skull and Bones of Yale University.[469]

While Quigley could not name the specific funders for the writing of his books, he does define the major families involved, "The French economy was dominated by three powers (Rothschild, Mirabaud, and Schneider); the German economy was dominated by two (I. G. Farben and Vereinigte Stahl Werke); the United States was dominated by two (Morgan and Rockefeller). Other countries, like Italy or Britain, were dominated by somewhat larger numbers."[470] The Group is principally made up of a powerful axis of financial and industrial people and families of Europe and the "Eastern Establishment"[471] of the United States. It all started with the banking influence on the industrial revolution and railroads. Says Quigley:

> Rothschild interests came to dominate many of the railroads of Europe, while Morgan dominated at least 26,000 miles of American railroads. Such bankers went further than this. In return for flotations of securities of industry, they took seats on the boards of directors of industrial firms, as they had already done on commercial banks, savings banks, insurance firms, and finance companies. From these lesser institutions they funneled capital to enterprises which yielded control and away from those who resisted. *These firms were controlled through interlocking directorships, holding companies, and lesser banks.*[472] (Italics added)

In time they brought into their financial network the provincial banking centers, organized as commercial banks and savings banks, as well as insurance companies, to form all of these into single financial system on an international scale which manipulated the quantity and flow of money so that they were able to *influence, if not control, governments on one side and industries on the other.*[473] (Italics added)

The Eastern Establishment, Quigley affirms, "reflects one of the most powerful influences in the twentieth-century American and world history."[474] Likewise, "The power and influence of this Rhodes-Milner group in British imperial affairs and in foreign policy since 1889, although not widely recognized, can hardly be exaggerated."[475] Sir Alfred Milner carried forth the Rhodes vision of controlling the entire world.

Ironically, OWS targeted Wall Street and banks as the villains that needed to be destroyed along with capitalism. However, the bottom line shows that in some ways Wall Street and banks were as much victims as the other "99 percent." An analysis done by the Daily Bell, a libertarian think tank, shows that the OWS protests "intended to move attention away from the proximate cause of modern financial disasters (central banks printing money-from-nothing) to 'Wall Street' and Goldman Sachs and other facilities that promote Anglosphere elite goals but are not in charge of the larger conspiracy."[476]

The conspiracy to run the world seems to emanate from a small group of banking families that control central banks along with their associates and enablers. This group—a cartel or mafia with religious and cultural homogeneity—creates war and chaos in order to build their longed-for new world order.[477] The current protests are likely part of the chaos that apparently is being willfully created by this power elite and funded in part by George Soros.

Quigley found that "The influence of these business leaders was so great that the Morgan and Rockefeller groups acting together, or even Morgan acting alone could have wrecked the economic system of the country merely by throwing securities on the stock market for sale.... Morgan came very close to it in precipitating the 'panic of 1907,' but they did not hesitate to wreck individual corporations, at the expense of the holders of common stocks, by driving them into bankruptcy."[478] As powerful as they are, however, Quigley says they are not invincible;

In no country was the power of these great complexes paramount and exclusive, and in no country were these powers able to control the situation to such a degree that they were able to prevent their own decline under the impact of world political and economic conditions, but their ability to dominate their spheres is undeniable. *In France, Rothschild and Schneider were not able to weather the assault of Hitler;... in the United States, Morgan was unable to prevent the economic swing from financial to monopoly capitalism, and yielded quite gracefully to the rising power of du Pont [and Rockefeller]....But all these shifts of power within the individual economic systems indicate merely that individuals or groups are unable to maintain their positions in the complex flux of modern life, and do not indicate any decentralization of control.*[479] (Italics added)

So, even though the political and economic fortunes of individual families or groups wax and wane, the power of the Group or financial cartel continues to increase. While the BIS is the center of their power, the greatest financial power block today is Great Britain and the United States. It is known as the Anglo-American Establishment or Faction. Although England no longer has the global economic power it once had, its dominance as a global financial center in spite of the introduction of the now threatened euro is still all powerful. Out of 48 international central banks, the Bank of England handles more than 30 percent of spot foreign exchange turnovers. This is unchanged since 1998.

London's slice of currency trading in 2001 was equal to that of its three nearest rivals with the U.S. taking 16 percent, Japan 9 percent and Singapore 6 percent.[480] Together, the U.S. and England handle nearly half of all monetary exchanges in the world. Link that with the raw economic power of the U.S., and the Anglo-American axis is all-powerful.

Tongue-in-cheek, Quigley summarizes the reality and power of this open conspiracy:

The two ends of this English-speaking axis have sometimes been called, perhaps facetiously, the English and American Establishments. There is, however, a *considerable degree of truth behind the joke*, a truth which reflects a very real power structure. It is this power structure which the *Radical Right in the United States has been attacking for years in the belief that they are attacking the Communists*. This is particularly true when these attacks are directed, as they so frequently are at 'Harvard Socialism,' or at 'Left-wing newspapers' like *The New York Times* and the Washington Post, or at foundations and their dependent establishments, such as the Institute of International Education.[481] (Italics added)

In one sweeping statement Quigley implicates some of the faculty of Harvard and the progressive liberal newspapers like the *New York Times* and *Washington Post* as being part of this power structure. It is no small wonder that in 1968 publication of Quigley's book *Tragedy and Hope* ceased. It was even pulled from the bookshelves and library stacks after people had already purchased nine thousand copies.[482]

Author Ted Flynn in *The Hope of the Wicked* explains why; "Quigley's book *Tragedy and Hope* was intended for an elite readership composed of scholars and network insiders. But unexpectedly it began to be quoted in the journals of the John Birch Society, which correctly had perceived that his work provided a valuable insight to the inner workings of a hidden power structure. That exposure triggered a large demand for the book by people who were opposed to the network...."[483]

In a personal letter by Quigley dated December 9, 1975, Quigley acknowledged the book "has brought me headaches as it apparently says something which powerful people do not want known."[484] In another letter Quigley said, "I am now quite sure that *Tragedy and Hope* was suppressed."[485]

It is a shock to some that the so-called radical right in America has been correct all along. There *is* a real global agenda, and its existence cannot be denied. Given the current global financial upheavals, especially in Europe, it is not too speculative to say that this cartel is about to unleash a global financial hell to force citizens to accept the Cartel's solutions in order to survive. Of course, that means global governance and an entirely new financial architecture that will likely use a brand new currency or type of currency.

From the vantage point of nearly forty years of additional history since Quigley wrote his book, the economy of the world *is* becoming more controlled. Just as Quigley predicted, it is increasingly feudalistic (no middle class) by the actions and laws created by progressives of both parties. They are forcing the Rousseau model of governance on us. How the Group (financial cartel) did it is at once appalling and fascinating.

CREATING THE GLOBAL FINANCIAL CARTEL

"THE CHIEF BACKBONE of this organization," informs Quigley, "grew up along the already existing financial cooperation running from the Morgan Bank in New York to a group of international financiers in London...."[486] Lord Alfred Milner initially started the Group, fulfilling a long-held dream of Cecil John Rhodes (1853-1902) for England to control the world. With the cooperation of the Bank of England and financiers like Lord Rothschild, Rhodes amassed one of the largest fortunes in the history of mankind. Rhodes exploited South African gold and diamonds and actually captured the global diamond market through DeBeers Consolidated Mines.[487]

Most people are aware of the Rhodes Scholarship at Oxford. What they may not know is that the Scholarship is designed to help bright, young, globally oriented men get the Rousseau-dominated education necessary in order to obtain positions of power in business, media or government. In many of these positions they could advance the long-held dream of Rhodes—many without even realizing they are doing it.

President Clinton was one such scholar and was mentored by Quigley himself. Receiving a Rhodes Scholarship doesn't mean the student automatically succeeds or becomes a die-hard one-worlder. These scholars are heavily screened, however, and if they show promise in their academics they will have doors opened in their career path that other, even brighter, graduates never get. It is easy to coerce very ambitious inexperienced and indoctrinated students into going with the flow so they can attain power and prestige for themselves.

The Rhodes Scholarship was only one avenue Rhodes devised to realize his dream. In *Confessions of Faith,* he laid out a plan to form a secret society with a goal to bring the entire world under British rule. He first heard of the idea from Professor John Ruskin while attending Oxford University,[488] "Why should we not form a secret society with but one object, the furtherance of the British Empire for the *bringing of the whole uncivilized world under British rule* for the recovery of the United States, for the making the *Anglo-Saxon race by one Empire.*"[489] (Italics added)

Rhodes organized his secret society on February 5, 1891. His first three recruits were journalist William T. Stead, Lord Milner, and a man named Brett, who later became Lord Esher.[490] Stead later wrote a book about the five wills of Rhodes in which he stated the magnitude of what Rhodes envisioned, "Mr. Rhodes was more than the founder of a dynasty. He aspired to be the creator of one of those vast semi-religious, quasi-political associations, which like the Society of Jesus (the Jesuits), have played so large a part in the history of the world. To be more strictly accurate, he wished to found an Order as the instrument of the will of the Dynasty."[491]

When Cecil Rhodes died in 1902, Lord Milner took control of the Rhodes Trust and the secret society, which became known as Milner's Kindergarten in South Africa. In 1909, the Kindergarten organized the first Round Table- Group in England. Seven other round tables were eventually formed, the key being the one in the United States. In 1919, the Round Tables formed the Royal Institute of International Affairs in England (known as the Chatham House) and the Institute of International Affairs in the United States.[492] In 1921, Col. Edward M. House, a key player in the creation of the Federal Reserve in 1913 and close advisor to President Woodrow Wilson, reorganized the U.S. branch into the Council on Foreign Relations (CFR). Quigley then picks up the story:

> The Round Table Groups were semi-secret discussion and lobbying groups organized… on behalf of Lord Milner, the dominant Trustee of the Rhodes Trust…. The original purpose of these groups was to seek to federate the English-speaking world along lines laid down by Cecil Rhodes…and William T. Stead…and the money for the organizational work came originally from the Rhodes trust. By 1915 Round Table Groups existed in seven countries, including England…[and] the United States…. Since 1925 there have been substantial contributions from wealthy individuals and from foundations and firms associated with the international banking fraternity, especially the Carnegie United Kingdom Trust, and other organizations associated with J. P. Morgan, the Rockefeller and Whitney families, and the associates of Lazard Brothers and of Morgan, Grenfell, and Company.[493]

According to Ted Flynn, the CFR was a spin-off from the failure of the U.S. to embrace the League of Nations following World War I. "It became clear to the master planners," says Flynn, "that they had been unrealistic in their expectations for rapid acceptance. If their plan were to be carried forward, it would have to be done on the basis of patient gradualism symbolized by the Fabian turtle, which still today is the symbol of the London School of Economics, a training ground for the elite."[494] The Fabians were a group of elite intellectuals who formed yet another secret society to peacefully bring socialism into the world.

Quigley also claimed that the CFR in New York was "a front for J. P. Morgan and Company in association with the very small American Round Table Group."[495] Originally associates of the Morgan Bank dominated the CFR. The CFR also had powerful members from academia, Wall Street and the Morgan-dominated media. Not only did the CFR serve as a front for the interests of J. P. Morgan, the secret U.S. Round Table Group was directing it in close concert with the British Round Table.

The same people established a third network in 1925 called the Institute of Pacific Affairs (IPA), which eventually expanded to ten nations. According to Quigley "The financing came from the same international banking groups and their subsidiary commercial and industrial firms." The IPA as an independent entity was short-lived, however. During the depression it became too expensive, and the CFR absorbed its activities in the United States and the seven other local Institutes of International Affairs where it continues its work.[496]

Since the creation of the Round Table Groups and the Institutes of International Affairs (including the CFR), the globalists have created three other organizations for specific purposes; the Bilderbergers, (economic), the Club of Rome (occult), and the Trilateral Commission (political):

- Bilderbergers (founded in 1954): The Bilderbergers are a sort of international, but smaller, CFR. The European Economic Community is a product of the Bilderberger Group. Their membership, which consists of the world's elite, meets once a year to coordinate and disseminate plans for the New World Order.
- Club of Rome (founded in 1968, in part by David Rockefeller): With less than one hundred members, the occult-driven organization is charged with the task of overseeing regionalization, then unification, of the entire world. [Seven of the ten economic regions originally envisioned by the Club are now in place or are being created]. Most of

the planning directives for world government come from this group, including the original concept of sustainable development that led to the UN's Agenda 21.

- Trilateral Commission (founded by David Rockefeller and Zbigniew Brzezinski, 1973): Members of the economic superpowers, North America, Western Europe and Japan, hence the term "trilateral." This multinational planning commission seeks to unite superpowers into a one-world socialist government, requiring the voluntary demise of American independence.[497]

Lust for World Government

The objectives of the CFR and its offspring, and the success at which they have been implemented, are nothing short of shocking for most Americans. Paul Warburg, Wall Street financier and CFR leader, told the U.S. Senate Foreign Relations Committee during a hearing on February 17, 1950; "We shall have world government whether or not you like it—by conquest or consent."[498] Warburg was the son of Paul Warburg Sr., one of the principle architects of the creation of the Federal Reserve in 1913. The Warburg family still owns a substantial share of the Fed.

The CFR's Roundtable, not necessarily its members, seeks to undermine all that this nation stands for in their lust for world government—with them at the helm! In 1954, Senator William Jenner entered into the Congressional Record a warning about the CFR, which was completely ignored by Congress, to the detriment of the peoples of the United States:

> Today the path to total dictatorship in the U.S. can be laid by strictly legal means, unseen and unheard by Congress, the President or the people.... We have a well-organized political-action group in this country, determined to destroy our Constitution and establish a one-party state.... It is a dynamic, aggressive, elite corps, forcing its way through every opening, to make a breach for a collectivist one party state. It operates secretly, silently, continuously to transform our Government without suspecting that change is under way....
>
> It is difficult for people governed by reasonableness and morality to imagine the existence of a movement which ignores reasonableness and boasts of its determination to destroy, which ignores morality, and boasts of its cleverness in outwitting its opponents by abandoning

all scruples. This ruthless power-seeking elite is a disease of our century.... This group...is answerable neither to the President, the Congress, nor the courts. It is practically irremovable.[499]

Rear Admiral Chester Ward, former Judge Advocate General (JAG) and a former CFR member said in his book, coauthored with Phyllis Schlafly, *Kissinger on the Couch,* that the goal of the CFR was the,

submergence of U.S. sovereignty and national independence into an all-powerful one-world government....Once the ruling members of the CFR have decided that the U.S. Government should adopt a particular policy, the very substantial research facilities of CFR are put to work to *develop arguments, intellectual and emotional, to support the new policy, and to confound and discredit, intellectually and politically, any opposition.*[500] (Italics added)

Senator Barry Goldwater, in his 1979 book, *With No Apologies*, tried to warn the American people about the CFR. "Their goal is to impose a benign stability on the quarreling family of nations through merger and consolidation. They see the elimination of national boundaries, the suppression of racial and ethnic loyalties as the most expeditious avenue to world peace."[501]

Many have noted that this agenda draws power to Washington to aid in the creation of a one-world government. It occurs whether we have a Democrat or Republican administration. One of the primary goals of the Round Table group controlling the CFR is to manipulate American politics so that voters elect people having a globalist mentality and give them key positions of power. It really doesn't matter which party is in office, the agenda always stays the same. Quigley proudly defines this horrifying, manipulative agenda:

The chief problem of American political life for a long time has been how to make the two Congressional parties more national and international. The argument that the two parties should represent opposed ideals and policies, one, perhaps, of the Right and the other of the Left, is a foolish idea acceptable only to doctrinaire and academic thinkers. Instead, the two parties should be almost identical, so that the American people can "throw the rascals out" at any election *without leading to any profound or extensive shifts in policy.*[502] (Italics added)

The September 2, 1961, issue of the liberal Christian Science Monitor described the CFR as "probably one of the most influential, semi-public organizations in the field of foreign policy.... It has staffed almost every key position of every administration since FDR." The November 21, 1971, issue of the New York Times stated, "For the last three decades American foreign policy has remained largely in the hands of men – the overwhelming majority of them Council members [CFR].... One of the most remarkable aspects of this remarkable organization...is how little is known about it outside a narrow circle of East Coast insiders." As a result, most voters go into the ballot box completely blind.

Voter Beware

The progressive Democrats are the ideologues easily controlled and manipulated by the global financial cartel. Stroke their giant egos and give them some money along with a concocted goal or problem like man-caused global warming, and they become blind, pit bull automatons who have pre-packaged vitriol for anyone who disagrees with them. President Obama, his Czars, and the progressive Democrats in Congress are classic examples of this.

Progressive liberals now totally dominate the Democratic Party. Although they are globalists, they manipulate the poor, minorities, environmentalists and labor unions by promising the moon if they are voted into office. Yet, as described in the proceeding chapters, their policies are bankrupting the U.S. so that in the end, no one receives anything except heartache and poverty as these empty promises turn to ashes.

Likewise, the progressive Republicans and their fascist-like goals attempt to blend private corporations and the government into public-private partnerships. Neocons especially can be led by the nose with the promise of dollars into new governance arrangements that are in no way accountable to the people such as regional planning boards. Texas Governor Rick Perry exemplified this when he created a public/private partnership with the Spanish firm Centra to construct the Trans-Texas Corridor, the first segment of the NAFTA Superhighway.[503] In either case the Constitution would be thrown out the window.

As discussed in previous chapters, neocons are globalists who want to control the world through financial and military power. The Republican Party is essentially controlled by progressive Republicans or neocons who actively promote these globalist ideals. That is why the Republican Party disavowed or undermined Tea Party candidates in the 2010 elections and during the 112th Congress. While the Tea Party freshmen forced Congress to look at reducing the deficit and debt for the first time in memory, the neocons always settled for something that sounded impressive but was a bag of hot air. They are doing it. It is happening again in the 2012 election cycle. Voter beware! We got into this mess through manipulation and deception. We can only get out of it by education and action.

9 – INSTITUTIONS AND PEOPLE

With the help of the Internet and the ability for mass communication without the mainstream media over the past ten to twelve years, the global agenda is no longer secret—if you know what to look for. It is still helpful, however, to briefly explain some of the institutions involved in advancing this evil agenda to plunder America, and expose at least one of the principle players who have caused harm to hundreds of millions of people around the world. Although there are many institutions that advance this agenda, there is one whose members infest key governmental and corporate segments of our economy—the Council on Foreign Relations (CFR).

PENETRATION OF THE CFR INTO AMERICAN POLICY AND POLITICS

WHILE THE NEW YORK-BASED CFR has a membership of only 4,500 people and more than 200 corporations, these members hold the pinnacles of power in American government, finance, media and other key American institutions. According to its own website, "CFR's ranks include top government officials, renowned scholars, business leaders, acclaimed journalists, prominent lawyers, and distinguished nonprofit professionals.[504]

CFR members participate in meetings, panel discussions, interviews, lectures, book clubs, and film screenings to discuss and debate the major foreign policy issues of our time. Members have unparalleled access to world leaders, senior government officials, members of Congress, and prominent thinkers."[505]

During the mid-twentieth century, conservatives documented this bi-partisan control. Senator Barry Goldwater noted in his 1979 book *With No Apologies*, "When we change Presidents, it is understood to mean the voters are ordering a change in national policy. With the exception of the first seven years of the Eisenhower administration, there has been no appreciable change in foreign or domestic policy direction." That remains true today and bears repeating; when a new president comes on board, there is a great turnover in personnel but no significant change in policy.[506]

Ironically, the global agenda often makes greater gains in a Republican administration because conservatives let their guard down when they believe a conservative is in charge. The president doesn't even have to be part of the agenda—he merely appoints globalists to key positions and *they* advance the agenda. The majority of members and supporters of the CFR are not knowledgeable about the true purpose of the organization and provide the perfect cover to the more inflammatory activities of its leadership. Carroll Quigley believed the "outer circle [of The Group] were not conscious they were being used by a secret society."[507] That way, CFR members can claim familiarity with the agenda and yet honestly deny its true goals.

It is important to realize that CFR members rarely take direct orders from the CFR's controlling Round Table core. There is no lockstep control. Rather, as members of the CFR, they have demonstrated that they support a globalist viewpoint. Therefore, when they achieve positions of power in commerce or government they will generally make decisions that favor the global agenda. Friendly suggestions with a back slap or phone call while 'discussing business' can be very effective. Of course, if the person is subject to blackmail, the financial cartel can apply even more direct pressure.

A flood of CFR propaganda as well as *Foreign Affairs*, the CFR periodical that is published five times a year, helps them justify their support. A modern day example of this is the Intergovernmental Panel for Climate Change (IPCC). Since 2007, a number of embarrassing revelations have been made clearly showing that much of the so-called science used by the IPCC is manufactured or manipulated to show a predetermined conclusion: man causes global warming. The cover-ups for these distortions have been massive—and very successful.[508] As will be discussed in Chapter 12, the very organizations manipulating the data for the IPCC were forced in January of 2012 to admit that there is a 92 percent probability that there will be 30 to 70 years of dramatic cooling, not warming.[509]

Although the IPCC has been discredited, every progressive liberal politician, reporter, or blogger uses the IPCC as the final say on the global warming debate. Even the EPA based their finding that CO_2 was a pollutant using IPCC science, which then allowed them to declare the polar bear as endangered. Once that was done the EPA was free to issue thousands of new punitive regulations for coal-fired electrical generation facilities and oil refineries.[510]

This dominance of key administration positions by progressive CFR members is not unique to presidents. Most Republican presidents and almost every secretary of state, CIA Director, National Security Advisor, Secretary of War/Defense, Joint Chiefs of Staff Chairmen, and other key administrative positions since 1929 held membership in the CFR. Retired members of Congress in both parties are also CFR members.

Not only has the financial cartel penetrated our political institutions with CFR members, Carroll Quigley notes that historically they have

...expected that they would be able to control both political parties equally. Indeed, some of them intended to contribute to both and to allow an alternation of the two parties in public office in order to conceal their own influence, inhibit any exhibition of independence by politicians, and allow the electorate to believe that they were exercising their own free choice.[511]

Indeed, they have been very successful at controlling both sides of the political spectrum while giving the appearance that there are strong differences between the candidates. Quigley continues by saying that, "The policies that are vital and necessary for America [i.e. to the financial cartel] are no longer subjects of significant disagreement, but are disputable only in details of procedure, priority, or method...."[512] Republicans talk about smaller government. However, most programs Republican Neocon candidates propose are different from those of the progressive Democratic candidates by mere degree of socialism, or the type of plunder they will employ, not a matter of returning to a Constitutional form of self-government.

The classic example of this is 2012 presidential candidate Mitt Romney. While running for governor of Massachusetts in 2003 he was the star example of the "moderate" Republican, espousing many social positions held by liberal Democrats. Since he started running for president he has flip-flopped on most of his liberal social views. People can certainly change, but it is obvious he is not a principled conservative. He promoted what became known as Romneycare which was based on socialist principles and which closely parallels Obamacare. Some of the same people were involved in crafting both plans. It is astonishing that so-called Tea Party advocates voted for him in the early Republican primaries when the overriding concern of the Tea Party movement was opposition to Obamacare.

The CATO Institute declared Romneycare to be the walking dead in 2008.[513] Romneycare has failed miserably to contain costs and has left Massachusetts taxpayers paying the highest insurance rates in the nation.[514] It has also created doctor shortages.[515] Yet, Romney refuses to acknowledge its failure. While it is likely Romney will greatly slow down Obama's warp speed blitz to implement a Rousseau/Soviet statist government should he become president, it is unlikely he will stop and reverse the global agenda.

Although President G. W. Bush did many things to seemingly slow the global agenda, he angered conservatives by also increasing the size and invasiveness of the federal government far more than the conservatives' arch-enemy, Bill Clinton, ever dreamed of doing. Following 9-11, the so called Patriot and the Homeland Security Acts did more to centralize power to the federal government and to threaten civil liberties than any two laws ever passed.

President Bush also greatly expanded federal control of public education through the Leave No Child Behind Act. Obama has continued the assault with Race to the Top. Both parties also continue to advance the financial cartel's globalist goals and the transfer of sovereignty from local governments to the federal government and eventually to the United Nations. President G. W. Bush's push for the Free Trade Area of the Americas is but one example of the effort to drastically reduce national sovereignty in favor of a European Union-like economic block.

In saying this, it is important to understand that not everything done in the name of globalism is bad. After all, we do live in a global economy. What is bad for America is relinquishing sovereignty in the name of free trade or fighting terrorism—or something else in which the American people lose their sovereignty. By doing so, America squanders the ability to control its own destiny. Instead, those agreements allow others outside the U.S. to control U.S. policy.

9 – Institutions and People

Now that the Tea Party, 9/12, conservative, and Patriot movements are trying to turn America back to a Constitutional Republic, they are demonized and vilified by both Democrats and Neocon Republicans. It was no accident that every time a seemingly conservative candidate started to rise in the polls in the Republican primary campaign during 2011 they were viciously attacked, and pummeled with innuendo and slander.

Since both parties are advancing the same policies, Quigley says that changing political parties in the White House and Congress is desirable because it invigorates the drive to enact the financial cartel's goals. Therefore every candidate for office, regardless of party, according to Quigley, must meet a litmus test before they receive decent media coverage;

> We must remain strong, continue to function as a great world Power in cooperation with other Powers, avoid high-level war, keep the economy moving without significant slump, help other countries do the same, *provide the basic social necessities for all our citizens, open up opportunities for social shifts for those willing to work to achieve them,* and defend the basic Western outlook of diversity, pluralism, cooperation, and the rest of it, as already described. These things any national American party hoping to win a presidential election must accept. But either party in office becomes in time corrupt, tired, unenterprising, and vigorless. Then it should be possible to replace it, every four years if necessary, by the other party, which will be none of these things but will still pursue, with new vigor, approximately the same basic policies.[516] (Italics added)

The 2012 Republican primary proves Quigley's point. Mitt Romney, the establishment's Neocon candidate, was flush with money and outspent his nearest rival, Newt Gingrich 5 to 1 in Florida. George Soros—the elite of the elite—said the day before the Florida Primary that there isn't "all that much difference" between Obama and Romney.[517] Soros is right. Not surprisingly, the progressive mainstream media has anointed Romney as having the best chance of beating Obama. Many Tea Party advocates voted for Romney out of outright fear that Obama will get reelected. The cartel is bamboozling even the most conservative of conservatives—once again.

The cartel tries to marginalize candidates who do not pass the litmus test described by Quigley. A wayward candidate's more globally-minded opponent suddenly finds money flowing into his campaign coffers, along with help framing vicious campaign ads to defeat the conservative candidate. Compare Mitt Romney and Ron Paul. Romney is swimming in donations and media coverage. Ron Paul has to scrimp for every dime from individual supporters and is ignored by the media. The cartel ignores any threat to the global agenda unless the person starts gaining credibility, then marginalizes the candidate, and finally demonizes him or her. If that doesn't work they will try to destroy the candidate. The result? Although the person and his party change from election to election, the cartel continues to advance the same global policies.

This pattern was obvious in the 2010 congressional elections and is becoming obvious in the 2012 presidential campaigns. Without endorsing any particular candidate, Paul, Bachmann, Santorum and Cain were ignored and marginalized (especially Paul), even though each of them have done well in some states. Some of that, of course is the natural tendency of the media to focus on the front runners. However, Paul is a staunch constitutional libertarian. Paul's detractors claim his policies border on anarchy. As just noted, he got very little media coverage, even when he did well in a primary. When he is mentioned, it was almost always accompanied by some negative caveat. Paul's attack on the Federal Reserve was cause in itself to neutralize him. Add to that his strict constitutional position and he is a major threat to the global agenda.

Next to Paul, Bachmann has demonstrated the greatest adherence to constitutional principles in Congress. The one big exception was her yes vote on the Patriot Act, arguably one of the greatest infringements on our civil rights ever passed before Obamacare. She claims that we have a new war and tactics that impose such a great threat that expanded ability to gain intelligence is justified. She insists, however, this pertained only to potential terrorist activity. She adamantly said that the right to roving wiretaps must never extend to business and individuals.[518] With that exception, however, she stands on constitutional principles. She too was a real danger to the global agenda.

Santorum almost never made it out of the cellar in the primaries, but when he did, he came roaring out, catching the media and his opposition off guard. While he is a strong social conservative, his fiscal voting record in Congress was a bit checkered. He voted for a lot of spending increases, although many of them were riders on otherwise good bills. He also voted to raise the national debt (but so did everyone else) and loved pork barrel projects for his state. However, even with these caveats, Santorum is a conservative and therefore a threat to the global agenda. After weeks of being demonized, Santorum was forced to drop out of the primaries.

Cain didn't have a political track record so he was a more difficult presidential candidate to evaluate. He did, however, have more business experience. Real, on the ground experience rubbing shoulders and dealing with employees, unlike that of Romney whose experience was in the much needed, but sterile world of venture capitalism.

Many conservatives, however, were concerned that Cain was Chairman of the Board for the Federal Reserve of Kansas City. However, not only does the Kansas City Fed not have the global power that the New York City Fed has,[519] Cain's position as Chairman of the Board was more ceremonial than functional. What he did was, "not much," and "a little more than not much."[520] Cain's biggest threat to Obama, however, was his business experience and that he was black. Progressives wouldn't be able to play the race card, or as effectively wage class warfare. He had to go.

Enter the women who suddenly, out of nowhere, confronted Cain with allegations of sexual harassment and assault—many years after the alleged incidents took place. Although it can never be proven either way, the allegations had the appearance of being contrived, or at least spun into something they were not. In any event, it worked. By withdrawing from the race, Cain was no longer a threat to the real progressives running in the election.

Newt Gingrich's record, on the other hand, resembles a schizophrenic internal battle over whether he wants to be a conservative or a progressive. He tends to be philosophically conservative, but was also vindictive and unpredictable. He is very intelligent, so much so that he sometimes runs down a rabbit trail like global warming without thinking it through. When Gingrich started to be a threat, his former wife suddenly revealed that he said years ago he wanted an open marriage. The effort failed when Gingrich's children staunchly defended him.

Each of these candidates represented some level of threat to the global agenda and none ever had the financing to be successful in the primaries except perhaps Cain. Meanwhile Romney was constantly in the headlines and spent tens of millions of dollars on negative ads bashing his opposition—especially Gingrich, then Santorum when he became a threat.

Exposure is 80 percent of the battle to become elected and he is getting loads of it. Yes, his mistakes are reported, but usually couched with other positive statements, and he is *always* in the news as the odds-on favorite to win the primary.

If Romney becomes the Republican nominee, and if elected president, he will be a breath of fresh air compared to the ideologue Obama. The plunge into socialism will greatly slow down. However, be advised not to go to sleep just because a Republican is elected president.

BSTEP AND THE PLANNED SOCIETY

SOCIALISTIC PLANNING REQUIRES PEOPLE give up their freedom of choice and God-given civil rights, or at least severely limit their freedom of choice and rights to a narrowly defined set of options allowed by the government. Ironically, Quigley saw this coming as early as 1966 when he published *Tragedy and Hope*:

> It is increasingly clear that, in the twentieth century, the expert will replace the industrial tycoon in control of the economic system even as he will replace the democratic voter in control of the political system. This is because *planning* will inevitably replace laissez faire in the relationships between [government and business]. This planning may not be single or unified, but it will be *planning*, in which the main framework and operational forces of the [economic] system *will be established and limited by the experts on the governmental side*; then the experts…on the economic side will do their *planning within these established limitations.*[521] (Italics added)

Even as Quigley penned these words, a planned society was already being formed through education and was about to be launched in land use control.

Control by Planning "Experts"

Now, reflect back to Chapter 1 and the BSTEP education program that also claimed the future would be run by planners. The 1965 HEW funded report entitled; "The Behavioral Science Teacher Education Program" (BSTEP) at Michigan State University stated exactly the same thing more than 40 years ago:

We are getting closer to developing effective methods for shaping the future and are advancing in fundamental social and individual evolution....[522] *Long-range planning and implementation of plans will be made by a technological-scientific elite....* The *Protestant Ethic will atrophy* as more and more enjoy varied leisure and guaranteed sustenance. *No major sense of self-worth will replace the protestant Ethic.*[523] (Italics added)

The reality of these Rousseau-laden words in the twenty-first century should send chills of horror down the back of every reader. The so-called "expert" or "planner" will make more and more decisions for us as leisure and pleasure destroy the need for God and the moral ethics that such belief ingrains in the population.

During his intensive twenty-year study of the global financial cartel, Quigley found that they realized that "by 1960...a new economic organization of society was both needed and available."[524] The financial elite, according to Quigley, called this new economic organization the "pluralist economy" and characterized "its social structure as one which provides prestige, rewards, and power to managerial groups of experts whose contributions to the system are derived from their expertise and 'know-how.'"[525] Quigley said that the globalists put into motion a plan to achieve this goal:

Thus the pluralist economy and the managerial society, from the early 1940's, have forced the growth of a new kind of economic organization which will be totally unlike the four types of pre-1939 (American laissez faire, Stalinist Communism, authoritarian Fascism, and underdeveloped areas.).... The method of operation of this newly formed pluralist-managerial system may be called "*planning*," if it be understood that *planning* may be both public and private and does not necessarily have to be centralized in either, but is rather concerned with the general method of a *scientific and rational utilization of resources, in both time and space, to achieve consciously envisioned future goals.*[526] (Italics added)

The global financial cartel controlled the education process that created BSTEP , which in turn, helped make planning by so-called experts the future of America. Of course, these elite planners would be brainwashed in public schools using Rousseau socialism in order to achieve the cartels "consciously envisioned future goals." Go into almost any city, county, state, or federal agency and you will find that planners define goals and their implementation, while elected officials merely rubber stamp the recommendations of the planners. This planning is being implemented by the United Nations through a process called Agenda 21 around the entire world. More on this in a later chapter.[527]

This does not mean that *all* planning is bad. Every person, business, corporation, government department and agency has to plan. What makes the managerial society and BSTEP diabolical is that educationally brainwashed planners control the process with *their vision of the future*, not the individual, communities, business or corporation. That vision just happens to be guided by the global financial cartel. As we are now witnessing with nearly a $16 trillion debt and $118 trillion unfunded liability, the results have been disastrous.

Quigley knew the goals of the cartel would severely limit people's freedom, yet hoped they would have some choice left to make them feel good. At the same time, he knew it would be meaningless in securing real change because of the extremely tight controls that they imposed:

> Hopefully the elements of choice and freedom may survive for the ordinary individual in that he may be free to make a choice between two opposing political groups (even if these groups have little policy choice within the parameters of policy established by the experts) and he may have the choice to switch his economic support from one large unit to another. But, in general, *his freedom and choice will be controlled within very narrow alternatives* by the fact that he will be numbered from birth and followed, as a number through his educational training, his required military or other public service, his tax contributions, his health and medical requirements, and his final retirement and death benefits.[528] (Italics added)

Amazingly, in classic Rousseau thinking, Quigley acknowledges that the global cartel is subverting the freedoms guaranteed by the Constitution because he believes, as do the elite, that the masses apparently are unable to think for themselves. Everything has to be planned for them. The goals of BSTEP and the goals set forth by Quigley have been nearly fulfilled by 2012. The Tea Party/conservative revivals have awakened many Americans. Unfortunately, the majority of voters are still indoctrinated with the siren song and propaganda sung by the progressives of both parties who control the key institutions of America. Hopefully, that will have changed by the 2012 election.

The global agenda to control the world, including you and your family, does exist. Far more evidence is available to support this than has been presented here. What makes this insidious is that it is out in the open. It is obvious to anyone who has eyes and can think critically. Yet, the average American citizen, regardless of their intelligence, cannot see it because they have been programmed NOT to see it. As mentioned throughout this book, progressives of both parties make ideal candidates for manipulation by the elites. However, they are not the only victims of this indoctrination. Most of us have become Le Bon's automatons to some extent, dutifully quacking when we are told to quack. Worse, we defend, often violently, the very programs and ideology that are destroying us.

We must define what is happening, how it happened, and what people can do to defend against it. These solutions will be covered later.

GEORGE SOROS – ANATOMY OF A MODERN GLOBAL ELITIST

MOST AMERICANS WOULD BE APPALLED if they knew the beliefs of these would-be global masters. Although most lead very secret lives, detailed information has recently been exposed for the world to see about one of these masters.

Almost unknown until recently, multi-billionaire George Soros has been quietly bringing down governments around the world for decades. David Kupelian, managing editor of WorldNetDaily.com and editor of Whistleblower magazine calls Soros a "God-hating atheist, a self-hating Jew, a capitalism-hating socialist, and an America-hating globalist."[529]

That is just the start. Soros supports euthanasia, socialism, and global governance. He opposes free enterprise, Israel (even though he is a Jew!) and U.S. sovereignty.[530] He wants to devalue the U.S. dollar, telling the *Financial Times* in October 2009 that "an orderly decline of the dollar is actually desirable." It is even more chilling to realize that he knows Americans would suffer if it were to happen.[531] In other words, Soros is the classic elitist carved from the same mold of all Rousseau's haters of peace and individualism.

Replacing the Dollar as World's Reserve Currency

Soros wants to replace the U.S. dollar as the world's reserve currency with "a new currency system."[532] As noted earlier in the book, if that were to happen it would have a catastrophic effect on the U.S. There is a huge demand for dollars in the world because the dollar is the world's reserve currency. Every nation must use dollars to buy oil and other commodities in international trade.[533] This keeps the demand, (and therefore the value) for dollars high. Yet, there is growing evidence that this catastrophe is imminent within the next few years.

There have been efforts to dump the dollar as the reserve currency in the past. In the most recent effort, Gulf Arab states, along with China, Russia, Japan and France have announced plans to do this by 2018.[534] That effort seems to have been stalled for now. If the dollar ever loses its reserve currency status, there would suddenly be a huge surplus of dollars flooding back to the U.S. causing high inflation, even hyperinflation.[535] Americans would have to carry their money in wheelbarrows to buy a loaf of bread as happened in the Weimar Republic which led to Hitler's rise to power.

Can Soros do this? Soros made $7.5 billion in 2010. With a net worth estimated at $22 billion,[536] he is worth more than the Gross Domestic Product of half of all the nations in the world.[537] He helped to bring down the Russian government in the late 1990s.[538] He is famously known as "the man who broke the Bank of England" by shorting the British pound on September 16, 1992.[539] The international banking community now calls it Black Wednesday.

Soros brags about making a billion or more dollars by crashing of the Bank of England,[540] and says it is "fun" to bring down entire nations he labels "repressive" based on his Marxist ideology." The innocent casualties of his subversive activities are "unintended" but a necessary cost of doing good (as Soros defines it).[541] In a 2008 interview with Charlie Rose, Soros seemed amused by the collateral damage resulting from his escapades.[542]

Glenn Beck calls Soros "spooky dude" because he actually looks and acts a lot like the evil Emperor Palpatine of Star Wars fame. Soros's raspy voice even sounds like Palpatine as the Emperor spins his evil throughout his empire. There is some truth in this comparison. Soros was responsible for collapsing the national currency of Malaysia in 1997. Years later he would deny this, but when originally confronted with this evil, Soros casually justifies himself by saying that if he hadn't speculated with the Malaysian currency, someone else would have.[543]

The Making of a Twisted Psyche?

Soros's birth name was György Schwarz.[544] Soros was thirteen when his homeland of Hungary was invaded by the Nazis in 1944. His Jewish, but anti-Semitic father, saw this inevitability and gave Soros a false Christian identity at age 6 so he would not be identified as a Jew.[545] A government official responsible for confiscating the property of the Jews and shipping them off to death camps took Soros in as a godson at age 14. Soros accompanied his godfather in this activity and he eventually participated in the grisly process.[546]

In an interview on December 20, 1998 with 60 Minutes' Steve Kroft, Soros boasted, "that's when my character was made." Soros admitted to Kroft that he actually participated in the confiscation of the Jews' property. When Kroft responded that it would cause psychiatric problems for most people, Soros responded, "Not—not at all. Not at all. Maybe as a child you don't—you don't see the connection. But it was—it created no—no problem at all." Soros went on to say he had no feelings of guilt whatsoever.[547] He felt no guilt even two years later when the atrocities committed by Hitler in his death camps were exposed to the world.[548]

Soros' parents were never seen again and were apparently among those shipped off to the death camps. There is no evidence that Soros witnessed this, but he had to have known it. The loss of parents in this way would be a major trauma to any 14 year-old. For Soros to say that it created no emotional problem at all would require that he severed his emotions from his psyche. It allowed him to survive, but at a terrible cost. Perhaps that is why Soros can have "fun" deliberately causing incredible pain for hundreds of thousands, perhaps millions of people in his twisted logic. It is just a cost of doing business.

Soros learned how to manipulate people and events early in life. His actions are destructive, yet he admits he feels no remorse. He believes, after all, he is actually helping the people he harms because he is punishing the evil government that created their poverty. He identifies himself as a progressive and has stated publicly that he has messianic tendencies.[549]

An Army of Tax-Exempt Radical NGOs

Soros is committed to saving the world from itself, no matter what the cost. This is also the goal of most, if not all progressives. The two go hand in hand. Therefore, it is not surprising that Soros provides hundreds of millions of dollars to radical progressive groups, and these progressive groups provide the shock troops needed to destabilize and destroy the United States.

The funding by Soros goes to hundreds, if not thousands of these radical progressive groups. WorldNetDaily's December 2010, Whistleblower magazine identifies 150 of these non-governmental organizations (NGOs).[550] They range from his flagship Open Society Institute, to the Tides Foundation, and MoveOn.org (which labeled General Petraeus, "General Betray Us").

Glenn Beck did a series of programs on Soros to expose the almost unbelievable network of anti-American NGOs funded or manipulated by Soros. He even funds media groups like the Huffington Post and National Public Radio, whose programming is very liberal.[551] In late 2010 Soros donated a million dollars to the leftist Media Matters to attack Fox News in general and Glenn Beck in particular by targeting their advertisers.[552] Many observers believe these attacks eventually forced Fox to terminate Beck's contract in the summer of 2011. Media Matters also takes credit for the firing of Lou Dobbs from CNN.[553]

Tucker Carlson, of The Daily Caller, investigated Media Matters and found

> ...that Media Matters has been in regular contact with political operatives in the Obama administration. According to visitor logs, on June 16, 2010, [Media Matter founder and head David] Brock and then-Media Matters president Eric Burns traveled to the White House for a meeting with Valerie Jarrett, arguably the president's closest adviser.... Media Matters also began a weekly strategy call with the White House, which continues today.[554]

Media Matters also brags about how "the entire progressive blogosphere picked up our stuff...," including all of the progressive media.[555] Karl Frisch of Media Matters also said, "We should hire private investigators to look into the personal lives of Fox News anchors, hosts, reporters, prominent contributors, senior network and corporate staff." While not illegal, it speaks volumes of the blatant bias and hatchet mentality of Media Matters,[556] and by extension, the White House. This isn't news. Media Matters has turned the mainstream media into the progressive "Ministry of Propaganda," not unlike Joseph Goebbels' Propaganda Ministry created to control the news for Adolph Hitler. Although the story is every bit as explosive as Watergate during the Nixon administration, the mainstream media barely mentioned it.

Soros doesn't do this entirely by himself. Compatriots like billionaires Herb and Marion Sandler and their ProPublica organization also contribute to the anti-American effort.[557] They are the top funders of ACORN, MoveOn.org, the American Civil Liberties Union and other far-leftist NGOs.[558] In just one example, the Sandlers funded ACORN to trash Wells Fargo, a direct competitor of Sandlers' World Savings Bank.[559]

The Open Society Institute (OSI), recently renamed the Open Society Foundations, is the principle organization that Soros uses to distribute $450 million dollars every single year to progressive NGOs. Most telling, Soros originally selected Aryeh Neier to head OSI. Neier was the founder of the violent radical group SDS (Students for a Democratic Society) in the 1960s.[560] Soros has stated publically that he wants his vast network of organizations to be the "conscience of the world."[561] In other words, Soros's conscience. What does Soros's conscience tell him? "The main obstacle to a stable and just world order is the United States."[562]

Towards this goal, Soros has spent at least $45 million from 2000-2008 on efforts to restructure the judicial system in America. He is promoting what he calls the "merit selection" of judges. Instead of voting for judges in elections, Soros wants the process to be one of appointment by a body of unelected, unaccountable commission of lawyers, most of whom are liberal progressives. Soros has funded dozens of NGOs under the umbrella of the Justice at Stake Campaign to advance his agenda. All of this is funded by the Soros-controlled Open Society Foundations.[563]

Soros publicly explained that he has historically brought down nations and currencies by destabilizing the nation, its currency or both using his vast army of NGOs as a "shadow government" to create what he calls "subversive activities."[564] This is the same strategy used by the communists to spread communism since the First World War. More recently, it is the same model advocated by Saul Alinsky and radical socialists Richard

Cloward and Frances Piven discussed in Chapter 6.[565] It is so successful that the thousands of pages of new regulations continually passed by liberal progressives in Congress and our federal agencies may be designed to collapse the system in addition to meeting their unrealistic ideology.

THE LATE, GREAT U.S. DOLLAR

IMPOSSIBLE, YOU SAY? Just how do you think the U.S. has accumulated a $15.8 trillion debt? In their relentless quest to solve the unending evils they see in America, radical NGOs, many funded by Soros, have lobbied social legislation through Congress that the United States cannot afford. When there was no longer any tax money to fund the bloated programs, the U.S. began to borrow money to fund them.

Obama's budget includes a $1.4 trillion budget deficit in 2012 to add to our $15.8 trillion debt.[566] At this rate it will be $18.5 trillion by 2015, even more if Congress does not get the budget under control.[567] This is not free money. In 2010 the interest payment alone on the debt was $414 billion, an amount second only to Social Security and National Defense.[568]

The National Debt to Gross Domestic Product ratio is 100 percent. That means the U.S. owes as much as it produces every year. That is not sustainable, which means the financial condition of the United States is very unstable—exactly what the likes of Soros as well as Cloward and Piven have been striving to accomplish for decades. Yet, the mainstream media is strangely quiet on this precarious predicament. Two things can happen that could totally collapse the dollar overnight. First, during his U.S. visit the week of January 24, 2011, Chinese President Hu said that the U.S. dollar should no longer be used as the world's reserve currency. Most people don't understand the drastic implications of this, if it were to happen.

Is this likely to happen? Other nations want the dollar gone, but a sudden collapse would also collapse their economies so they are reluctant to attack the dollar. China is slowly selling U.S. debt[569] and is seemingly panic buying massive amounts of gold, property and commodities.[570] That's not a good sign. Porter Stansberry, a global financial advisor, warned on February 22, 2012:

We (Americans) are stuck with an enormous debt we can never realistically repay... And the Chinese are trapped with an

176

outstanding loan they can neither get rid of, nor hope to collect.... The Chinese "State Administration of Foreign Exchange" (SAFE) is now engaged in a full-fledged currency war with the United States. The ultimate goal—as the Chinese have publicly stated—is to create a new dominant world currency, dislodge the U.S. dollar from its current reserve role, and recover as much of the $1.5 trillion the U.S. government has borrowed as possible.[571]

This chilling warning is especially troubling since Stansberry is usually right on his predictions. Stansberry also warns that if the U.S. dollar loses its reserve currency status, the U.S. will not be able to borrow money. "And if we can't borrow money, banks will shut down. Government services will be disrupted and more likely, eliminated. No business, local government, or citizen will be able to get a loan at a reasonable rate. Everything we import... food, furniture, clothing, and oil, just to name a few, will get much, much more expensive. Our quality of life will plummet... in a matter of weeks."

China's action was brought on because of the reckless increase in U.S. debt. If China does not solve its problem (at our expense) it would cause massive unemployment and almost certain violent riots within its borders.[572] It's one of the real fears that give Chinese leadership nightmares.[573]

Soros retired from managing investors' money in 2011. Regardless, he has consistently shown that he can take advantage of economic instability to make billions, while causing the collapse of whatever currency he attacks. While unlikely at the moment, we should be concerned that Soros will find a critical lynchpin that when pulled, could cause a cascade effect that would collapse the dollar, while Soros makes billions in gold or another currency.

In an interview with Newsweek in mid-January 2012, Soros explained—almost gleefully according to Newsweek—about a potential Western economic collapse, massive civil unrest and the end of the free market. "It will be an excuse for cracking down and using strong-arm tactics to maintain law and order, which, carried to an extreme, could bring about a repressive political system, a society where individual liberty is much more constrained, which would be a break with the tradition of the United States," Soros told Newsweek. "We are facing an extremely difficult time, comparable in many ways to the 1930s, the Great Depression."[574]

The second thing that could happen would be far less serious, but far more likely. With the total disregard by progressive Democrats of our debt and the Standard and Poor's downgrade of our credit rating on August 5, 2011, China and our other debt holders are starting to say 'no more.' As noted above and in Chapter 7, it may have already started. During the last week of December 2011, foreign holders of U.S. Treasuries dumped a record $69 billion ($3.6 trillion annually) in Treasury Notes.[575] If that trend were to continue, our interest payments on the $16 billion debt could skyrocket from the $414 billion paid in 2010 to as much as $1 trillion annually.[576] While not initially catastrophic, it precipitates a vicious cycle of having to borrow more money to pay the skyrocketing interest on what we already owe, which will cause a further decline in the U.S.'s credit rating.

Many will say that just the opposite happened in mid-2011. The interest rate the U.S. pays on its new debt is going down, not up. That is a mirage. Europe and the Euro are in such desperate shape that the *only* safe haven (as tenuous as it is) is the U.S. dollar. When the EU and Euro collapse, which seems almost certain at the time of this writing, the fatal debt crisis will domino into the U.S. and there will be no safe haven for investment anywhere in the world. No one will want to buy U.S. debt and interest rates will necessarily skyrocket.

The result of either of these possibilities would eventually collapse the dollar and cause pandemonium on the scale of what we have seen in the PIIGS nations. Worse, it would likely cause the unraveling of our economic and political system, allowing Soros and other globalists to come riding in on their white horses to save the day with global governance and a new global currency—something that the progressive elites have been planning for a hundred years.

The United States is in very serious trouble. We hope that the unthinkable does not happen. But there are many in the world, including Soros and most progressives, who would like to see the dollar collapse and capitalism be abandoned so they can implement their radical progressive agenda. That is the type of "change" progressives, including President Obama, really mean when they use the code word "change" or "transformation."

Thousands, perhaps millions, of citizens who call themselves part of the Tea Party movement, conservatives, Constitutionalists and others are fighting the various elements of this agenda (including *Agenda 21*) without knowing the full magnitude of the problem. But that is like a General fighting a battle without the knowledge that the enemy is flanking his troops on both sides where his defenses are weakest. He might even be pushing back the enemy on the front lines. But ignorance will defeat them.

The same is true for developing an effective defense against the global agenda. Most citizens fighting the battle are not aware of the full magnitude of the war and that the enemy is flanking them. To effectively neutralize this agenda, we must all understand how the globalists have gradually overcome any opposition to their goals in the media, our free markets, education, science, property rights and environmentalism.

This radical progressive agenda must be exposed very soon so the American people can intelligently vote most progressives in Congress and our State Legislatures out of office. In the meantime, we must develop a plan to quickly reduce our national debt and deficit spending—as painful as that may be. As long as the progressive Democrats have any power whatsoever in Congress and our state legislatures, or local governments, our state and federal debts and our stifling regulations will continue to grow larger until they break the back of this great nation and cause massive suffering for the very citizens they claim to be helping.

PLUNDERED

10 – CORRUPTING EDUCATION 1800-1945

As discussed previously, the global elite couldn't implement BSTEP (See Chapters 1 and 9) or their soviet model of government unless American citizens were completely dumbed down. Only when citizens no longer understand the Constitution or the fact that they are being used as "useful idiots" could the elite secure final victory. The plundering of America has now put us on the verge of that fateful day. What you are about to read is stunning in its magnitude and sickening in its duplicity. The dumbing down of the American educational machine has been no accident.

THE TRAGIC STATE OF AMERICAN EDUCATION

FORTY-TWO MILLION AMERICANS cannot read, write or perform simple math. Another 50 million Americans cannot read past the 4th grade level. And 7,000 high school students drop out every day.[577]

A report that came out in the fall of 2011 found that as many as 75 percent of college freshmen need some kind of remedial work before they are ready for their core classes. These refresher courses at the college level taken to fill gaps left by the nation's high schools carry a price tag of $5.6 billion.[578] A report by the education advocacy group Strong American Schools released in 2008 found that 80 percent of college students who take remedial classes had a high school GPA of 3.0 or better.[579]

Dr. Samuel Blumenfeld, one of the foremost scholars on education in America, claims that it is easy to dumb down the education system. "Destroy its literacy and you've dumbed it down. And, once it's dumbed down, it becomes the potential victim of any power that wants to dominate it."[580] The most illiterate nations of the world are normally ruled by despots. "That doesn't mean that literate nations, like Germany, can't produce monsters," notes Blumenfeld. "But when they do, we know that satanic influences are behind it."[581]

Charlotte Iserbyt, in her Magnum Opus book *The Deliberate Dumbing Down of America,* states that investigators of this agenda,

> ...have continued to amass—over a thirty- to fifty-year period—what must surely amount to *tons* of materials containing irrefutable proof...of deliberate, malicious intent to achieve behavioral changes in students/parents/society which have nothing to do with commonly understood educational objectives.[582]

Iserbyt knows what she is talking about. As Senior Policy Advisor in the Office of Educational Research and Improvement in the U.S. Department of Education during the first term of the Reagan administration, she discovered:

> An alien collectivist (socialist) philosophy, much of which came from Europe, crashed onto the shores of our nation, bringing with it radical changes in economics, politics, and education, funded—surprisingly enough—by several wealthy American families and their tax-exempt foundations.... Only a dumbed down population, with no memory of America's roots as a prideful nation, could be expected to willingly succumb to the global workforce training planned by the Carnegie and the John D. Rockefellers, I and II, in the early twentieth century which is being implemented by the United States Congress....[583]

The volumes of government and private documents Iserbyt presents in her book are literally stunning. The enormous power of tax-exempt foundations has been used to pervert the United States educational system. Their implication for the future is staggering. It took two entire chapters to discuss what has happened to education in America. And even that is incomplete.

THE ATTACK ON EDUCATION, 1800-1945

WHILE MOST POLITICAL GAINS BY THE ELITE using progressive ideology has been made over the past one hundred years, the elite's attack on education goes back two hundred and fifty years.

Horace Mann (1800-1850's)

In his book *NEA, The Trojan Horse in American Education*, Samuel Blumenfeld traces the problem back to Horace Mann (1796-1859) who, perhaps unwittingly, assisted Rousseau's model of state-controlled governance. Rousseau introduced some radical new ideas on education. In his book *Emile* he proposed "a permissive education" avoiding "strict discipline and tiresome lessons." Furthermore, the "whole child" should be educated by "doing"—and religion should not be a guiding principle in education.[584] Horace Mann and his successors saw these ideas as a way to change the American education system.

Mann, often called the father of public education in America, went to Prussia in the mid-1830s and learned the "Parens Patriae" method of education. By definition, according to Blumenfeld, the fatherland is the parent of children in Parens Patriae. Therefore the children belong to the state. The purpose of state schooling was the conditioning of children to "obedience, subordination, and collective life." In Parens Patriae, Mann saw the means to correct the horrid conditions of the common schools of his youth. [585]

Upon returning to the United States, Mann began to extol the virtues of Parens Patriae for America and in 1837 became the secretary of the Board of Education for the State of Massachusetts. In that role he rejected Christian primers because he "found that they described the fearsome eternal fate of young children who die horribly after committing some small offense."[586] Mann's overzealous minister had tragically turned him from Christianity by callously using the drowning death of Mann's older brother as an example of what happens to wayward boys, rather than consoling the grieving family.[587]

Mann started the first public school and the first state-controlled and financed teacher college (Normal School) in Lexington to prepare teachers using Parens Patriae methods. He instilled a process that eventually would lead to the downfall of public education—psychoanalysis of the student and the use of the whole language approach to reading rather than the proven, tried and true phonics method.[588]

Mann also mocked the primers and *"Noah Webster's American Spelling Book"* that taught children the alphabet before they learned to read words. The "old method," the names of the letters—the ABC's—were first taught so students could learn words phonetically. "Instead,

Mann argued for the virtues of a 'new method,' which sounded very similar to that pushed by proponents of whole language teaching in the twentieth and twenty-first centuries."[589]

Stanley Hall

Horace Mann did much good by changing the public school system to allow all children the opportunity to get an education. However, he also planted the seeds of state-controlled education that fostered the dumbing down of America. Following Horace Mann was his student Stanley Hall (1844-1944), who also studied in Prussia and returned a convinced atheist and evolutionist.

Hall believed superior men should rule over the inferior. He studied under Georg Wilhelm Friedrich Hegel, who, as a student of Rousseau taught what Karl Marx would later expand into Marxism. Hegelian philosophy thoroughly indoctrinated Hall during his studies at the University of Berlin in 1870-71.[590] Upon returning to the United States in 1871, he took a chair position at the very liberal Antioch College (formerly held by Horace Mann) and taught Hegelian philosophy.[591]

After spending four years at Antioch, Hall went back to Germany to get his Ph.D. in psychology at the University of Leipzig under Wilhelm Wundt. Wundt believed that "man is only the summation of his experience."[592] Refining Rousseau philosophy, Wundt claimed that man is merely a captive of his experiences, a pawn needing guidance. Antony Sutton, a former Research Fellow at the Hoover Institute, spent a lifetime studying this agenda. Sutton concludes;

> Wilhelm Wundt (1832-1920), Professor of Philosophy at University of Leipzig, was undoubtedly the major influence on G. Stanley Hall. Modern education practice stems from Hegelian social theory combined with the experimental psychology of Wilhelm Wundt. Whereas Karl Marx and von Bismarck applied Hegelian theory to the political field, it was Wilhelm Wundt...who applied Hegel to education, which in turn, was picked up by Hall and John Dewey and modern educational theorists in the United States."[593]

Hall was one of the most popular speakers at National Education Association (NEA) conventions. He also helped create the NEA Child Study department—the beginning of experimental psychology labs on children. Hall believed that literacy was bad for all but a few people in society. Illiteracy was much more virtuous; "The knowledge that illiterates acquire," claims Hall, "is probably on the whole more personal, direct, environmental and probably a much larger proportion of it practical. Moreover, they escape much eyestrain and mental excitement, and other things being equal, are probably more active and less sedentary...."[594] As will be discussed in the next chapter, education in the twenty-first century put Hall's ideals into practice.

John Dewey

Upon receiving his Ph.D. under Wundt at the University of Leipzig, Hall was hired by Johns Hopkins University where he met and heavily influenced doctoral candidate John Dewey (1859-1952). Dewey would later be known as the father of progressive education.

When Hall arrived at Johns Hopkins University, Dewey had already been working on his Ph.D. under Hegelian philosopher George Sylvester Morris. Morris had also studied Rousseau, Hegel and others while working on his doctorate at the University of Berlin.

Upon graduating from Hopkins, Dewey went to the University of Michigan and "in 1886 published *Psychology*, a blend of Hegelian philosophy applied to Wundtian experimental psychology."[595] It should be noted that Psychology was published nine years before psychologist Gustav Le Bon wrote his scathing analysis of the precursor to progressivism. (See Chapter 4) *Psychology* was destined to become the most widely-read and quoted textbook in schools of education in this country. Dewey's purpose was to show how education could be reformed "to create little socialists instead of little capitalists," who would eventually change America's economic system.[596]

Dewey became head of the Columbia Education Department in 1904 where he began "to mold twentieth century educational thought"[597] into American education. Following Rousseau's and Hegel's philosophies, Dewey believed there is no such thing as individual freedom. Freedom to Dewey "is the participation of every mature human being in formation of the values that regulate the living of men together."[598]

The purpose of education, claimed Dewey, is to "use his own powers for social ends. Education, therefore, is a *process of living* and not a preparation for future living."[599] (Italics added) This is definitely from Rousseau, Hegel and Marx. The only freedom an individual has is to support the general will of the superior social state. Education is merely a tool in that process.

Dewey's foundational belief is totally antithetical to the principles of individual liberty enshrined in the Declaration of Independence and the Bill of Rights of the United States Constitution. It is no small wonder that modern education has virtually eliminated the history of America's formation and the intent of the Founders to create a government of the people, by the people and for the people.

Education, to modern theorists, is merely a tool to create the socialized citizen rather than to prepare the student to contribute to society. Today's students are not given the tools to maximize their individual talents in society. Nor are they taught to think for themselves. Rather, they are taught, "to function as a unit in an organic whole—in blunt terms a cog in the wheel of an organic society."[600] Is it any wonder that Americans have become Le Bon's "automatons"?

While at Columbia, Dewey was the first to teach "functionalism." Functionalism incorporated the ideas that man was without purpose, the importance of the mind above all else, and the theory that a person is a product of his or her experience and nothing else. Since he theorized that all knowledge and ability come from experience, then all values must be found within the social context. Values therefore are relative and ethics are based on custom, inclination or utilitarianism.[601]

In 1913 John D. Rockefeller, Jr.'s director of charity for the Rockefeller Foundation, Frederick T. Gates, set up the General Education Board (GEB). Following the classic Rousseau rhetoric, Gates wrote a precursor to BSTEP discussed in Chapters 1 and 9:

Is there aught of remedy for this neglect of rural life? Let us, at least, yield ourselves to the gratifications of a beautiful dream that there is. In our dream, we have limitless resources, and *the people yield themselves with perfect docility to our molding hand.* The present educational conventions fade from our minds; and, unhampered by tradition, *we work our own good will upon a grateful and responsive rural folk. We shall not try to make these people or any of their children into philosophers or men of learning or of science.* We are not to raise up from among them authors, orators, poets, or men of letters.... Nor will we cherish even the humbler ambition to raise up from among them lawyers, doctors, preachers, politicians, statesmen, of whom we now have ample supply.[602] (Italics added)

Remember, in 1913 more than half of the population of the United States lived in rural America. What Gates, and by default, Rockefeller, was calling for was a plan to keep the majority of Americans dumbed down and content with a life that was entirely planned for them by the elite.

Blumenfeld notes, "Since the beginning of Western civilization, the school curriculum was centered on the development of academic skills, the intellectual faculties, and high literacy. Dewey wanted to change all of that. Why? He believed high literacy produced independent intelligence and critical thinking, which he insisted was anti-social, selfish and deplorable."[603]

Dewey's model has "no obvious social motive for the acquirement of mere learning."[604] Blumenfeld explains, "To Dewey, the greatest enemy to socialism was the private consciousness that seeks knowledge in order to exercise its own individual judgment and authority. High literacy gave the individual the means to seek knowledge independently…. The goal was to produce inferior readers with inferior intelligence dependent on socialist educational elites for guidance, wisdom, and control."[605]

Columbia University and its Dewey-dominated Teacher Colleges became the undisputed training center for "progressive education." Its activist graduates were then placed in strategic prominent positions as the heads of teacher colleges, universities, superintendents of schools across the nation where they made sure they taught only the "progressive," socialist philosophy of education.

According to estimates, Columbia gave advanced degrees to as many as one-fourth of all high school superintendents and half of teachers' college heads by the beginning of the twenty-first century.[606] Because of Dewey's ideas of atheism, socialism and evolution these graduates began to remove God from the classroom and establish the ideology of no absolutes, no moral standards, situational ethics, and eventually boundary free sex, self-esteem and values clarification.

DELIBERATE DUMBING DOWN OF AMERICA

DEWEY OPPOSED EVERYTHING AMERICA REPRESENTED. He was a member of the globalist Council on Foreign Relations (CFR), a Fabian Socialist,

Marxist, Darwinist and co-authored the *Humanist Manifesto I* in 1933.[607] Yet, with funding by the Rockefeller Foundation, Dewey created and organized the Progressive Education Association (P.E.A.) in 1919.

As World War II was concluding in 1943, the board of the P.E.A. published a statement in its journal *Progressive Education* which stated, in part, "This is a global war, and the peace now in the making will determine what our national life will be for the next century. It will demonstrate the degree of our national morality. We are writing now the credo by which our children must live…"[608] What was this new credo by which our children must live? Dr. Augustus Thomas, Commissioner of Education for the State of Maine had already told the World Federation of Education Associations (WFEA) on August 8, 1927:

If there are those who think we are to jump immediately into a new world order, [i.e. world government] actuated by complete under-standing and brotherly love, they are doomed to disappointment…. It will [only come] after patient and persistent effort of long duration. The present international situation of mistrust and fear can only be corrected by a formula of *equal status* [i.e. socialism], continuously applied, to every phase of international contacts, until the cobwebs of the old order are brushed out of the minds of the people of all lands. This means that the world must await *a long process of education and a building up of public conscience and an international morality…*[609] (Italics added)

A year later, O. A. Nelson, a retired high school assistant principal, gave a lecture on teaching functional physics in high school at an American Association for the Advancement of Science conference on December 27, 1928. The next day Dr. Ziegler, chairman of the Educational Committee of the CFR, asked Nelson to attend a private meeting where they informed him that "the purpose of 'new math' was to dumb down students."[610] Also attending the December 28 meeting were John Dewey, Edward Thorndike and other CFR members. In 1979 Nelson revealed in the July issue of the *National Educator* what occurred in the 1928 meeting:

We were 13 at the meeting. Two things caused Dr. Ziegler…to ask me to attend,…my talk of the teaching of functional physics in high school, and the fact that I was a member of a group known as the Progressive Education Association, which was nothing but a Communist front. I thought the word "progressive" meant progress for better schools. Eleven of those attending the meeting were leaders in education. Drs. John Dewey and Edward Thorndike, from Columbia University, were there, and the others were of equal rank. I checked later and found that ALL were paid members of the Communist Party of Russia. I was classified as a member of the Party, but I did not know it at the time.

The sole work of the group was to destroy our schools! We spent one hour and forty-five minutes discussing the so-called "Modern Math." At one point I objected because there was too much memory work, and math is reasoning; not memory. Dr. Ziegler turned to me and said, "Nelson, wake up! That is what we want…a math that the pupils cannot apply to life situations when they get out of school!" That math was not introduced until much later, as those present thought it was too radical a change. A milder course by Dr. Breckner was substituted but it was also worthless… The radical change was introduced in 1952. It was the one we are using now. So, if pupils come out of high school now, not knowing any math, don't blame them. The results are *supposed to be* worthless.[611]

The effort to turn America into math morons succeeded with blazing colors by the end of the twentieth century. Now, more than a decade into the twenty-first century, our 15-year-olds placed 25th out of 34 countries in math according to the Paris-based Organization for Economic Cooperation & Development. With its release of these disgraceful results in 2009, it was revealed to the world that we are mathematically outmatched by 9 nations including South Korea, Japan, Singapore, as well as Finland, with the city of Shanghai scoring at the top.[612]

The U.S. government considers this test one of the most comprehensive measures of international achievement. When all subjects tested were considered, we were humiliatingly outmatched by 17 nations out of the 34 tested.

THE ROLE OF TAX-EXEMPT FOUNDATIONS

IN 1953, U.S. REPRESENTATIVE CARROLL REECE (R-TN) formed the U.S. Congressional Reece Committee to investigate the impact of tax-exempt foundations on education and the constitutional government of the United States. Norman Dodd served as its Director of Research and wrote the report, while René Wormser was the committee's general legal counsel. The findings were so frightening that Wormser wrote *Foundations; Their Power and Influence* to expose the findings to the American people.

The Reece Committee found that foundations have "already come to exercise very extensive, practical control over most research in the social sciences, much of our educational process, and a good part of government administration.... The aggregate thought control power of this foundation and foundation-supported bureaucracy can hardly be exaggerated."[613]

Very little was ever heard of the Reece Report because of the awesome power of these foundations. The Report goes on to say that,

> The far-reaching power of the large foundations…has so influenced the press, the radio, and even the government that it has become extremely difficult for objective criticism of foundation practices to get into news channels without having first been distorted, slanted, discredited, and at times ridiculed.[614]

A pamphlet written by Professor George S. Counts entitled "A Call to the Teachers of the Nation" revealed to the Reece Committee the elitist and militant nature of the P.E.A. (Progressive Education Association),

> The progressive minded teachers of the country must unite in a powerful organization militantly devoted to the building of a better social order, in the defense of its members against the ignorance of the masses and the malevolence of the privileged. Such an organization would have to be equipped…to wage successful war in the press, the courts, and the legislative chambers of the nation." [615]

The Rockefeller Foundation, the Carnegie Corporation and the Ford Foundation are ultimately responsible for the attack on education in America and around the world starting about 1902.[616] "The largest of the foundation giants, The Ford Foundation, is a latecomer."[617] The Reece

Report also concluded that "The impact of foundation money upon education has been very heavy, largely tending to promote uniformity in approach and method, tending to induce the educator to become an agent for social change and a propagandist for the development of our society in the direction of some form of collectivism."[618]

The foundations did it by first controlling universities training future teachers. Money talks, and most colleges and universities of the first half of the twentieth century were starving for funds. Said Wormser, "It was a case of conform, or no grant. When to conform meant bathing in a stream of millions, college and university administrators and their faculties were inclined to conform."[619] Law, history, education and liberal arts schools and colleges were soon filled with professors steeped in progressive ideology.

Foundations dictated what the colleges and universities did. Said Wormser, "Accrediting organizations and other instruments in the form of civic, professional, and school associations were created or supported to implement the reform plans of these three foundations,…[including] The National Education Association… The Progressive Education Association, The John Dewey Society, The National Council on Parent Education, and The American Youth Commission."[620]

The power of foundation money was so great that it forced colleges, even the colleges originally founded as religious colleges like Harvard and Yale, to abandon "their religious affiliations in or even before 1915 in order to conform to requirements established by foundations."[621] As a result, it eliminated religion, the very foundation of a free people described by French judge, statesman and political writer Alexis de Tocqueville, as the basis for its peoples' education. It would not be until 1962, however, that they would be able to get religion totally banned in schools.

One of the key witnesses before the Reece Committee was Aaron Sargent, a lawyer who specialized in investigating and researching the changes in education and subversion. He had served as a consultant to the Senate Internal Security Committee in 1952 and had conducted extensive research into the subversive activities of the various foundations in America.

Sargent testified that Fabian Socialism was beginning to dominate our upper education system through the activities of John Dewey and The Intercollegiate Socialist Society.[622] The Fabian Society was a political organization founded in Britain in 1884 with the aim of bringing about socialism by gradual and lawful means rather than by revolution. "John Dewey denied that there was any such thing as absolute truth," testified Sargent. "...everything was relative, everything was doubtful, that there were no basic values and nothing which was specifically true."[623] With this philosophy, "you automatically wipe the slate clean, you throw historical experience and background to the wind and you begin all over again, which is just exactly what the Marxians want someone to do."[624]

This kind of socialism, testified Sargent, does not originate with the masses via a grass-roots movement. Citing a quote from Professor Ludwig Von Mises, Sargent said that such socialism is "instigated by intellectuals 'that form themselves into a clique and bore from within and operate that way. It is not a people's movement at all. It is a capitalization on the people's emotions and sympathies toward a point they wish people to reach.'" [625]

In 1934 the Carnegie Corporation commissioned and funded the Commission on Social Studies of the American Historical Association to conduct a huge study. Their goal? How they could structure social studies in order to present socialism as desirable. They funded the study to the tune of $340,000—which would have the equivalent buying power of a whopping $5.6 million in 2012. The Commission published the results of the foundation-funded study entitled Conclusions and Recommendations *for the Social Studies*:

> The commission was also driven to this broader conception of its task by the obvious fact that American civilization, in common with Western civilization, is passing through one of the great critical ages of history, *is modifying its traditional faith in economic individualism [free enterprise], and is embarking upon vast experiments in social planning and control which call for large-scale cooperation on the part of the people...*[626]
>
> ...Cumulative evidence supports the conclusion that in the United States and in other countries the age of "laissez fair" in economy and government is closing and that *a new age of collectivism is emerging....* As to the specific form which this "collectivism," this integration and interdependence,... it *may involve the limiting or supplanting of private property by public property or it may entail the preservation of private property,*

extended and distributed among the masses.... Almost certainly it will involve a larger measure of *compulsory* as well as voluntary cooperation of citizens in the conduct of the functions of government, and an *increasing state of intervention in fundamental branches of economy previously left to the individual discretion and initiative.*[627] (Italics added)

These are the same goals of the UN's *Agenda 21* and the U.S. *Sustainable America* discussed in the next chapter. Like *Agenda 21* and *Sustainable America, Conclusions and Recommendations for the Social Studies* takes direct aim at the liberty and wealth producing capacity of private property, calling for the state to control all private property, whether directly through collectivism, or indirectly by sharing the benefits of private property through socialist regulatory restrictions. British philosopher and socialist Professor Harold Laski said of this report, "At bottom, and stripped of its carefully neutral phrases, the Report is an educational program for a Socialist America."[628]

Every American should be shocked to the core to discover that there has been a systematic plan to revise America's cultural history to strip us of private property rights and destroy our free market foundation. Even more shocking is the realization that such an overwhelming change in America's culture could be accomplished without the average, otherwise intelligent citizen even being aware of it. Controlling the American education system was the key.

Revising History Textbooks

The Reece Congressional Committee found that, "Foundations have supported text books (and books intended for inclusion in collateral reading lists) which are destructive of our basic governmental and social principles and highly critical of some of our cherished institutions."[629] In his testimony Aaron Sargent revealed that "writers of textbooks are to be expected to revamp and rewrite their old works in accordance with this frame of reference..."[630] (i.e. the *Conclusions and Recommendations for the Social Studies* by the American Historical Association). Sargent concluded that "this report became the basis for a definite slanting in the curriculum by selecting certain historical facts and by no longer presenting others...."[631]

With the help of millions of dollars in foundation grants, "schools in the United States were flooded with books which disparaged the free-enterprise system and American traditions."[632] Wormser noted that classical or conservative textbook writers "have difficulty in getting the funds to enable him to produce his work.... In contrast, a foundation-supported textbook writer, as a rule, can apply a substantial part of his time, or all of it, to his writing. Moreover, the very fact of foundation support...and the consequent inference of approval will create a favorable climate of opinion for the acceptance of his work by schools."[633]

In one example, the Rockefeller Foundation amply funded the writing and publication of the 'Rugg textbooks.' Professor Harold Rugg, who began in Columbia's Lincoln Experimental School, initially wrote pamphlets written from a socialist perspective. With Rockefeller funding, the pamphlets were expanded into a series of textbooks called *Building America*. Rugg's philosophy followed that of the *Conclusions and Recommendations for the Social Studies*, and involves, "implementing an expectancy of change; *picturing the America of today as a failure*; *disparaging the American Constitution and the motives of the Founders of the Republic*; and presenting a 'New Social Order.'"[634] (Italics added).

Not surprisingly, the National Education Association, intensively promoted the *Building America* series, and poured more than five million copies of the textbooks into American schools up to 1940. Wormser didn't know how many were sold between 1940 and 1958, when he wrote his book, but they were still on the market when the Reece committee held its hearings.[635] The subversive ideas promoted in the series include:

- Public enterprise must become a major constituent of our economy, if we are really going to have economic prosperity....
- It is necessary to have public ownership of basic natural resources (mines, oil fields, timber, coal, etc.)
- In order to ensure that the public corporations act in accordance with the competitive "rules of the game," a special economic court (enjoying the same independence as the courts of justice) be established...and that the economic court be given the power to repeal any rules of Congress, of legislatures, or of the municipal councils.[636]

These concepts are raw Rousseau socialism and form the heart of the twenty-first century effort to create what is known as global governance—

a euphemism for world government in the United Nations. Wormser suspected that the propaganda was already having a deleterious effect on America when he wrote his book in 1958:

> These texts, financed by the Rockefeller Foundation and distributed by the National Education Association, must have influenced the thinking of hundreds of thousands of defenseless young Americans. They may well have contributed to the recent philosophy of reckless public spending and overgrowth of government.[637]

The Reece Committee report characterized the series as nothing less than an "attempt by radical educators financed by foundations to suborn the schools."[638] Every evidence in the twenty-first century leads to the conclusion that they are succeeding so far. The state increasingly controls private property. The so-called public good (the collective) drives many of the laws and policy decisions in the United States. Thousands of regulations control land-use and whether natural resources even can be extracted. The World Trade Organization and NAFTA are increasingly able to overrule laws passed by Congress.

The *Building America* series was so anti-American and pro socialist-Soviet that it was banned from the schools in the State of California after the legislature-impaneled the Dilworth Committee, which concluded that they were subtle attempts to "play up Marxism and to destroy our traditions."[639] The San Francisco Board of Education also reviewed the series and unanimously held them to be "reprehensible." The board found:

> ... the books contain a constant emphasis on our national defects. Certainly we should think it a great mistake to picture our nation as perfect or flawless either in its past or in its present, but it is our conviction that these books give a decidedly distorted impression through over-stressing weaknesses and injustices. They therefore tend to weaken the student's love for his country, respect for its past and confidence in its future.[640]

The Rockefeller Foundation and Carnegie Corporation as well as others did not confine these gross distortions to textbooks. Financed by the Rockefeller Foundation, Columbia University and Cornell University established courses in Russian history that displayed the same revisionism found in *Building America*. This work was then incorporated into *The Encyclopedia Americana*, which with the permission of *The Encyclopedia Americana*, was turned into the college textbook *USSR*. *USSR* was adopted by Cornell, Columbia, Rutgers, Swarthmore, Chicago, Pennsylvania, Michigan, Southern California, Washington and Yale universities.[641]

The manipulations of American education by foundations through World War II are almost beyond belief, but the Reece Committee thoroughly documented them. The hundreds of millions of dollars spent by the foundations did not initially accomplish what the global elite needed— a dumbed-down citizen who would support world government. Why? Because dedicated teachers and parents had enough influence over their children to nullify much of what the global elite were attempting to do. It was not enough to revise the textbooks and hope the teachers would brainlessly teach known error, or that children would absorb the propaganda as fact, unchallenged by their parents. The global elite needed some help in their efforts to dumb-down the American education system. They began in earnest following World War II in partnership with the brand new United Nations.

THE ROLE OF UNESCO

THE FAMOUS TENNESSEE VS. JOHN THOMAS SCOPES, or the Scopes "Monkey Trial" which provided the landmark decision institutionalizing evolution took place in 1925. After this trial, Fabian Socialist[642] and first head of the United Nations Educational, Scientific, and Cultural Organization (UNESCO) Sir Julian Huxley claimed that humanism's "keynote, the central concept to which all its details are related, is evolution."[643] By the end of World War II evolution was firmly entrenched in the public school systems and creationism was on the way out, regardless of how flimsy the science was for evolution or how strong it was for creation science.

Evolution was a key concept for these early American education socialists. "Evolution is at the very basis of modern public education," notes Blumenfeld, "where the child is taught that he is an animal linked by evolution to monkeys. His school materials have been designed to teach him as an animal with stimuli-response techniques which are now universally used throughout American education. So we ought not to be surprised when students act like animals and call their school The Zoo."[644]

Julian Huxley was the prime mover of UNESCO and served as its first Director-General. Huxley had served on Britain's Population Investigation Commission before World War II and was vice president of the Eugenics Society from 1937 to 1944. Evolution was the cornerstone of eugenics and Huxley founded UNESCO, in part, to promote selective breeding of people to "advance humanity" like Hitler did. In a 1947 document entitled *UNESCO: Its Purpose and Its Philosophy,* Huxley wrote:

> Thus even though it is quite true that any radical eugenic policy will be for many years politically and psychologically impossible, it will be important for UNESCO to see that the eugenic problem is examined with the greatest care, and that the public mind is informed of the issues at stake so that much that now is unthinkable may at least become thinkable.[645]

Internationalization of education also became a primary goal of the education change artists. The ink on the UN Charter had not yet dried when the Charter for UNESCO was presented in London, November, 1945. The primary goal of UNESCO was to construct a world-wide education system to promote global government.[646]

Huxley wanted to replace our Constitution with a single, world government: "*Political unification in some sort of world government will be required for the definitive attainment*" of the next stage of social development. (Italics original) He saw UNESCO as an instrument to "*help in the speedy and satisfactory realization of the process*" and designed programs from the beginning to capture children at the earliest possible age to begin the educational process.[647] UNESCO advisor, Bertrand Russell, writing for the UNESCO Journal, *The Impact of Science on Society,* said,

> Every government that has been in control of education for a generation will be able to control its subjects securely without the need of armies or policemen...."[648]

In 1946, William Benton, Assistant U.S. Secretary of State told UNESCO that, "We are at the beginning of a long process of breaking down the walls of national sovereignty. UNESCO must be the pioneer."[649]

Just how was UNESCO going to accomplish that goal? UNESCO publication No. 356, In the Classroom: Toward World Understanding states:

> As long as a child breathes the poisoned air of nationalism, education in world-mindedness can produce only precarious results. As we have pointed out, it is frequently the family that infects the child with extremism nationalism. The school should therefore use the means described earlier to combat family attitudes that favour jingoism [nationalism].... We shall presently recognize in nationalism the major obstacle to development of world-mindedness.

Not surprisingly, the National Education Association (NEA) was a major advocate for UNESCO. When the United Nations was created in 1945, the plan to create the global student was well developed by the NEA, though not yet implemented. A year after the creation of the UN, Joy Elmer Morgan wrote in a NEA journal article entitled "The Teacher and World Government." In it he claimed, "In the struggle to establish an adequate world government, the teacher has many parts to play. He must begin with his own attitude and knowledge and purpose. He can do much to prepare the hearts and minds of children for global understanding and cooperation..."[650]

According to education scholar, Charlotte Iserbyt, former Senior Policy Advisor in the Office of Educational Research and Improvement in the U.S. Department of Education, "United States membership in... UNESCO in 1946 set in motion the destabilization of our society through the rejection of absolute morals and values, Judeo-Christian tradition, and Roman law."[651] Membership in UNESCO, continues Iserbyt, "marked the end of United States autonomy in a very crucial area: that of education. From this time on UNESCO would dictate education policy to our government..."[652]

Dr. Raymond Moore, author and educational expert warned about the use of institutional settings for the education of children at too early an age. Known as the Grandfather of Homeschooling, Dr. Moore was graduate programs officer with the Education Department at the beginning of Head Start. This federal program was instrumental in getting very small children out of home settings and into classrooms at historically record setting young ages.

Dr. Moore advocated that the most important thing that children need is to be in a loving, stable home environment for as long as possible in order to retain their parents' values and to become free thinkers. According to Dr. Moore, the real danger for children is peer dependence,

"Most children, before they get out of the 3rd or 4th grade today, are already tired of learning. They're on a motivational learning plateau and most of them never get off it. What we need to make as a bigger thing is the child's character traits. Is he responsible, is he dependable, is he orderly, does he have a sense of self-worth? This is the big thing; not that a child is dependent upon his peers.... [The system keeps] him in there just until he almost gets started then thrusts him out into the crowd way before he's ready.... He's thrown out into the group with other children, he's never given the chance to be an independent thinker.[653]

When the young child is thrust into formal, institutional educational settings before he is of an age to reason consistently from cause to effect, which is somewhere between 7 and 12 depending on the child, he is in grave danger of never being able to make decisions desirably on his own. Rather, he may fall prey to peer dependency—too many times creating a progressive in the process.

At an age when he is still learning manners and habits and correct speech content, he is thrown in with the other children and he learns from the other little children rather than his parents. Then he comes home with bad manners and doesn't understand the parents' attempts to alter this behavior which has made him acceptable to his new social group. This puts children at risk of rejecting the values parents want to instill. A child learning a good sense of self-worth is the essential dynamic of positive sociability. Dr. Moore said it is really very simple; "Let him start working as soon as he can start walking... putting his toys away... making the bed, etc. Read with the child, eat with the child, rest with the child... do life with the child."[654]

It is obvious that for the entities that have coopted American education in the past century, independent thinking is the LAST thing they want in a citizenry. Early on in our nation, character was developed in the home where families were in far better shape than they are now. We saw generations of independent, free thinkers who built on the solid foundation of our fledgling nation and made it into the strongest in human history, in innovation, in prosperity, in character, in opportunity and in freedom.

The breakdown of the traditional family has made this educational model advocated by Moore virtually impossible. Financial strains on families such as a poor economy and a high tax burden make it extremely difficult even for intact families to keep children in the home for any effective length of time.

11 – CORRUPTING EDUCATION, 1945-2012

With the entrance of the United Nations into the education process of America and the world, the restructuring of the American education process got underway in earnest—although initially it was not readily apparent. The education change artists realized that to be successful in plundering America, students had to first be deprogrammed and then reprogrammed to create the perfect global citizen—despite the child's native intelligence.

USING PSYCHOLOGY TO PROGRAM STUDENTS

A LEGION OF PSYCHOLOGISTS AND EDUCATORS advanced the goals and methodology of Dewey following World War II. In 1946, General Brock Chisholm, a Canadian psychiatrist and friend of Soviet agent and United Nations founder Alger Hess, began to attack the concept of right and wrong. In a paper published in *Psychiatry* in 1946 Chisholm wrote,

> We have swallowed all manner of poisonous certainties fed us by our parents, or Sunday and day school teachers. The results are frustration, inferiority, neurosis and inability to make the world fit to live in. The re-interpretation and eventually eradication of the concept of right and wrong, which has been the basis of child training, these are the belated objectives of practically all effective psychotherapy. Psychology and sociology should be taught to all children in primary and secondary schools, while the study of such things as trigonometry, Latin, religions and others of specialist concern should be left to universities. Only so can we help our children carry their responsibilities as world citizens.[655]

Chisholm presented the same message to the United Nations World Health Organization (WHO) the same year in a paper entitled "The Psychiatry of Enduring Peace and Social Progress."[656] Education specialist Charlotte Iserbyt notes in her book *The Deliberate Dumbing Down of America*, that it was "Brock Chisholm who recommended that teachers all over the world be trained in the 'no right/no wrong'" psychotherapeutic techniques. The concept permeates schools today and has led to, among other things, situational ethics.[657] With no boundaries is it any wonder that children are confused and resentful to the point of outright hatred of their parents when they try to establish boundaries?

The Skinner, Kinsey, Bloom Psychiatry Gang (1940s-1980s)

Like Dewey in the first half of the twentieth century, one man stood above all others—Burrhus Frederic Skinner (1904-1990). In 1945, Skinner became chairman of the Psychology Department of Indiana University where he joined long-term faculty member Alfred C. Kinsey. Foundations heavily funded both men, especially the Rockefeller Foundation.

By 1948, Professors Skinner and Kinsey published their books, Walden *Two* and *Sexual Behavior in the Human Male,* respectively. Skinner recommended, among other radical ideas, that children be reared by the state, to be trained from birth to demonstrate only desirable characteristics and behavior."[658] Kinsey "wrested human sexuality from the constraints of love and marriage in order to advance the grand scheme to move America and the world toward the eugenic future."[659]

In conjunction with the American Law Institute, Kinsey launched a national assault against sex crimes legislation. Again, funding came from the Rockefeller Foundation. They had a hit list of definitions of crimes they targeted for radical revision, including laws concerning prostitution, rape, sodomy, bestiality, incest, adultery, and pornography. In 1955, the American Law Institute developed the Model Penal Code based on Kinsey's repugnant research. Today, all of the code's references referring to data concerning sexual behavior cite Kinsey.

Kinsey "insisted that children could benefit from early sex, and even incest. He succeeded in demonizing the Judeo-Christian concept of sex only within marriage. By doing so, he opened the door to the sexual revolution and school sex education of the last half of the twentieth century."[660] Since 1955, lawyers and judges have cited Kinsey in case after case to overturn laws that protect us from criminal sex offenders. Even now, Kinsey is the most cited sex scientist in legal indices, including *Westlaw*, which is the most commonly used legal reference source in America. Kinsey's research has been discredited, at the least, as very bad science:

> The sample of test subjects that he used didn't come close to being random or representative. His sample consisted primarily of pedophiles, pederasts, convicts, pimps, and other sexually aggressive males whom he recruited at homosexual bars and bath houses. Their sexual behavior was recorded and then reported as being consistent with that of the average American male. The perpetrators of these acts are criminally culpable. Two generations of children have grown into adults who are horribly scarred because of the heinous perversions this man and his successors have promoted as science.[661]

In 1956 Professor Benjamin Bloom, the man known as 'the father of Outcome-Based Education (OBE)' and a contemporary of Kinsey and Skinner, published *Taxonomy of Educational Objectives*. Also funded by foundations, *Taxonomy of Educational Objectives* defined and classified learning behavior that broke behavior into measurable categories that deny the personality and spiritual side of a person. By doing so, they stripped students of their individuality.

Iserbyt notes that, "Bloom changed the focus of education from a general, liberal arts education which benefitted man as a whole to a narrow training which would be based on behavioral psychologists' determination of what changes in 'thoughts, feelings, and actions' would be desirable and, perhaps, necessary for the benefit of *society as a whole*."[662] (Italics original) It eventually led to BSTEP.

The ideas of Kinsey, Bloom and Skinner came together to eventually form "Mastery Learning" followed by "Outcome-Based Education," "Direct Instruction" (formally Goals 2000) and finally Schools to Work. In 1953 Skinner published Science and Human Behavior in which he said, "Operant conditioning shapes behavior as a sculptor shapes a lump of clay."[663]

Skinner's work with pigeons and rats provides the basis for operant conditioning. "When a bit of behavior is followed by a certain consequence, it is more likely to occur again, and a consequence having this effect is called a reinforcer."[664] Like Pavlov's conditioning of dogs, "anything the organism does that is followed by the receipt of food is more likely to be done again whenever the organism is hungry."[665]

Skinner insisted that the Pavolovian reinforcer had to be positive, not negative. Positive reinforcers will condition long-term responses, while negative reinforcers will only cause the desired response as long as the negative stimulus is applied. Modern-day examples of Skinner's positive reinforcers are the thousands of unconstitutional government benefits that have created the $15.8 trillion debt. Nearly 50 percent of the American population now depends at some level on government handouts.[666] These people typically vote for the candidate who promises even more benefits.

Conversely, the Soviet Union's KGB is an example of a negative reinforcer. If the Soviet citizen didn't conform, he or she often disappeared. By adopting positive reinforcement, the door was opened to systematically implement BSTEP with enormous success. However, remember the Soviet Union—the model progressives want to implement—also had cradle to grave benefits.

The problem of the Rousseau/Soviet model of governance is that it does not work. It never has. So just like the economy of the Soviet Union tanked under the Soviet model, the U.S. economy is stagnating as Obama imposes his Rousseau/Soviet model. Discontent naturally arises. Just like Rousseau recommended in his "Social Compact," the Soviet's solution was punishment by death or banishment to Siberia.[667] Hence the KGB. Although Obama has not done anything close to that draconian, numerous examples have been cited in this book that suggests he would if he could.

Perhaps one of the most telling examples of Obama's deftly hidden megalomania is his dressing down of the U.S. Supreme Court following oral arguments on March 26-28, 2012, in which the justices suggested Obamacare was unconstitutional. In response to a question on the oral arguments during a press conference on April 3, 2012, Obama said, "...I think the American people understand, and I think the Justices *should* understand that in the absence of an individual mandate you cannot have a mechanism to ensure people with preexisting conditions can actually get healthcare."[668]

Really? Obama telling the Supreme Court justices what they should/ must understand? The purpose of the Supreme Court is to determine whether a law is constitutional, not whether the intentions for the law were good or bad. The law's good intention is not up for consideration. The road to hell is paved with good intentions. But good intentions are everything for liberal progressives, including Obama. Their entire existence is based on good intentions, not reality. That's why we have a $15.8 trillion debt and a $118 trillion unfunded liability.

Obama then astonished even the mainstream press when he slammed the Supreme Court by saying its decision would be "unprecedented, extraordinary" by an "unelected group of people" who will have turned to "judicial activism or a lack of judicial restraint" if they decide to strike down Obamacare. Come again? This is exactly what the Supreme Court is supposed to decide. To say that it would be "unprecedented" is beyond belief. The Court has found more than 165 laws unconstitutional.[669]

Obama claims to be a constitutional lawyer. He knows better. This was a direct attack on the independence of the Supreme Court and clearly shows what Obama would do if he had the power of a king or dictator.

Obama's attack didn't go unanswered. The following day a three-judge panel of the Fifth Circuit Court of Appeals hearing an unrelated Obamacare case suddenly required the Department of Justice to submit a three-page, single-spaced letter within 48 hours on whether the Executive Branch believes that courts can strike down laws that are found to be unconstitutional. They treated Eric Holder and the Justice Department like an errant fifth grader who was being punished by having to write an essay.

The fiasco was so outrageous that Holder did quietly write the three pages. What the Fifth Circuit Court did was trite to be sure. Or was it? Obama had begun to act like a god whose very words were truth and law, and he needed to be called on it. The Fifth Court succeeded in doing that.

MARCHING TOWARDS BSTEP

AS NOTED IN CHAPTER 10, the findings of the 1953-54 Congressional Reece Committee were nothing short of astonishing.

The trustee minutes of the Carnegie Endowment subpoenaed by the Reece Committee revealed that the foundations did not want life to return to what it had been before the WWII. Carnegie asked the Rockefeller Foundation to assist in the monumental task of radically changing the direction of the nation. According to the Reece Committee Report: "They divided the task in parts, giving to the Rockefeller Foundation the responsibility of altering education as it pertains to domestic subjects, but Carnegie retained the task of altering our education in foreign affairs and about international relations."[670] Given the state of education today, they have wildly succeeded.

During a subsequent personal meeting between the committees' head, Norman Dodd and President Rowan Gaither of the Ford Foundation, Gaither made this stunning statement:

> Mr. Dodd, all of us here at the policy making level of the foundations have at one time or another served in the OSS [Office of Strategic Services, CIA forerunner] or the European Economic Administration, operating under directives from the White House. We operate under those same directives. The substance under which we operate is that we shall use our grant making power to so alter life in the United States that we can be comfortably merged with the Soviet Union." [671]

Dodd revealed this discussion publicly many times and eventually he was anonymously warned, "If you proceed with the investigation as you have outlined, you will be killed."[672] Although the Soviet Union has failed and is no longer here, the United States is rapidly approaching the goal Gaither had revealed. It is no surprise the U.S. is now facing the same problems that brought down the Soviet Union. Something to think about.

UNESCO, The Soviet Union and Mastery Learning

In 1960, Gaither's comment began to solidify in the publication of *Soviet Education Programs Foundations, Curriculums, Teacher Preparation* by William K. Medlin, specialist in Comparative Education for Eastern Europe, Division of International Education and others. It was written under the direction of the U.S. Department of Health, Education and Welfare Secretary Arthur S. Flemming and Office of Education Commissioner Lawrence G. Derthick:

> The ideas and practices of Soviet education form a philosophy of education in which the authoritarian concept predominates.... Major efforts of U.S.S.R schools during the past 30 years have been to train youngsters for the Government's planned economic programs to inculcate devotion to its political and social system. U.S.S.R plans are to bring all secondary school children into labor education and training experiences through the regular school

program. The "school of general education" is now named the "labor-polytechnic school of general education."

…Employing primarily the conditioned reflex theory as elaborated by Pavlov (1849-1936), Soviet psychologists have worked out a system of didactics which are strict and fixed in their conception and application. School children and students are engaged in a total education program which aims to teach all the same basic subjects, morals and habits in order to provide society with future workers and employees whose general education will make them socialist [Communist] citizens and contribute to their productivity upon learning a vocation [profession].[673]

Education specialist Charlotte Iserbyt notes that those "familiar with the details of American school-to-work restructuring will see that the United States is adopting the Soviet polytechnic system. The Pavolovian conditioned reflex theory' discussed is the Skinnerian mastery learning/ direct instruction method required in order to implement outcome-based education and school-to-work."[674]

Since its creation in 1946, UNESCO was also busy in restructuring education using the Skinner-Kinsey-Bloom models. UNESCO had much to do with incorporating Kinsey's sexual perversions into American education by sponsoring the International Symposium on Health Education, Sex Education and Education for Home and Family Living in Hamburg, Germany, in 1964. At this UN meeting, the participants concluded that sex education was necessary at an early age because children rarely learn about sex in their own homes.[675]

Within months of the Hamburg meeting, Sexuality Information and Education Council of the United States (SIECUS) was formed and evolved into the "most influential provider of sex education material in the country."[676] SIECUS still exists and although it seems benign, it advocates extreme and licentious sexual practices.

According to SIECUS, educational material should teach adolescents that their sexual orientation, by definition, "describes one's erotic, romantic and affectional attraction to the same gender, the opposite gender, or both."[677] Sex education should therefore "provide an opportunity for young people to question, explore, and assess their sexual attitudes in order to develop their values, increase self-esteem, develop insights concerning relationships with members of both genders, and understand their obligations and responsibilities to others."[678]

On December 6, 2011, U.S. Secretary of State Hillary Clinton gave a speech at the United Nations meeting on International Human Rights, laying out President Obama's new, aggressive campaign to promote Lesbian, Gay, Bisexual and Transgendered (individuals) "LGBT rights" worldwide. In her speech, she actually compared this move by Obama to the historic fight to end slavery and apartheid.[679] It was no accident that on the same day, President Obama issued a memorandum commanding all U.S. government agencies that engage in any international activities to make advancing "LGBT rights" in the countries where they work a major priority.[680]

This new presidential memorandum purports to be merely an effort to prevent violence against LGBT individuals, which would be considered by most to be a noble cause. One need only look at what Obama has already done to know that it won't stop there;

- "In order to celebrate the U.S.'s "Gay Pride" month in June, the U.S. Embassy in Pakistan held a "Gay Pride" event to promote LGBT rights in Pakistan. This was understandably seen as an overt attack on Muslim culture. The event initiated major protests throughout Pakistan and fueled anti-American sentiment in the Middle East. Government leaders in Pakistan said the event was an act of "cultural terrorism."

- "In one of the first official acts Obama made after taking office he signed on January 23, 2009 an order to direct U.S. funds to organizations that perform and promote abortion overseas. In this directive, Obama overturned the so-called "Mexico City Policy," a vital pro-life policy that had been advocated by presidents before him back to 1961. This move put millions of tax-payer dollars into the hands of organizations that provide abortions overseas.[681]

Progressive LGBT activists around the world are vehemently trying to remove all laws protecting traditional marriage between one man and one woman, saying that prohibition of same-sex marriages is a violation of human rights. They say the same of laws requiring a traditional family model for adopted children. And these activists insist upon the instruction of even very young school children in the knowledge and inclusion of homosexual behavior as acceptable and normal. The same agenda that has been successful here will be pushed in other countries, regardless of the cultural or moral beliefs of the people in that nation;

- "Decriminalizing homosexual behavior in the 70 countries where it is illegal. (This is necessary to be able to implement the rest of this list below because once homosexual sex is legal, people can pressure governments for special rights based on that behavior. As long as it remains illegal, at least as a civil offense, the rest of the LBGT agenda can never be realized.)
- Prohibiting discrimination against LGBT people in housing or employment, regardless of the nature of the job.
- Enacting "hate crimes" laws that criminalize criticism of same-sex behavior.
- Legalizing civil unions or domestic partnerships.
- Legalizing same-sex marriages.
- Legalizing same-sex adoption.
- Mandating comprehensive sexuality education in public schools, which teaches children that homosexual behavior is healthy and normal." [682]

Make no mistake. It is a done deal in the U.S. This is the agenda LGBT activists want pushed worldwide, and Obama is using tax dollars to see it done.

God is Dead, Mastery Learning and Outcome-Based Education

Out of this primeval soup, Mastery Learning began to take shape using Skinner and Bloom's model. Certain stimuli can change children in predictable ways to optimize their abilities to obtain certain skills. The education change artists sold the concept on the basis that every child can learn—eventually. But learn what? Certainly not facts as is done in the traditional liberal arts education. Instead, the public school system increasingly subjects students to the psychological process of behavior modification to a new way of thinking by manipulating their emotions and systematically indoctrinating them into the desired world view. [683]

In spite of the spreading of socialism through our schools and the all-out attack on literacy, somehow good teachers still managed to provide students the basics of a decent education. Test scores were fairly high; students were basically moral and decent. Then something happened on June 25, 1962, and June 17, 1963, that drastically changed all that—the Supreme Court officially took God out of the school in *Engel v. Vitale*[684] and *Abington School Dist. v. Schempp.*[685]

The Court decisions specifically forbid school sponsored prayer and Bible readings. It was not long, however, before the schools forbade any expression of religion. This has had an enormous effect, not only on our schools, but also on the whole nation.[686] The explosion in drug use, unrestrained sex, teenage pregnancies, plummeting SAT scores, and a host of other social ills that are now common in 2012 can all be traced to 1962-63 when the global elites finally got God out of the school.

The dumbing down of the American education system to create the compliant citizen took a leap forward when the education change artists took control of education within the U.S. Department of Health, Education and Welfare (HEW). In 1965, HEW funded the "The Behavioral Science Teacher Education Program (BSTEP) at Michigan State University discussed in Chapter 1 and 9.

Reading the goals of this anti-American program is not for the faint-hearted and is sickening to the average American. BSTEP's "purpose was to change the teacher from a transmitter of knowledge/content to a social change agent/facilitator/clinician"[687] by applying Skinner's theories. A small segment of its purpose was given in Chapter 1. Below is a more complete version:

> The program is designed to focus the skills and knowledge of Behavioral Scientists on education problems, translating research into viable programs for pre-service and in-service teachers.[688] *Calculations of the future and how to modify it are no longer considered obscure academic pursuits.* Instead, they are the business of many who are concerned about and responsible for devising various modes of social change. We are getting closer to developing effective methods for shaping the future and are advancing *in fundamental social and individual evolution.*[689] (Italics added)

Long-range planning and implementation of plans will be made by a technological-scientific elite. This will *strain the democratic fabric to a ripping point.* The Protestant Ethic will atrophy as more and more enjoy varied leisure and guaranteed sustenance. Work as the means and end of living will diminish. No major source of a sense of worth and dignity will replace the Protestant Ethic. *Most people will tend to be hedonistic, and a dominant elite will provide 'bread and circuses' to keep social dissension and disruption at a minimum.* A small elite will carry society's burdens. *The resulting impersonal manipulation of most people's lifestyles will be softened by provisions for pleasure-seeking and guaranteed physical necessities.*[690] (Italics added)

The use of the systems approach to problem solving and of cybernetics to manage automation *will remold the nation.* Most of the population *will seek meaning through other means or devote themselves to pleasure seeking.* The *controlling elite will engage in power plays largely without the involvement of most of the people.* The society will be a leisurely one. People will study, play, and travel; *some will be in various stages of the drug-induced experiences.*[691] (Italics added)

Each individual will receive at birth a multipurpose identification which will have, among other things, extensive communications uses. None will be out of touch with those authorized to reach him. Routine jobs to be done in any setting can be initiated automatically by those responsible for the task; all will be in constant communication with their employers, or other controllers, and thus exposed to direct and subliminal influence. Each individual will be saturated with ideas and information. Some will be self-selected; other kinds will be imposed overtly by those who assume responsibility for others' actions. *Relatively few individuals will be able to maintain control over their opinions. Most will be pawns of competing opinion molders.*[692] (Italics added for emphasis)

Remember, HEW and many major institutions, key universities and corporations funded this report. It was written in 1969 after four years of study. With a controlled media, Digital Angel,[a, 693] the Internet, the FBI's Carnivore,[694] NSA's Echelon and its spinoffs,[695] the Patriot and Homeland Security Acts, plus a host of other new technologies[696] and laws that diminish our civil liberties, most of the report's goals are reality today. Just as predicted, the strain is bringing our "democratic fabric to the ripping point."

The National Education Association

As BSTEP evolved after 1967, the NEA declared war on the American people. Its executive secretary arrogantly, but accurately proclaimed: "NEA will become a political power second to no other special interest group... NEA will organize this profession from top to bottom into logical operational units that can move swiftly and effectively and with power unmatched by any other organized group in the nation."[697] The NEA is coming closer and closer to that goal, and is now the most powerful and largest labor union within the Democratic Party.

Since its inception in Philadelphia in 1857, the NEA has assisted in every way possible to push ahead the globalization and psycho manipulation coup d'état of U.S. public education. Largely funded by the Rockefeller Foundation and Carnegie Corporation,[698] the NEA's goal was always to establish a national, then a global system of education. The NEA reaffirmed this in its 1976 U.S. Bicentennial report entitled *A Declaration of Interdependence: Education for a Global Community*, "We are committed to the idea of Education for Global Community. You are invited to help turn the commitment into action and mobilizing world education for development of a world community."

The NEA's ideal centers on the Prussian system as refined by Hegel from Rousseau and other like philosophers discussed in the Chapter 10. Along with UNESCO, the NEA was deeply involved in developing Mastery Learning in the 1970s to mold the student into a global citizen.

---

[a] Digital Angel is a microchip the size of a grain of rice inserted under the skin. It can record a person's entire life history and allow satellite tracking of the person's every movement. It is a nightmare greater than George Orwell's *1984*, and yet most Americans are completely ignorant of what is happening. Because of this unawareness, the American people are doing exactly what this study projected they would do in less than forty years. The Behaviorists and Humanists who are rapidly becoming the major directors of public education are creating this nightmare.

Tremendous opposition to it arose as critics began to help parents understand what it really meant in the 1970s and early 1980s. Rather than abandoning this immoral program, however, the change artists merely repackaged it under the name Outcome-Based Education (OBE).

These change artists hoped that OBE would be more acceptable by shifting the focus from the psychological manipulative process to reprogram the student, to the "outcomes" of the psycho-manipulation. When parents learned of that deception, the name was changed yet again to Direct Instruction. It became fully integrated into former President Clinton's Goals 2000, President Bush's No Child Left Behind and Obama's Race to the Top. It is the same wolf dressed in sheep's clothing. Education expert Berit Kjos explains the strategy:

> To stay ahead of the critics, leading educators keep changing the labels. Thus, what many know as Outcome-Based Education, or OBE, is also called Quality Learning, Total Quality School Restructuring, Performance- or Achievement-based Education. Whatever the label, it refers primarily to the national/international system that demands specific "outcomes" from students and uses the psychological strategies of Mastery Learning to achieve the planned result.[699]

THE UN WORLD CORE CURRICULUM AND GOALS 2000

DURING THE 1970S, the works of Skinner, Bloom, and Kinsey exploded into a broad front to totally restructure American and global education. In 1978, former Undersecretary General of the United Nations Robert Muller, and social anthropologist and new age guru Margaret Mead, challenged the people of the world to prepare for the year 2000 by a "worldwide collaborative process of unparalleled thinking, education and planning for a just and sustainable human world order."[700]

Mead's challenge led to the creation of the U.S. Department of Education in 1978 with the committed help of the NEA, and the eventual development of the United Nations World Core Curriculum program. It also spawned the Project Global 2000 in the United Nations and the America 2000/Goals 2000 program in the United States. In 1981, the World Bank committed $900 million a year to this education and training.[701]

The global agenda for education began to accelerate in 1985. First, "the U.S. Department of State gave the Carnegie Corporation authority to negotiate with the Soviet Academy of Sciences, known to be an intelligence-gathering arm of the KGB, regarding 'curriculum development and the restructuring of American education.'"[702] The same year, the Netherlands hosted a twelve-nation international-curriculum symposium in November.

According to the introduction to the World Core Curriculum, the purpose is to, "Assist the child in becoming an integrated individual who can deal with personal experience while seeing himself as part of 'the greater whole.'" In other words, promote collectivism so that group good, group understanding, group interrelations and group goodwill replace all limited, self-centered objectives, leading to group consciousness." That, of course, is exactly the goal of the Rousseau-Hegel model throughout the book.

In 1987 the Rockefeller, Ford and Exxon Foundations funded a study called the Commission on Global Education,[703] which included (then) Governor Bill Clinton, Professor John Goodlad of the Carnegie Foundation for the Advancement of Teaching, and Frank Newman, president of the Education Commission of the United States.

With Arkansas Governor Clinton on board, the tables were set to carry out OBE. But the elite needed one more key step. In 1989, President George H. W. Bush convened the National Governors' Association (NGA) Education Summit at the University of Virginia in Charlottesville, Virginia. The NGA unveiled America 2000, now known as Goals 2000, and its six national education goals. These six goals were later increased to eight.[704] While these goals seemed noble and based in traditional education, in fact the fine print still enabled OBE with links into the World Core Curriculum.

Shirley McCune, Senior Director with MCREL (Mid-continent Regional Educational Laboratory, a curriculum developer) claimed; "What's happening in America today is a total *transformation of our society*. We have moved into a new era. I am not sure we have really begun to comprehend the incredible amount of organizational restructuring and human resource development restructuring. *What the revolution has been in curriculum is that we **no longer are teaching facts** to children.*"[705] (Italics & bold added)

Education expert Berit Kjos laments in her book *Brave New Schools*, "In the absence of foundational facts, those *higher-order thinking skills* can only lead to subjective uncertain answers. Without a broad knowledge base, children are rudderless and headed for disaster. Deprived of the factual comprehension needed for moral, spiritual and intellectual discernment, they cannot recognize deception." The fact that 45 percent of the American people in a January 12-14, 2012 Fox News poll believe Obama is doing a good job,[706] when in fact he is driving America into the ground testifies as to how easy it is to deceive so many people.

When the same people in the Fox News poll were asked if they were satisfied in the way things were going, the satisfied rating only dropped to 40 percent.[707] The only possible reason for this is that 40-45 percent belongs to the 49 percent of the population that receive government benefits in a substantial way.[708]

The Dangers of OBE and Goals 2000

During Clinton's presidency America 2000 was renamed Goals 2000. Goals 2000 seeks to create the perfect global citizen for the twenty-first century. The right attitudes, beliefs and behaviors replace academics as the main outcome of education.[709]

Benjamin Bloom developed taxonomically ranked facts and knowledge at the bottom of his evaluation system, effectively making them lower-order thinking skills. Reading, English, math and other traditional subjects were relatively insignificant in his taxonomy. In contrast, he ranked subjective processes application, analysis, synthesis, and evaluation at the highest level, making them higher-order thinking skills.[710] Emotion reigns.

How does a student analyze, synthesize, and evaluate without the facts, especially when the information contradicts what parents have taught them at home? They can't. The purpose is to create conflict in the student. The deliberate strategy to create conflict and discomfort about what is being taught as right in school and what the parents have taught causes cognitive dissonance. It is designed to make the student more susceptible to the subjective conditioning being given by the teacher. In other words, it is manipulation and the teacher may even be unaware of it.

For instance, parents might teach their children that sex is something reserved for marriage, while the school *will* teach that sex outside of marriage is perfectly normal and acceptable. This sets up a dissonance that must be resolved. Since the teenager is told premarital sex is natural, which is supported by his or her raging hormones, what they are taught by the school wins. It also provides one more reason their parents are clueless and unreasonable, and no one the teenager should pay attention to.

Following World War II, the whole language method of teaching reading had spread across America. Today it is the most "widely used method of teaching reading in the U.S.;"[711] replacing the proven technique of learning the alphabet and then phonetically sounding out a word. It literally involves the student memorizing every word in the English language in order to spell it.[712] With whole language reading becomes a chore. Unless a child had previously memorized all the words in a sentence, the student had no way of understanding what it was phonetically because he or she possesses no tools to decipher non-memorized words.

Predictably, reading ability and literacy began a long downward spiral in America that continues today. By the 1990s, the whole language method had dumbed down so many children, and caused more who subsequently hated to read, that programs like "Hooked On Phonics" became overnight best sellers as desperate parents tried to find some way to get their kids interested in reading. Parents were amazed; phonics worked miracles for many, if not most of their kids.

Amazingly, phonics is not a new method. It merely reaffirms a program that had been taught to their great grandparents and it worked! But for those students forced to use the whole language approach, reading became frustrating. They turned to television & video games for entertainment to numb their minds. In the process, television, videos and games desensitized them to sex and violence. The systematic deconstruction of America's public education system by progressive change artists can only be described as diabolical.

Federal Takeover of Education in 1994

In 1994, Congress signed into law H.R. 1804, Goals 2000 Act,[713] H.R. 2884, the School-to-Work Opportunities Act [714] and H.R. 6, Elementary and Secondary Education Acts.[715] In 1995, they passed companion legislation H.R. 1617, The CAREERS Act.[716] All passed with strong Republican support.

Space does not permit an in-depth review of the mind-bending results of these bills. To provide a flavor of just how they revolutionized education in American, H.R. 6 states:

(1)(A) The Secretary [of Education] is authorized to carry out a program to enhance the third and sixth National Education Goals [of Goals 2000] by educating students about the history and principles

216

of the United States, including the Bill of Rights, and to foster civic competence and responsibility.[717]

The federal government now controls the teaching (or lack of teaching) of history and civil rights via testing. Specifically H.R. 6 stated that federal control would be administered through a non-governmental organization (NGO) called the Center for Civic Education, "(B) Such programs shall be known as *'We the People: The citizen and the Constitution'*…[and shall be] administered by the Center for Civic Education…"[718]

In other words, a single NGO now controls the entire curricula covering the U.S. Constitution, the Bill of Rights and civics—by law! Allen Quist, three-term Minnesota legislator serving on the House Education Committee and currently a professor of political science at Bethany Lutheran College, laments:

This single organization would dictate what was true and what was important in these academic areas. There would be no review of its dictates by Congress. There would be no review of its dictates by American citizens. Our schools would have nothing to say about what this one group determined was true and important regarding civics and government. One organization (NGO) would determine the new National Curriculum in these areas, and no one else would have anything to say about it.[719]

Remember, H.R. 6 was passed overwhelmingly by Republicans. Worse, similar language authorizing and funding the Center for Civic Education to continue its control of the federal curriculum was in President Bush's "No Child Left Behind" education bill in 2002. What does *We the People: The Citizen and the Constitution* say? Page 207 of the book states:

As fundamental and lasting as its guarantees have been, the Bill of Rights is a document of the eighteenth century, reflecting the issues and concerns of the age in which it was written.

When written in this way it does not take a rocket scientist to realize that a student who has little, if any, knowledge of the importance of the Bill of Rights will assume it is no longer relevant to today's society. The twist and distortion is obvious. *We the People* does not mention national sovereignty once in the book. It does, however, extensively promote the concept of the global village and world citizenship in Lesson 37 for high school students. Lesson 40 on page 214 even encourages the student to challenge the foundational principles of the U.S. Constitution that have made the United States the greatest nation in the world,

> The Founders, themselves, were vigorous critics of the wisdom they inherited and the principles in which they believed. They were articulate, opinionated individuals who loved to examine ideas, to analyze, argue and debate them. They expected no less of future generations. They would expect no less of you.

We the People provides only one side of the information needed to challenge the foundational principles of the United States. It leads the student to believe the U.S. Constitution and unalienable rights are disposable relics to be replaced by positive rights. Therefore, the only rights Americans should have are those defined by the federal government. How can a student possibly analyze and debate the foundational principles when they receive no information on why these principles might be critically important?

It should therefore be no surprise that the *National Standards for Civics and Government* written by the Center for Civic Education are so biased that they can be described as little more than propaganda. The material references environmentalism 17 times, multiculturalism 42 times, First Amendment (especially separation of church and state) 81 times, and references the Second Amendment 0 times. [720]

Regardless of the reader's position on gun control, the Second Amendment is one of the Bill of Rights and a discussion of the reasons it was included should be included in any textbook discussing the Bill of Rights. This glaring omission distorts any historical discussion of the founding documents of the United States and predisposes the student to anti-gun propaganda. Why is the Second Amendment not included? Political science professor Allen Quist states: "The purpose of the Federal Curriculum is to indoctrinate, not to inform."[721]

In summary, Eagle Forum's president, Phyllis Schlafly, warned these laws were intended to restructure the public schools by:

- Bypassing all elected officials on school boards and in state legislatures by making federal funds flow to the Governor and his appointees on workforce development boards.

- Using a computer database, a.k.a. "a labor market information system," into which school personnel would scan all information about every schoolchild and his family, identified by the child's social security number: academic, medical, mental, psychological, behavioral, and interrogations by counselors. The computerized data would be available to the school, the government, and future employers.

- Using "national standards" and "national testing" to cement national control of tests, assessments, school honors and rewards, financial aid, and the Certificate of Initial Mastery (CIM), which is designed to replace the high school diploma.[722]

GOODBYE HISTORY AND MATH

ONE OF THE CASUALTIES OF OBE and Goals 2000 is U.S. history. Cutting off a student from his or her cultural and historical roots makes it much easier to manipulate the student using Skinner's methods. The pride and history of a nation is what creates patriotism, which is hard to overcome when attempting to create the global citizen. Therefore, education change artists must minimize national pride, history and patriotism.

This shows up in dismal history scores. In the 2010 National Assessment of Educational Progress called the Nation's Report Card—found that just 13 percent of high school seniors who took the test showed solid academic performance in American history. Fourth-grade students did slightly better at just 22 percent, while eighth graders scored at only 18 percent proficient or better.[723] It is hard to believe that is exactly the goal of these progressive change artists.

In spite of a few victories, this dumbing-down agenda has affected all core subject areas—including geography. A year and a half after the tragedy of 9-11, as the U.S. was readying to go to war with Iraq, a National Geographic survey found that only 14 percent of Americans aged between 18 and 24 could even find Iraq or Iran on a map. While 58 percent knew about Afghanistan, only 17 percent could find it on a world map![724] Only half of the students could find New York and 11 percent could not find the U.S. on the map. How can our youth begin to understand the global geopolitics that threatens their future if they cannot even find New York City—where cave-dwelling hate-filled barbarians living some 10,000 miles away snuffed out nearly 3,000 precious lives? This is more than tragic. It is despicable.

By distorting or teaching false history, it drives a wedge between parents and children. Poll after poll shows American adults still believe in God, but their children learn that Judeo-Christian values are either incorrect or have failed us, and it is time to discard the old beliefs and adopt the correct view—that of earth-centered cultures.[725]

The insidious Skinner psycho manipulation perpetrated on our children has also affected science and math skills. By 2007 (the last comparable data available), however, the United States ranked 15th out of 16 in advanced math skills and 16th out of 16 in science skills in the Trends in International Mathematics and Science Study (TIMSS).[726]

The 2011 National Center for Education Statistics' "Condition of Education 2011" report showed 15-year-olds in the U.S. scored 23rd out of 34 nations having advanced economies in math literacy. The same 15-year-olds scored only slightly better in science literacy, 12th out of 34.[727] Considering that the U.S. used to be at the top in these areas illustrates how dumbed down math and science has become.

This dismal performance came in spite of huge increases in education spending at local, state and federal levels. Jay P. Greene, with the Manhattan Institute's Education Research Office, reports in his book, *Education Myths: What Special-Interest Groups Want You to Believe About Our Schools—and Why It Isn't So,* "Inflation-adjusted per-pupil public school spending has doubled in the past thirty years, but test scores and graduation rates are flat. Public schools spent much more money on education, but they taught less."

According to an Eagle Forum *Education Report* "A comparison study of California math and science textbooks between 1963 and 1988 found that, over the 25-year period, *7th-grade textbooks moved up to the 9th grade.* The later textbooks were more colorful and 'slick,' but the content had been watered down."[728]

NO CHILD LEFT BEHIND

THE ELECTION OF GEORGE W. BUSH to the presidency in 2000 initially heartened those against OBE. However, President Bush passed into law the granddaddy of all federal education laws, the No Child Left Behind Act of 2001. The Act proposed to achieve this lofty goal by making schools *accountable to the federal government* by controlling testing. Sen. Paul Wellstone (D-MN) called the bill "a stunning federal mandate" that strikes at "the essence of local control." Teachers have dubbed the law the "No Teacher Left Standing Act" because of the mountain of paperwork it requires.

Education analysts note that Leave No Child Behind Act continues a failed strategy that began with President Lyndon Johnson's "Great Society" in 1965. Johnson's program promised to "close the gap" between achieving and non-achieving students. Eagle Forum President Phyllis Schlafly wrote, "Even though the government's own evaluations prove that billions of dollars have produced no measurable results, this law's only approach is still more federal spending and control."[729] "The problem remains," writes Eagle Forum Legislative Director Lori Waters, "that whoever controls the test controls the curriculum, and schools will be held accountable to the federal government, not parents."[730]

Federal intrusion into U.S. education has been a disaster. In the period between 1970 and 2012 the Department of Education will have spent $1.4 trillion.[731] The result? Plummeting SAT scores for public schools.[732] SAT scores have fallen an incredible 18 points since 2006, the first year of No Child Left Behind.[733] In 2011 only 43 percent of public school students taking the test met the 1550 combined score that most colleges use for admission, the lowest ever.

The only exceptions to this growing education tragedy are home schooled kids and a few teachers, schools and school districts that still teach, or try to teach classical education. These fortunate kids excel in education and exhibit respect for others compared to their OBE and Goals 2000 public school-educated peers.

Homeschooled students typically score 15 to 30 percentile points above public school students on standardized academic achievement tests—regardless of their parents' level of education.[734] Homeschooled kids score so much higher in SAT exams that the public school system refuses to include homeschooled student scores in their SAT overall statistics. Why? Homeschooled children are more successful because they learn by using the proven, historical approach to education.

No longer does America have an education system that imparts knowledge of languages, math, scientific reasoning, history and literature. The federally manipulated public education today focuses on feelings, belongingness, positive self-esteem, group will, sexual freedom, obedience to the state, political correctness and becoming a global citizen. Neocon Republican presidents since Reagan have promised to eliminate the U.S. Department of Education. Instead, its budget keeps getting bigger and bigger.

U.S. citizens must ask a basic question. Why are all these highly educated "experts" so willing to corrupt America's public education system when it is blatantly obvious that it is destroying kids? In the 1950s and 60s the worst problems we had in the school were the kids shooting spit wads and the occasional fight after school. Today kids are shooting other kids, suicide has become the number one killer of teens and anything-goes-sex is the norm. Meanwhile, test scores are plummeting. Even a casual observer can see this.

If the progressive education change artists really thought what they were doing was so good, why did they keep it secret from the American people? Why did they lie to the American people about their goal of creating a socialist state out of a constitutional republic of free citizens? Can raw arrogance and super-sized egos explain it? Or, are they deceived and deluded. Or, do they have an agenda knowing full well what they are doing?

Certainly, most progressives are arrogant and seem to be delusional. But most are very intelligent. There is no way of knowing for sure, but at least some of the so-called progressive "experts" have to know they are deliberately destroying our youth.

12 – AGENDA 21

By the last half of the twentieth century the global financial cartel was gradually exerting more and more influence over the federal government, education and finance. Two major roadblocks remained that prevented them from shifting the Locke form of constitutional and limited government to Rousseau's state-controlled socialist government that would allow the unimpeded plundering of America.

The first problem involved the millennia-old tactic of creating a fear of war as a mechanism to focus a population's efforts in a direction that benefited the nation's power elite. The threat of war originates from real or contrived animosities between two nations. Kings and tyrants over the millennia have used this strategy to refocus their nation's population from internal problems to an external threat. However, if a peaceful world government were instituted, the threat of war would evaporate as an tool that could distract the population's attention. A substitute was required.

The second problem was the Constitutional protection of private property. As discussed in Chapter 2, private property is essential to the creation of liberty and wealth. It was therefore an obstacle to the Rousseau model of state control over the people and their resources. As explained in my previous book, *Rescuing a Broken America*, the global elite looked at a variety of mechanisms in the late 1960s to replace the threat of war as a mechanism to keep the general population under control. What they found was that the threat of environmental destruction was more than sufficient to convince a mostly urban dumbed-down population that we were destroying the environment, and humanity along with it.

Suddenly, the focus of the nation quickly turned to the environment. Congress passed the National Environmental Policy Act in 1969 and the Clean Air Act in 1970, the same year it created the Environmental Protection

Agency (EPA). The Clean Water Act passed in 1972 with a stronger version in 1977, and the Endangered Species Act passed in 1973—along with dozens of other environmental laws following Rousseau's statist philosophies. Just as predicted by Carroll Quigley and planned by the BSTEP education program, every one of these laws put the future of America into the hands of planning technocrats. Quigley's "managerial society"[735] was born.

As with education activism, the big foundations began to pour hundreds of millions of dollars annually into environmental activism to achieve the progressive concept of environmental justice. This has created one of the most powerful political forces in the twentieth century alongside the National Education Association (NEA), SEIU and ACORN. Federal agencies also began to fund environmental organizations through a host of federal projects.

By the mid-1990s, the Boston Globe estimated the combined revenue for environmental groups was $4 *billion* annually, dwarfing any organized opposition.[736] Today, federal spending on global warming alone is $4-5 billion a year. Meanwhile the well-oiled propaganda machine ensured that the public's perception was that environmentalists were underpaid souls defending the environment from evil corporations.

Not all of this was bad. America's rivers and air are much cleaner today than in the early 1970s. People do need to protect the environment. The question is how best to do it. Rousseau's model of state control and forced compliance formed the basis of nearly all federal environmental laws passed since 1967. If instead of using the Rousseau model, Congress used the Locke model, the same results may have been legally attainable without the loss of private property rights and usurpation of local and state sovereignty by the federal government.[a]

THE BIRTH OF AGENDA 21

IT WAS CLEAR RIGHT FROM THE START that there was a deliberate effort by the elite to shift control of property rights from the individual to the state or federal government. David Rockefeller co-founded the Club of Rome in

---

[a] To understand better the Locke approach to sustainable development and a point by point comparison to *Agenda 21* read the *Freedom 21; Promoting Sustainability through Political and Economic Freedom*. http://www.freedom21agenda.org/Freedom21Agenda.pdf

1968.[737] The Club of Rome published *Limits to Growth* in 1972, which called for severe limits on human population and the control of all development in the world to achieve "sustainable development." Sustainable development was eventually formalized into a United Nations global action plan called *Agenda 21*, which President Bush committed the U.S. to at the 1992 Earth Summit in Rio de Janeiro.

David Rockefeller also co-founded the Trilateral Commission in 1973, another globalist group dedicated to world government. At the same time Laurence Rockefeller commissioned and led the study entitled *Use of Land: A Citizen's Policy Guide to Urban Growth* that was published in 1973. The nationally based *Use of Land* was a companion to the Club of Rome's internationally based *Limits of Growth*. The *Use of Land* was edited by William Reilly, who would later be appointed by George H. W. Bush as the administrator of the Environmental Protection Agency in 1989. A third effort was achieved by Nelson Rockefeller, New York's Governor, to create the Adirondack Park Agency, which was patterned exactly after the *Use of Land*.

Although utterly evil, the Rockefeller's effort to destroy the constitutional basis of property rights was brilliant. The thrust of the *Use of Land* report supported the premise that development rights of private property should be at the discretion of the government for the "good of society:"

"Landowners expect to be able to develop their property as they choose, even at the expense of scenic, ecological, and cultural assets treasured by the public....[However], with private property rights go obligations that *society can define and property owners should respect.*"[738] (Italics added)

This verbiage could be ripped from the pages of Rousseau's description of the general will in his *Social Contract*, Book 1. The government, not the individual should define the property rights permitted the individual. Environmental protection would occur "not by purchase but through the police power of the federal government." The *Use of Land* then goes on to say,

It is time that the U.S. Supreme Court re-examine its precedents that seem to require a balancing of public benefit against value loss in every case and declare that, when the protection of natural, cultural, or aesthetic resources or the assurance of orderly development are involved, a mere loss in land value is no justification for invalidating the regulation of land use.[739]

Think about this for a moment. *Use of Land* recommends that the Supreme Court throw away 200 years of constitutional law to justify constantly changing regulatory law. This new interpretation of the Constitution would allow the government to pass laws and create legislation at the whim of some arbitrary natural, cultural, or even aesthetic reason.

Wait a minute! Isn't that what most environmental laws in the past 50 years are based on? Not only that, but the book's recommendations are precisely what the Supreme Court has done since the book was published. Page after page of the *Use of Land* describes what has happened to create the Rousseau model of state control today.

Federal land use legislation was introduced in Congress in the mid-1970s based on the *Use of Land* to implement government control over all land use in the nation. They all failed; primarily because most Republicans and Democrats still had enough constitutional knowledge to realize the federal government should *never* be allowed to control land use.

The Adirondack Park Template

Concurrent to the writing of *Use of Land* and the failure to pass legislation, Laurence Rockefeller teamed up with his brother, New York Governor Nelson Rockefeller, to launch a study in 1968 that led to the creation of the Adirondack Park Agency (APA) in upstate New York three years later.

Laurence Rockefeller provided foundation funding to a dozen activist environmental organizations which joined to form the Adirondack Council in Upstate New York. In turn, the council demanded state control over land-use in the Adirondacks. At the same time, Governor Nelson Rockefeller provided the political hammer to force the APA bill through the legislature.

To cap it off, the progressive New York Times promoted blatantly false propaganda to a largely ignorant, but politically powerful urban majority in New York City. The New York Times falsely asserted that unless the APA Act passed immediately, development would overrun the Adirondacks. Although over 80 percent of the Adirondack citizens were against the bill, the cartel's machine prevailed and the APA Act passed in 1971.

This "unless we do it now the world is going to end" Hegelian Dialectic is standard operating procedure for the cartel specifically, and progressive liberals in general. Two recent successes are TARP in 2008 and the Stimulus Bill in 2009.

The APA perfectly reflects the *Use of Land* and Rousseau model of state control of private property. It controls all land-use activity on private property within the 6.1 million acre blue line of the park boundary. Fifty-five percent of that is private property. The Act dictates the number of acres required per home (up to forty acres per home), all new home construction or renovations, and a host of regulations that have stifled most development.

Except in the exempted cities and communities, driving through the Adirondacks today is like driving through a 1960s landscape. Urban New Yorkers who want a bucolic experience may love the effect in order to sooth their hyper-stressed nerves, but the APA has locked the Adirondack citizens into a Rousseau socialist time warp that has denied them the rights enjoyed by other American citizens. The raw ugly power of the APA used on the citizens of the Adirondacks would shock most Americans.

Intoxicated by the successful effort to control land development in the Adirondacks, the APA model became the template for what is now called sustainable development and environmental justice across America and around the world. Without knowing it, residents of the New Jersey Pinelands had the APA template applied with the creation of the New Jersey Pinelands Commission in 1978. Likewise, residents of the Columbia River Gorge in Oregon had the APA model forced on them with the creation of the Columbia River Gorge National Scenic Area in 1986.

The federal government then attempted a two pronged effort in the 1990s to advance the APA model on a regional scale. The Northeast had the Northern Forest Lands encompassing 20 million acres almost forced on them by the federally driven Northern Forest Lands Council. At the same time, the federal government attempted to swallow up the entire Interior Columbia River basin with the proposed Interior Columbia Basin Ecosystem Management Project (ICBEMP) during the Clinton Administration.

ICBEMP is the biggest effort to date, encompassing most of Washington, Oregon and Idaho as well as portions of Montana and Utah. Both the Northern Forest Lands Council and ICBEMP were eventually rejected by the people, but neither has been fully deactivated. They live on like latent cancer cells waiting for the moment they can once again metastasize.

Smart Growth/Comprehensive Planning

Smart growth is another means of attempting to control property rights in urban areas. Like the Adirondack Park Agency, smart growth had its origins with the *Use of Land*. Not surprisingly, the same foundations promoting the education and environmental agendas are funding the smart growth agenda.

Smart growth seeks to preserve land in a natural or agricultural state by encouraging individuals to live in denser communities that take up smaller amounts of land per housing unit. Such communities also encourage residents to rely more on walking or public transit than on cars for mobility. Retail and other commercial facilities are also more closely mixed with residential units to foster easy access to jobs and shopping.

While smart growth seems so smart, it has a fundamental flaw. In order for the Rousseau concept to work, government bureaucrats must control property rights. There is simply no other way to implement smart growth. The government must have the ability to tell landowners what they can and cannot do. Otherwise, urban sprawl results.

Smart growth is supposed to solve urban problems from air pollution and traffic congestion to providing access to single-family dwellings for the poor. Smart growth not only does none of these things, it actually accelerates the ills it is supposed to cure. The worst casualty of smart growth is the housing collapse of 2007-2010 that was caused by giving toxic mortgages to the poor who couldn't pay them. The entire fiasco was a component of smart growth to get low-income families into single family housing.

Likewise, increased numbers of people in a small area brings increased congestion. As a rule, more dense areas cost more to build, tend to have higher taxes, higher levels of pollution, and a higher cost of living. The transient nature of the apartment dwellers can lead to crime or a reduction in property values.[740] As a result of smart growth, the poor in any community are hit the hardest.

The Adirondack model attempts to force people into higher density urban areas, while depopulating rural areas by demanding multi-acre lot sizes. No matter how they cut it, urban planning and smart growth is a bald-faced fraud that is creating a nightmare for people across America. It is artificially driving up the equity value for existing homeowners while denying access to the poor and lower middle class. During the 2007-2010 housing crash, those properties having the greatest devaluation *always* occurred in smart growth communities.[741]

Land-use zoning has a devastating impact on the cost of land. The Harvard Institute of Economic Research showed that zoning dramatically increases the cost of land in urban areas. The study found that when zoning is based upon historical harm and nuisance, it does not artificially drive up the price of a quarter-acre lot. This condition exists in urban Kansas City, Baltimore, Houston, Philadelphia and other cities that have not imposed smart growth regulations.[742]

However, in San Francisco, Los Angeles, Anaheim, San Diego, New York City, Seattle and others cities like them, the difference between the cost of an extra quarter-acre in a lot, and a separate buildable quarter-acre lot is in the hundreds of thousands of dollars. "In these areas," claims the Harvard study, "only a small percentage of the value of the lot comes from an intrinsically high land price; the rest is due to restrictions on construction." Although many other variables were tested, land-use regulation was the only one correlated with the huge cost increases. [743]

Another in-depth study by Randal O'Tool published in *The Planning Penalty* found that in 2005, smart growth and other land-use restrictions cost U.S. homebuyers at least $275 billion. Almost all of the more than 124 metropolitan areas having affordability problems in 2005 were directly caused by comprehensive planning and smart growth. Most enlightening, the report found that, "more than 30 percent of the total value of homes in this country is attributable to prices inflated by planning-induced housing shortages."[744] This contributed to the wild increases and speculation in housing prices from 2000-2006, which inevitably led to the housing crash in 2007-2010, and the financial crash of 2008.

The comprehensive planning/smart growth model is taught in college planning programs today. It is vigorously advanced by the American Planning Association (APA) and International Council on Local Environmental Initiatives (ICLEI). Although it now denies it, ICLEI is an international NGO directly tied to the United Nations and the implementation of *Agenda 21*. More specifically, it encourages regulations limiting CO_2 emissions into the atmosphere.[745] ICLEI currently has contracts with over 500 cities and counties in the U.S. to implement its toxic plans.[746] Both the

APA and ICLEI have boilerplate plans and solutions that cash-strapped local cities, towns and counties can quickly adapt to their community without spending a lot of money. They are deadly.

The Tea Party almost universally has been dedicated to eliminating ICLEI in their local communities. Fortunately, in just over one year the Tea Party has succeeded in getting over 50 local communities to not renew their contracts with ICLEI[747] and succeeded in passing a resolution condemning *Agenda 21* and ICLEI in Tennessee.[748] Other states, like New Hampshire, are studying it. Some states are even passing legislation to stop smart growth. Even in those success stories, however, in most cases the local government has already passed ordinances implementing the Rousseau-laden APA or ICLEI plans. Getting rid of ICLEI is not going to remove those toxic plans. Worse, the reason the community signed the contract with ICLEI in the first place is because they had progressive elected officials. These progressives will strongly resist any effort to dilute their power over their citizens.

The only way to get the plan revoked when the elected officials do not want to, is to vote them out of office by replacing them with constitutionally faithful candidates in the 2012 election. The toxic plan can then be revoked by reinstating an older, more traditional ordinance that is based on historical harm and nuisance provisions.

Like the Adirondack example, this misguided Rousseau experiment in land control has spread like cancer despite overwhelming evidence that it does not work.[a] The persistence of these beliefs, despite all facts to the contrary, is a tribute to the power of a small group of progressive elitists to make a ruinous idea fashionable in order to increase federal control.

AGENDA 21

WHILE ALL OF THIS HAD BEEN GOING ON at the national level, the same effort had been underway at the international level.[b] The effort by the United Nations to control land and property rights is long and complex. As previously noted, the concept of sustainable development had evolved into

---

[a] For a more thorough discussion on this subject, review the hundreds of papers and links found on: http://www.americandreamcoalition.org.

[b] For a more thorough list of references and discussion of this effort go to our website at   http://www.sovereignty.net/p/land/index.html

a forty chapter United Nations plan called *Agenda 21*.[749] It represents the single-greatest attack on constitutional principles ever made. It was done very quietly under the seemingly motherhood-and-apple-pie banner of 'sustainable development.'

Agenda 21 covers everything from human population, urban development, global warming, biodiversity destruction to much, much more. It is stunning in its magnitude. *Agenda 21* and its existing and proposed enforcement treaties would provide a web of interlocking international laws that would regulate virtually *every* aspect of human interactions with the environment. It is the primary mechanism by which the global elite are building the structure for global governance.

Agenda 21 was signed by President George H. W. Bush at the 1992 Earth Summit in Rio de Janeiro. Most Americans have never heard of it. Until recently, progressives of both parties had viciously attacked anyone who even mentioned *Agenda 21* as being a kook and ill-informed. That is changing. Most conservatives Tea Party and 9/12 groups are now well aware of *Agenda 21* and are actively and successfully protesting against it.

Key to *Agenda 21* is the Rousseau model of state-controlled property rights. This has been the foundation of all United Nations treaties since its 1976 Habitat I Conference in Vancouver, British Columbia:

Land...cannot be treated as an ordinary asset, controlled by individuals and subject to the pressures and inefficiencies of the market. Private land ownership is also a principal instrument of accumulation and concentration of wealth and therefore contributes to social injustice; if unchecked, it may become a major obstacle in the planning and implementation of development schemes. The provision of decent dwellings and healthy conditions for the people can only be achieved if land is used in the interests of society as a whole. Public control of land use is therefore indispensable.[750]

Sustainable America

These words could have been taken from Rousseau's *Social Compact* as well as Rockefeller's *Use of Land*. *Agenda 21* was made into United States policy in a 1996 policy document entitled *Sustainable America*.[751] *Sustainable America* and a host of sub documents were written by Clinton's President's Council on Sustainable Development (PCSD).[752] *Sustainable America* quietly, but effectively changed the mission statement for every federal agency in the United States without a single vote in Congress and totally unknown by the American people.

Once the federal agencies accepted *Sustainable America*, no longer was their mission to "serve the citizens." Under *Sustainable America,* the mission of federal agencies is to "control citizens" in order to protect the environment and ensure "sustainable development." The changes required by Agenda 21 and *Sustainable America* meant a complete shift from the constitutional basis of "life, liberty and the pursuit of happiness" to one of protecting nature *from citizens* at all costs.

The Earth Charter

In spite of these advances, *Agenda 21* was never intended to have the force of law by itself. That was to change with the acceptance by the United Nations of the Earth Charter at the 2002 World Summit on Sustainable Development in Johannesburg, South Africa. The Earth Charter was originally written for acceptance in the 1992 Earth Summit, but was refused because it was so blatantly pantheistic. Briefly, pantheism is the broad belief that nature (or earth) is god (or goddess) and that the central organizing principle of humanity must be to serve and protect mother earth. Some adherents actually state that mankind is a cancer to the earth.

When the Earth Charter was rejected in 1992, the task to sanitize it for public consumption was given to billionaire Maurice Strong, founder of the Earth Council, and Mikhail Gorbachev, former president of the USSR and founder of Green Cross International. Both Strong and Gorbachev were also members of the Club of Rome. Steven Rockefeller (son of Nelson Rockefeller, governor of New York), was given the responsibility to write the various drafts.

According to Elaine Dewar's stunning revelations in her book *Cloak of Green,* Strong was the almost superhuman mastermind behind global environmentalism from the 1970s into the late 1990s. Strong was a close friend of the Rockefellers and was brilliant in implementing the Rockefeller agenda.[753] He was a member of the occult Club of Rome and was the Secretary General of the UN's first Earth Summit in Stockholm in 1972 and the second Earth Summit in Rio in 1992. In opening the 1992 session Strong said,

It is clear that current lifestyles and consumption patterns of the affluent middle class—Involving high meat intake, consumption of large amounts of frozen and convenience foods, use of fossil fuels, appliances, home and work-place air-conditioning, and suburban housing—are not sustainable. A shift is necessary toward lifestyles less geared to environmentally damaging consumption patterns.

In a nutshell this is what sustainable development intends to do. Officially, sustainable development was defined by the World Commission on Environment and Development's report *Our Common Future* as being, "Development that meets the needs of the present without compromising the ability of future generations to meet their own needs."[754] However, Steven Rockefeller, son of Nelson Rockefeller, provides the occult definition in his and John Elder's book *Spirit and Nature*:

Sustainable by definition, means not only indefinitely prolonged, but nourishing, as the earth is nourishing to life and the self-actualizing of persons and communities. The word development need not be restricted to economic activity, but can mean the evolution, unfolding growth and fulfillment of any and all aspects of life. Thus sustainable development may be defined as the *kind of human activity that nourishes and perpetuates the fulfillment of the whole community of life on earth.* [755] (Italics Added)

Steven Rockefeller was the primary driver for the Earth Charter—both its inception and its sanitation. He chaired the Rockefeller Brothers Fund until 2006, and still serves as a trustee.[756] The Rockefeller Brothers Fund is one of numerous Rockefeller foundations which have funded many environmental organizations supporting sustainable development to the tune of tens of millions of dollars.

The sanitized version of the Earth Charter was taken to the 2002 World Summit on Sustainable Development in Johannesburg, South Africa, in what they called the "Ark of Hope." The Ark of Hope was patterned after the Biblical Ark of the Covenant, except it had dozens of occult symbols painted on its exterior. The Earth Charter was in the final consensus document for the conference as *the* new world ethic (read: world religion).

However, the Committee for a Constructive Tomorrow (CFACT), probably along with others, convinced the U.S. State Department Delegates that the Earth Charter was a very dangerous document. Hours before the

Summit delegates were to accept the UN consensus document, the United States demanded that the Earth Charter be removed.

The removal of the Earth Charter proved to be a wrenching blow to the Cartel's agenda. In the wings, the Cartel had another treaty waiting called the Covenant on Environment and Development (CED). This treaty was designed to put the force of international law behind the Earth Charter and *Agenda 21*, and lay the foundation for a world religion based on pantheism. Since the Earth Charter failed, the CED was never introduced to nations for ratification. The world came within hours of that reality.

Entire books can, and have been written on *Agenda 21*. Googling *Agenda 21* will yield 223 *million* references. Yet, thanks to suppression by the mainstream media, these issues are never discussed, so most people have never heard of them. They even have a hard time believing them. Yet, the global agenda is being implemented. Lest you think this effort has not had much impact, 1153 legislative bills or amendments have been introduced in Congress that are based on *Agenda 21* or sustainable development between the 100th and 112th (1987-2012) Congresses.[757] That's 46 per year! The deep divisions that presently exist in America are, in part, a direct result of this agenda.

The good news is that as the devastating impact of sustainable development become more widely known, citizens are increasingly demanding their local government not implement, or repeal if already passed, sustainable development ordinances. This has become so prevalent that the American Planning Association has issued a warning not to use language associated with sustainable development:

> Some opponents of planning argue...sustainable development... adversely affects not only an individual's rights and freedoms, regionalism, livability and the like...in a way that emphasizes the economic value, long-lasting benefits and positive outcomes that result from good planning and plan implementation....Planners [should] frame what they say in positive terms, avoid jargon and technical words...and use...messages...that emphasize value, choice, and engagement...[758]
> These include,

- APA members help create communities of lasting value.

- Good planning helps create communities that offer better choices for where and how people work and live.
- Planning enables civic leaders, business interests, and citizens to play a meaningful role in creating communities that enrich people's lives.

In other words, ignore reality and use emotion-laden phrases to convince uninformed citizens and government officials that sustainable development planning is the answer to all their problems. In fact, programs like sustainable development, Sustainable America and *Agenda 21* do none of the things they promise to do. Worse, they destroy private property rights and make the problems of the community much, much worse by severely limiting development, increasing traffic congestion— therefore pollution—and increasing the cost of living.

The jaws of this trap are about to close on America. While there are forty goals of *Agenda 21* currently being implemented, space and time allow only two to be very briefly discussed in this book. These two goals almost had, or may yet have an incalculable devastating impact on American citizens. They are global warming and biodiversity in Chapters 9 and 15 of *Agenda 21*, respectively. Both are enormous frauds, based in a grain of truth, and designed to justify global control over the economy of the United States and private property rights.

Global Warming

Most people do not know that CO_2 by itself does not cause most of the warming in the global warming theory. Instead, CO_2 theoretically causes just enough warming in the tropical zone around the equator to cause more thunderstorms, which puts more water vapor into the higher elevations of the atmosphere. When the thunderstorms decay, the water vapor and cirrus (thin high elevation) clouds are left behind. It is the increased water vapor and cirrus clouds that trap the heat and cause the warming, not CO_2. Although this is generally unknown by the lay public, it is the foundation upon which the man-caused theory is built. There is no disagreement about this within the scientific community.

Dr. Roy Spencer, former head of NASA's Advanced Microwave Scanning Radiometer unit and now principal research scientist at the University of Alabama at Huntsville, found that the man-caused theory's required increase in water vapor and cirrus clouds is just not happening.[759]

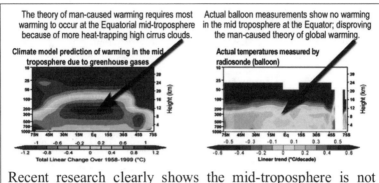

The theory of man-caused warming requires most warming to occur at the Equatorial mid-troposphere because of more heat-trapping high cirrus clouds.

Actual balloon measurements show no warming in the mid troposphere at the Equator; disproving the man-caused theory of global warming.

Climate model prediction of warming in the mid troposphere due to greenhouse gases

Actual temperatures measured by radiosonde (balloon)

Total Linear Change Over 1958-1999 (°C)

Linear trend (°C/decade)

Recent research clearly shows the mid-troposphere is not warming as the man-caused theory demands it must, and which is the basis of every computer model.[759] Source of graphics: S. Fred Singer. Nature, Not Human Activity Rules the Climate. The Heartland Institute, 2008, p. 6. http://www.globalwarmingglobalgovernance.com/NIPCC.pdf Used by permission.

In fact, he found that "the satellite observations suggest there is much more heat energy lost to space during and after warming than the climate models show." Therefore, the man-caused theory of global warming cannot be correct. So far the challenges to Spencer's research by alarmist scientists have not shown that Spencer's analysis is wrong.[760] As usual, the mainstream media is ignoring this proof that the man-caused theory is wrong and is not causing the majority of the warming.

Additionally, after months of dragging their feet, NOAA and NASA have had to admit that the sun is going into hibernation—similar to the Dalton and Maunder Minimums in the 1700s and 1800s in which earth's temperatures were much colder than today.[761] A rapidly increasing number of scientists now believe we may be heading into 25-30 plus years of significant cooling, not warming.

Even more telling, the British Met Office and the University of East Anglia Climate Research Office (CRU) have released data showing that there is a *92 percent probability* that because the sun is entering hibernation we may be entering a long period (as much as 70 years) of dramatic cooling in which earth's temperature could decline by a whopping 2°C.[762] The Met later tried to backpedal, but the cat was out of the bag.

Both the Met and CRU are two key proponents of global warming and have been at the heart of the Climategate email scandals. For NOAA, NASA, The Met and CRU to admit to this represent a near total capitulation.

This comes on the heels of the 2009 Climategate email scandal, which revealed a series of revelations that the IPCC's 2007 report was fraught with pseudoscience and errors. The emails had all but thoroughly discredited the IPCC as a source despite a huge government effort to whitewash the revelations by glossing over the hard evidence of data manipulation and other malfeasances.[763]

The accusations of a whitewash by the two studies were ultimately condemned by the Commons Science Select Committee in Britain's Parliament as ineffective and too secretive.[764] The committee also said the emails review "did not fully investigate the serious allegation" relating to the deletion of emails and instead relied on a verbal reassurance from the perpetrators themselves that the messages still exist. This, in spite of other emails advising recipients to delete certain damning emails.[764]

Another 5,000 emails were released in November, 2011. This new damning set of pirated emails is being called Climategate 2.0,[765] and demonstrates not only how various data sets were manipulated to show warming, but also how investigations into fraud were rigged from the start. One of the Climategate II emails stated, "The trick may be to decide on the main message and use that to guide what's included and what is left out."[766]

This small group of scientists not only controlled what was included in the IPCC reports, but also controlled what peer-reviewed science would be published. It explains why peer-reviewed contrary science was neither published nor included in the IPPC reports. In another email, Phil Jones, the leader of the group even admitted that "the basic problem is that all of the models are wrong."[767] Yet, the only "evidence" that man is causing global warming is what these models predict!

Timothy Carter of the Finnish Environmental Institute wrote, "It seems that a few people have a very strong say, and no matter how much talking goes on beforehand, the big decisions are made at the eleventh hour by a select core group."[768] Carter concluded, "Decisions at the highest levels of what specific figures and conclusions were to appear in the short 'summary for policy makers'—usually the only part of the IPCC's multivolume reports that the media and politicians read—required changing what appeared in individual chapters, a case of the conclusions driving the findings in the detailed chapters instead of the other way around."[769]

In spite of this avalanche of contrary evidence, the EPA did none of its own research to show CO_2 was truly a pollutant, as is required by law. Instead, it ignores the fact that CO_2 is absolutely essential for life on earth (it is the basic food for all plant life), and bases its endangerment ruling solely on the corrupted and now discredited "findings" of the IPCC.

In March of 2009, Alan Carlin, a senior scientist in the EPA since 1967, wrote a critical 98 page internal report asserting, "We believe our concerns and reservations are sufficiently important to warrant a serious review of the science by the EPA." Backed by citation after citation of peer-reviewed science, he showed how the EPA decision to declare CO_2 a pollutant was based on incomplete science that ignored research refuting the EPA position. Carlin's supervisor (an Obama appointee), quashed his report and warned him in an email, "I don't want you to spend any additional EPA time on climate change. No papers, no research, etc."[770] The EPA would condone no dissent to its mantra of man-caused global warming.

The EPA's ruling is so bad that the EPA's Inspector General (IG) released its own highly critical report on September 26, 2011 stating the EPA's scientific findings "were not made available to the public as would be required for reviews of highly influential scientific assessments." The report went on to say, the EPA "did not fully meet the independence requirements for reviews of highly influential scientific assessments because one of the panelists was an EPA employee."[771]

The evidence the EPA is no longer science-based but purely political is overwhelming. After an in-depth study of EPA actions, Kathleen Hartnett White, Director of the Armstrong Center for Energy and Environment, reported the EPA is "misusing the Clean Air Act to force an anti-fossil fuel energy policy repeatedly rejected by Congress. Under cover of the broad law-like authority delegated to EPA in the CAA, the EPA increasingly acts like a fourth branch of government—one unaccountable to the three constitutional branches...." Never before has the EPA used such "speculative, manipulated science to justify this most aggressive regulatory agenda to date." She concludes, "Cumulatively, EPA rules scheduled to become effective in the next three years could cost more than $1 trillion and destroy hundreds of thousands of jobs."[772]

The same is true for the IPCC. After being slapped in the face with reality, the IPCC seems to be backing off its 2007 man-is-destroying-the-earth. In a complete reversal, the draft executive summary of the IPCC's upcoming 2012 report states,

> Projected changes in climate extremes under different emissions scenarios generally do not strongly diverge in the coming two to three decades, *but these [man-made] signals are relatively small compared to natural climate variability over this time frame.* Even the sign of projected changes in some climate extremes over this time frame is uncertain.[773] (Italics added)

This astonishing admission is likely due to the realization the sun's hibernation is going to cool the earth indefinitely.

Nonetheless, even as the IPCC may be backpedaling, the EPA seems to be on a drunken binge to impose economy-killing regulations to reduce CO_2 emissions. These new regulations are based on what amounts to religious tenants of faith that humans are destroying mother earth. Another, more politically troubling reason for the EPA's insane regulations may be that the U.S. economy is totally dependent on cheap energy, which in turn is mostly dependent on carbon-based fuels. If the EPA can control CO_2 emissions, it can control the economy and every citizen—something that causes progressives to salivate.

So zealous is the EPA in ignoring real science that it had to bend the Clean Air Act to the breaking point to implement its new regulations. The Act requires the EPA to regulate any facility emitting more than 250 tons of pollutant a year (in this case CO_2). According to the Competitive Enterprise Institute, however, this would include "literally millions of small entities—big box stores, apartment and office buildings, hospitals, schools, large houses of worship, Dunkin' Donut shops." It would also require an army of 230,000 full-time EPA employees, producing 1.4 billion work hours to administer,[774] cost billions of dollars and wipe out millions of jobs, year after year."[775]

The EPA knew that fielding an army of 230,000 EPA storm troopers to stop Dunkin' Donuts from baking pastries would never fly. So the EPA simply, unilaterally and arbitrarily rewrote the Clean Air Act, revising the emission minimum for CO_2 from 240 tons to 25,000 tons, a mere 100 times what the law required. Never fear though, the regulation will be incrementally increased to include more and more businesses and people as environmentalists file premeditated lawsuits in the future.

The EPA's new minimum of 25,000 tons per year affects coal and natural gas fired electrical generating facilities and refineries—two primary targets that Obama has said during his 2008 campaign that he wanted to either put out of business or make so expensive that his green energy program would look cost competitive.

According to a major report by Paul Driessen, senior policy advisor at CFACT (Committee For A More Constructive Tomorrow) and author of *Eco-Imperialism: Green Power Black Death*, Obama's plan is working. Along with other new EPA regulations, "many coal-fired generating facilities will just close their doors. Analysts predict the United States as a whole will lose 17,000 to 60,000 megawatts per year by 2017."[776] That's not all. Driessen gives this warning:

Consumers in many states will pay 20% more for electricity by 2014 or shortly thereafter. In Illinois, electricity rates are expected to skyrocket 40-60%. For businesses, these price hikes will be major disincentives to hiring new workers. Struggling families will have even less for basic necessities…. Even the International Brotherhood of Electrical Workers says within a few years EPA's new rules will cost up to 50,000 jobs in the utility, coal mining and railroad industries alone—and 200,000 jobs overall.[777]

In summarizing this blatant overreach of the EPA in its April 2012 report "Economy Derailed," The American Legislation Exchange Council (ALEC), the nation's largest nonpartisan, individual membership organization of state legislators, made this observation:

The U.S. Environmental Protection Agency (EPA) has begun a war on the American standard of living. During the past couple of years, the Agency has undertaken the most expansive regulatory assault in history on the production and distribution of affordable and reliable energy…. The standards are so stringent that even recently permitted plants employing the best available technology cannot meet them, and no new coal plants are likely to be built…. These impacts are far worse for lower-income populations, because energy makes up a larger proportion of their budget.[778]

Apparently Obama doesn't care as much about jobs and affordable living for the poor as he claims. He is hell-bent to force us to use green energy at any cost to the citizens of America; rich or poor. The EPA claims the benefits of its new regulations will exceed costs by tens of billions of dollars while allegedly improving the health for millions of Americans. To paraphrase Driessen, only environmental and community organizer ideologues can believe in the tortured logic used to justify such hogwash.

Biodiversity

Chapter 15 of *Agenda 21* calls for the conservation of biological diversity. It demands that the earth's biological diversity be protected by the ratification by each nation of the Convention on Biological Diversity (Biodiversity Treaty). In typical Hegelian Dialectic, *Agenda 21* demands biodiversity must be protected to save the earth from certain collapse of her ecosystems.

In classic Rousseau progressive and/or pantheistic logic, humanity is guilty of destroying ecosystems with development. Therefore, all development must be severely limited. Yet, as a research scientist who has conducted research into biological diversity, this author has found this belief is not based in scientific fact, but in religious belief or progressive nihilistic belief that man is the cause of all evil. Biodiversity is important, but it is not as fragile as *Agenda 21* and the Biodiversity Treaty makes it out to be.

The need for the Biodiversity Treaty is predicated on a new science called Conservation Biology, which in turn is based in pantheistic ideas that "nature knows best" and natural ecosystems have to be managed, well, naturally. Artificial management (i.e. cattle ranching, forest management, modern agriculture, and other management manipulations) are generally destructive. This anti-human underpinning of conservation biology is revealed in its purpose that was defined in the first issue of its journal, Conservation Biology:

The society is a response…to the biological diversity crisis that will reach a crescendo in the first half of the twenty-first century. We assume implicitly that…the worst biological disaster in the last 65 million years can be averted…. We assume implicitly that environmental wounds inflicted by *ignorant humans* and destructive technologies can be treated by *wiser humans* and by wholesome technologies.[779] (Italics added)

Although there is a small place in science for conservation biology, this wild-eyed purpose gives a flavor of the extreme zeal and endgame of those who support *Agenda 21*. Such a radical ideology seems bizarre for the average American. Yet, it is fully entrenched in our universities today because foundations provided endowed chairs and millions of dollars of research money to entice universities. Federal agencies are full of graduates having this indoctrination.

Conservation biology provides the basis for how the UN's Biodiversity Treaty was supposed to protect biodiversity.[a] If a person pictures the human body with its network of arteries and veins, you have a picture of what is called for in the treaty. Real zealots would even include a nervous system because they believe the earth (Gaia) is a living, sentient being. At any rate, the treaty calls for establishing a system of huge core wilderness areas called core reserves that are interconnected by wilderness corridors and all surrounded by buffer zones.

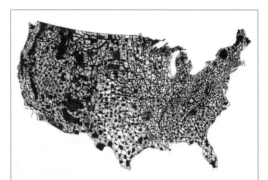

A depiction of what the Convention on Biological Diversity would have done over the next 50 years if it was fully implemented according to recommendations by the UN funded Global Biodiversity Assessment. The black areas are wilderness reserves and corridors and the gray areas buffer zones. The author used an earlier color version of this map to stop the ratification of the Convention on Biological Diversity in the U.S. Senate. (Used by permission from Environmental Perspectives Incorporated, Bangor Maine 207/945-9878)

Four of us succeeded in temporarily stopping U.S. Senate ratification of the treaty in August of 1994.[780] It was brought up for another vote in the

---

[a] For more background information on the treaty go to
http://freedom.org/reports/srbio.htm

Senate on September 29, 1994. The ratification of the treaty was certain. In the meantime, however, the four of us had received the actual UN documentation[781] the day before the vote was scheduled. Called the UN Global Biodiversity Assessment (GBA), the document proved this treaty was literally going to destroy the integrity of the United States.

A full color map depicting what the treaty would do had been under construction for two years by this author. It was overnighted (see black and white map) to the U.S. Senate along with the UN documentation. The map was blown up into a 4 x 6 foot poster and taken out on the Senate floor an hour before the cloture vote.

It stopped the ratification dead in its tracks. The Senate never voted on it.[783] The United States was within one hour of ratifying a United Nations treaty that would have destroyed constitutional property rights and divided America up into human occupation zones. The machinations and intrigue behind the Convention on Biological Diversity would make a best-selling novel.[784]

Reserve and Corridor Map prepared for the California Dept. Transportation and California Dept. Fish and Game. Source: California Essential Habitat Connectivity Project.[782]

Nonetheless, environmental NGOs, as well as federal and state agencies (usually staffed with conservation biologists) have continued to implement the treaty piecemeal. Most states now have plans of some sort of how and where they will create reserves and corridors, such as the California Essential Habitat Connectivity Project: *A Strategy for Conserving a*

Connected California.[785] (See map, previous page) No provisions to protect private property rights are discussed. The rights of Mother Earth trump any human right. The only thing the landowner gets is a discount in his annual taxes.

These are just a few examples of the gross distortion and machinations of all the global environmental and financial crises that most Americans have accepted at face value. While America has a responsibility to protect the environment, the financial elite have squandered enormous sums of money to distort environmental problems into crises of global proportions—all to justify the need for global governance and government control of the lives of all people on earth.[a]

---

[a] To better understand the Locke approach to sustainable development and a point-by-point comparison to Agenda 21 read the *Freedom 21; Promoting Sustainability Through Political and Economic Freedom.*
http://www.freedom21agenda.org/Freedom21Agenda.pdf

13 – What Must be Done

Plundered has provided a very brief overview of why, how and what has happened to America over the past 100 years. A well-planned agenda of plundering has been pushed by the global elite to slowly create a world government having occult roots. Although this world government would be administered by an international organization like the UN (there are several that could be substituted if the UN becomes shunned), the real decision makers would be the global elite.

To be successful, this elite group realized decades ago that the citizens of the world must be dumbed down and made compliant in a manner similar to the U.S. BSTEP program of the late 1960s discussed in Chapters 1 and 9. BSTEP indoctrination is now almost complete. Americans now willingly accepted the Rousseau, state controlled model of government as desirable over the John Locke model set up by our Founding Fathers. In most cases these American's have never even heard of Locke and how his principles have made the U.S. the greatest nation in history. The agenda to subvert America's Locke-based Constitution has been well-documented by insiders and outsiders with impeccable credentials. We are in the final stages of its implementation.

America, with its Locke form of government, was the major obstacle to this effort. This is changing, however. Through foundations, corrupt courts, and progressive politics, the powerful elite are systematically destroying the Locke-based foundation of the U.S. Constitution. They are implementing legalized plunder through the destructive application of "expert planning" and the "public good" doctrine inherent within the Rousseau model of governance. And because of our Rousseau-oriented education, media, and environmental propaganda machine, most Americans are totally ignorant of what these globalists are doing to our children and grandchildren's future.

Americans are not stupid. Indeed they are very intelligent. Except in a few cases, however, intelligence cannot stand up to generation after generation of indoctrination in which all opposing ideas are ignored, denigrated or vilified and dismissed as conspiracy theories. Or, where nearly fifty percent of the population is dumbed down and desensitized through a BSTEP process so they are totally dependent upon the government for their very day-to-day lives. Then there is a vast number that are so busy with the aftermath of disintegrating families and working themselves into the ground just to eke out a living. It is up to each individual American whether our country returns to its Locke roots, or continues its progression into Rousseau socialism, fascism and global control. We are out of time. We must act now.

The most common rebuttal for this warning is, 'It can't happen in America.' Hiding behind empty platitudes, however, will not change the outcome. The 2012 election will likely be either the turning point at which we begin to restore the republic, or the final nail in America's coffin. The ultimate solution, however, goes beyond electing good people to office in 2012. We need to be reminded of a few of the goals Karl Marx included in his Communist Manifesto:

- The theory of the Communists may be summed up in the single phrase: Abolition of private property.

- The middle-class owner of property. This person must, indeed, be swept out of the way, and made impossible.

- Abolition of the family!

- Communism abolishes eternal truths, it abolishes all religion, and all morality.

- Communists everywhere support every revolutionary movement against the existing social and political order of things.[786]

These, of course, are exactly the goals of the progressives today. We also need to be reminded of the prophetic warning of Joseph Stalin; "America is like a healthy body and its resistance is threefold: its patriotism, its morality, and its spiritual life. If we can undermine these three areas, America will collapse from within."[787]

13 – What Must be Done

Unless a person lives in utter delusion, it is impossible not to see that all three of these pillars of liberty and prosperity have now been essentially neutered, and what remains is under ferocious and unrelenting attack. Patriotism has become a quaint idea now scorned in a 'global' society. Morality is in a free fall in a society where 'anything goes,' or 'if it feels good, do it.' Studies show that church attendance and Bible reading has plummeted from 1991 to 2011, especially among baby boomers.[788] While 84 percent of Americans still call themselves Christian, most no longer have a good understanding of what that means.[789]

In Chapter 2 we discussed the importance of Christianity in forming the Constitution and the foundations for building the most successful civilization in the history of mankind. So imperative are the Biblical roots of our Constitution that John Adams wrote, "Our Constitution was made only for a moral and religious people. It is wholly inadequate to the government of any other."[790] If that is true, the only way America can be restored over the long term is to return to its Judeo-Christian roots.

Of course, progressives, with their self-serving superior intellect reject this thesis with utter contempt. However, many patriots who sincerely want to restore our constitutional footing will have a hard time accepting this if they are ambivalent or have rejected their Christian or Jewish roots. Yet, history makes the need to return to our Godly roots imperative.

THE IMPORTANCE OF AMERICA'S JUDEO-CHRISTIAN FOUNDATION

AFTER SPENDING DECADES STUDYING the history of American education and why modern U.S. literacy rates were plummeting, Dr. Blumenfeld found that the reason our early education was so good was because, "The people were governed by the precepts of the Bible, and Biblical literacy was paramount in the education of the nation's children."[791] All students were well grounded in both the Bible and the purpose of the Constitution. Why the study of the Bible in America's early schools? The answer may surprise many Americans who believe that the Constitution forbids the teaching of the Bible.

Contrary to what most public schools teach students today, the Constitution does not forbid the teaching of the Bible in schools. Rather, our Founders proclaimed that they founded America as a Christian nation. Patrick Henry, the famous fiery Founder that shouted, "Give me liberty or give me death," also proclaimed:

It cannot be emphasized too strongly or too often that this great nation was founded, not by religionists, but by Christians; not on religions, but on the Gospel of Jesus Christ. For this very reason peoples of other faiths have been afforded asylum, prosperity, and freedom of worship here.[792]

The Founders built the entire Constitution of the United States on Christian principles of freedom, property rights, love and respect, repudiating the modern day dogma that the Constitution of the United States demands a separation of church and state. People who have not even read the First Amendment that supposedly establishes this rigid separation will be surprised that it states, "Congress shall make no law respecting an establishment of religion, or prohibiting *the free exercise thereof.*" (Emphasis added)

In other words, neither Congress nor a state can establish a state religion—as was the case in England with the Anglican Church. Nor can it prohibit the free exercise of a religion. Very few people now understand that at the time the states ratified the U.S. Constitution seven of the thirteen states had officially established religions:

1. Connecticut (Congregational Church)
2. New Hampshire (Protestant faith)
3. Delaware (Christian faith)
4. New Jersey (Protestant faith)
5. Maryland (Christian faith)
6. South Carolina (Protestant faith)
7. Massachusetts (Congregational Church)[793]

The Founders realized that forcing people to accept a specific denomination would politicize the Christian faith. They had studied what had happened in England's Anglican Church *and* what eventually became the Catholic Church following the edict of Theodosius I to make Christianity the official religion of the Roman Empire. Such a church would lose its moral power to political power.

Consequently, the Founders forbade the states the ability to declare a state religion. At the same time, they recognized that true wisdom and knowledge came from the Bible. So important was this concept that both the U.S. House of Representatives and the U.S. Senate investigated in 1853 how to separate Christian principles from government. Both Houses presented similar reports. The March 27, 1854 House report stated:

At the time of the adoption of the Constitution and the amendments, the universal sentiment was that Christianity should be encouraged, but any one sect (denomination) not dominate.... [T]here is no substitute for Christianity.... That was the religion of the founders of the republic, and they expected it to remain the religion of their ancestors.[794]

The commonly held belief in the twenty-first century that the First Amendment to the Constitution does not allow any Christian influence in government was foreign to the Congress of that day. The House report continues: "Had the people during the Revolution, had a suspicion of any attempt to war against Christianity, the Revolution would have been strangled in its cradle."[795]

As many of the states had established denominations early on, and concerned about rumors that Congregationalism was going to become the national religion, the Baptist Association of Danbury, Connecticut sent off a letter to Thomas Jefferson expressing their deep concern over this. Jefferson wrote a reply in 1801 assuring them that "the First Amendment has erected a wall of separation between church and state," meaning there would be no national religion.

It was not until 1947, after President Roosevelt packed the Supreme Court with progressive judges, that the jargon of "separation of church and state" was taken out of context[796] and became a repeated mantra. In *Everson v. Board of Education*,[797] the Court proclaimed "The First Amendment has erected 'a wall of separation between church and state.' That wall must be kept high and impregnable."[798] Thus the progressive lie of separation of church and state was born, grown and multiplied with great virulence, so much so that many Americans today believe that the actual phrase can be found in the Constitution.

The state did not dictate school curriculum in early America. Rather, local families and communities held that responsibility. Hence, schools were free to use the Bible—letting Biblical moral principles speak for themselves, free from denominational dogma. French judge, statesman and political writer Alexis de Tocqueville, in his two-volume and highly acclaimed book,

Democracy in America, wrote that the success of a free people not only depends upon education, but also in its morality:

> It cannot be doubted that in the United States the instruction of the people powerfully contributes to the support of the democratic republic.... Such must always be the case, I believe, where the instruction which enlightens the understanding is not separated from the moral education.[799]

Above all else, de Tocqueville saw that Christianity was central to the education of Americans: "The religious aspect of the country was the first thing that struck me on arrival in the United States."[800] Free men must, according to de Tocqueville, have a solid foundation in a religion that does not define its doctrine in political will, but in moral character and accountability to God. In contrasting the Koran and the Bible, de Tocqueville notes that the Koran espouses

> ...not only religious doctrines, but political maxims, civil and criminal laws, and theories of science. The Gospel, on the contrary, speaks only of the general relations of men to God and to each other, beyond which it inculcates and imposes no point of faith. This alone, besides a thousand other reasons, would suffice to prove that the former of these religions [Islam] will never long predominate in a cultivated and democratic age, while the latter [Christianity] is destined to retain its sway at these as at all other periods.[801]

Yet, for some inexplicable reason progressives continue to extol Sharia law, which completely violates the U.S. Constitution and even tramples many of the sacred tenets of progressives such as women's rights and complete acceptance of homosexuality. Just as Le Bon observed in 1895, progressive ideology blinds progressives from connecting the reality that Sharia law is totally against their beliefs. De Tocqueville continues:

> ...Men who are similar and equal in the world readily conceive the idea of the one God, governing every man by the same laws and granting to every man future happiness on the same conditions. The idea of the unity of mankind constantly leads them back to the idea of the unity of the Creator; while on the contrary in a state of society

where men are broken up into very unequal ranks, they are apt to devise as many deities as there are nations, castes, classes, or families, and to trace a thousand private roads to heaven."[802]

Christianity, then, was the catalyst in America's early educational process and the glue that helped make the Constitution work. Christianity reinforced the idea that all men were created equally and all had a God-given unalienable right to life, liberty and the pursuit of happiness. Most important, *each person was accountable to a higher authority than the government.*

The American constitutional model was not the historical norm for governments, however. De Tocqueville notes that following the fall of the Roman Empire, the peoples divided into factions each seeking religious privilege and power:

A scale of ranks soon grew up in the bosom of these nations; the different races were more sharply defined, and each nation was divided by castes into several peoples.... Men continue to worship one God, the Creator and Preserver of all things; but every people, every city, and, so to speak, every man thought to obtain some distinct privilege and win the favor of a special protector near the throne of grace.[803]

Thus, as the nations of post Roman Empire politicized Christianity, the equality of men and law broke down causing the nations to become weak and continuously at war. When Europe attempted to unite into the European Union, they did not do it based on God's law, but by what seemed right in the mind of man. Proverbs 14:12 and 16:25 warn, "There is a way *that seems* right to a man, but its end *is* the way of death."[a] Of course, there is no way of proving that this warning is the root of what is happening today, but history and current events strongly support it. Ironically, a quick read of Proverbs 14 and 16 alone suggests that everything we are doing today is counter to God's way of doing things.

Only when men understand that they are accountable to God, who holds all men as equal, will there be equality and justice in the law. Because

---

[a] NKJV, italics original

the Founders designed the republican form of government to place checks and balances on abuse of power based on God's moral code as the final authority, harmony existed between government and the church.

The First Amendment to the U.S. Constitution prevented a state religion from being established, but did not prevent government leaders from accountability to God. Except for the blight of the slavery issue, this type of accountability was dominant in early America. Said de Tocqueville:

> It may be asserted, then that in the United States no religious doctrine displays the slightest hostility to democratic and republican institutions. The clergy of all the different sects there hold the same language; their opinions are in agreement with the laws, and the human mind flows onwards, so to speak, in one undivided current.... There is no country in the world where the Christian religion retains a greater influence over the souls of men than in America; and there can be no greater proof of its utility and of its conformity to human nature than that its influence is powerfully felt over the most enlightened and free nation of the earth.... The Americans combine the notions of Christianity and of liberty so intimately in their minds that it is impossible to make them conceive the one without the other.[804]

This Judeo-Christian spirit still exists, albeit, rarely. In December 1995 textile producer Malden Mills in Lawrence, Massachusetts, suffered total destruction when its factory burned to the ground. Instead of closing the doors and putting hundreds of employees on the streets, its CEO, Aaron Feuerstein continued to pay the employees month after month until the factory was rebuilt. He didn't have to do it. So why did he? Christianity and Judaism share the same moral roots. Feuerstein was a devout Jew and believed the Torah when it says he had a responsibility to take care of his poor employees.[805]

"The fundamental difference is that I consider our workers an asset, not an expense," said Feuerstein. "I have a responsibility to the worker, both blue-collar and white-collar," he added. "I have an equal responsibility to the community. It would have been unconscionable to put 3000 people on the streets and deliver a death blow to the cities of Lawrence and Methuen. Maybe on paper our company is worth less to Wall Street, but I can tell you it's worth more."[806]

Many said that good intentions do not make for good business decisions. Malden Mills was $180 million in debt and had to declare Chapter 10 bankruptcy in November 2001.[807] But it is not because he helped the employees. It is because he did not bother to patent Polartec fleece, one of the best synthetic fabrics used to make and insulate clothing.[808] This allowed the unscrupulous to steal his process. Even so, by August of 2002, with the help of the sale of some property and some substantial military contracts,[809] Malden Mills recovered.[810]

In 2007, the company's assets were sold to a private investment firm and the company was reorganized and renamed Polartec. Today, many of the employees kept on by Feuerstein after the fire are still employed there, unlike most workers in the textile industry who lost their jobs when their companies moved overseas.[811]

Christian Morality Constitutional Glue

De Tocqueville never claimed that all Americans were Christians, but that Christian *morality* is the glue which maintains their republican institutions:

> Among the Anglo-Americans some profess the doctrines of Christianity from a sincere belief in them, and others do the same because they fear to be suspected of unbelief. Christianity, therefore, reigns without obstacle, by universal consent... Thus, while the law permits the Americans to do what they please, religion prevents them from conceiving, and forbids them to commit, what is rash or unjust.... Religion in America takes no direct part in the government of society, but it must be regarded as the first of their political institutions; for if it does not impart a taste for freedom, it facilitates the use of it.... I do not know whether all Americans have a sincere faith in their religion—for who can search the human heart?—but I am certain that they hold it to be indispensable to the maintenance of republican institutions."[812]

Despite relentless efforts by some progressive "scholars" to discount the Christian belief of the Founders, almost all were self-proclaimed Christians. The possible exceptions are Benjamin Franklin and Thomas

Jefferson. Many claim Franklin and Jefferson followed in the footsteps of John Locke as a deist,a not a Christian. Yet, Franklin wrote, God "sometimes interferes by his particular providence and sets aside the effects which would otherwise have been produced...."[813] During a particularly rancorous month in the Constitutional Convention of 1787, James Madison recorded Franklin as saying,

> I have lived, Sir, a long time, and the longer I live the more convincing proofs I see of this truth—that God Governs in the affairs of men. And if a sparrow cannot fall to the ground without his notice, is it probable that an empire can rise without his aide? We have been assured, Sire, in the sacred writings, that 'except the Lord build the House they labour in vain that build it. I firmly believe this; and I also believe that without his concurring aid we shall succeed in this political building no better than the Builders of Babel.[814]

These are hardly the words of a man who believed the creator to be a hands-off deity. Likewise, there is no disagreement that Thomas Jefferson understood the critical importance of God-given unalienable rights and equality of all men when he wrote the Declaration of Independence. However, he eschewed dogmatism.[815] It is no accident that Jefferson claimed, "...Nay, we have heard it said that there is not a Quaker or a Baptist, a Presbyterian or an Episcopalian, a Catholic or a Protestant in heaven; that on entering that gate, we leave those badges of schism behind."[816]

Denominations are institutions that can become dogmatic over time leading to divisions. Paul warned of this in Chapter one of 1 Corinthians, especially 1:10 where he implores Christians to "all speak the same thing, and that there be no divisions among you, but that you be perfectly joined together in the same mind and the same judgment."[b]

It is the message of Christianity that all men are equal and accountable to God, not to make the sects or denominations more important. "The Christian Religion," claimed Jefferson, "when divested of the rags in which

---

[a] Deism was a popular 18th century philosophy whose adherents believed in God the Creator, but considers him an absent master, unconcerned with his creation.
[b] 1 Corinthians 1:10, NKJV

they [the clergy] have enveloped it, and brought to the original purity and simplicity of its benevolent institutor, is a religion of all others most friendly to liberty, science, and the freest expansion of the human mind."[817]

Contrary to modern day political correctness, Christianity liberates and provides freedom for scientific discovery. Conversely, modern fads of political correctness seek to lock humanity into narrow-minded and destructive "truths" that supposedly throw off the shackles of religious repression, but in fact create prisons of their own.

Because Jefferson and the other Founders realized that Christianity was the catalyst as well as the glue that would make the constitutional republic work, its precepts became the foundation of the Declaration of Independence, the U.S. Constitution and of early education. However, Christian morality was an obstacle for self-appointed elitists of the twentieth century. Like most elitists, they believed they were "superior," "gods among mere mortals." They saw in the Rousseau model of governance the ability to manipulate the masses into doing the "general will." Of course the general will would be whatever these elitists defined it to be.

These elitists did not (and still do not) believe themselves accountable to God. Therefore, to the elite the belief that "every knee shall bow to Me, and every tongue shall confess to God" in Isaiah 45:23 and Romans 14:11 (KJV) is superstition or a lie. The elites are their own god and are not accountable to God. The Founders had established the education system in America on the Judeo-Christian principle of freedom, dedicated to preparing each student to excel in whatever endeavor he or she chose. The elite and their progressive minions have essentially destroyed what was once the best education system in the world.

The elites could never allow such freedom in a controlled society. If the elite cabal was going to succeed in gaining the control that it desired over the American people, it had to eliminate the foundation of Biblical Christianity and Judaism in the culture of American society, which meant controlling the American educational system.

In a historically unprecedented move that certainly violates the constitutional right of the free exercise of religion, the Obama administration issued a mandate in January 2012 that all employers would be required to offer free contraceptive services to employee insurance benefits. This includes the morning after pill, which can be interpreted as an abortion. The key here is all employers including the Catholic Church and other religious organizations are mandated to provide these services. In the statement put out by the U.S. Department of Human Services, Secretary Kathleen Sebelius said:

> After evaluating comments, we have decided to add an additional element to the final rule. Nonprofit employers who, based on religious beliefs, do not currently provide contraceptive coverage in their insurance plan, will be provided an additional year, until August 1, 2013, to comply with the new law.

Religious organizations would have been forced to comply regardless of doctrinal beliefs, violating the very heart of the First Amendment. The outrage by the Catholic Church and many Protestant denominations forced the president to make an "accommodation" on February 10, 2012. The religious institution would no longer have to provide free contraceptives, but their insurer would. The accommodation is absurd and does nothing to reduce the direct attack on religious freedoms. The religious organization would still have to buy insurance that attacks its fundamental beliefs, and the cost of these services would still be borne by the organization.[818]

The birth control provision took a radical turn on February 23, 2012 when unmarried Georgetown Law student, Sandra Fluke, testified at a meeting of the House Democratic Steering and Policy Committee. She claimed that it can cost $3000 for birth control while at Georgetown University Law School and it wasn't 'fair' that she had to pay for it. Most Americans asked themselves, 'Why does an employer have to pay for contraceptives for optional activities when seniors have to provide copays for heart or arthritis medication?'[819]

The issue took off like a wildfire when Rush Limbaugh attacked Fluke, calling her a 'slut' among other hateful descriptions. Although Limbaugh later apologized, saying he had sunk to the level of leftist liberals, the progressive slogan machine immediately cranked up calling Republicans 'hate-filled' and 'waging war on women.'[820] Yet, Super PAC for Obama had no problem accepting a $1 million donation from comedian Bill Maher who has repeatedly used profane language like 's---' and 'c---' on air to describe 2008 Vice-Presidential candidate Sara Palin.[821]

Apparently the hypocritical attack on Limbaugh in particular and the Republicans in general backfired. A CBS/NYT poll showed Obama's favorability plummeted from 50 percent to 41 percent overnight,[822] although some of the drop may be due to his repressive energy policy that has allowed gasoline prices to skyrocket.[823] One can hope this poll is not an aberration and the American people finally understand the duplicity of progressive Democrats. If so, hopefully they will also understand the duplicity of progressive Republicans.

The overriding fact remains, however, that the Obama administration didn't seem to have any problem with plowing right over the Constitution or the deeply held tenets of faith of millions of Americans. It is just another example of the arrogance and linear thinking by progressives to deviously destroy the foundations of our nation. History has shown what happens to people of faith when a government starts infringing upon religious freedoms. When nothing is done by the populace, those infringements can become much more far reaching and eventually even deadly.

Although the forced contraceptive issue is a major violation of the First Amendment, progressive liberals deftly used Limbaugh's attack on Fluke to turn the debate from a First Amendment violation to a Republican war on women. The speed in which they did this was astonishing.

The global elite have all but destroyed true Christianity in Europe. Much of Judaism was purged by the Russian pogroms and Nazism. While that in itself has not directly caused the economic collapse now being witnessed in Europe, it set up the moral collapse needed for the corruption and greed that has undermined many of the nations of Europe.

There are positive signs however. Bible reading and volunteer work in America has gone up 9 percent during 1991 to 2011 for young adults (born from 1965-1983). Additionally, there has been a 12 percent increase in the number of young adults making a personal commitment to Jesus Christ. At the same time there has been a 60 percent increase in the number of young adults who say they have been "born again."[a] That's precisely the opposite of what baby boomers did during the same period from 1991 to 2011.[824] Unfortunately, no similar studies could be found for Jewish trends and their commitment to God.

Another positive sign has shocked the establishment Republicans; the strong support for presidential candidate Ron Paul by the youth of

---

[a] "Born again" is the acceptance by faith (not works) by Jesus of a person as Savior *and* Lord of their lives, followed by a life of good works resulting from that decision.

America. While it is true that they are idealists, some of whom undoubtedly supported Obama in 2008, they are sick of the lies and empty promises of the progressives of both parties.[825]

The college campus organization, Young Americans for Liberty, strongly supports Paul and actively invites him on their campuses.[826] They have done their homework, unlike many in their parents' generation, and now realize that real hope and change doesn't come from Obama's growing government control, but in constitutionally limited governance and congressionally driven foreign policy. These youth apparently like this, even when many conservatives and Tea Party members of their parents' generation do not like Paul for other reasons, primarily his foreign policy.

On the downside, the number of young adults not attending church in the past six months increased by 8 percent.[827] Combined with the increased interest in Biblical Christianity, it suggests that young adults are looking for more than the narcissistic world their baby boomer parents have created. However, they are finding it in the Bible and in volunteer activity, not so much in the institutional church. Why?

A Case in Point

In one example, George Barna, the leading pollster/writer on Christian issues, found that young adults and families favored a church service which utilizes contemporary or blended music style in their corporate worship with upbeat choruses rather than a traditional one with hymns. The young adults seeking to find God in an otherwise black hole of our materialistic society find the Psalm-like hymns foreign and hard to relate to. Although church leadership tried to adapt by having contemporary or blended services, about 20 percent of the long-term church attenders, however, strongly objected. They prefer traditional services. They are displeased with the changes and make their objections known. This has caused division in the church. In his studies Barna found,

> Church leaders foster the problem by focusing on how to please people with music or how to offer enough styles of music to meet everyone's tastes rather dealing with the underlying issues of limited interest in, comprehension of, and investment in fervent worship of a holy, deserving God.[828]

13 – What Must be Done

Barna notes that nearly 50 percent of churchgoers believe the worship service is there for their personal benefit and enjoyment.[828] American churchgoers have in many cases fallen into the mindset of "what's in it for me?" when it comes to church, rather than "how can I love and serve this body?" Barna notes that such members have missed the point of worship entirely. "Music is just a tool meant to enable people to express themselves to God, yet we sometimes spend more time arguing over the tool than over the product and purpose of the tool."[829] In other words, the focus of worship is God, not whether the church uses 'my' style of music.

This goes to the issue of concern in this book. Even within the church, believers are focused more on themselves than on God. While Barna found that more than 80 percent of all self-identified Christian adults say they have made a personal commitment to Jesus Christ, less than 20 percent claim to be totally committed to being built up in Biblical faith.[830]

Worse, Barna goes on to say that "the evidence is quite clear that relatively few self-identified Christians are serious about abandoning the lure of sin and handing total control of their life to God. In fact, only 12 percent of self-identified Christians even grasp the significance of their sin and of their accountability to God. While most self-identified Christians are *comfortable* in their church, they don't take their faith that seriously.[830] If self-identified Christians don't take God seriously, how can they have any impact on the non-Christian political world? They can't. That's the problem.

As noted earlier in the chapter, many in the first few generations after the creation of the U.S. Constitution were nominal Christians. Nonetheless, Christian morality was the foundation of America. Non-Christians were certainly plentiful, but they had to operate in a Christian culture. Even though Christians in those days were far from perfect, they at least understood the nature of sin. They understood that was why Christ died on the cross. They understood that they could have forgiveness *when* they acknowledged their sin and repented as John explains in 1 John 1, especially 1:8-10:

> If we say that we have no sin, we deceive ourselves, and the truth is not in us. If we confess our sins, He is faithful and just to forgive us *our* sins and to cleanse us from all unrighteousness. If we say that we have not sinned, we make Him a liar, and His word is not in us. (NKJV)

Fifty years ago many children did things wrong or "sinned," just as they have since time began. They knew they were sinning. They did it anyway. That was immorality at work. Today, most kids don't even know "I shouldn't move in with my boy- or girlfriend." They really don't even know it is wrong. Why not? That is amorality at work—not knowing right from wrong. Most "Christians" don't know what sin is or why it is important. Many treat sin as irrelevant, even titillating.

When the extra marital affairs of pro-golfer Tiger Woods became public, on December 2, 2009, the athlete made a very public apology in which he said, "I have let my family down and I regret those transgressions with all of my heart." On that day in 2009, out of three billion searches on Google, the number one search was "transgression"; the number five was "definition of transgression." Between our public school education, the news media and TV programing, our society has had the concept of sin removed from its consciousness—with devastating consequences.

Is it any wonder then that morality is plummeting, crimes of violence are increasing, children can't even be allowed to play in their front yards unsupervised, or that kids are shooting kids in school? In comparison, when this author was a child and old enough, I was allowed to roam the neighborhood with my parents having no fear that something terrible might happen to me. That's not true any longer. Our culture has been corrupted by progressive ideology and actions.

The point is that most Americans no longer even make an effort not to sin. Psalms 36:1-4, along with many other verses, makes it clear that when "there is no fear of God before his eyes, [man] flatters himself in his own eyes," and iniquity and hatred result. "The words of his mouth are wickedness and deceit; He has ceased to be wise and to do good. He devises wickedness on his bed; He sets himself in a way that is not good; He does not abhor evil." (NKJV) This is a perfect description of what Saul Alinsky's book, *Rules for Radicals* actually teaches the reader to do. As noted earlier, Alinsky even dedicated the book to Lucifer, otherwise known as Satan or the Devil—the leader of rebellion and discord. Also noted before, Alinsky's book has been described as the bible for progressive liberals.

Think about that. In 1991, 74 percent of all Americans believed that God is "the all-knowing, all-powerful and perfect Creator of the universe who still rules the world today."[831] In 2011 it was 67 percent. In 1991 46 percent of all Americans strongly believed that the "Bible is totally accurate

260

in all of the principles it teaches." That dropped to 38 percent in 2011.[831] This is not only a cultural war; it is also more fundamentally a spiritual war. Worse, the statistics say that evil is winning. What does that mean?

This presents a dilemma. If a Christian (or Jew) does not believe everything in the Bible is God's truth, such as sin and God's judgment of it, how can they decide which of God's promises are true? The answer is simple, they cannot. So when tragedy or hardship come, as they surely will, how can they stand on God's promises that He loves them and will never leave them or forsake them? Again, they cannot, and the tragic event can make their lives a living hell with no refuge.

Conversely, a Christian (or Jew) who depends on God's promises, while still feeling the pain or uncertainty, knows that God will see them through the crisis and they *depend* on God's strength and provision to do it. This is the real hope and change, something Obama and the progressives can never provide.

The simple fact is that because Christian or Jewish Americans do not trust God, then the church or synagogue is no different than society. Why would anyone want to darken the door of a church or synagogue if there is no evidence that God is interacting and impacting the people in it? The world has coopted many churches and synagogues, rather than the churches and synagogues leading the world. Many Christians have lost their saltiness. In Matthew 5:13 Jesus warned that when that happened, all the so-called good works of the church become worthless.

Entire books are written on these subjects. The point is not to delve into theology, but to emphasize that the Founders knew that the Constitution would never survive once the nation turned away from God as its foundation *in practice*.[a] The elite also knew this and attacked Christianity at the same time they attacked the Constitution and our original form of education.

NEEDED GOVERNMENTAL CHANGES

THE TENTH AMENDMENT to the Constitution of the United States affirms

---

[a] Saying you are a Christian is meaningless. Do you practice it (with God's help) with the commitment, mercy, forgiveness and love as God commands? Or, do you take what God teaches in the Bible or Torah and twist it into impossible demands as did the Pharisees? Or worse, ignore it entirely as the progressives and many lukewarm Christians do today? Unless we return God to His proper position, we can win everything in 2012 and still lose the nation.

that, "The powers not delegated to the United States by the Constitution, nor prohibited by it to the States, are reserved to the States respectively, or to the people." In other words, state power or the people trump federal power except for the specific powers delegated to the federal government in Article 1 Section 8 of the Constitution. Thomas Jefferson warned,

> When all government, domestic and foreign, in little as in great things, shall be drawn to Washington as the center of all power, it will render powerless the checks provided of one government on another and will become as venal and oppressive as the government from which we separated.[832]

As defined throughout this book, our Founders understood the dangers of a powerful central government. Therefore, they designed the structure of governance so that the powers delegated to the federal government are very few and well defined. The Tenth Amendment was designed to guarantee that most government power resides with the individual states or its people. However, the usurpation of state powers by the federal government has all but eliminated the protection of the people by the Tenth Amendment.

The erosion of the Tenth Amendment started when the Seventeenth Amendment was ratified in 1913 after being promoted by the progressives of the era. This transferred the selection of a state's two Senators by each state's legislature, to popular election by the people of each state. The Constitution originally had Senators represent the states' interest, which would have all but prevented any legislation from passing that weakened the states' powers in relation to the federal government. With the ratification of the Seventeenth Amendment, however, Senators were elected by the people, who were heavily influenced by party propaganda.

Every department and agency of the federal government must be reviewed for constitutionality and need. There is no constitutional justification for the Department of Education, Department of Housing and Urban Development, the Department of Energy or the Environmental Protection Agency (EPA), to name but four. All have mission statements to implement the UN's *Agenda 21* via the U.S.'s *Sustainable America*. Education has always been a state and local issue, but for the global elite to dumb down Americans, it had to control the educational process through grants. The Department of Energy is systematically preventing almost all development of coal and oil, causing escalating energy costs and more dependence on foreign oil.

The EPA wasn't even created by an act of Congress, but was created out of thin air by the executive branch. Yet, it has become the high priest of the entire nation, dictating tens of thousands of unneeded new pages of regulations every year. These regulations are based on flimsy pseudo-science and politics that destroy lives, smother commerce and the free market while doing almost nothing to protect the environment. As noted earlier, at least one EPA director admitted he "crucified" violators like the Romans to make examples of them.[833]

The elimination of these four departments or agencies by themselves would reduce the 2012 proposed budget by nearly $200 billion. Other department budgets must also be slashed. The economic benefit would be even greater as the enormous drag of voodoo progressive regulations is reduced.

All future laws, as well as the laws passed in the last 100 years, should go through the litmus test of Constitutionality. The continued passage of unconstitutional laws must stop NOW. However, it must also be understood that 100 years of systematic destruction of Constitutional governance cannot be undone overnight.

Our entire economy and culture is now built around the Soviet/Rousseau socialist/fascist model of governance. For example, those citizens who have been forced to pay into social security, and whose retirement plan was built around it, cannot suddenly have it taken away. Even so, entitlements must be restructured to make them solvent.

The restoration of constitutional governance must also be done with wisdom to minimize unnecessary turmoil. It will take time to undo the indoctrination and the destructive laws passed over the last 100 years. The first step will be to reinstate local control of our public schools and demand textbooks based on true facts—rather than revisionist theory and politically correct history that is common in today's textbooks.

Equally important, the new Congress must uphold their Constitutional responsibility to impeach judges in the various courts if they stray from the Constitution. Under Article III of the Constitution, judges "hold their offices during good behavior." For the most part that means till death, resignation, or retirement, but judges who undermine the Constitution can be removed from office by impeachment—the same as for the president and "all civil officers of the United States."

Although activist judges and courts have rewritten or even written laws, contrary to the Constitution, to date only 13 federal judges have had impeachment proceedings started against them in the House of Representatives. Of the 11 tried by the Senate (the other two resigned first), only seven were convicted and removed from office.[834] While impeachment must never be taken lightly, it is imperative that the destroyers of constitutional governance be quickly impeached. It won't take long before other rogue judges get the point that they are not permitted to be legislators.

The Rousseau mentality that pervades the bureaucratic culture of federal, state and local governments won't disappear overnight either. An increasing majority of today's bureaucrats believe it is their responsibility to control citizens in their jurisdictions rather than to serve them. The abuse of urbanites by smart growth laws and rural citizens by environmental laws are examples of jack-booted regulations. Unfortunately, these examples are becoming the norm, not the exception.

Be warned, however, that when a lawsuit is necessary, do so in the Court of Federal Claims. Never file in Federal District Court. Your attorney will demand you go to District Court because that is what he or she has always done. If you do, you will lose.

District Court is the administrative court. It does not decide constitutional issues. That belongs in the Court of Federal Claims, where the injured party can demand discovery (review of all documents) and can sue the individual bureaucrat as well as the agency. The threat of being sued personally gets the attention of offending bureaucrats very quickly.[835]

These are but a few of the things that must be done. Some should be done as soon as possible, others will take longer to accomplish. The restoration of the Constitution must be started however, and the best way to start is on Election Day, 2012.

THE ROAD TO NOVEMBER

AMERICA IS ABOUT TO FAIL DISASTROUSLY as a nation, because we have drifted far from the truth of God's Word and fallen for the siren song of progressive ideology. The safest way to cure this is to begin to roll back a hundred years of progressive re-interpretation of the Constitution. That will take decades. America does not have decades. The turning point must be NOW.

Throw the Rascals Out

The progressives' unbelievable state of denial affects too many people to be delusional. It doesn't make any sense politically. Instead of moving toward the political center as such a historic defeat would call for, they are charging ahead as if they have won. Are they committing political suicide?

The seemingly political schizophrenia by the progressive liberals only makes sense if they are following the Saul Alinsky formula for winning and radically transforming America. Alinsky advised that when you are surrounded and in trouble, step on the gas and viciously attack the opposition. They have gradually come into power over the last few decades through the relentless attack against anyone who opposes them by demonization and false accusations. For them, the end justifies the means even if it means lying, cheating, and conducting criminal activities.[836] The strategy has worked for ACORN and the SEIU. It also worked in passing the extremely unpopular Obamacare.

What this means is that progressive liberals will not give up, will ignore reason and common sense, and will intensify their attacks on anyone who opposes them. This, of course, is exactly what has happened in Congress in 2011 after the Republicans took over the House of Representatives. The controversial Glenn Beck warned that the first victims would be any Democrat in Congress who opposes the progressive Democrats—even if it means destroying the traditional Democrat party in the process. That's exactly what happened in the 2010 election. It appears some of these progressives don't care, or may even desire the destruction of the party and the United States as we have historically known it.

Every effort by states to tighten up the voter registration process to reduce fraud has been met with howls of rage from progressives. They claim that it somehow discriminates against minorities. Understand that is nothing but a progressive power play to manipulate the electoral process.

The power in the Tea Party movement is the thousands of like-minded, but independent grass roots organizations at the local level. As difficult as it would be, it is far easier to work effectively within the Republican Party to roll back neocon dominance and get the party back to its original conservative constitutional principles than to start a new party. Unfortunately, it will be far more difficult for constitutional Democrats to work within the Democrat Party; it has been totally hijacked by Rousseau progressive liberals.

The biggest obstacle is that the American people, especially Republican leadership, still do not get it. Many, in fact, do get it and actively promote the destruction of the Constitution. Very few people realize we are in a literal war to the death over what model of governance we will have; Rousseau's progressive liberalism or Locke's Constitutional conservatism.

To sugar coat this war by saying progressivism is only a difference of opinion is to ignore the declaration of war actually made by progressive liberals. They are the ones defining this war. As just stated, they are the ones willing to lie, cheat and destroy anything that gets in the way of their goal to transform America into the Soviet model based in Rousseau ideology. It is time to expose their lies and go on the offensive.

Only one form of government will survive. It is not politics as usual (Democrats vs. Republicans). Both parties are now controlled at the top by progressives. Most Republicans, even Tea Party and conservative Republicans are woefully ignorant of the war to the death in which they are entrenched. Many people still do not truly understand *why* we are in the mess we are in. A huge educational challenge lies ahead if the voters are to be brought up to speed as to *why* they are so upset. The intent of this book is to provide the framework of understanding to make intelligent decisions.

We are witnessing a "paradigm" or fundamental shift in American politics as people begin to understand the dangerous progressive ideology that finally came out of the shadows in 2009 when progressives went for America's jugular. We must return to constitutional principles as laid out by John Locke. Much of the electorate is not yet aware why that is so critically important. Once the electorate is educated, even true Democrats (not progressives) have a chance to win in the November 2012 elections if they adopt constitutional principles.

That raises another problem. Many neoconservatives and progressive Democrats will take on a more conservative image in order to win the 2012 election as they did in 1994 and 2010. They will not *truly* change their anti-constitutional and big government ideology. Because of their arrogance, however, they will not understand why their beliefs are ultimately destructive. If they are reelected it will be business as usual. Therefore, it is imperative that they be identified in the primary elections and exposed.

To do this, local activists can develop a list of pledge statements they can submit to candidates to force them to support Constitutional principles.

13 – What Must be Done

Freedom 21[837] has put together such a list to which candidates must pledge agreement in order to get the organization's endorsement:

1. I will vote for only that legislation which contains a citation to the specific authority granted in Article 1, Section 8 of the U.S. Constitution.
2. I will vote *against* any legislation that infringes on the individual right to keep and bear arms.
3. I will vote *for* legislation that allows the use of domestic resources to achieve energy and food independence.
4. I will vote *for* only that legislation which applies equally to the public, and to members of the judicial, legislative, and executive branches of the federal government.
5. I will vote *against* any legislation that results in a federal takeover of any private corporation, institution, or entity.
6. I will vote *against* any legislation that raises the pay of legislators in any year without a balanced budget.
7. I will vote *against* any legislation that authorizes the United Nations to impose a tax, levy, fee or royalty on the United States or any of its citizens.
8. I will vote *against* any legislation that attempts to implement provisions of any treaty not approved by two-thirds vote of the Senate (as mandated by the Constitution in Article 2, Section 2).

This is only the starting point for ideas. Obviously, these principles apply best to congressional candidates, but they provide a template that is easily modified for other levels of government as well. If their past record does not support these principles, challenge them on it. Some candidates will have truly changed, but many who pledge to uphold these principles do so only to garner the conservative vote. Their commitment is only skin deep. If possible, vote for someone who clearly upholds these principles in their heart.

It is imperative to the future of America that candidates holding these constitutional principles be elected to office. They should be heavily supported. Never will we have the chance to reform our political offices that we have now. If the elected offices are not taken back during the 2012 elections, it is highly likely that the Constitution will be made a worthless piece of paper and it will be nearly impossible to recapture the freedoms the Founders valiantly provided for us, if we would but protect them.

These are but a few of the things that need to be changed in the future if we are to save America. Many books have been written describing in detail why changes are needed. Additional books will be written on each issue in the future. For now, however, it is imperative that every American understand that enormous amounts of money and energy are being drained from the economy keeping these progressive mechanisms of control going and expanding. It must be stopped NOW. Total reversal will take time, but stopping its expansion can begin in the 2012 election by electing constitutionally literate candidates—at every level of government.

When signing the Declaration of Independence, our Founders mutually pledged to each other their "Lives, our Fortunes, and our sacred Honor." Hundreds of thousands more have made the supreme sacrifice to protect our liberties. If we do not do the same, our great nation, our liberties and our prosperity will be lost—perhaps forever.

CITATIONS AND ENDNOTES

Chapter 1 – A War of Worldviews and Crushing Debt

1   Thomas Dilorenzo. *The Real Lincoln; A New Look at Abraham Lincoln, His Agenda, and an Unnecessary War*. New York: Three Rivers Press, 2002). Pp. 2-3

2   Ibid, P. 3.

3   Irving Kristol. Neoconservative Persuasion: What it Was, and What It Is. The Weekly Standard, August 25, 2003. http://www.amnation.com/vfr/archives/001679.html

4   Matt Bai. Does Anyone Have a Grip on the G.O.P.? New York Times Magazine, October 16, 2011.
     http://www.nytimes.com/2011/10/16/magazine/does-anyone-have-a-grip-on-the-gop.html?_r=1&ref=magazine

5   Henry Reske. Exit Polls: Tea Party Supporters Went for Romney. Newsmax.com, January 10, 2012.
     http://www.newsmax.com/InsideCover/romney-tea-party-paul/2012/01/10/id/423732?s=al&promo_code=DE6C-1

6   National Defense Authorization Act, S. 1867 http://www.gpo.gov/fdsys/pkg/BILLS-112s1867pcs/pdf/BILLS-112s1867pcs.pdf

7   Ibid, P. 359.
     Also: Joe Wolverton II, J.D. Belligerent Amcericans. New American, Vol. 28, No. I, January 9, 2012. P. 18.

8   Ibid, Joe Wolverton II, P. 19.

9   Ibid, P. 20.

10   Joe Wolverton. Obama Signs National Defense Authorization Act into Law. January 2, 2012, http://www.thenewamerican.com/usnews/constitution/10396-president-obama-signs-national-defense-authorization-act-into-law; http://www.whitehouse.gov/the-press-office/2011/12/31/statement-president-hr-1540

11   Matt Bai. Does Anyone Have a Grip on the G.O.P.? New York Times Magazine, October 16, 2011.
     http://www.nytimes.com/2011/10/16/magazine/does-anyone-have-a-grip-on-the-gop.html?_r=1&ref=magazine

12   C. Bradley Thompson and Yaron Brook. *Neoconservatism: An Obituary for an Idea*. (Boulder, London: Paradigm Publishers, 2010). Preface, P. i.

13   Ibid. Preface, P. ix.

14   Ibid. P 8.

15   Ibid. P. 251.

16   Irving Kristol. *Reflections of a Neoconservative*. (New York, NY: Basic Books, Inc., 1983), P 34.

http://books.google.com/books/about/Reflections_of_a_neoconservative.html?id=6PF3AAA AIAAJ

17 Charlotte Thomson Iserbyt. *The Deliberate Dumbing Down of America*, (Ravenna, Ohio: Conscience Press, 1999) see "Futurism as a Social Tool and Decision-Making by an Elite," p. 248-255. and p. A-25.

18 Ibid, p. 259. Ibid.

19 Ibid, p. 261. Ibid.

20 Keynesian Economics. Investopedia. http://www.investopedia.com/terms/k/keynesianeconomics.asp

21 Randal Holcombe. The Growth of the Federal Government in the 1920s. The CATO Journal Vol. 16, No. 2. (no date). http://www.cato.org/pubs/journal/cj16n2-2.html

22 Internal Revenue Service (12/12/2008). "Table 23. U.S. Individual Income Taxes". http://www.irs.gov/pub/irs-soi/histab23.xls. Retrieved July15, 2011.

23 Internal Revenue Service (12/12/2008). "Table 23. U.S. Individual Income Taxes". http://www.irs.gov/pub/irs-soi/histab23.xls. Retrieved July15, 2011.

24 Thomas Woods. The Forgotten Depression of 1920. Mises Daily, November 27, 2009. http://mises.org/daily/3788#ref3.

25 On Japan, see Benjamin M. Anderson, *Economics and the Public Welfare: A Financial and Economic History of the United States, 1914–1946* (Indianapolis: Liberty Press, 1979 [1949]), pp. 88–89, 90. http://books.google.ca/books?id=5beaAAAAIAAJ&q=Economics+and+the+Public+Welfare& dq=Economics+and+the+Public+Welfare

26 Thomas Woods. The Forgotten Depression of 1920. Mises Daily, November 27, 2009. http://mises.org/daily/3788#ref3.

27 Michael Coffman and Kristie Pelletier. Playing Politics with U.S. Deficits and Debt. Rescuing America Book. July 11, 2011. http://www.rescuingamericabook.com/opeds/Playing_Politics_with_the_U_S_Debt.pdf

28 Warren G. Harding. Wikipedia. (no date). http://en.wikipedia.org/wiki/Warren_G._Harding

29 Eugene P. Trani and David L. Wilson, *The Presidency of Warren G. Harding* (Lawrence, KS: University Press of Kansas, 1977), p. 72. http://books.google.ca/books?id=kJ13AAAAMAAJ&dq=The+Presidency+of+Warren+G.+Har ding&q=The+tax+cuts%2C+along+with+the+emphasis+on+repayment+

30 Thomas Woods. The Forgotten Depression of 1920. Mises Daily, November 27, 2009. http://mises.org/daily/3788#ref3.

31 The Austrian School of Economics. Investopedia. July 31, 2009. http://www.investopedia.com/articles/economics/09/austrian-school-of-economics.asp#axzz1SHwPxQay

32 Thomas Woods. The Forgotten Depression of 1920. Mises Daily, November 27, 2009. http://mises.org/daily/3788#ref3.

33 Ibid.

34 Murray Rothbard. *America's Great Depression*. (New York, NY: Van Nostrand Reinhold, 1963). Part II, Pp 85-169. http://books.google.com/books?id=RHINtHpq8p0C&printsec=frontcover#v=onepage&q&f=fa lse

35 Michael Coffman and Kristie Pelletier. Playing Politics with U.S. Deficits and Debt. Rescuing America. July, 11, 2011. http://www.rescuingamericabook.com/opeds/Playing_Politics_with_the_U_S_Debt.pdf

36 Ferrell, Robert H. *The Presidency of Calvin Coolidge*. (Lawrence, KS: University Press of Kansas, 1998). P 195.

37 Herbert Hoover, American President: An Online Reference Resource. The Miller Center, University of Virginia. (no date). http://millercenter.org/academic/americanpresident/hoover/essays/biography/1

38 Glen Abel. The Harding/Coolidge Prosperity of the 1920's. (no date). http://www.calvin-coolidge.org/html/the_harding_coolidge_prosperit.html

39 Milton Friedman and Anna Jacobson Schwartz. *Monetary History of the United States, 1867-1960*. (Princeton, NJ: Princeton University Press, 1963) P 352

http://books.google.com/books?hl=en&lr=&id=Q7J_EUM3RfoC&oi=fnd&pg=PA710&dq=a+monetary+history+of+the+united+states&ots=17nxlLz1x3&sig=3PpMK_alHmOpx6vcYUaSTAHuBis#v=onepage&q&f=false

40 Ben Bernanke. Remarks by Governor Ben S. Bernanke; Honoring Milton Friedman on Friedman's Ninetieth Birthday. The Federal Reserve Board. November 8, 2002. http://www.federalreserve.gov/BOARDDOCS/SPEECHES/2002/20021108/default.htm

41 Glen Abel. The Harding/Coolidge Prosperity of the 1920's. (no date). http://www.calvin-coolidge.org/html/the_harding_coolidge_prosperit.html
Also: Smoot-Hawley Tariff Act. Wikipedia. http://en.wikipedia.org/wiki/Smoot-Hawley_Tariff_Act

42 Herbert Hoover. Wikipedia. http://en.wikipedia.org/wiki/Herbert_Hoover#cite_ref-51

43 James Ciment. Encyclopedia of the Great Depression and the New Deal. Sharpe Reference, 2001. Originally from the University of Michigan. Vol. 2. p. 396
Also, Internal Revenue Service (12/12/2008). "Table 23. U.S. Individual Income Taxes". http://www.irs.gov/pub/irs-soi/histab23.xls. Retrieved July15, 2011.

44 Lekachman, Robert. The age of Keynes. (New York, NY: Random House, 1966). p. 114. http://books.google.com/?id=noGaAAAAIAAJ.

45 Friedrich, Otto. F.D.R.'s Disputed Legacy. Time Magazine, February 1, 1982. http://www.time.com/time/magazine/article/0,9171,954983-4,00.html. Retrieved March 24, 2008.

46 Ralph Reiland. Not Just Another Speech. New American, Vol. 28(2):20, January 23, 2012.

47 Ibid, Pp. 19--20

48 Meg Handley. Home Values Down $6.4 Trillion Since Housing Crash. US News, December 23, 2011. http://www.usnews.com/news/blogs/home-front/2011/12/23/home-values-down-64-trillion-since-housing-crash

49 Ralph Reiland. Not Just Another Speech. New American, Vol. 28(2):19, January 23, 2012.

50 Barack Obama. Remarks by the President on the Economy in Osawatomie, Kansas. Office of the White House Press Secretary, December 6, 2011. http://www.whitehouse.gov/the-press-office/2011/12/06/remarks-president-economy-osawatomie-kansas

51 Mike Brownfield. Morning Bell: Tangled Up in Washington's Red Tape. The Foundry. July 27, 2011. http://blog.heritage.org/2011/07/27/morning-bell-tangled-up-in-washingtons-red-tape/

52 Clyde Wayne Crews Jr. Ten Thousand Commandments. Competitive Enterprise Institute. 2011. P 2. http://cei.org/sites/default/files/Wayne%20Crews%20-%2010,000%20Commandments%202011.pdf

53 Steve Stanek. Federal Regs: 231 Billion Dollars, 133 million Paperwork Hours. Heartland Institute, January 4, 2012. http://news.heartland.org/newspaper-article/2012/01/04/federal-regs-231-billion-dollars-133-million-paperwork-hours

54 Ashe Schow. Regulations Don't Hurt Business? Heritage in Action. Heritage Foundation, November 17, 2011. http://heritageaction.com/2011/11/regulations-don%E2%80%99t-hurt-business/

55 Small Business Outlook Survey. Harris Interactive, July 11, 2011. http://www.uschambersmallbusinessnation.com/docs/US-Chamber-of-Commerce-Summit-Presentation-from-Harris-Interactive.pdf

56 Lydia Saad. U.S. Political Ideology Stable with Conservatives Leading. Gallup, August 1, 2011. http://www.gallup.com/poll/148745/Political-Ideology-Stable-Conservatives-Leading.aspx

57 Lydia Saad. U.S. Political Ideology Stable with Conservatives Leading. Gallup, August 1, 2011. http://www.gallup.com/poll/148745/Political-Ideology-Stable-Conservatives-Leading.aspx

58 Historical Treasury Rates. U.S. Treasury Resource Center. July 1, 2011. http://www.treasury.gov/resource-center/data-chart-center/interest-rates/Pages/Historic-LongTerm-Rate-Data-Visualization.aspx

59 Tyler Durden. The Fed's $600 Billion Stealth Bailout of Foreign Banks at the Expense of the Domestic Economy. Zerohedge.com, June 12, 2011.

http://www.zerohedge.com/article/exclusive-feds-600-billion-stealth-bailout-foreign-banks-continues-expense-domestic-economy-

60   Valentina Pop. Greece to Face 'Restricted Default' as Bailout Details Emerge. EU Observer. July 22, 2011. http://euobserver.com/9/32653

61   Super-Eurocrats to the Rescue/Eurozone in Chaos? The Daily Bell, October 10, 2011. http://www.thedailybell.com/3063/Super-Eurocrats-to-the-Rescue

62   EU Tackles Crisis With 50% Greek Writedown, $1.4 Trillion Fund. Bloomberg, November 2, 2011. http://www.businessweek.com/news/2011-11-02/eu-tackles-crisis-with-50-greek-writedown-1-4-trillion-fund.html

63   Porter Stansberry. The S&A Digest, October 11, 2011. http://www.stansberryresearch.com/secure/digest/2011/html/index/908

64   Staff. Greece to Hold New Election on 17 June. BBC News Europe. May 16, 2012. http://www.bbc.co.uk/news/world-europe-18082552

65   Michael Coffman and Kristie Pelletier. The Brink of Total Financial Collapse. Rescuing America, July 5, 2011. http://www.rescuingamericabook.com/opeds/financial_collapse.pdf

66   Mark Perry. Anti-Keynseian Supply Side Tax and Spending Cuts in Sweden, and the Finance Minister Behind it. The Daily Crux as posted from Carpe Diem, May8- 9, 2012. http://thedailycrux.com/Article/40242/Government_Stupidity
Also http://mjperry.blogspot.com/2012/05/anti-keynesian-supply-side-tax-and.html

67   Ibid.

68   Ibid.

Chapter 2 – Philosophical Origins of the Two Warring Worldviews

69   Kenneth Weinstein. "Individual Rights v. The General Will: An historical perspective on John Locke & Jean-Jacques Rousseau and a look at how today's environmental movement is rapidly advancing one above the other." CFACT Briefing Paper #111 - Part A, August 2002. http://www.cfact.org/IssueArchive/Limited%20Government%20Under%20Assault%20Jean-Jacques%20Rousseau%20Versus%20John%20Locke.pdf

70   John Locke, Second Treatise on Government. Chapter II, Of the State of Nature, Section 6. http://www.constitution.org/jl/2ndtr02.htm

71   William Blackstone,. Commentaries on the Laws of England. Ed. William Carey Jones, 2 Vols (San Francisco; Bancroft-Whitney Company, 1916), 1:63 and 93.

72   Letter to the Officers of the First Brigade of the Third Division of the Militia of Massachusetts, 11 October 1798, In: Revolutionary Services and Civil Life of General William Hull (New York, 1848), Pp 265-6.
http://books.google.com/books?id=E2kFAAAAQAAJ&dq=editions%3AVsZcW99fWPgC&pg=PA265#v=onepage&q&f=false
There are some differences in the version that appeared in The Works of John Adams (Boston, 1854), vol. 9, pp. 228-9, most notably the words "or gallantry" instead of "and licentiousness
http://books.google.com/books?id=PZYKAQAAIAAJ&pg=PA228#v=onepage&q&f=false

73   2 Timothy 3:1-9, especially verse 5.
http://www.biblegateway.com/passage/?search=2%20tim%203:1-9&version=NKJV

74   John Locke. Second Treatise Government. Chapter Fourteen, 1690. http://libertyonline.hypermall.com/Locke/second/second_frame.html

75   Nancie and Roger Marzulla, Property Rights, Understanding Government Takings and Environmental Regulation. (Rockville, Maryland: Government Institutes, Inc., 1997), p. 2.

76   Ibid.

77   Lynch v. Household Finance Corporation, 405 U.S. 538, 92 S. Ct. 1113, March 23, 1972. http://laws.findlaw.com/us/405/538.html

78   Noah Webster, "An Examination into the Leading Principles of the Federal Constitution," Pamphlets (October 10, 1787), p. 58-61. In: Philip Kurland and Ralph Lerner, Eds, The Founders Constitution (Chicago: University of Chicago Press, 1986), Ch. 16(17). http://press-pubs.uchicago.edu/founders/documents/v1ch16s17.html

79   Nancie and Roger Marzulla, pp. 2-3.

80 Ken Weinstein. Individual Rights v. The Genral Will. CFACT, 2002, Briefing Paper 111

81 Jean-Jacques Rousseau. The Social Contract. Book I, 7-The Sovereign, Paragraph 8. 1762. http://www.constitution.org/jjr/socon_01.htm

82 Ibid.

83 Jean-Jacques Rousseau. Discourse on the Origin of Inequality, Part II, Paragraph 1. 1754. http://www.constitution.org/jjr/ineq_04.htm

84 Ibid, paragraph 38.

85 Coffman, *Saviors of the Earth? The Politics and Religion of the Modern Environmental Movement.* (Chicago: Moody Press, 1994), pp. 273-274.

86 Jean-Jacques Rousseau. *The Social Contract.* Book 4, 8-Civil Religion, Paragraph 9. 1762. http://www.constitution.org/jjr/socon_04.htm

87 Ibid, Paragraph 18.

88 Bill O'Reilly. Demonizing Christianity. BillOreilly.com. July 28, 2011. http://www.billoreilly.com/site/rd?satype=13&said=12&url=%2Fnewslettercolumn%3Fpid%3 D33094

89 Anders Behring Breivik. New York Times, July 27, 2011. http://topics.nytimes.com/top/reference/timestopics/people/b/anders_behring_breivik/index.h tml

90 O'Reilly: Christianity Demonized. NewsMax, July 30, 2011. http://www.newsmax.com/InsideCover/OReilly-Christianity-Demonized/2011/07/30/id/405403

91 Steven Kreis. The Origins of the French Revolution. The History Guide, Lectures on Modern European Intellectual History. 2000. http://www.historyguide.org/intellect/lecture11a.html

92 1789 French Revolution. Roman Catholic Church, Buildings and Religion. The Other Side. October 23, 2000. http://www.theotherside.co.uk/tm-heritage/background/church.htm#frenchrev

93 Steven Kreis. The Origins of the French Revolution. The History Guide, Lectures on Modern European Intellectual History. 2000. http://www.historyguide.org/intellect/lecture11a.html

94 New International Version

95 Jean-Jacques Rousseau. *The Social Contract.* Book 4, 8-Civil Religion, Paragraph 33. 1762. http://www.constitution.org/jjr/socon_04.htm

96 Ibid.

97 Gustave Le Bon. *The Crowd: A Study of the Popular Mind.* (Kitchener, Ontario: Batoche Books, 2001, org. 1896), P.19. http://socserv.socsci.mcmaster.ca/~econ/ugcm/3ll3/lebon/Crowds.pdf

98 Ibid, P. 65. http://socserv.socsci.mcmaster.ca/~econ/ugcm/3ll3/lebon/Crowds.pdf

99 Ibid, P. 68. http://socserv.socsci.mcmaster.ca/~econ/ugcm/3ll3/lebon/Crowds.pdf

100 Mathew White. French Revolutionary Wars. Statistics of Wars, Oppressions and Atrocities of the Eighteenth Century. 2004-2010. http://users.erols.com/mwhite28/wars18c.htm

101 Maximilien Robespierre "Speech to National Convention: The Terror Justified. My History Lab. 2009. http://dev.prenhall.com/divisions/hss/app/BW_TEST/Western_History/documents/Maximilien _Robespierre_Speech_to_National_Convention_The_Terror_Justified_.htm
    In: Maximilien Robespierre, "Speech to the National Convention, February 6, 1794: The Terror Justified," in Pageant of Europe, ed. Raymond P. Stearns (New York: Harcourt Brace, 1947), 404-405. http://dev.prenhall.com/divisions/hss/app/BW_TEST/Western_History/documents/Maximilien _Robespierre_Speech_to_National_Convention_The_Terror_Justified_.htm

102 Grace Denison. Jean Jacques Rousseau – —Father of the French Revolution. Reading Revolutions: Intellectual History, University of Maine, 2005-2006. http://hua.umf.maine.edu/Reading_Revolutions/Rousseau.html

103 Mass Killings Under Communist Regimes. Wikipedia. http://en.wikipedia.org/wiki/Mass_killings_under_Communist_regimes

104 Gustave Le Bon. *The Crowd: A Study of the Popular Mind.* (Kitchener, Ontario: Batoche Books, 2001, org. 1896), P. 31. http://socserv.socsci.mcmaster.ca/~econ/ugcm/3ll3/lebon/Crowds.pdf

105 Jean-Jacques Rousseau. *The Social Contract.* Book 4, 8-Civil Religion, Paragraph 33. 1762. http://www.constitution.org/jjr/socon_04.htm

Chapter 3 – Using the Law to Plunder

106 Frederic Bastiat. *The Law* (Foundation for Economic Education, 30 South Broadway, Irvington-on-the- Hudson, NY 10533), 1998) (Originally published in 1850).1849. http://www.econlib.org/library/Bastiat/basEss2.html#Chapter 2, The Law, 2.1 Note: the web version is a different translation from the original French than the quotes from the book. They say the same thing, but in different words.

107 Frederic Bastiat, http://www.econlib.org/library/Bastiat/basEss2.html#Chapter 2, *The Law*, 2.14

108 Ibid, 2.57

109 Farmer Should be Free, Say Campaigners. Mail Online, Undated, circa September 29, 2011. http://www.dailymail.co.uk/news/article-81359/Farmer-free-say-campaigners.html Manslaughter Verdict for Martin. BBC News, October 30, 2001. http://news.bbc.co.uk/2/hi/uk_news/1627540.stm Tony Martin (farmer). Wikipedia. http://en.wikipedia.org/wiki/Tony_Martin_(farmer). Ginny Simone. English Warning to Americans: Don't Give Up your Guns! YouTube, August 12, 2011. http://www.youtube.com/watch?v=KCkr2psNvCs&NR=1

110 Ibid.

111 Ibid.

112 James Chapman and Jack Doyle. The Legal Right to Protect Your Home: Owners Will be Able to Fight Off Burglars Without Fear of Prosecution. Mail Online, June 22, 2011. http://www.dailymail.co.uk/news/article-2006245/Criminal-justice-Legal-right-protect-home-fear-prosecution.html

113 YouTube video of Obama Joe the Plumber exchange. http://www.youtube.com/watch?v=BRPbCSSXyp0

114 Jean-Jacques Rousseau. *The Social Contract.* Book I, 7-The Sovereign, Paragraph 8. 1762. http://www.constitution.org/jjr/socon_01.htm

115. Frederic Bastiat, p. 17. http://www.econlib.org/library/Bastiat/basEss2.html#Chapter 2, The Law, 2.58

116 Milton Friedman Destroys Phil Donahue. Encyclopedia Britannica Blog. July 31, 2009. http://www.britannica.com/blogs/2009/07/milton-friedman-happy-birthday-destroys-phil-donahue/ Also: Milton Friedman Calmly Destroys Phil Donahue. Transcript of 1979 interview posted by vote for David, posted August 26, 2009. http://votefordavid.blogspot.com/2009/08/milton-friedman-calmly-destroys-phil.html

117 Ibid.

118 Ibid.

119 Ibid.

120 Barack Obama. Remarks by the President on the Economy in Osawatomie, Kansas. Office of the White House Press Secretary, December 6, 2011. http://www.whitehouse.gov/the-press-office/2011/12/06/remarks-president-economy-osawatomie-kansas

121 Frederic Bastiat, *The Law*, p. 5., http://www.econlib.org/library/Bastiat/basEss2.html#Chapter 2, The Law, 2.20

122 Ibid 2.23

123 Ibid, 2.89

124 Ibid, 2.27

125 Ibid, 2.27

126 Poverty in the United States; Frequently Asked Questions. National Poverty Center, University of Michigan. Viewed on September 3, 2011. http://www.npc.umich.edu/poverty/#3

127 Poverty: 2000 Highlights, U.S. Department of Census.
     http://www.census.gov/hhes/poverty/poverty00/pov00hi.html
128 Poverty in the United States, Frequently Asked Questions. National Poverty Center,
     Reviewed on February 2, 2012. http://www.npc.umich.edu/poverty/
129 Peter Beckmann. *What Attracts Intellectuals to Socialism?* (Boulder, CO: Golem Press,
     1978), p. 1-2.
130 Benjamin Franklin. *On the Price of Corn and Management of the Poor.* 29 November, 1766.
     http://www.founding.com/founders_library/pageID.2146/default.asp
131 Benjamin Franklin. *On the Price of Corn and Management of the Poor.* 29 November, 1766.
     http://www.founding.com/founders_library/pageID.2146/default.asp
132 2 Thessalonians 3:10. NKJ
133 James 1:27. NKJ
134 Donna Fen. "Give me your poor." *Inc. magazine*, June 2000, Vol. 22, Issue 8.
135 Frederick Bastiat, *The Law*, p. 21. http://www.econlib.org/library/Bastiat/basEss2a.html, L.80
136 John Stossel and Kristina Kendall. Who Gives, Who Doesn't. ABC 20/20. November 28,
     2006. http://abcnews.go.com/2020/story?id=2682730&page=1 Note: This is a little old, but it
     is highly doubtful the percentages have changed much.
137 Ibid.
138. Jon Carlisle, "1998 National Directory of National Environmental and Regulatory Victims,"
     National Center for Public Policy Research, Washington, D.C.
     http://www.nationalcenter.org/VictimDirectory98.html#B
139. Ibid.
140. Ibid.
141 Charles Rice, "Net Loss of Freedom," The New American, Vol. 8(11), P 29, June 1, 1992.
142. Ibid
143. Michael Coffman, *Saviors of the Earth*, Pp. 239-240.
144 Becket Adams. Supreme Court Justices 'Blast' EPA for Telling Idaho Couple They Can't
     Build on 'Protected Wetlands.' The Blaze, January 9, 2012.
     http://www.theblaze.com/stories/supreme-court-justices-blast-epa-for-telling-couple-they-
     cant-build-on-protected-wetlands/
145 Ibid.
146 Bob Unruh. Supremes: EPA Actions 'Outrageous.' WorldNetDaily, January 10, 2012.
     http://www.wnd.com/2012/01/supremes-epa-actions-outrageous/
147 Ibid.
148 SACKETT ET VIR v. ENVIRONMENTAL PROTECTION AGENCY ET AL. Supreme Court of
     the United States, March 21, 2012. http://www.supremecourt.gov/opinions/11pdf/10-
     1062.pdf
149 Ibid.
150 EPA Video Reveals Team Obama's Scary Crusade Against Affordable, Reliable Energy.
     Fox News, April 27, 2012. http://www.foxnews.com/opinion/2012/04/27/epa-video-reveals-
     team-obama-scary-crusade-against-affordable-reliable-energy/
     Also: EPa Seeks to 'Crucify' US Energy Producers?
     http://video.foxnews.com/v/1590459174001/epa-seeks-to-crucify-us-energy-producers
151 Internal Revenue Service. Internal Revenue Costs, Collections, Employees, and U.S.
     Population, Fiscal Years 1969-1998. 1998 IRS Data Book, Publication 55B. September 13,
     2000. File 98DB37CS.XLS. http://www.irs.gov/pub/irs-soi/98db37cs.xls
152 Internal Revenue Gross Collections, by Type of Tax, Fiscal Years 1972-2001. 2001 IRS
     Data Book, Publication 55B. March 18, 2002. File 01DB07CO.XLS.
     http://www.irs.gov/pub/irs-soi/01db07co.xls
     SOI Tax Stats - Gross Collections, by Type of Tax and State, Fiscal Year - IRS Data Book
     Table 5. http://www.irs.gov/taxstats/article/0,,id=206488,00.html
153 Moody, J. "Scott. America Celebrates Tax Freedom Day," Special Report No. 122, Tax
     Foundation, April 2003. http://www.taxfoundation.org/SR122.pdf
154 Terence P. Jeffrey. "Bush Drove Down Tax Burden." Human Events. April 24, 2002.
     http://www.humanevents.org/articles/04-22-02/jeffrey.htm

155 America Celebrates Tax Freedom Day. Tax Foundation. Viewed September 3, 2011. http://www.taxfoundation.org/taxfreedomday/
156 U.S. Federal Spending—Fiscal Year 2010.
http://en.wikipedia.org/wiki/File:U.S._Federal_Spending_-_FY_2007.png
Table S-1 President's Ten Year Plan. In: A Blueprint For New Beginnings, A Responsible Budget for America's Beginnings. 2001.
http://www.whitehouse.gov/news/usbudget/blueprint/budx.html
157 Frederic Bastiat, *The Law*, http://www.econlib.org/library/Bastiat/basEss2.html#Chapter 2
158 Ibid, 2.101
159 Ibid, 2.105
160 Ibid, 2.167
161 Ibid, 2.114
162 Ibid, 2.83
163 Ibid, 2.87
164. Hernando de Soto. *The Mystery of Capital* (New York: Basic Books, 2000), p. 83.
165 Ibid, p. 155.
166 Ibid, p. 83.
167 Frederic Bastiat, *The Law*, http://www.econlib.org/library/Bastiat/basEss2.html#Chapter 2
2.32
168 Ibid, 2.34
169 Ibid, 2.51
170 Ibid, 2.52
171 Bergh, Albert Ellery, ed. *The Writings of Thomas Jefferson*, 20 Vols (Washington: Thomas Jefferson Memorial Association, 1907), 15:278
172 *Thomas Jefferson to Edward Carrington, 1788.* In: *The Writings of Thomas Jefferson*, Memorial Edition (Lipscomb and Bergh, editors) 20 Vols., Washington, D.C., 1903-04. Vol 7:3.
173 Frederic Bastiat, p. 8. http://www.econlib.org/library/Bastiat/basEss2a.html, 2.35
174 Ibid, 2.27
175 Ibid, 2.90
176 Ibid, 2.59

Chapter 4 – History of Progressivism

177 Gustave Le Bon. *The Crowd: A Study of the Popular Mind.* (Kitchener, Ontario: Batoche Books, 2001, org. 1896). Pp. 13.
http://socserv.socsci.mcmaster.ca/~econ/ugcm/3ll3/lebon/Crowds.pdf
178 Gustave Le Bon. *The Crowd: A Study of the Popular Mind.* (Kitchener, Ontario: Batoche Books, 2001, org. 1896). 129 Pp.
http://socserv.socsci.mcmaster.ca/~econ/ugcm/3ll3/lebon/Crowds.pdf
179 Ibid, P. 13.
180 Stuart Jeffries. Hands Up If You Are an Individual. The Guardian, March 7, 2009.
http://www.guardian.co.uk/lifeandstyle/2009/mar/07/social-psychology-group-mentality?INTCMP=SRCH
181 Aditya Chakrabortty. Just How Similar Are Humans to Rats? The Guardian, April 6,2010.
http://www.guardian.co.uk/commentisfree/2010/apr/06/rats-humans-brain-food?INTCMP=SRCH
182 Jay Y. Gonen. *The roots of Nazi Psychology: Hitler's Utopian Barbarism.* (Lexington, KY: University Press of Kentucky, 2000, orig. 1934). P. 92.
http://books.google.com/books?id=By44SoKlLuwC&pg=PA92&lpg=PA92&dq=Le+Bon+Hitler&source=bl&ots=SFflU9_FKc&sig=XRhseXPa9Na0LeDDLSMMBHvHAkl&hl=en&ei=LyhAToP9Fe650AG0kfX5Aw&sa=X&oi=book_result&ct=result&resnum=6&ved=0CDYQ6AEwBQ#v=onepage&q=Le%20Bon%20Hitler&f=false
Gonen was referencing the book *The Psychopathic God: Adolf Hitler* by Robert Waite. 1977. P. 122.
183 Ibid, Pp 44-45.

184 Ibid, P. 43 & 44.
185 Gustave Le Bon. *The Crowd: A Study of the Popular Mind*. (Kitchener, Ontario: Batoche Books, 2001, org. 1896). Pp. 16-18
     http://socserv.socsci.mcmaster.ca/~econ/ugcm/3ll3/lebon/Crowds.pdf
186 Ibid, P. 19.
187 Ibid, P. 24.
188 Ibid
189 Gretchen Carlson. The Left's Use of One Liner Slogans. Fox and Friends. Fox News, August 5, 2011.
190 Blind Spot? RNC Says DNC Chair Wasserman Schultz Denied Unemployment is Up Under Obama. St. Petersburg Times • The Miami Herald, December 12, 2011.
     http://www.politifact.com/florida/statements/2011/dec/15/republican-national-committee-republican/did-dnc-chair-wasserman-schultz-deny-unemployment-/
191 Ibid.
192 Gustave Le Bon. *The Crowd: A Study of the Popular Mind*. (Kitchener, Ontario: Batoche Books, 2001, org. 1896), P. 20.
     http://socserv.socsci.mcmaster.ca/~econ/ugcm/3ll3/lebon/Crowds.pdf
193 Nia-Malika Henderson. Maxine Waters to Tea Party: Go to Hell. Washington Post, August 22, 2011. http://www.washingtonpost.com/politics/maxine-waters-to-tea-party-go-to-hell/2011/08/22/glQAjgEeWJ_story.html
194 Maxine Waters Calls Republican Leaders "Demons." Fox News, February 15, 2012.
     http://www.foxnews.com/politics/2012/02/15/maxine-waters-calls-republican-leaders-demons/
195 Ashe Schow. Regulations Don't Hurt Business? Heritage in Action. Heritage Foundation, November 17, 2011. http://heritageaction.com/2011/11/regulations-don%E2%80%99t-hurt-business/
196 Keach Hagey. John Kerry Wants Media to "Not Give Equal Time" to Tea Party. Politico, August 5, 2011.
     http://www.politico.com/blogs/onmedia/0811/John_Kerry_wants_media_to_not_give_equal_time_to_Tea_Party.html
197 Gustave Le Bon. *The Crowd: A Study of the Popular Mind*. (Kitchener, Ontario: Batoche Books, 2001, org. 1896), Pp. 119-120.
     http://socserv.socsci.mcmaster.ca/~econ/ugcm/3ll3/lebon/Crowds.pdf
198 Ibid, P 17.
199 Michael Coffman and Kristie Pelletier. Unions, Protests and the Collapse of the U.S. Economy, Part 1. Rescuing America, March 31, 2011.
     http://www.rescuingamericabook.com/opeds/Unions1.pdf
200 Occupational Employment Statistics. Bureau of Labor Statistics, U.S. Dept. of Labor. May, 2010. http://www.bls.gov/oes/current/oes_wi.htm#otherlinks
201 The Budget-Repair Bill's Impact on Wisconsin State Employee Health Benefit Costs. HC Trends. (no date). http://maciverinstitute.com/wp-content/uploads/2011/02/State-Employee-Health-Plan-Contributions-Final.pdf
202 Michael Coffman and Kristie Pelletier. Unions, Protests and the Collapse of the U.S. Economy, Part 1. Rescuing America, March 31, 2011.
     http://www.rescuingamericabook.com/opeds/Unions1.pdf
203 Ibid.
204 Gov. Walker's Advice for Washington. Fox News, Fox and Friends, August 3, 2011.
     http://video.foxnews.com/v/1091983144001/gov-walkers-advice-for-washington
205 Gov. Walker's Advice for Washington. Fox News, Fox and Friends, August 3, 2011.
     http://video.foxnews.com/v/1091983144001/gov-walkers-advice-for-washington
206 Staff. 52% in Wisconsin Support Recall of Governor Walker. Rasmussen Reports, April 2, 2012.
     http://www.rasmussenreports.com/public_content/politics/general_state_surveys/wisconsin/52_in_wisconsin_support_recall_of_governor_walker
207 Greta Van Susteren. Leader Pelosi is Trying to Save the World from Republican Budget. Fox News, GretaWire. July 28, 2011.

http://gretawire.foxnewsinsider.com/2011/07/28/leader-pelosi-is-trying-to-save-world-from-republican-budget/

208 Lyle Rossiter Jr. M.D. *The Liberal Mind; The Psychological Causes of political Madness*. (St. Charles, IL: Free World Books, LLC., 2006). P 330.

209 Ibid, P 384.

210 Gustave Le Bon. *The Crowd: A Study of the Popular Mind*. (Kitchener, Ontario: Batoche Books, 2001, org. 1896), P. 30.
http://socserv.socsci.mcmaster.ca/~econ/ugcm/3ll3/lebon/Crowds.pdf

211 Lyle Rossiter Jr. M.D. *The Liberal Mind; The Psychological Causes of political Madness*. Free World Books, LLC. 2006, p 329.

212 U.S. Ties Iran to Assassination Plot Against Saudi Diplomat on U.S. Soil. Fox News, October 11, 2011. http://www.foxnews.com/us/2011/10/11/iranians-charged-over-terror-plot-in-us/

213 Gustave Le Bon. *The Crowd: A Study of the Popular Mind*. (Kitchener, Ontario: Batoche Books, 2001, org. 1896), P. 31.
http://socserv.socsci.mcmaster.ca/~econ/ugcm/3ll3/lebon/Crowds.pdf

214 John Stossel. The Mob on Wall Street. Fox News Special. October 14, 2011.
http://www.foxbusiness.com/on-air/stossel/index.html

215 Joyce Lee Malcom. Gun Control's Twisted Outcome. Reason Magazine. November, 2002.
http://reason.com/archives/2002/11/01/gun-controls-twisted-outcome

216 Katrina Tweedie. Scotland Tops List of World's Most Violent Countries. London Times, September 19, 2005. http://www.freerepublic.com/focus/f-news/1487949/posts

217 Ginny Simone. English Warning to Americans: Don't Give Up your Guns! YouTube, August 12, 2011. http://www.youtube.com/watch?v=KCkr2psNvCs&NR=1

218 Sharyl Attkisson. Documents:ATF Used "Fast and Furious" to Make the Case for Gun Regulations. CBS News, December 7, 2011. http://www.cbsnews.com/8301-31727_162-57338546-10391695/documents-atf-used-fast-and-furious-to-make-the-case-for-gun-regulations/

219 Joan Neubauer. Conspiracy Theory: Fast and Furious an Attempt to Further Gun Control. Canada Free Press, October 11, 2011. http://canadafreepress.com/index.php/article/41202

220 Jeffrey Kuhner. Kuhner: Obama's Watergate. The Washington Times, December 15, 2011.
http://www.washingtontimes.com/news/2011/dec/15/obamas-watergate-758295296/

221 Jonathan Strong. Pressure Builds on Lanny Breuer in Fast and furious Fallout. Roll Call, December 7, 2011.
http://www.rollcall.com/news/pressure_builds_on_lanny_breuer_in_fast_and_furious_fallout-210858-1.html

222 Jeffrey Kuhner. Kuhner: Obama's Watergate. The Washington Times, December 15, 2011.
http://www.washingtontimes.com/news/2011/dec/15/obamas-watergate-758295296/

223 Ibid.

224 Ibid.

225 Gun sales increase; violent crime decreases; gun control advocates conspicuously mum. National Rifle Association, May 27, 2011.
http://www.cafemom.com/answers/857470/Gun_sales_increase_violent_crime_decreases_gun_control_advocates_conspicuously_mum

226 Jonathan Elliot, Ed. June 14, 1788, *The Debates in the Several State Conventions on the adoption of the Federal Constitution*, 2nd Ed. Vol. 3,1836
http://econfaculty.gmu.edu/wew/quotes/arms.html

227 Samuel Adams. *Debates and Proceedings in the Convention of the Commonwealth of Massachusetts*, (Pierce & Hale, eds., Boston, 1850), Pp. 86-87.
http://econfaculty.gmu.edu/wew/quotes/arms.html

228 Gustave Le Bon. *The Crowd: A Study of the Popular Mind*. (Kitchener, Ontario: Batoche Books, 2001, org. 1896), P. 21.
http://socserv.socsci.mcmaster.ca/~econ/ugcm/3ll3/lebon/Crowds.pdf

229 Video: Union Hate Rally in Wisconsin: Protests Rife With Hitler, Gun Targets, Death Threats. Fox Nation, February 17, 2011.

http://nation.foxnews.com/politics/2011/02/17/union-hate-rally-wisconsin-protests-rife-hitler-gun-targets-death-threats

230 Saul Relative. Jared Lee Loughner: Left-Wing, Right-Wing, or Just Plain Nutcase? Yahoo! News, January 9, 2010.

231 Video: Union Hate Rally in Wisconsin: Protests Rife With Hitler, Gun Targets, Death Threats. Fox Nation, February 17, 2011.

232 Hoffa on Tea Party: "Take These Son-of-a-Bitches out.' Fox News, September 5, 2011. http://www.foxnews.com/politics/2011/09/05/hoffa-on-tea-party-take-these-sons-bitches-out/

233 Ann Coulter. *Demonic; How the Liberal Mob is Endangering America*. (New York: Crown Forum-Random House, 2011) 354 pages.

234 Rossiter, Lyle Jr. M.D. *The Liberal Mind; The Psychological Causes of political Madness*. Free World Books, LLC. 2006, P 330.

235 Ibid, Pp 330-331

Chapter 5 – Politics of Deceit and the U.S/Global Debt Crisis

236 China Boosts Holdings of US Treasury Debt. MoneyNews.com. November 16, 2011. http://www.moneynews.com/StreetTalk/China-Holdings-US-Treasury/2011/11/16/id/418216?s=al&promo_code=D869-1
Major Foreign Holders of Treasure Securities (through October 2011). http://www.treasury.gov/resource-center/data-chart-center/tic/Documents/mfh.txt

237 Interest Expense on the Debt Outstanding. Treasury Direct. November 11, 2011. http://www.treasurydirect.gov/govt/reports/ir/ir_expense.htm

238 Historical Treasury Rates. U.S. Treasury Resource Center. July 1, 2011. http://www.treasury.gov/resource-center/data-chart-center/interest-rates/Pages/Historic-LongTerm-Rate-Data-Visualization.aspx

239 United States National Debt & Budget Deficits. Intellectual Takeout. No date, but sometime in 2010. http://www.intellectualtakeout.org/library/articles-commentary-blog/national-debt-faq-questions-answers

240 Josh Tauberer. Kill Bill: How Many Bills are There? How Many are Enacted? GovTrack.us. http://www.govtrack.us/blog/2011/08/04/kill-bill-how-many-bills-are-there-how-many-are-enacted/

241 Chris Edwards. George W. Bush: Biggest Spender Since LBJ. CATO. December 19, 2009. http://www.cato-at-liberty.org/george-w-bush-biggest-spender-since-lbj/

242 US Debt Clock as of 12-15-2011. http://www.usdebtclock.org/

243 Gerald Prante and Mark Robyn. Summary of Latest Federal Individual Income Tax Data. Tax Foundation, Fiscal Fact No. 249. October 6, 2010. http://www.taxfoundation.org/news/show/250.html#table3

244 Curtis Dubay. You Can't Tax the Rich Enough to Close the Deficit. The Foundry, The Heritage Foundation, October 7, 2010. http://blog.heritage.org/2010/10/07/you-can%E2%80%99t-tax-the-rich-enough-to-close-the-deficit/

245 Reid: "Millionaire Job Creators Are Like Unicorns" …They "Don't Exist." Real Clear Politics Video. December 12, 2011. http://www.realclearpolitics.com/video/2011/12/12/reid_millionaire_job_creators_are_like_un icorns_because_they_dont_exist.html

246 Tamara Keith. GOP Objects To 'Millionaires Surtax'; Millionaires We Found? Not So Much. NPR, December 9, 2011. http://m.npr.org/news/Business/143398685

247 Ibid.

248 Alan Reynolds. Tax Rates, Inequality and the 1%. Wall Street Journal. December 6, 2011. http://online.wsj.com/article/SB10001424052970204630904577062661910819078.html

249 Alan Reynolds. Tax Rates, Inequality and the 1%. Wall Street Journal. December 6, 2011. http://online.wsj.com/article/SB10001424052970204630904577062661910819078.html

250 U.S Debt Clock. July, 2011. http://www.usdebtclock.org/

251 Liberal Group's Medicare Ad Shows Paul Ryan Throwing Grandma Off The Cliff. http://Www.Youtube.Com/Watch?V=Unnaeohxfyi

252 Charles Krauthammer. The Elmendorf Rule. Washington Post Opinions, July 8, 2011. http://www.washingtonpost.com/opinions/the-elmendorf-rule/2011/07/07/gIQAPagk2H_story.html

253 Penny Singer. Luxury-Tax Repeal Encourages Sellers. New York Times. October 3, 1993. http://www.nytimes.com/1993/10/03/nyregion/luxury-tax-repeal-encourages-sellers.html

254 Bret Baier. Who Are the Media Blaming for Debt Crisis. Special Report, Fox News, July 27, 2011. http://video.foxnews.com/v/1083087600001/grapevine-who-are-media-blaming-for-debt-crisis

255 Charles Krauthammer. The Elmendorf Rule. Washington Post Opinions, July 8, 2011. http://www.washingtonpost.com/opinions/the-elmendorf-rule/2011/07/07/gIQAPagk2H_story.html

256 Con Carroll. Budget Lies. Washington Examiner, February 13, 2012. http://campaign2012.washingtonexaminer.com/blogs/beltway-confidential/morning-examiner-obama%E2%80%99s-budget-lies/372101

257 Transcript of Obama's News Conference on the Debt Ceiling. Wall Street Journal, July 22, 2011. http://blogs.wsj.com/washwire/2011/07/22/transcript-of-obamas-news-conference-on-the-debt-ceiling/

258 Ibid.

259 Boehner on Debt Limit: White House Insisted on Raising Taxes, Moved Goalposts. Boehner Website, July 22, 2011. http://johnboehner.house.gov/News/DocumentSingle.aspx?DocumentID=253430

260 Mike Emanuel. Boehner: The President and I "Just Come from Two Different Planets." Fox News, January 24, 2012. http://politics.blogs.foxnews.com/2012/01/24/boehner-president-i-just-come-two-different-planets

261 Krugman, Paul. Nobody Understands Debt. The New York Times, January 1, 2012. http://www.nytimes.com/2012/01/02/opinion/krugman-nobody-understands-debt.html

262 Ibid.

263 Ibid.

264 Ibid.

265 Porter Stansberry. How the Chinese Will Establish a New Financial Order. Daily Wealth, February 22, 2012. http://www.dailywealth.com/1994/How-the-Chinese-Will-Establish-a-New-Financial-Order

266 Ibid.

267 Greta Van Susteren. Leader Pelosi is Trying to Save the World from Republican Budget. Fox News, GretaWire. July 28, 2011. http://gretawire.foxnewsinsider.com/2011/07/28/leader-pelosi-is-trying-to-save-world-from-republican-budget/

268 Charles Krauthammer. The Washington Post Writers Group, July 25, 2011. http://www.postwritersgroup.com/krauthammer.htm

269 Barna Survey: Americans Think Obama is the Smartest and Most Honest Major Candidate. The Barna Group, October 4, 2011. http://www.barna.org/culture-articles/530-barna-survey-americans-think-obama-is-the-smartest-and-most-honest-major-candidate

270 Ibid.

271 Jonathon Weil. Geithner: No Risk U.S. Will Lose AAA Credit Rating – —Ever. The Daily Bail. April 19, 2011. http://dailybail.com/home/geithner-no-risk-us-will-lose-aaa-credit-rating-ever.html

272 Graham Bowley and Christine Hauser. Volatile Wall Street Ends the Day Mixed. The New York Times Business Day, August 5, 2011. http://www.nytimes.com/2011/08/06/business/daily-stock-market-activity.html

273 Nikola G. Swann and John Chambers. United States of America Long-Term Rating Lowered to AA+ on Political Risks and Raising Debt Burden; Outlook Negative. Standard & Poors, Global Credit Portal, August 5, 2011. http://www.standardandpoors.com/servlet/BlobServer?blobheadername3=MDT-Type&blobcol=urldata&blobtable=MungoBlobs&blobheadervalue2=inline%3B+filename%3D US_Downgraded_AA%2B.pdf&blobheadername2=Content-

Disposition&blobheadervalue1=application%2Fpdf&blobkey=id&blobheadername1=content-type&blobwhere=1243942957443&blobheadervalue3=UTF-8

274 Ibid.

275 Blame Game Vitriol Demonstrates S&P Disgust. Fox News. August 7, 2011. http://www.foxnews.com/politics/2011/08/07/blame-game-vitriol-demonstrates-sp-disgust/

276 Greta Van Susteren. Top Obama Guy—David AxelRod —Says it is the 'Tea Party." Fox News, GretaWire, August 7, 2011. http://gretawire.foxnewsinsider.com/2011/08/07/top-obama-guy-david-axelrod-blames-tea-party/

277 http://paulryan.house.gov/UploadedFiles/PathToProsperityFY2012.pdf

278 An excellent resource: Ron Paul's Roadmap. The Claremont Institute. April, 2011. http://www.claremont.org/publications/crb/id.1749/article_detail.asp

279 Richard Wagner and Martin Gould. Obamacare's Gross Costs Double to $1.76 Trillion, CBO Projects. NewsMax, March 14, 2012. http://www.newsmax.com/Newsfront/Obamacare-costs-double-CBO/2012/03/14/id/432506

280 Jeffrey Anderson. CBO: Obamacare Would Cost Over $2 Trillion. The Weekly Standard, March 18, 2011. http://www.weeklystandard.com/blogs/cbo-obamacare-would-cost-over-2-trillion?page=2

281 Analyzing the President's New Budget Framework. Committee for a Responsible Federal Budget. April 21, 2011. http://crfb.org/sites/default/files/Analyzing_the_Presidents_New_Budget_Framework.pdf

282 Anthony Salvanto. Poll: 71% Shun GOP Handling of Debt Crisis. CBS News, July 18, 2011. http://www.cbsnews.com/8301-503544_162-20080250-503544.html?tag=pop

283 CNN/ORC Poll. July 21, 2011. http://i2.cdn.turner.com/cnn/2011/images/07/21/rel11b.pdf

284 Anthony Salvanto. Poll: 71% Shun GOP Handling of Debt Crisis. CBS News, July 18, 2011. http://www.cbsnews.com/8301-503544_162-20080250-503544.html?tag=pop

285 CNN/ORC Poll. July 21, 2011. http://i2.cdn.turner.com/cnn/2011/images/07/21/rel11b.pdf

286 Dana Blanton. Fox News Poll: Trust in Federal Government Hits New Low. Fox News, July 20, 2011. http://www.foxnews.com/politics/2011/07/20/fox-news-poll-trust-in-federal-government-hits-new-low/

287 Fox News Poll Raw Data: Romney Hits Record High, But Still Tied with Obama. Fox News, July 20, 2011. http://www.foxnews.com/interactive/politics/2012/01/15/fox-news-poll-raw-data-romney-hits-record-high-but-still-tied-with-obama/

288 Aaron Klein and Brenda Elliott. *Red Army; The Radical network That Must Be Defeated to Save America.* (New York: Broadside Books, Harper Collins Publisher, 2011). Pp 80-81.

289 Words We Use. Herndon Alliance. July 7, 2010. http://herndonalliance.org/resources/basics-american-values/words-we-use.html

Chapter 6 – Collapsing America

290 Aaron Klein and Brenda Elliott. *Red Army, The Radical Network that Must be Defeated to Save America.* (New York: Broadside Books, Harper-Collins Publishers, 2011) P. Cover Flap

291 Saul Alinsky: Prophet of Power to the People. Time Magazine, March 2, 1970. http://www.time.com/time/magazine/article/0,9171,904228,00.html

292 Saul Alinsky. *Rules for Radicals; A Pragmatic Primer for Realistic Radicals.* (New York: Vintage Books/Random House, 1971). P.29.

293. Scott Herron. Saul Alinsky's Rules for Radicals. Heirs of Liberty Press. May 9, 2009 http://www.heirsoflibertypress.org/article.php?id=52

294 Ibid, P. 166.

295 Ibid.

296 Ibid, P. 116

297 Scott Herron. Saul Alinsky's Rules for Radicals. Heirs of Liberty Press. May 9, 2009 http://www.heirsoflibertypress.org/article.php?id=52

298 Saul Alinsky. *Rules for Radicals; A Pragmatic Primer for Realistic Radicals.* (New York: Vintage Books/Random House, 1971). P. 3.

299 Saul Alinsky: Prophet of Power to the People. Time Magazine, March 2, 1970.
     http://www.time.com/time/magazine/article/0,9171,904228,00.html
300 Ibid.
301 Glenn Beck. Manufacturing Czar Says "the Free Market is Nonsense." The Glenn Beck
     Program. October 20, 2009. Beck played an actual recording of Bloom's speech.
     http://www.glennbeck.com/content/articles/article/198/32133/
302 Saul Alinsky: Prophet of Power to the People. Time Magazine, March 2, 1970.
     http://www.time.com/time/magazine/article/0,9171,904228,00.html Rules for Radicals. Heirs
     of Liberty Press. May 9, 2009 http://www.heirsoflibertypress.org/article.php?id=52
303 Nina Easton. What's really behind SEIU's Bank of America Protests? Fortune, May 19,
     2010.
     http://money.cnn.com/2010/05/19/news/companies/SEIU_Bank_of_America_protest.fortune/
     index.htm
304 Capital Confidential. Police Report on "Gladney Beatings by SEIU Thugs. Big
     Government.com, November 9, 2009.
     http://biggovernment.com/capitolconfidential/2009/11/09/exclusive-police-report-on-gladney-
     beating-by-seiu-thugs/
305 Sammy Benoit. Obama, ACOPRN, and the SEIU? They Go Way Back. Pajamas Media,
     August 18, 2009. http://pajamasmedia.com/blog/obama-acorn-and-the-seiu-they-go-way-
     back/
306 Capital Confidential. Police Report on "Gladney Beatings by SEIU Thugs. Big
     Government.com. November 9, 2009.
     http://biggovernment.com/capitolconfidential/2009/11/09/exclusive-police-report-on-gladney-
     beating-by-seiu-thugs/
307 Pelosi: We'll Pole Vault, Parachute in To Get Health Care Passed. Fox News, January 28,
     2010. http://www.breitbart.tv/pelosi-well-pole-vault-parachute-in-to-get-health-care-passed/
308 Glenn Beck. Obama Is Transforming Us. The Glenn Beck Program, July 29, 2009. Beck
     played actual video of Obama's speech.
     http://www.glennbeck.com/content/articles/article/198/28610/
309 Editorial. Solyndra Scandal Exposes the Lie of Government 'Investment.' Washington
     Examiner. September 17, 2011. http://washingtonexaminer.com/opinion/2011/09/solyndra-
     scandal-exposes-lie-government-investment
310 Ibid.
311 John Kass. Obama's Solyndra Scandal Reeks of the Chicago Way. Chicago Tribune,
     September 18, 2011. http://articles.chicagotribune.com/2011-09-18/news/ct-met-kass-0918-
     20110918_1_solyndra-loan-guarantee-obama-fundraisers-obama-white-house
312 Adrian Krieg. Stupid People Do Stupid Things. The Daily Bell, October 22, 2011.
     http://thedailybell.com/3122/Adrian-Krieg-Stupid-people-do-stupid-things
313 Ibid.
314 David Almasi. Al Gore and Obama's Job Panel Member John Doerr Benefit from Clean
     Energy Loan to Fisker Automotive. National Center for Public Policy Research, October 26,
     2011. http://www.nationalcenter.org/PR-Crony_102611.html
315 Parent of Obama-backed Battery Maker Goes Bankrupt. Fox News, January 27, 2012.
     http://www.foxnews.com/politics/2012/01/27/parent-obama-backed-battery-maker-goes-
     bankrupt/
316 Another Solyndra? Fox News, January 27, 2012
     http://video.foxnews.com/v/1417296599001/another-solyndra
317 Solar Panels Maker Q-Cells to File Bankruptcy. BBC News/Business. April 2, 2012.
     http://www.bbc.co.uk/news/business-17587830
318 Alexander Neubacher. Re-Evaluating Germany[s "Blind Faith in the Sun. der Spiegel,
     January 18, 2012. http://www.spiegel.de/international/germany/0,1518,809439,00.html
     Also, Kirsty Buchanan. MPs' Bid to Halt Hot Air Chris Huhne's Wind Farms. Express,
     January 22, 2012. http://www.express.co.uk/posts/view/297150/MPS-bid-to-halt-hot-air-
     Chris-Huhne-s-wind-farms

319 Lachian Markay. The Foundry, The Heritage Foundation, November 14, 2011. (Taken from Peter Schweizer's book, *Throw them All Out*. http://blog.heritage.org/2011/11/14/report-80-of-doe-green-energy-loans-went-to-obama-backers/

320 David Almasi and Judy Kent. More Crony Capitalism from Federal Government's Clean Energy Push. The National Center for Public Policy Research. October 26, 2011. http://www.nationalcenter.org/PR-Crony_102611.html

321 Robert Bryce, Energy Smackdown: Keystone XL vs. Solyndra. National Review, November 21, 2011. http://www.ncpa.org/sub/dpd/index.php?Article_ID=21346&utm_source=newsletter&utm_medium=email&utm_campaign=DPD

322 Michael Coffman. Obama's All-Out War. Range magazine, Summer 2011. http://www.rangemagazine.com/features/summer-11/range-su11-obamas_war.pdf

323 Arctic National Wildlife Refuge (ANWR). U.S. Department of Energy, National Energy Technology Laboratory. No date. http://www.netl.doe.gov/publications/factsheets/policy/Policy006.pdf

324 Co-existing With Oil Development, Central Arctic Caribou Heard Thrives, Population at Record High. ANWR.org, 2009. http://www.anwr.org/images/pdf/Cariboufinal_6-09.pdf

325 Michael Coffman. Obama's All-Out War. Range Magazine, Summer, 2011. http://www.rangemagazine.com/features/summer-11/range-su11-obamas_war.pdf

326 Are the Chinese Drilling off the Coast of Cuba?. FactCheck.com, June 26, 2008. http://www.factcheck.org/2008/06/drilling-off-the-coast-of-cuba/

327 Bill Cornwell. Is Drilling 60 Miles off the Coast of Florida too Close for Comfort? Florida Weekly, November 24, 2011. http://palmbeachgardens.floridaweekly.com/news/2011-11-24/Top_News/Is_drilling_60_miles_off_the_coast_of_Florida_too_.html

328 Glenn Kessler. U.S. Oil Resources: President Obama's 'Non Sequitur Facts'. Washington Post, March 15, 2012. Quote was from a speech made in North Carolina, March 7, 2012. http://www.washingtonpost.com/blogs/fact-checker/post/us-oil-resources-president-obamas-non-sequitur-facts/2012/03/14/gIQApP14CS_blog.html

329 Ibid.

330 Bill Cornwell. Is Drilling 60 Miles off the Coast of Florida too Close for Comfort? Florida Weekly, November 24, 2011. http://palmbeachgardens.floridaweekly.com/news/2011-11-24/Top_News/Is_drilling_60_miles_off_the_coast_of_Florida_too_.html   Ibid.

331 Erin Bock. Federal Judge Rules Against EPA Coal Permit Regulations. The Jurist, October 8, 2011. http://jurist.org/paperchase/2011/10/federal-judge-rules-against-epa-coal-permit-regulations.php

332 Forrest Jones. Former Shell CEO: Get Ready for $5 Gasoline. Money News, February 14, 2011. http://www.moneynews.com/StreetTalk/Former-Shell-Gasoline-price/2012/02/13/id/429217

333 Phil Taylor. Oil and Gas: Production on Federal Tracts Fell in 2011. EnergyWire, February 27, 2012.

334 Robert Rapier. Are President Obama's Polices Causing U.S. Oil Production to Rise? Consumer Energy Report, January 25, 2012. http://www.consumerenergyreport.com/2012/01/23/are-president-obamas-policies-causing-a-rise-in-u-s-oil-production/

335 Ibid.

336 UK Faces Green Agenda Backlash as Energy Prices Rise. Reuters Africa. July 24, 2011. http://af.reuters.com/article/energyOilNews/idAFL6E7IM1AM20110724?sp=true
     Also: Andrew Gilligan. British Jobs Gone with the Wind. The London Telegraph, July 17, 2011. http://www.telegraph.co.uk/journalists/andrew-gilligan/8642659/British-jobs-gone-with-the-wind.html

337 Editorial. Investor's Business Daily, June 20, 2010. http://news.investors.com/Article/534696/201005201839/The-Green-Jobs-Myth.htm

338 Nancy Pelosi and Newt Gingrich Commercial on Climate Change. YouTube, April 27, 2008. http://www.youtube.com/watch?v=qi6n_-wB154

339 Richard Cloward and Frances Piven. The Weight of the Poor, A Strategy to End Poverty. Discover the Networks, May 2, 1966. http://www.discoverthenetworks.org/Articles/A%20Strategy%20to%20End%20Poverty2.html

340 The Cloward-Piven Strategy. Discover The Networks, no date. http://www.discoverthenetworks.org/groupProfile.asp?grpid=6967

341 Richard Cloward and Frances Piven. The Weight of the Poor, A Strategy to End Poverty. Discover the Networks, May 2, 1966 http://www.discoverthenetworks.org/Articles/A%20Strategy%20to%20End%20Poverty2.html

342 The Cloward-Piven Strategy. Discover The Networks, no date. http://www.discoverthenetworks.org/groupProfile.asp?grpid=6967

343 Ibid.

344 Ibid.

345 Ibid.

346 Eric Shawn. ACORN's Troubled Past Leads to Stunning Election Day Announcement. Fox News, November 2, 2010. http://politics.blogs.foxnews.com/2010/11/02/acorn-s-troubled-past-leads-stunning-election-day-announcement

347 Stephen Clark and Nicole Collins. Obama Violated ACORN Funding Ban With Housing Grant to Offshoot, Watchdog Says. Fox News, July 6, 2011. http://www.foxnews.com/politics/2011/07/06/obama-violates-acorn-funding-ban-with-housing-grant-to-offshoot-watchdog-says/#ixzz1UB2IfOe2

348 Ibid.

349 Recent Efforts to Overload the American System. DiscoverTheNetworks.org, January 2010. http://archive.frontpagemag.com/readArticle.aspx?ARTID=33989

350 Katherine Bradley and Robert Rector. Welfare Spendathon: House Stimulus Bill Will Cost Taxpayers $787 Billion in New Welfare Spending. Heritage Foundation, Webmemo #2276, February 6, 2009. http://www.heritage.org/research/reports/2009/02/welfare-spendathon-house-stimulus-bill-will-cost-taxpayers-787-billion-in-new-welfare-spending

351 Ibid.

352 Robert Rector and Katherine Bradley. Welfare Spendathon. FrontPage Magazine, February 9, 2009. http://archive.frontpagemag.com/readArticle.aspx?ARTID=33989

353 Dick Morris and Eileen McGann. Catastrophe, Obama's War on Prosperity (HarperCollins Publishers, New York, 2009), p 47. http://books.google.com/books?id=kWtYU7IKVgQC&pg=PA47&lpg=PA47&dq=Under+the+guise+of+a+stimulus+package+to+bring+the+economy+out+of+recession+Dick+Morris&source=bl&ots=pSAO86Eju0&sig=9zha59bkljFlp5dV5oDhJdpDVWw&hl=en&ei=8XzmTriEAuj40gGtmOHEDA&sa=X&oi=book_result&ct=result&resnum=4&ved=0CDQQ6AEwAw#v=onepage&q&f=false

354 Katherine Bradley and Robert Rector. Welfare Spendathon: House Stimulus Bill Will Cost Taxpayers $787 Billion in New Welfare Spending. Heritage Foundation, Webmemo #2276, February 6, 2009. http://www.heritage.org/research/reports/2009/02/welfare-spendathon-house-stimulus-bill-will-cost-taxpayers-787-billion-in-new-welfare-spending

355 Jeffrey Anderson. Obama's Economists: 'Stimulus' Has Cost $278,000 per job. The Weekly Standard, July 3, 2011. http://www.weeklystandard.com/blogs/obama-s-economists-stimulus-has-cost-278000-job_576014.html

356 Ibid.

357 William McBride. Global Evidence on Taxes and Economic Growth: Payroll Taxes Have No Effect. Tax Foundation, February 8, 2012. http://www.taxfoundation.org/publications/show/27959.html

358 Alexander Bolton. Senate Democrats Buck Obama on Jobs Proposal by Changing 'Pay-Fors'. The Hill, October 4, 2011. http://thehill.com/homenews/senate/185577-senate-dems-buck-obama-on-jobs-plan

359 Scott Conroy. Palin Unleashes New Attack Against Obama on Coal, CBS News, November 2, 2008. http://www.cbsnews.com/8301-502443_162-4564043-502443.html

360 Keystone Pipeline Decision a Political Ploy or a Political Problem? Fox News, November 11, 2011. http://www.foxnews.com/politics/2011/11/11/keystone-pipeline-decision-political-ploy-or-political-problem/

361 Obama Administration Rejects Keystone Pipeline Permit. Fox News, January 18, 2012. http://www.foxnews.com/politics/2012/01/18/industry-source-state-department-will-reject-keystone-pipeline-reroute/

362 Ed Hiserodt. Hungry for Power. New American, Vol 28(4), February 20, 2012.

363 Bob Beauprez. Pipeline Pushover: What Obama's Keystone XL Decision Really Tells the American Public. Fox News Opinion, January 18, 2012. http://www.foxnews.com/opinion/2012/01/18/pipeline-pushover-what-obamas-keystone-xl-decision-really-tells-american-public/

364 Recent Efforts to Overload the American System. Discoverthenetworks.org, January 2010. http://www.discoverthenetworks.org/Articles/recenteffortstooverloadtheamericansystem.html

365 Ibid.

366 Peter Roff. Pelosi: Pass Health Reform So You Can Find Out What's In It. US News. March 9, 2010. http://www.usnews.com/opinion/blogs/peter-roff/2010/03/09/pelosi-pass-health-reform-so-you-can-find-out-whats-in-it

367 Aaron Klein and Brenda Elliott. *Red Army, The Radical Network that Must be Defeated to Save America.* (New York: Broadside Books, Harper-Collins Publishers, 2011) P. 66.

368 Ibid, P 67.

369 Ibid, Pp 67-69.

370 Ibid, Pp 14-15.

371 Ibid, P 17.

372 Ibid, P 13.

373 Ibid, P 27.

374 Ibid, P 32.

375 Ibid, P 63.

376 Ibid.

377 Ibid. P 207

378 Julia Seymour. Obama the Taxcutter: A Network Fairytale: Executive Summary. Business and Media Institute; Media Research Center. October 19, 2010. http://www.mrc.org/bmi/reports/2010/Obama_the_Tax_Cutter_A_Network_Fairy_Tale.html

379 Still Thrilled by Obama. Executive Summary. Media Research Center, November, 2011. http://www.mrc.org/Static/uploads/StillThrilled.pdf

380 Jonathan Strong. Documents Show Media Plotting to Kill Stories About Rev. Jeremiah Wright. The Daily Caller, July 20, 2010. http://dailycaller.com/2010/07/20/documents-show-media-plotting-to-kill-stories-about-rev-jeremiah-wright/

381 Ibid.

382 Ibid.

383 Jonathan Strong. Liberal journalists suggest government censor Fox News. The Daily Caller, July 21, 2010. http://dailycaller.com/2010/07/21/liberal-journalists-suggest-government-shut-down-fox-news/

384 Lyle Rossiter Jr. M.D. *The Liberal Mind; The Psychological Causes of Political Madness.* (St. Charles, IL: Free World Books, LLC., 2006). P 384.

385 Jonathan Strong. Liberal journalists suggest government censor Fox News. The Daily Caller, July 21, 2010. http://dailycaller.com/2010/07/21/liberal-journalists-suggest-government-shut-down-fox-news/

386 Lyle Rossiter Jr. M.D. *The Liberal Mind; The Psychological Causes of Political Madness.* (St. Charles, IL: Free World Books, LLC., 2006). Chapter 2

387 Ibid, P 31.

Chapter 7 – The Final Collapse?

388 The Invisible Committee. The Coming Insurrection. (Los Angeles: Semiotext(e), 2007, first published in French in 2005). P 128. http://tarnac9.wordpress.com/texts/the-coming-insurrection/

389 Ibid, Pp. 119, 121, 124, 126 and 130.

390 Revealed—The Left's Economic Terrorism Playbook: The Chase Campaign by a Coalition of Unions, Community Groups, Lawmakers and Students to Take Down US Capitalism and Redistribute Wealth & Power. The Blaze, March 22, 2011. http://www.theblaze.com/stories/revealed-the-lefts-economic-terrorism-playbook-the-chase-campaign-for-a-coalition-of-unions-community-groups-lawmakers-and-students-to-take-down-us-capitalism-and-redistribute-wealth-power/

391 Stephen Lerner. Speaker at the Left Forum 2011 "Towards a Politics of Solidarity" Pace University March 19, 2011; read more, http://www.businessinsider.com/seiu-union-plan-to-destroy-jpmorgan#ixzz1HvhSaie1

392 Stephen Lerner. Speaker at the Left Forum 2011 "Towards a Politics of Solidarity" Pace University March 19, 2011; read more, http://www.businessinsider.com/seiu-union-plan-to-destroy-jpmorgan#ixzz1HvhSaie1

393 Stephen Lerner. Speaker at the Left Forum 2011 "Towards a Politics of Solidarity" Pace University March 19, 2011; read more, http://www.businessinsider.com/seiu-union-plan-to-destroy-jpmorgan#ixzz1HvhSaie1

394 Revealed—The Left's Economic Terrorism Playbook: The Chase Campaign by a Coalition of Unions, Community Groups, Lawmakers and Students to Take Down US Capitalism and Redistribute Wealth & Power. The Blaze, March 22, 2011. http://www.theblaze.com/stories/revealed-the-lefts-economic-terrorism-playbook-the-chase-campaign-for-a-coalition-of-unions-community-groups-lawmakers-and-students-to-take-down-us-capitalism-and-redistribute-wealth-power/

395 Ibid.

396 William Jasper. Occupy Wall Street; Lawlessness and Communist Revolution Masquerading as Idealism. The New American, December 19, 2011. P 17.

397 Thomas Lifson. OWS Arrest Total Nearing 5000. American Thinker, November 27, 2011. http://www.americanthinker.com/blog/2011/11/ows_arrest_total_nearing_5000.html

398 William Jasper. Occupy Wall Street; Lawlessness and Communist Revolution Masquerading as Idealism. The New American, December 19, 2011. P 17.

399 Jim Hoft. Nazi Party and Communist Party Support Occupy Wall Street. Human Events. October 15, 2011. http://www.humanevents.com/article.php?id=46893
Glenn Beck. The Truth Behind Occupy Wall Street. GBTV, October 24, 2011. http://web.gbtv.com/media/video.jsp

400 William Jasper. Occupy Wall Street; Lawlessness and Communist Revolution Masquerading as Idealism. The New American, December 19, 2011. Pp 18-19.

401 Ibid.

402 President Obama Endorses Occupy Wall Street Protesters; Looking to Politicize Anger? ForexTV, October 6, 2011. http://www.forextv.com/forex-news-story/president-obama-endorses-occupy-wall-street-protesters-looking-to-politicize-anger

403 JWF. Democrats Circulate Petition in Support of Occupy Wall Street Mob. October 10, 2011. http://www.humanevents.com/article.php?id=46758&keywords=Occupy+Wall+Street

404 Ibid.

405 Glenn Beck. The Truth Behind Occupy Wall Street. GBTV, October 24, 2011. http://web.gbtv.com/media/video.jsp

406 Ibid.

407 Ibid.

408 Ibid.

409 Ibid.

410 Ibid.

411 Ibid.

412 Matthew Vadum. George Soros Funds Occupy Wall Street. Human Events, October 21, 2011. http://www.humanevents.com/article.php?id=47009

413 Ed Lasky. All the News that Fits Soros' Agenda. Whistleblower magazine, December 2010. Pp 34-37.

414 Matthew Vadum. George Soros Funds Occupy Wall Street. Human Events, October 21, 2011. http://www.humanevents.com/article.php?id=47009

415 Staff Report. Occupy Wall Street Demands Global UN Tax and Worldwide G20 Protest. The Daily Bell, October 20, 2011. http://www.thedailybell.com/3111/Occupy-Wall-Street-Demands-Global-UN-Tax-and-Worldwide-G20-Protest

416 David Almasi. Black Conservatives Demand Pelosi, NAACP and Other Liberals Renounce and Apologize for Occupy Wall Street Outrageousness. National Center for Public Policy Research., November 17, 2011.

417 China's Meltdown Continues. The Daily Bell, December 15, 2011. http://www.thedailybell.com/3354/Chinas-Meltdown-Continues

418 Porter Stansberry. Why Europe's Banks Are in Such Bad Shape. S&A Digest, September 2, 2011 http://www.stansberryresearch.com/secure/digest/2011/html/index/882

419 Chris Giles. Alternative Scenarios for Greek Debt Crisis. Financial Times, June, 22, 2011. http://www.ft.com/intl/cms/s/0/f4b8c97c-9cf6-11e0-8678-00144feabdc0.html#axzz1QQhZ1Krh

420 Kerin Hope and Ralph Atkins. Violence Escalates After Greek Vote. Financial Times, June 29, 2011. http://www.ft.com/intl/cms/s/0/714cbba8-a281-11e0-9760-00144feabdc0.html#axzz1QsRLugo3

421 Chris Giles. Ibid.

422 Weekend Edition: Porter Stansberry: The World's Global Currency System Is Collapsing. The Growth Stock Wire. June 25, 2011.

423 Michael Birnbaum. Euro Zone Pumps Up Bailout Fund to nearly $1 Trillion. Washington Post, March 30, 2012. http://www.washingtonpost.com/world/euro-zone-pumps-up-bailout-fund-to-nearly-1-trillion/2012/03/30/gIQAneD7kS_story.html

424 Dan Ferris. The S&A Digest. Why Greece is Toast, January 23, 2012. http://www.stansberryresearch.com/secure/digest/2012/html/index/984

425 James Neuger and Stephanie Bodoni. EU Sets 50% Writedown, $1.4T in Crisis Fight. Bloomberg, October 27, 2011. http://www.bloomberg.com/news/2011-10-27/europe-leaders-set-50-greek-writedown-1-4-trillion-in-debt-crisis-fight.html
Porter Stansberry. The U.S. Will Print, Print, Print. S&A Digest, October 14, 2011. http://www.stansberryresearch.com/secure/digest/2011/html/index/911

426 Ibid.

427 Porter Stansberry. The U.S. Will Print, Print, Print. S&A Digest, October 14, 2011. http://www.stansberryresearch.com/secure/digest/2011/html/index/911

428 Shai Ahmed. Greek Debt Writedown of 100 Percent Needed: Analyst. CNBC, October 18, 2011. http://www.cnbc.com/id/44941628/Greek_Debt_Writedown_of_100_Percent_Needed_Analyst

429 The Trilateral Commission Appoints Lucas Papademos and Mario Monti. A Freak Show, November 11, 2011. http://afreakshow.com/2011/11/the-trilateral-commission-appoints-lucas-papademos-and-mario-monti/

430 Porter Stansberry. Moody's Wakes Up to Europe/Euro Banks Can't Fund the Gap. The S&A Digest, November 30, 2011. http://www.stansberryresearch.com/secure/digest/2011/html/index/943

431 Ibid.

432 FAQ on Europe's 'fiscal compact.' CBC News and The Associated Press, December 9, 2011 (updated December 12). http://www.cbc.ca/news/business/story/2011/12/09/faq-europe-fiscal-union.html

433 Ibid.

434 Porter Stansberry. The Problem with Europe's Latest Deal. S&A Digest, December 13, 2011. http://www.stansberryresearch.com/secure/digest/2011/html/index/953

435 Gabi Thesing and Rainer Buergin. ECB Lends 489 Billion Euros for Three Years, Exceeding Forecast. Bloomberg, December 28, 2011. http://www.businessweek.com/news/2011-12-28/ecb-lends-489-billion-euros-for-three-years-exceeding-forecast.html

436 Sean Goldsmith. The ECB's Latest, Lame Effort. S&A Digest, December 21, 2011. http://www.stansberryresearch.com/secure/digest/2011/html/index/961

437 Forrest Jones. European Banks Have $10 Trillion in Claims Against US Rivals. MoneyNews, December 30, 2011. http://www.moneynews.com/StreetTalk/Forbes-European-Banks-US/2011/12/30/id/422564?s=al&promo_code=DD16-1

438 Tyler Durden. The Fed's $6oo Billion Stealth Bailout of Foreign Banks at the Expense of the Domestic Economy.Zerohedge.com, June 12, 2011. http://www.zerohedge.com/article/exclusive-feds-600-billion-stealth-bailout-foreign-banks-continues-expense-domestic-economy-

439 Robin Wigglesworth. $6.3tn Wiped Off Markets in 2011. Financial Times, December 30, 2011. http://www.ft.com/intl/cms/s/0/483069d8-32f3-11e1-8e0d-00144feabdc0.html#axzz1iKGDsW5u

440 Forest Jones. Foreigners Dump Record $69 Billion in US Treasurys. MoneyNews.com, December 31, 2011. http://www.moneynews.com/StreetTalk/Foreigners-Dump-US-Treasurys/2011/12/30/id/422563?s=al&promo_code=DD38-1

441 Maria Sarycheva. US Debt is "Flushed" Into the Market. RT, January 12, 2012. http://rt.com/politics/press/izvestiya/us-debt-market-treasury/en/

442 Brian Faler. Senate Vote Will Allow $1.2 Trillion Debt-Limit Increase. Washington Post Business, January 26, 2012. http://www.washingtonpost.com/business/senate-vote-will-allow-12-trillion-debt-limit-increase/2012/01/26/gIQA5omUVQ_story.html

443 Alternate Inflation Charts. Shadow Government Statistics. As of March 13, 2012. http://www.shadowstats.com/alternate_data/inflation-charts

444 William Jasper. Now, More than Ever, Time to Audit the Fed. New American, vol 28(4):25-28, February 20, 2012.

445 Economic and Social Affairs of the United Nations. Towards a New International Financial Architecture. United Nations, January 21, 1999. http://www.rescuingamericabook.com/financial_arch.htm.

446 Ibid.

447 Obama: North America Needs 'Aggressive Action.' USA Today, August 8, 2009. http://www.usatoday.com/news/world/2009-08-09-obama-mexico-summit_N.htm?csp=34

448 Ibid.

449 History. Financial Stability Board. Referenced on October 24, 2011. http://www.financialstabilityboard.org/about/history.htm

450 Mandate. Financial Stability Board. Referenced on October 24, 2011. http://www.financialstabilityboard.org/about/mandate.htm

451 Kofi Annan, Sec. Gen of UN. "Towards a stable international financial system, responsive to the challenges of development, especially in the developing countries." Report of the Secretary General, A/55/187. July 27, 2001, paragraph 24, 32, 40, 71 p. 8-10, 16.
Also: See General Assembly Resolution: Towards a strengthened and stable international financial architecture responsive to the priorities of growth and development, especially in developing countries, and to the promotion of economic and social equity. A/RES/55/186. January 25, 2001.
And: General Assembly Resolution: "Role of the United Nations in promoting development in the context of globalization and interdependence." A/RES/55/212. February 22, 2001.
And: International Conference on Financing for Development. March 18-22, 2002.
And: Monterrey Consensus, (The); Report of the International Conference on Financing for Development. UN General Assembly A/CONF.198/11. January 27, 2002. http://ods-dds-ny.un.org/doc/UNDOC/GEN/N02/392/67/PDF/N0239267.pdf?OpenElement

452 Monterrey Consensus of the International Conference on Financing for Development, numerous pages. http://www.un.org/esa/ffd/monterrey/MonterreyConsensus.pdf

Chapter 8 – The Anglo-American Establishment

453 Alex de Tocqueville. Democracy in America, 12th ed., 2 vol. (New York: Vintage Books, 1945), 1:329-30. http://xroads.virginia.edu/~HYPER/DETOC/1_ch17.htm

454 Christopher Columbus Langell—Further Readings. American Law and Legal Information. No date. http://law.jrank.org/pages/8072/Langdell-Christopher-Columbus.html

455 Ted Flynn. *Hope for the Wicked, The Master Plan to Rule the World*. (Sterling, Virginia: MaxKol Communications, Inc., 2000), p.4-5.

456 Woodrow Wilson. *The New Freedom*. (New York: Doubleday, Page and Co., 1913). http://www.cbc.cc.tx.us/acdem/social/mdwlwn/1302/doc15.htm

457 President Woodrow Wilson (National Economy and the Banking System, Senate Documents, Col. 3 No. 23) http://www.worldnewsstand.net/2002/article/3-15.htm

458 *Colonel Houses' Papers*, Sterling library, Yale University. Quoted in Dennis Cuddy, *Secret Records Revealed*. (Oklahoma City: Hearthstone Publishing, 1999), p.. 53.

459 Carroll Quigley. *Tragedy & Hope, A History of the World in Our Time*. (New York: The Macmillian Company, 1966), P 950.

460 Ibid, p. 324.

461 Kofi Annan, Sec. Gen of UN. "Towards a stable international financial system, responsive to the challenges of development, especially in the developing countries." *Report of the Secretary General, A/55/187*. July 27, 2001, paragraph 24, 32, 40, 71 p. 8-10, 16.
     Also: See General Assembly Resolution: Towards a strengthened and stable international financial architecture responsive to the priorities of growth and development, especially in developing countries, and to the promotion of economic and social equity. *A/RES/55/186*. January 25, 2001.
     And: General Assembly Resolution: "Role of the United Nations in promoting development in the context of globalization and interdependence." *A/RES/55/212*. February 22, 2001.
     And: International Conference on Financing for Development. March 18-22, 2002.
     And: *Monterrey Consensus, (The); Report of the International Conference on Financing for Development*. UN General Assembly A/CONF.198/11. January 27, 2002. http://ods-dds-ny.un.org/doc/UNDOC/GEN/N02/392/67/PDF/N0239267.pdf?OpenElement

462 Henry Lamb. "Global Taxation Moves Closer," WorldNetDaily, September 8, 2001. http://www.wnd.com/2001/09/10686/

463 Ibid.

464 Shannon Bond. Wall Street Protesters Seek to Create Structure. Financial Times, October 27, 2011. http://www.ft.com/intl/cms/s/0/68eae5d0-fe51-11e0-bac4-00144feabdc0.html#axzz1I94Kw3Lh

465 Carroll Quigley. *The Anglo-American Establishment* (NY: Books in Focus, 1981), preface, p. xi.

466 Ibid, p. ix, xi.
     Gurudas. *Treason, The New World Order*. (San Rafael, California: Cassandra Press, 1996), p. 17.

467 Carroll Quigley. *The Anglo-American Establishment*, p.ix, 32.

468 Ibid, x.

469 Antony Sutton. *America's Secret Establishment*, (Waterville, Oregon: Trine Day:, 1983, 1986, 2002), pp.1-58.

470 Carroll Quigley, *Tragedy and Hope*, p. 539.

471 Ibid, p. 950.

472. Ibid, p. 60-61.

473. Ibid, p. 51.

474. Ibid, p. 956.

475. Ibid, p. 133.

476 Foment OWS Terror, Open Camps? The Daily Bell, December 8, 2011. http://www.thedailybell.com/3330/Foment-OWS-Terror-Open-Camps

477 Carroll Quigley. *Tragedy & Hope, A History of the World in Our Time*. (New York: The Macmillian Company, 1966), P. 539.

478 Ibid, p. 72.

479 Ibid, p. 539-540.

480 Christopher Swan. "London Still Dominant as Finance Center." Bank of International Settlements, October 10, 2001. This is the last report found having this information. There is no reason, however, to believe it has changed substantially unless the Fed and Bank of England now have an even bigger share.

481 Ibid, p. 956.
482 Gurudas, p. 15.
483 Ted Flynn, p. 82.
484 Ibid.
485 Ibid, p. 83. In: G. Edward Griffin. *The Creature from Jekyll Island.* (Westlake Village, California: American Media, 1994), p. 269.
486 Carroll Quigley, *Tragedy and Hope*, p. 951.
487 Ted Flynn, p. 79.
488 Carroll Quigley, *Tragedy and Hope*, p. 130-131.
489 H. G. Wells, *Experiment in Autobiography*, (New York: The Macmillian Company, 1934), p. 651.
490 Carroll Quigley. *The Anglo-American Establishment*, op cit. p. 30, 31, 58, 137. In: Stanley Monteith, p. 95.
491 Ted Flynn, p. 79.
492 Carroll Quigley, *Tragedy and Hope*, p. 130-132.
493 Ibid, p. 950-951.
494 Ted Flynn, p. 80.
495 Carroll Quigley, *Tragedy and Hope*, p. 952.
496 Ibid, p. 954.
497 Ted Flynn, p. 85. In: Debra Rae. *ABC's of Globalism*, (Lafayette, La.: Huntington House, 1999) p. 91.
498 U.S., Congress, Senate, Subcommittee on Foreign Relations, Revision of the U.N. Charter, Hearings, 81st Congress, 2d Session. February 17, 1950. (Washington, D.C.: Government Printing Office, 1950), p. 494.
499 U.S., Congress, Senate, *Congressional Record,* February 23, 1954 Vol. 100, Part 2, P. S 2121. In: Gurudas. *Treason, The New World Order*, p. 21.
500 Phyllis Schlafly and Chester Ward. *Kissinger on the Couch* (New Rochelle, N.Y.: Arlington House, 1975), p. 151.
501 Goldwater; op cit., p. 278. In: Phyllis Schlafly and Chester Ward.
502 Carroll Quigley. *Tragedy & Hope, A History of the World in Our Time.* (New York: The Macmillian Company, 1966),p. 1247-1248.
503 One state's Solution to Coordination. American Stewards. http://www.americanstewards.us/news-publications/coordination-works/coordination-works-previous-articles/one-solution-to-get-state-agencies-to-coordinate

Chapter 9 – Institution and People

504 Membership, Council on Foreign Relations. (as of September 27, 2011) http://www.cfr.org/about/membership/
505 Ibid.
506 Barry Goldwater. *With No Apologies* (William Marrow and Co., 1979) op cit., p. 277-278. In: Phyllis Schlafly and Chester Ward.
507 Carroll Quigley. *The Anglo-American Establishment.* (New York: Books in Focus, 1981). Preface, p. x.
508 James Delingpole. Climategate: the Official Coverup Continues. The Telegraph, February 12, 2010. http://blogs.telegraph.co.uk/news/jamesdelingpole/100025934/climategate-the-official-cover-up-continues/
509 Dave Rose. Forget Global warming—It's Cycle 25 We Need to Worry About (and if NASA Scientists are Right, the Tames Will Be Freezing over Again). Daily Mail, January 29, 2012. http://www.dailymail.co.uk/sciencetech/article-2093264/Forget-global-warming--Cycle-25-need-worry-NASA-scientists-right-Thames-freezing-again.html?ito=feeds-newsxml
510 Michael Coffman. The Green Energy Fraud—Americans be Damned. Range magazine. Spring, 2012. http://www.rangemagazine.com/
511 Carroll Quigley. *Tragedy & Hope, A History of the World in Our Time.* (New York: The Macmillian Company, 1966), p. 73.

512 Ibid, p. 1248

513 Michael Tanner. Individual Liberty, Free Markets, and Peace. CATO Institute, Public Policy Report, January/February, 2008. http://www.cato.org/pubs/policy_report/v30n1/cpr30n1-1.html

514 J. Robert Smith. The Businessman Versus the Career Politician. American Thinker, September 10, 2011. http://www.americanthinker.com/2011/09/the_businessman_versus_the_career_politician.html

515 Philip Klein. The Failure of RomneyCare, Doctor Shortage Edition. The Washington Examiner, May, 9, 2011. http://washingtonexaminer.com/blogs/beltway-confidential/2011/05/failure-romneycare-doctor-shortage-edition

516 Carroll Quigley. *Tragedy & Hope, A History of the World in Our Time*. (New York: The Macmillian Company, 1966), p. 1248.

517 George Soros: Not "Much Difference" Between Romney and Obama. Real Clear Politics, January 30, 2012. http://www.realclearpolitics.com/video/2012/01/30/george_soros_not_much_difference_between_romney_and_obama.html

518 Pete Kasperowicz. Bachmann Defends Vote for Patriot Act After Fielding Complaints about Government Over-reach. The Hill, May 26, 2911. http://thehill.com/blogs/floor-action/house/163633-bachmann-defends-vote-for-patriot-act-after-fielding-complaints-about-government-over-reach

519 G. Edward Griffin. The Creature From Jekyll Island (Appleton, Wisconsin: American Opinion Publishing, Inc., 1994-1995), p. 438

520 David Weigel. Hermain Cain: The Fed Years. State, October 17, 2011. http://www.slate.com/articles/news_and_politics/politics/2011/10/herman_cain_s_fed_years_what_did_he_actually_do_.html

521 Carroll Quigley. *Tragedy & Hope, A History of the World in Our Time*. (New York: The Macmillian Company, 1966),p. 866.

522 "Systematic Analysis of Future Society." *The Behavioral Science Teacher Education Program* (Washington, D.C: U.S. Office of Education, Dept. of Health Education and Welfare, 1969), p. 237. In: Charlotte Iserbyt, p. A-24.

523 Ibid, p. 259, Ibid, p. A-25.

524 Carroll Quigley, *Tragedy and Hope*, p. 550.

525 Ibid, p. 551.

526 Ibid, pp. 551, 553.

527 A Short Intro to Agenda 21. Freedom Advocates, http://www.freedomadvocates.org/video/watch/145_short_intro_to_agenda_21/

528 Ibid, p. 866.

529 David Kupelian. The Emperor. Whistleblower, December 2010, p 3.

530 Ibid.

531 Chrystia Freeland. Transcript: George Soros Interview. Financial Times, October 23, 2009. http://www.ft.com/cms/s/0/6e2dfb82-c018-11de-aed2-00144feab49a.html#axzz1CjpoFGVa

532 Ibid.

533 Ian Welsh. What Not Buying Oil With Dollars Means. Ian Welsh, October 7, 2009. http://www.ianwelsh.net/what-not-buying-oil-with-dollars-means/

534 Robert Fisk. Oil Not Priced In Dollars by 2018? Business Week, October 6, 2009. http://www.businessweek.com/globalbiz/content/oct2009/gb2009106_736291.htm

535 Ian Welsh. What Not Buying Oil With Dollars Means. Ian Welsh, October 7, 2009. http://www.ianwelsh.net/what-not-buying-oil-with-dollars-means/

536 Matthew Vadum. George Soros Funds Occupy Wall Street. Human Events, October 21, 2011. http://www.humanevents.com/article.php?id=47009

537 List of Countries by GDP (nominal). Wikipedia. Accessed October 27, 2011. http://en.wikipedia.org/wiki/List_of_countries_by_GDP_(nominal)

538 The Man Who Broke the Bank of England. BBC News, December 6, 1998. http://news.bbc.co.uk/2/hi/229012.stm

539 Alice Thomson and Rachel Sylvester. George Soros, the Man Who Broke the Bank, Sees a Global Meltdown. The Sunday Times, March 28, 2009. http://www.timesonline.co.uk/tol/news/uk/article5989163.ece

540 Glenn Beck. George Soros, the Puppet Master, Part 2. November 10, 2010. Video. http://www.youtube.com/watch?v=yKK1QcQwzwE&feature=related

541 Arlen Williams. George Soros Video: Having Fun Subverting Nations. RenewAmerica.com, November 12, 2010. http://www.renewamerica.com/columns/williams/101112

542 Charlie Rose. A Conversation with George Soros. http://www.charlierose.com/view/interview/9031

543 James Lewis. George Soros the Guiltless. American Thinker, February 2, 2011. http://www.americanthinker.com/2007/10/soros_the_guiltless.html

544 James Lewis. Soros the Guiltless. American Thinker, February 2, 2011. http://www.americanthinker.com/2007/10/soros_the_guiltless.html

545 Alice Thomson and Rachel Sylvester. George Soros, the Man Who Broke the Bank, Sees a global Meltdown. The Sunday Times, March 28, 2009. http://www.timesonline.co.uk/tol/news/uk/article5989163.ece

546 George Soros, Nazi Collaborator. Snopes.com, April 25, 2009. Transcript from 60 Minutes Broadcast, December 20, 1998. http://message.snopes.com/showthread.php?t=43876

547 George Soros, Nazi Collaborator. Snopes.com, April 25, 2009. Transcript from 60 Minutes Broadcast, December 20, 1998. http://message.snopes.com/showthread.php?t=43876

548 James Lewis. Soros the Guiltless. American Thinker, February 2, 2011. http://www.americanthinker.com/2007/10/soros_the_guiltless.html

549 Glenn Beck. George Soros, the Puppet Master Part 1, November 9, 2010. Video http://www.youtube.com/watch?v=puLL0Eh5HZc

550 Whistleblower, December 2010 (the entire issue)

551 Glenn Beck. George Soros, the Puppet Master Part 1, November 9, 2010. Video http://www.youtube.com/watch?v=puLL0Eh5HZc

552 Aaron Klein. George Soros Minions Step Up War on Fox News. World Net Daily, May 25, 2011. http://www.wnd.com/2011/05/302733/

553 Tucker Carlson with Alex Pappas and Will Rahn. Inside Media Matters: Sources, Memos reveal Erratic Behavior, Close Coordination with White House and News Organizations. The Daily Caller, February 12, 2012. http://dailycaller.com/2012/02/12/inside-media-matters-sources-memos-reveal-erratic-behavior-close-coordination-with-white-house-and-news-organizations/3/

554 Ibid. http://dailycaller.com/2012/02/12/inside-media-matters-sources-memos-reveal-erratic-behavior-close-coordination-with-white-house-and-news-organizations/2/
Also: Jeffrey Lord. Is Media Matters Obama's Watergate. American Spectator, February 21, 2012. http://spectator.org/archives/2012/02/21/is-media-matters-obamas-waterg/1

555 Ibid. http://dailycaller.com/2012/02/12/inside-media-matters-sources-memos-reveal-erratic-behavior-close-coordination-with-white-house-and-news-organizations/3/

556 Jeffrey Lord. Is Media Matters Obama's Watergate. American Spectator, February 21, 2012. http://spectator.org/archives/2012/02/21/is-media-matters-obamas-waterg/1

557 Ed Lasky. All the News that Fits Soros' Agenda. Whistleblower magazine, December 2010. Pp 34-37.

558 Aaron Klein. George Soros Minions Step Up War on Fox News. World Net Daily, May 25, 2011. http://www.wnd.com/2011/05/302733/

559 Matthew Vadum. Liberal Billionaire Bankers Herb and Marion Sandler Paid ACORN to Hurt Wells Fargo. June 2, 2011. http://spectator.org/blog/2011/06/02/liberal-billionaire-bankers-he

560 Ibid.

561 Glenn Beck. George Soros, the Puppet Master, Part 2. November 10, 2010. Video. http://www.youtube.com/watch?v=yKK1QcQwzwE&feature=related

562 Ibid.

563 Matt Kauffman. Courting Justice. Citizen Magazine, Vol. 26(1):15, January, 2012.

564 Glenn Beck. George Soros, the Puppet Master, Part 2. November 10, 2010. Video. http://www.youtube.com/watch?v=yKK1QcQwzwE&feature=related

565 Richard Cloward and Frances Piven. The Weight of the Poor, A Strategy to End Poverty. Discover the Networks, May 2, 1966. http://www.discoverthenetworks.org/Articles/A%20Strategy%20to%20End%20Poverty2.html

566 Associated Press. Obama Budget Predicts $1.3T Deficit for 2012. http://www.foxnews.com/politics/2012/02/10/budget-ducks-big-benefit-cuts/

567 Brian Faler. Government Deficit Reports Inflames, Illustrates Budget Debate. Bloomberg, February 1, 2012. http://www.bloomberg.com/news/2012-01-31/budget-deficit-of-u-s-will-shrink-15-to-1-1-trillion-in-2012-cbo-says.html

568 Interest Expense on the Debt Outstanding. U.S. Treasury Dept. http://www.treasurydirect.gov/govt/reports/ir/ir_expense.htm

569 Min Zeng. Treasury Bond Market Unscathed by China's Reduced Buying. Wall Street Journal, January 20, 2012. http://online.wsj.com/article/BT-CO-20120120-705494.html

570 Porter Stansberry. The Largest Gold-Accumulation Plan of All Time. Daily Wealth, February 23, 2012. http://www.dailywealth.com/1995/The-Largest-Gold-Accumulation-Plan-of-All-Time
Also: Esther Tanquintic-Misa. Massive Gold Buying Mirrors Fear of Chinese Populace. IBTimes Gold, January 24, 2012. http://au.ibtimes.com/articles/286399/20120123/massive-gold-buying-mirrors-fear-chinese-populace.htm

571 Porter Stansberry. How the Chinese Will Establish a New Financial Order. Daily Wealth, February 22, 2012. http://www.dailywealth.com/1994/How-the-Chinese-Will-Establish-a-New-Financial-Order

572 Ian Welsh. What Not Buying Oil With Dollars Means. Ian Welsh, October 7, 2009. http://www.ianwelsh.net/what-not-buying-oil-with-dollars-means/

573 Min Zeng. Treasury Bond Market Unscathed by China's Reduced Buying. Wall Street Journal, January 20, 2012. http://online.wsj.com/article/BT-CO-20120120-705494.html

574 George Soros: Collapsing US Economy to Spark Street Violence. http://www.moneynews.com/StreetTalk/Soros-US-Economy-Violence/2012/01/23/id/425096

575 Forest Jones. Foreigners Dump Record $69 Billion in US Treasurys. MoneyNews.com, December 31, 2011. http://www.moneynews.com/StreetTalk/Foreigners-Dump-US-Treasurys/2011/12/30/id/422563?s=al&promo_code=DD38-1

576 Michael Coffman and Kristie Pelletier. Playing Politics with U.S. Deficits and Debt. Rescuing America Book. http://www.rescuingamericabook.com/opeds/Playing_Politics_with_the_U_S_Debt.pdf

Chapter 10 – Corrupting Education, 1800 to 1945

577 Frosty Woodridge. Illiteracy In America: 7,000 High School Kids Drop Out Every Day. WorldNetDaily, September 6, 2010) http://www.newswithviews.com/Wooldridge/frosty590.htm

578 Beverly Eakman. Education's Armageddon. The New American, Vol. 27(21):25-29, November 7, 2011. http://thenewamerican.com/culture/education/9475-educations-armageddon)

579 Ben Wolfgang. Scores Show Students Aren't Ready For College. The Washington Times, August 17, 2011) http://www.washingtontimes.com/news/2011/aug/17/scores-show-students-not-ready-college/?page=all

580 Sam Rosenfeld. "How To Dumb Down A Nation." WorldNetDaily, March 9, 2002 http://wnd.com/news/article.asp?ARTICLE_ID'26767

581 Ibid.

582 Charlotte Thomson Iserbyt. The Deliberate Dumbing Down of America, (Ravenna, Ohio: Conscience Press, 1999), p. xiv.

583 Ibid, p. 7.

584 Jean-Jacques Rousseau. Emile, (1762). In: Charlotte Thomson Iserbyt, The Deliberate Dumbing Down of America, Ravenna, Ohio: Conscience Press, 1999), p. 2.

585 Samuel Blumenfeld, NEA, The Trojan Horse of American Education, (Boise, ID: Paradigm Company), p. 17.

586 Ibid.

587 Ibid.

588 Ibid.

589 Ibid.

590 Antony C. Sutton. *America's Secret Establishment, An introduction to the Order of Skull & Bones* (Walterville, OR: Trine Day, 1983, 1986, 2002), p. 82.

591 Ibid, p. 83.

592 Ibid, p. 87.

593 Ibid, p. 86.

594 Samuel Blumenfeld, NEA, *The Trojan Horse of American Education*, p. 106.

595 Antony Sutton, *America's Secret Establishment*, p. 101.

596 Samuel Blumenfeld, *NEA, The Trojan Horse of American Education*, (Boise, ID: Paradigm Company), p. 53.

597 Ted Flynn. *Hope for the Wicked, The Master Plan to Rule the World*. (Sterling, Virginia: MaxKol Communications, Inc., 2000), p. 4.

598 John Dewey. *Democracy and Educational Administration* (School & Society, XVL, 1937), p. 457. In. Antony Sutton, *America's Secret Establishment*, p. 103.

599 John Dewey, My Pedagogic Creed. In. Antony Sutton, *America's Secret Establishment*, p. 102.

600 Antony Sutton, *America's Secret Establishment*, p. 102-103.

601 Microsoft Encarta, 2001.

602 Frederick T. Gates, "A Vision of the Remedy", *The Country School of Tomorrow: Occasional Papers No. 1*, (New York: General Education Board, 1913). In: Charlotte Iserbyt, P. 9.

603 Samuel Blumenfeld, *NEA: Trojan Horse in American Education*, P. 105.

604 Ibid.

605 Ibid, p. 106.

606 Debra Rae, *ABC's of Globalism*, (Lafayette, La.: Huntington House, 1999). p. 202. In: Ted Flynn, p. 4.

607 Charlotte Thomson Iserbyt, *The Deliberate Dumbing Down of America*, (Ravenna, Ohio: Conscience Press, 1999), p. 21.

608 *Progressive Journal*, (December 1943, Vol. XX, No. 8). In Charlotte Iserbyt, p. 11.

609 Charlotte Iserbyt, p. 14.

610 Ibid.

611 Ibid, p. 14-15.

612 John Hechinger. U.S. Teens Lag as China Soars on International Test. Bloomberg, December 7, 2010. http://www.bloomberg.com/news/2010-12-07/teens-in-u-s-rank-25th-on-math-test-trail-in-science-reading.html

613 "Findings and Concluding Observations of the Reece Committee." *Reece Committee Report*, 1954. In: Rene Wormser, *Foundations; Their Power and Influence* (New York: The Devin-Adair Company, 1958), p. 303.

614 Ibid.

615 *The Reece Committee Report*, 1954, p. 151. In: Rene Wormser, *Foundations; Their Power and Influence*, p. 153.

616 Rene Wormser, *Foundations; Their Power and Influence*, pp. 139, 144.

617 Ibid, p. 139.

618 "Findings and Concluding Observations of the Reece Committee." Ibid, p. 304.

619 Rene Wormser, *Foundations; Their Power and Influence*, p. 140.

620 Ibid, p. 142.

621 Ibid, p. 141.

622 Ibid, p. 144.

623 Ibid.

624 Ibid.

625 *Reece Committee Report*, p. 147. In: Rene Wormser, *Foundations; Their Power and Influence*, p. 145.

626 *Conclusions and Recommendations for the Social Studies* (New York: Charles Scribner's Sons, 1934), p. 1-2. In: Charlotte Iserbyt, p. 265.

627 Ibid, p. 16. In: Rene Wormser, *Foundations; Their Power and Influence*, p. 146-147.

628 Charlotte Iserbyt, p. 265.

629 "Findings and Concluding Observations of the Reece Committee." *Reece Committee Report*, 1954. In: Rene Wormser, *Foundations; Their Power and Influence*, p. 304.

630 Ibid, p. 149.

631 Ibid, p. 150.

632 Rene Wormser, *Foundations; Their Power and Influence,* p. 157.

633 Ibid.

634 Ibid, p. 159.

635. Ibid, p. 157.

636 Ibid, pp. 164-165.

637 Ibid, p. 165.

638 *The Reece Committee Report*, p. 154, In: Rene Wormser, *Foundations; Their Power and Influence,* p. 160.

639 Rene Wormser, Ibid, pp. 160-161.

640 Ibid, pp. 157-158.

641 Ibid, p. 168.

642 The Fabian Society was a political organization founded in Britain in 1884 with the aim of bringing about socialism by gradual and lawful means rather than by revolution.

643 Charlotte Iserbyt, p. 13.

644 Samuel Blumenfeld, *NEA, The Trojan Horse of American Education*, (Boise, ID: Paradigm Company), p. 53

645 William F. Jasper. *Global Tyranny, Step by Step* (Appleton, Wisconsin: Western Island Publishers, 1993) p. 165.

646 Henry Lamb, 1996-1998. http://www.eco.freedom.org/reports/rise/g_part03.html

647. Henry Lamb, 1996-1998. http://www.eco.freedom.org/reports/rise/g_part03.html

648 William Norman Grigg, *Freedom on the Altar: The UN''s Crusade Against God and Family*. (Appleton, Wisconsin: American Opinion Publishing, Inc., 1995), p. 18-19.

649 UNESCO publication No. 356. "In the Classroom: Toward World Understanding" (Paris: Georges Lang, 1949) p.58. William Benton, Assistant U.S. Secretary of State, in his initial address before the first meeting of the U.S. National Commission for UNESCO. September 23, 1946, included in *"Review of the United Nations Charter: A Collection of Documents,"* U.S. Senate Document #87, a report of the Subcommittee on the United Nations Charter, 83rd Congress, 2nd Session, January 7, 1954.

650 Ibid. Ibid.

651 Charlotte Thomson Iserbyt, *The Deliberate Dumbing Down of America*, (Ravenna, Ohio: Conscience Press, 1999), p. 27.

652 Ibid, p. 27-28.

653 Dr. Raymond Moore interview with Dr. James Dobson. School can Wait: Family Talk. Focus on the Family, Episode Sept, 1, 2010 http://www.oneplace.com/ministries/family-talk/custom-player/school-can-wait-130443.html & http://www.drjamesdobson.org/

654 Ibid.

Chapter 11 – Corrupting Education, 1945-2012

655 G. B. Chisholm. The Re-establishment of Peacetime Society," *Psychiatry*, February 1946, p. 7, 9-10. In: Berit Kjos, *Brave New Schools*, (Eugene, OR: Harvest House, 1995), p. 226.

656 Charlotte Thomson Iserbyt. The Deliberate Dumbing Down of America, (Ravenna, Ohio: Conscience Press, 1999), p. 28.

657 Ibid.

658 Charlotte Thomson Iserbyt, *The Deliberate Dumbing Down of America*, (Ravenna, Ohio: Conscience Press, 1999), p. 28.

659 Ibid.

660 Kristie Snyder. ""The Evil Legacy of Alfred Kinsey," *Discerning the Times Digest*, April, 2000, Vol 2(4):3.

661 Ibid.

662 Charlotte Thomson Iserbyt, *The Deliberate Dumbing Down of America*, (Ravenna, Ohio: Conscience Press, 1999), p. 29.

663 B.F. Skinner. *Science and Human Behavior*, (New York: Macmillan & Company, 1953). In: Charlotte Iserbyt, p. 28.

664 Francis Schaeffer, "A Christian View of Philosophy and Culture: Back to Freedom wand Dignity," *The Complete Works of Francis A. Schaeffer: A Christian Worldview, Volume One*, (Westchester, Ill. Crossway Books, 1982), p. 27. In: Charlotte Iserbyt, p.186.

665 Ibid, Ibid.

666 Sara Murray. Nearly Half of U.S. Lives in Household Receiving Government Benefits. Wall Street Journal, January 17, 2012. http://blogs.wsj.com/economics/2012/01/17/nearly-half-of-u-s-lives-in-household-receiving-government-benefits/?KEYWORDS=health+overhaul

667 Jean-Jacques Rousseau. *The Social Contract*, Book 4, 8-Civil Religion, Paragraph 33. 1762. http://www.constitution.org/jjr/socon_04.htm

668 Staff. Obama: Court Striking Down Obamacare Would be Judicial Activism. Real Clear Politics, April 2, 2012. http://www.realclearpolitics.com/video/2012/04/02/obama_supreme_court_striking_down_ob amacare_would_be_judicial_activism.html

669 Peter Wallsten and Robert Barnes. Obama's Supreme Court Comments Lead Some to Question His Strategy. Washington Post, April 4, 2012.

670 Charlotte Iserbyt, p. 47.

671 Charlotte Thomson Iserbyt, *The Deliberate Dumbing Down of America*, (Ravenna, Ohio: Conscience Press, 1999), p. 47. In: Robert H. Goldsbourgh. *Lines of Credit: Ropes of Bondage*. (Baltimore: The American Research Foundation, 1989). Read context of this interview between Senator Dodd and Gaither in a 1982 video-taped interview of Norman Dodd by Ed Griffin, author of *The Creature from Jekyll Island*, http://www.supremelaw.org/authors/dodd/interview.htm

672 Ibid, p 48.

673 William K. Medlin, et. al. *Soviet Education Programs: Foundations, Curriculum, Teacher Preparation*, Office of Education, OE-14037, Bulletin, 1950, No. 17. In: Charlotte Iserbyt, pp. 57-58.

674 Charlotte Thomson Iserbyt, *The Deliberate Dumbing Down of America*, (Ravenna, Ohio: Conscience Press, 1999), p. 57.

675 Ted Flynn. *Hope for the Wicked, The Master Plan to Rule the World*. (Sterling, Virginia: MaxKol Communications, Inc., 2000), p. 350. http://www.siecus.org/

676 Ibid.

677 Definitions of Sexually Related Health Terminology. Making the Connection: Sexuality and Reproductive Health. *SIECUS*, 2002. http://www.siecus.org/pubs/cnct/cnct0001.html

678 Comprehensive Sexuality Education. Making the Connection: Sexuality and Reproductive Health. *SIECUS*, 2002 http://www.siecus.org/pubs/cnct/cnct0003.html

679 Secretary of State Hillary Clinton. Remarks in Recognition of International Human Rights Day. U.S. Department of State, December 6, 2011. http://www.state.gov/secretary/rm/2011/12/178368.htm

680 President Barack Obama. Presidential Memorandum—International Initiatives to Advance the Human Rights of Lesbian, Gay, Bisexual, and Transgender Persons. The White House, December 6, 2011. http://www.whitehouse.gov/the-press-office/2011/12/06/presidential-memorandum-international-initiatives-advance-human-rights-l

681 President Barack Obama. Mexico City Policy—Voluntary Population Panning; Memorandum for the Secretary of State, January 23, 2009. http://www.whitehouse.gov/the_press_office/MexicoCityPolicy-VoluntaryPopulationPlanning

682 Sharon Slater. Obama Administration Officials: U.S. to Use Foreign Aid to Promote Gay Rights Abroad. The Family Watch, December 6, 2011 http://www.familywatchinternational.org/fwi/newsletter/0556.cfm)

683 Berit Kjos. *Brave New Schools* (Eugene Oregon, Harvest House 1995). p. 60.

684 *Engel et al v. Vitale et al.*, 370 U.S. 421, June 25, 1962.
     http://laws.findlaw.com/us/370/421.html
685 *Abington School Dist. V. Schempp*, 374 U.S. 203 (1963)
     http://caselaw.lp.findlaw.com/scripts/getcase.pl?navby'search&court'US&case'/us/374/203.h
     tml
686 Orlean Koehle. Eagle forum of Santa Rosa annual meeting, March 9, 2002.
687 Berit Kjos. *Brave New Schools* (Eugene Oregon, Harvest House 1995), p. 72.
688 "The Behavioral Science Teacher Education Program," p. 1. In: Charlotte Iserbyt, p. A-23
689 "Systematic Analysis of Future Society." "*The Behavioral Science Teacher Education
     Program*," p. 237. In: Charlotte Iserbyt, p. A-24.
690 "Futurism as a Social Tool and Decision-Making by an Elite," Ibid, p. 248-255. Ibid, p. A-25.
691 Ibid, p. 259. Ibid.
692 Ibid, p. 261. Ibid.
693 Digital Angel Unveiled. WorldNetDaily, November 1, 2000.
     http://www.wnd.com/2000/11/4324/
     Also, Becky McGlauflin. "Digital angel and Revelation 13:16-17." Discerning the Times
     Digest, November, 2000, Vol. 2(11):3.
     http://www.discerningtoday.org/members/Digest/2000Digest/November/digital_angels_and_
     revelation.htm
694 Michael Coffman. "'Carnivore' under siege." Discerning the Times Digest, Newsbytes, July
     24, 2000. http://www.discerningtoday.org/members/NewsBytes/2000NewsBytes/July/07-24-
     2000m.htm#7carnivore_under_seige
695 Michael Coffman. "NSA Finally Admits Echelon Spying on Americans," Discerning the Times
     Digest, Newsbytes, February 28, 2000.
     http://www.discerningtoday.org/members/NewsBytes/2000NewsBytes/Feb/02-28-
     2000m.htm#NSA finally admits Echelon spies on American citizens
696 Becky McGlauflin. "You Can Run but You Can't Hide." Discerning the Times Digest,
     October, 2000, Vol. 2(10):4
     http://www.discerningtoday.org/members/Digest/2000Digest/October/you_can_run_but_you
     _cant_hide.htm
697 Orlean Koehle. Eagle forum of Santa Rosa annual meeting, March 9, 2002.
698 Ted Flynn. *Hope for the Wicked, The Master Plan to Rule the World.* (Sterling, Virginia:
     MaxKol Communications, Inc., 2000), p. 4.
699 Berit Kjos. *Brave New Schools* (Eugene Oregon, Harvest House 1995), pp. 10, 12.
700 *Project Global 2000:Planning for a New Century* (New York: Global Education Associates,
     1991), p 2.
701 Human Intelligence International Newsletter, P.O. Box 1163, Birmingham, MI 48012
     (March/April 1981), p. 1. In: Berit Kjos, p. 230.
702 Berit Kjos. *Brave New Schools* (Eugene Oregon, Harvest House 1995), p. 231.
703 Dennis Laurence Cuddy. *Chronology of Education* (Highland City, FL Pro Family Forum,
     Inc., No date), p. 80. In: Berit Kjos, p. 232.
     http://www.crossroad.to/Books/BraveNewSchools/Chronology.htm
704 Charlotte Iserbyt, p. 254.
705 Transcribed from video tape of the conference. In: Berit Kjos, p. 234. Also see The Robert
     Muller School webpage on the World Core Curriculum, http://www.unol.org/rms/wcc.html
706 Fox News Poll Raw Data: Romney Hits Record High, But Still Tied with Obama. Fox News,
     January 14, 2012. http://www.foxnews.com/interactive/politics/2012/01/15/fox-news-poll-
     raw-data-romney-hits-record-high-but-still-tied-with-obama/
707 Ibid.
708 Sara Murray. Nearly Half of U.S. Lives in Household Receiving Government Benefits. WSJ,
     January 17, 2012. http://blogs.wsj.com/economics/2012/01/17/nearly-half-of-u-s-lives-in-
     household-receiving-government-benefits/?KEYWORDS=health+overhaul
709 Kristie Snyder, *Discerning the Times Digest*, December, 1999, Vol 1 (11):3.
     http://www.discerningtoday.org/members/Digest/1999Digest/December/The Occult.htm
710. Berit Kjos, pp. 66-67.

711 Whole Language vs. Phonics. Halcyon House, (no date). http://www.halcyon.org/wholelan.html

712 Ibid.

713 H.R. 1804. Bill Summary and Status for the 103rd Congress. Goals 2000 Act. http://thomas.loc.gov/cgi-bin/bdquery/z?d103:HR01804:|TOM:/bss/d103query.html| Also, http://www.ed.gov/legislation/GOALS2000/TheAct/index.html

714 H.R. 2884. Bill Summary and Status for the 103rd Congress. School-to-Work Act. http://thomas.loc.gov/cgi-bin/bdquery/z?d103:HR02884:|TOM:/bss/d103query.html||

715 H.R. 6. Bill Summary and Status for the 103rd Congress. Elementary and Secondary Education Act. http://thomas.loc.gov/cgi-bin/bdquery/z?d103:HR00006:|TOM:/bss/d103query.html|

716 H.R. 1617. Bill Summary and Status for the 103rd Congress. CAREERS Act. http://thomas.loc.gov/cgi-bin/bdquery/D?d104:2:./temp/~bdKR5m::|/bss/d104query.html|

717 Title X, Section 10601 a. *In:* Allen Quist. *Fed Ed, The New Federal Curriculum and How It's Enforced* (Glencoe, MN: NuCompass Publishing, 2002), p. 16. Bold added for emphasis in original.

718 Ibid. Ibid, p. 17. Bold added for emphasis in original.

719 Allen Quist. *Fed Ed, The New Federal Curriculum and How It's Enforced* (Glencoe, MN: NuCompass Publishing, 2002), *Fed Ed*, p. 17.

720 Ibid, p. 26.

721 Ibid, p. 29.

722 Phyllis Schlafly. *Eagle Forum.* http://www.eagleforum.org/educate/marc_tucker/marc_tucker_letter.html

723 Christine Armario. Report: Students Don't Know Much About US History. AP, June 14, 2011. http://www.msnbc.msn.com/id/43397386/ns/us_news-life/t/report-students-dont-know-much-about-us-history/#.Tx8GVPkr530

724 Samuel Blumenfeld. "Why Students Fail Geography," *WorldNetDaily*, November 23, 2002. http://www.wnd.com/news/article.asp?ARTICLE_ID'29763

725 Berit Kjos. *Brave New Schools* (Eugene Oregon, Harvest House 1995), p. 38.

726 Beverly Eakman. Education's Armageddon. The New American, Vol. 27(21):28, November 7, 2011.

727 The Condition of Education 2011. National Center for Education Statistics, Dept. of Education. May, 2011. P. 54. http://nces.ed.gov/pubs2011/2011033.pdf

728 U.S. Math Scores Fail the Test. Education Reporter, April, 1998. http://www.eagleforum.org/educate/1998/apr98/math_scores.html

729 "Will New Education Law Leave Every Child Behind?" *Education Reporter,* Eagle Forum, Jan. 2002), p. 1. http://www.eagleforum.org/educate/2002/jan02/hr1.shtml

730 Ibid.

731 Historical Tables, Budget of the U.S. Government—Fiscal Year 2012, Table 4.1 Outlays by Agency 1962-2016. Office of the President of the United States; U.S. Government Printing Office, Washington D.C. 2012. http://www.whitehouse.gov/sites/default/files/omb/budget/fy2012/assets/hist.pdf

732 Valerie Strauss. What the Decline in SAT Scores Really Means. Washington Post, September 14, 2011. http://www.washingtonpost.com/blogs/answer-sheet/post/what-the-decline-in-sat-scores-really-means/2011/09/14/gIQAdUzdSK_blog.html

733 Jason Koebler. SAT Scores Fall as Most Test Takers Miss College Benchmark. U.S. News, September 14, 2011. http://www.usnews.com/education/blogs/high-school-notes/2011/09/14/sat-scores-fall-as-most-test-takers-miss-college-benchmark

734 Brian Ray, Ph.D. Research Facts on Homeschooling. National Home Education Research Institute, January 11, 2011. http://www.nheri.org/Research-Facts-on-Homeschooling.html

Chapter 12 – Agenda 21

735 Carroll Quigley. *Tragedy & Hope, A History of the World in Our Time.* (New York: The Macmillian Company, 1966), pp. 551, 553.

736 Scott Allen. "Environmental Donors Set Tone—Activists Affected by Quest for Funds." Boston Globe, Monday, October 20, 1997, p. A1.

737 The Story of the Club of Rome. The Club of Rome. No date. http://www.cluborfome.org/eng/about/4/
Also: Club of Rome Organization. http://www.nndb.com/org/142/000056971/

738 William K. Reilly. Use of Land: A Citizen's Policy Guide to Urban Growth (New York: Tomas Y Crowell Co., 1973), pp 15-16.

739 Ibid, p 25.

740 Randal O'Toole. "Is Urban Planning "Creeping Socialism"? The Independent Review, Vol. IV, n. 4, Spring 2000, p. 504. http://www.independent.org/pdf/tir/tir_04_4_otoole.pdf

741 Randal O'Tool. How Urban Planners Caused the Housing Bubble. CATO Policy Analysis No. 646, October 1, 2009. http://americandreamcoalition.org/housing/pa646bubble.pdf

742 Edward Glaeser and Joseph Gyourko. The Impact of Zoning on Housing Affordability. Harvard Institute of Economic Research. Discussion Paper Number 1948. March 2002. http://www.economics.harvard.edu/pub/hier/2002/HIER1948.pdf

743 Ibid.

744 Randal O'Tool. The Planning Penalty. The American Dream Coalition. March, 2006. http://americandreamcoalition.org/Penalty.pdf

745 Understanding Sustainable Development, Agenda 21. Freedom Advocates, 2010. http://www.freedomadvocates.org/documents/download/white_paper_document_version_of _understanding_sustainable_development_-_agenda_21/

746 ICLEI United States Members as of May 5, 2011. http://www.freedomadvocates.org/images/pdf/iclei_usa_easy%20read_050511.pdf

747 Alex Newman. Irving, Texas, Becomes Latest City to Drop ICLEI & UN Agenda 21. The New American, March 19, 2012. http://www.thenewamerican.com/tech-mainmenu-30/environment/11234-irving-texas-becomes-latest-city-to-drop-iclei-a-un-agenda-21

748 Tennessee House Votes for the Anti-Agenda 21 Resolution. Virginia Right, March 15, 2012. http://www.varight.com/news/tennessee-house-votes-for-the-anti-agenda-21-resolution-on-to-the-tennessee-senate/

749 Agenda 21. Un Department of Economic and Social Affairs, Division for Sustainable Development. 1992. http://www.un.org/esa/dsd/agenda21/res_agenda21_00.shtml

750 Report of Habitat: United Nations Conference on Human Settlements, Chapter IID, Preamble. Vancouver May 31 to June 11, 1976. http://freedom.org/reports/human-settlements/land.html

751 The President's Council on Sustainable Development. Sustainable America, A New Consensus for the Prosperity, Opportunity and a Healthy Environment for the Future. (Washington D.C.: US Government Printing Office, 1996). 186 pages. http://clinton2.nara.gov/PCSD/Publications/TF_Reports/amer-top.html

752 These include: Eco-Efficiency (1996), Energy and Transportation (1996), Population and Consumption (1996), Public Linkage (1997), Dialogue, and Education (1997), Sustainable Agriculture (1996), Sustainable Communities Task Force Report (1997), and Natural Resources (1999). Downloadable at http://clinton2.nara.gov/PCSD/Publications/index.html

753 Elaine Dewar. Cloak of Green. (Toronto: James Lorimer & Company, 1995), pp 252-273.

754 Gro Brundtland, ed. Our Common Future. World Commission on Environment and Development. (Oxford: Oxford University Press, 1987). http://www.un-documents.net/ocf-02.htm/. Our Common Future was written by the Brundtland Commission, so named because its chairwoman was Norway's Prime Minister, Gro Brundtland. For the full document, see http://www.un-documents.net/wced-ocf.htm

755 Steven C. Rockefeller and John C. Elder. Spirit and Nature: Why the Environment Is a Religious Issue, (Boston: Beacon, 1992), p. 134.

756 Steven Rockefeller. Rockefeller Brothers Fund. As of January, 2012. http://www.rbf.org/people/steven-rockefeller

757 Debra Niwa. U.N. Agenda 21, "Sustainable Development" Introduced in the U.S. Congress. January 2012. http://dl.dropbox.com/u/26494838/Bills_SD_011712_dkn.pdf

758 Glossary For the Public. American Planning Association, no date. http://www.planning.org/policy/communicationsbootcamp/guide/pdf/glossaryforthepublic.pdf

759 James Taylor. New NASA Data Blow Gaping Hole in Global Warming Alarmism. Forbes. July 27, 2011. http://news.yahoo.com/nasa-data-blow-gaping-hold-global-warming-alarmism-192334971.html

Original research: Roy Spencer and William Braswell. On the diagnosis of radiative feedback in the presence of unknown radiative forcing. Journal of Geophysical Research, Vol 115, D16109, August 2010. http://www.drroyspencer.com/wp-content/uploads/Spencer-Braswell-JGR-2010.pdf

Also see: Why Climate Models are wrong. http://www.youtube.com/watch?v=3E-ryS5ehPo

760 Roy Spencer. Our Refutation of Dessler (2010) is Accepted for Publication. July 4, 2011. http://www.drroyspencer.com/2011/07/our-refutation-of-dessler-2010-is-accepted-for-publication/

761 Victoria Jaggard. Sun Headed into Hibernation, Solar Studies Predict. National Geographic, June 14, 2011. http://news.nationalgeographic.com/news/2011/06/110614-sun-hibernation-solar-cycle-sunspots-space-science/

762 Dave Rose. Forget Global Warming—It's Cycle 25 We Need to Worry About. Daily Mail, January 29, 2012. http://www.dailymail.co.uk/sciencetech/article-2093264/Forget-global-warming--Cycle-25-need-worry-NASA-scientists-right-Thames-freezing-again.html?ito=feeds-newsxml

763 Michael Coffman. *Rescuing a Broken America.* (New York: Morgan James, 2010) pp. 131-134. http://www.rescuingamericabook.com/

764 John Ingham. MPS Slam 'Secretive' Climategate Probes. UK Express, January 25, 2011. http://www.express.co.uk/posts/view/225108/MPs-slam-secretive-Climategate-probes

765 Leo Hickman. Fresh Round of Hacked Climate Science Emails Leaked Online. The Guardian, November 22, 2011. http://www.guardian.co.uk/environment/2011/nov/22/fresh-hacked-climate-science-emails

766 Ibid.

767 Jim Lacey. Scientists Behaving Badly. National Review Online. November 28, 2011. http://www.nationalreview.com/articles/284137/scientists-behaving-badly-jim-lacey

768 Climategate (Part II); A Sequel as Ugly as the Original. The Weekly Standard, December 12, 2011. http://www.weeklystandard.com/articles/climategate-part-ii_610926.html?nopager=1

769 Ibid.

770 Frank York. Former EAP Economist Alan Carlin Vindicated on Greenhouse Gas Report. EPA Abuse.com, November 8, 2011. http://epaabuse.com/2538/editorials/editorial-former-epa-economist-alan-carlin-vindicated-on-greenhouse-gas-report/

771 Stephen Dinan. Watchdog" EPA Cut Corners on Global-Warming Decision. The Washington Times, September 28, 2011. http://www.washingtontimes.com/news/2011/sep/28/watchdog-epa-cut-corners-global-warming-decision/

772 EPA's Approaching Regulatory Avalanche. Texas Public Policy Foundation, February, 2012. http://www.texaspolicy.com/pdf/2012-02-RR01-EPAsApproachingRegulatoryAvalanche-ACEE-KathleenHartnettWhite.pdf

773 Simon Allen, et.al. Special Report of the Intergovernmental Panel on Climate Change, Summary for Policy Makers. International Panel on Climate Change. Page 9. November 18, 2011. http://ipcc-wg2.gov/SREX/images/uploads/SREX-SPMbrochure_FINAL.pdf

774 Marlo Lewis. How Absurd Is Regulating Greenhouse Gases through the Clean Air Act? Global Warming.org, September 27, 2011. http://www.globalwarming.org/2011/09/27/how-absurd-is-regulating-greenhouse-gases-through-the-clean-air-act/

775 Paul Driessen. The EPA's Unrelenting Power Grab. CFACT, November, 2011. http://www.cfact.org/download2.asp

776 Ibid, p. 15.

777 Ibid, p. 16.

778 Economy Derailed; State-by-State Impacts of the EPA Regulatory Train Wreck. American Legislative Exchange Council, April, 2012. http://www.alec.org/docs/Economy_Derailed_April_2012.pdf

779 Michael Soule. "History and purpose of the society of conservation biology." *Conservation Biology*, 1(1987):4-5.

780 Henry Lamb and Michael Coffman. How the Convention on Biodiversity Was Defeated. Sovereignty International, Inc. 1994. http://www.sovereignty.net/p/land/biotreatystop.htm

781 V.H. Heywood and R.T. Watson, ed. *C Global Biodiversity Assessment*, World Resources Institute and UN Environmental Program (London, New York: Cambridge University Press, 1995). Section 13.4.2.2.3, p. 993

782 Spencer, W.D., P. Beier, K. Penrod, K. Winters, C. Paulman, H. Rustigian-Romsos, J. Stritholt, M. Parisi, and A. Pettler. 2010. California Essential Habitat Connectivity Project: A Strategy for Conserving a Connected California. Prepared for California Department of Transportation, California Department of Fish and Game, and Federal Highways Administration. http://www.scwildlands.org/reports/CEHC_Plan_MASTER_030210_3.pdf

783 V.H. Heywood and R.T. Watson, ed. *C Global Biodiversity Assessment*, World Resources Institute and UN Environmental Program (London, New York: Cambridge University Press, 1995). Section 13.4.2.2.3, p. 993

784 Henry Lamb. The Convention on Biological Diversity: Cornerstone of the New World Order. Eco•Logic *Special Report*, November 4, 1994 http://freedom.org/reports/srbio.htm

785 Spencer, W.D., P. Beier, K. Penrod, K. Winters, C. Paulman, H. Rustigian-Romsos, J. Stritholt, M. Parisi, and A. Pettler. 2010. California Essential Habitat Connectivity Project: A Strategy for Conserving a Connected California. Prepared for California Department of Transportation, California Department of Fish and Game, and Federal Highways Administration. http://www.scwildlands.org/reports/CEHC_Plan_MASTER_030210_3.pdf

786 From The Communist Manifesto written by Karl Marx and Friedrich engles in 1848.

Chapter 13 – What Must Be Done

787 Joseph Stalin. In: Quotes Daddy. http://www.quotesdaddy.com/quote/1401367/joseph-stalin/america-is-like-a-healthy-body-and-its-resistance

788 George Barna. Barna Describes Religious Changes Among Busters, Boomers, and Elders Since 1991. The Barna Group, July 27, 2011. http://www.barna.org/faith-spirituality/506-barna-describes-religious-changes-among-busters-boomers-and-elders-since-1991

789 George Barna. Barna Examines Trends in 14 Religious Factors Over 20 Years (1991-2011), July 26, 2011. http://www.barna.org/faith-spirituality/504-barna-examines-trends-in-14-religious-factors-over-20-years-1991-to-2011
Also: George Barna. 20 Years of Surveys Show Key Differences in the Faith of America's Men and Women. The Barna Group, August 1, 2011. http://www.barna.org/faith-spirituality/508-20-years-of-surveys-show-key-differences-in-the-faith-of-americas-men-and-women

790 Letter to the Officers of the First Brigade of the Third Division of the Militia of Massachusetts, 11 October 1798, In: *Revolutionary Services and Civil Life of General William Hull* (New York, 1848), Pp 265-6.
http://books.google.com/books?id=E2kFAAAAQAAJ&dq=editions%3AVsZcW99fWPgC&pg=PA265#v=onepage&q&f=false
There are some differences in the version that appeared in *The Works of John Adams* (Boston, 1854), vol. 9, pp. 228-9, most notably the words "or gallantry" instead of "and licentiousness
http://books.google.com/books?id=PZYKAQAAIAAJ&pg=PA228#v=onepage&q&f=false

791 Sam Rosenfeld, "How To Dumb Down A Nation." WorldNetDaily, March 9, 2002
http://wnd.com/news/article.asp?ARTICLE_ID'26767

792 Patrick Henry, March 23, 1775. In: William J. Federer. America's God and Country (St. Louis: Amerisearch, Inc., 1999), p. 289. Also see:
http://www.thinkexist.com/English/Author/x/Author_3831_1.htm It is generally understood that this quote is attributed to Patrick Henry, but there is no documented proof that he said or penned the words. However, on June 12, 1776 he penned article 16 of the Virginia Bill of Rights which confirms the same belief: "That religion, or the duty which we owe to our Creator, and the manner of discharging it, can be directed only by reason and conviction, not by force or violence; and ;therefore all men are equally entitled to the free exercise of

religion, according to the dictates of conscience; and that it is the mutual duty of all to practice Christian forbearance, love, and charity towards each other."

793 W. Cleon Skousen. *The Making of America* (Washington, D.C.: The National Center for Constitutional Studies, 1985), p. 680. In: C.B. Krouse, Jr., "The Historical Meaning and Judicial Construction of the Establishment of Religion Clause of the First Amendment," Washington Law Journal 2 (Winter 1962):65:94-107.

794 David Barton. "How Courts Invented Church-State 'Wall of Separation'", Whistleblower magazine, November 2003 Vol. 12(11):8.

795 Ibid.

796 Fr. Bill McCarthy, MSA. Not Separation of God from State. Free Republic, September 22, 2003. http://www.freerepublic.com/focus/news/987191/posts

797 Everson v. Board of Education of Ewing TP. 330 U.S. 1 (1947), http://laws.findlaw.com/us/330/1.html

798 David Barton, "How Courts Invented Church-State 'Wall of Separation ,'" p. 8.

799 Alex de Tocqueville. "Chapter 17, Principal Causes Which Tend To Maintain The Democratic Republic In The United States," *Democracy in America*, 1:329-30. http://xroads.virginia.edu/~HYPER/DETOC/1_ch17.htm

800 Ibid, 1:295.

801 Ibid, "How Religion in the United States Avails Itself of Democratic Tendencies." 2 Vol, Section 1, Chapter 5. http://xroads.virginia.edu/~HYPER/DETOC/ch1_05.htm

802 Ibid, "How Religion in the United States Avails Itself of Democratic Tendencies." 2 Vol, Section 1, Chapter 5. http://xroads.virginia.edu/~HYPER/DETOC/ch1_05.htm

803 Ibid.

804 Ibid, "Principle Causes Which Tend to Maintain the Democratic Republic in the United States." 1 Vol, Chapter 17 http://xroads.virginia.edu/~HYPER/DETOC/religion/ch1_17.htm

805 Morley Schaeffer, "Determined to Survive." Sixty Minutes, March 24, 2002.

806 Michael Ryan. "They Call Their Boss a Hero," Parade Magazine, September 8, 1997. In: Reputation Management, Selz Seabolt Communications, Chicago, IL. http://www.reputation-mgmt.com/malden.htm

807 Molly Manchenton. "Malden Mills to Sell Some Local Property." The Eagle Tribune, October 22, 2002. http://www.eagletribune.com/news/stories/20021022/BU_001.htm

808 Morley Schaeffer, "Determined to Survive," Sixty Minutes, March 24, 2002

809 "Malden Mills Lands $12.4 Military Contract," Boston Business Journal, October 21, 2002. http://www.bizjournals.com/boston/stories/2002/10/21/daily5.html

810 "Malden Mills prepares reorganization plan," Home Textiles Today, August 5, 2002. http://www.hometextilestoday.com/index.asp?layout'story&webzine'htt&publication'htt&articl eid'CA237521

811 David Gill. Was Aaron Feuerstein Wrong? Ethix, June 25, 2011. http://ethix.org/2011/06/25/was-aaron-feuerstein-wrong

812 Alex de Tocqueville. "Principal Causes Which Tend To Maintain The Democratic Republic In The United States," *Democracy in America*. http://xroads.virginia.edu/~HYPER/DETOC/1_ch17.htm.

813 Joe Wolverton II, J.D. Faith of the Founding Fathers. New American, December 19, 2011, Vol. 27(24):36. http://thenewamerican.com/history/american/10040-faith-of-the-founding-fathers

814 Ibid, P 36.

815 Ibid, P 38.

816 Thomas Jefferson. September 18, 1813, in a letter to William Canby. Compiled for Senator A. Willis Robertson, Letters of Thomas Jefferson on Religion. (Williamsburg, VA: The Williamsburg Foundation, April 27, 1960). In: Catherine Millard. *The Rewriting of America's History*, (Camp Hill, PA: Horizon House Publishers, 1991), p. 107-108.

817 Thomas Jefferson. March 23, 1801, in a letter from Washington, D.C. to Moses Robinson. Barnes May, ed. *Jefferson Himself–The personal Narrative of a many-sided American*, (Boston: Houghton Mifflin Company, 1942), p. 231. In: Catherine Millard, p. 92.

818 Immaculate Contraception. Wall Street Journal, February 13, 2012.
http://online.wsj.com/article/SB10001424052970203646004577215150068215494.html

819 Ira Stoll. Sandra Fluke's Amazing Testimony. Wall Street Journal, March 9, 2012.
http://online.wsj.com/article/SB10001424052970204603004577269491399954950.html

820 Otis. Rush Limbaugh's 'Slut' Comment Controversy Has Staying Power. ABC News, March 14, 2012. http://abcnews.go.com/blogs/politics/2012/03/rush-limbaughs-slut-comment-controversy-proves-it-has-staying-power/

821 Aliyah Shihad. Bill Maher: Me Calling Sara Palin a 'C---' Is Totally Different Than Limbaugh Calling Sandra Fluke a 'Slut.' New York Daily News, March 15, 2012.
http://www.nydailynews.com/news/politics/bill-maher-calling-sarah-palin-a-c-totally-limbaugh-calling-sandra-fluke-a-slut-article-1.1039705

822 Otis. Rush Limbaugh's 'Slut' Comment Controversy Has Staying Power. ABC News, March 14, 2012. http://abcnews.go.com/blogs/politics/2012/03/rush-limbaughs-slut-comment-controversy-proves-it-has-staying-power/

823 Stephanie Condon. Poll: Obama's Approval Rating Sinks to New Low. CBS News, March 12. 2012. http://www.cbsnews.com/8301-503544_162-57395703-503544/poll-obamas-approval-rating-sinks-to-new-low/?tag=cbsContent;cbsCarousel

824 George Barna. Barna Describes Religious Changes Among Busters, Boomers, and Elders Since 1991. The Barna Group, July 27, 2011. http://www.barna.org/faith-spirituality/506-barna-describes-religious-changes-among-busters-boomers-and-elders-since-1991

825 Andrew Romano. Ron Paul's Surprisingly Young Support Base. The Daily Beast, January 4, 2012. http://www.thedailybeast.com/articles/2012/01/03/ron-paul-s-surprisingly-young-support-base.html

826 Bring Ron Paul to Campus. Young Americans for Liberty, no date.
http://www.yaliberty.org/bringronpaultocampus

827 George Barna. Barna Describes Religious Changes Among Busters, Boomers, and Elders Since 1991. The Barna Group, July 27, 2011. http://www.barna.org/faith-spirituality/506-barna-describes-religious-changes-among-busters-boomers-and-elders-since-1991

828 Focus on "Worship Wars" Hides the Real Issues Regarding Connection to God. Barna Group, November 19, 2002. http://www.barna.org/barna-update/article/5-barna-update/85-focus-on-qworship-warsq-hides-the-real-issues-regarding-connection-to-god?q=contemporary+traditional

829 Ibid.

830 Self-described Christians Dominate America but Wrestle with Four Aspects of Spiritual Depth. The Barna Group, September 13, 2011. http://www.barna.org/faith-spirituality/524-self-described-christians-dominate-america-but-wrestle-with-four-aspects-of-spiritual-depth

831 George Barna. Barna Examines Trends in 15 Religious Factors over 20 Years (1991-1011). Barna Group, July 26, 2011. http://www.barna.org/faith-spirituality/504-barna-examines-trends-in-14-religious-factors-over-20-years-1991-to-2011

832 Albert Ellery Bergh, ed. The writings of Thomas Jefferson, 20 Vols. (Washington: Thomas Jefferson Memorial Association, 1907), 15:278

833 EPA Video Reveals Team Obama's Scary Crusade Against Affordable, Reliable Energy. Fox News, April 27, 2012. http://www.foxnews.com/opinion/2012/04/27/epa-video-reveals-team-obama-scary-crusade-against-affordable-reliable-energy/
Also: EPa Seeks to 'Crucify' US Energy Producers?
http://video.foxnews.com/v/1590459174001/epa-seeks-to-crucify-us-energy-producers

834 Cecil Adams. How Do We Get Rid of Whacked Out Judges? Straight Dope, February 9, 2007. http://www.straightdope.com/columns/read/2693/there-goes-the-judge

835 Michael Coffman. Our Federal Landlord. Range Magazine, Special Report. Winter 2012. Pp. 46-47. http://www.rangemagazine.com/specialreports/range-wi12-our_federal_landlord.pdf

836 Saul Alinsky. Rules for Radicals; A Pragmatic Primer for Realistic Radicals. (New York: Vintage Books, 1971), Pp. 24-47, especially Pp. 29 & 34.

837 Freedom 21 http://freedom21.org/

INDEX

314

De Soto   Mystery of
                 Capital ___
Gustave La Bon
  Saul D Alinsky
  Rules for Radicals
  _____
  Clinton 2. Nara. gov/